A HISTORY OF THE ENGLISH PEOPLE
IN THE NINETEENTH CENTURY

A HISTORY OF THE ENGLISH PEOPLE IN THE NINETEENTH CENTURY

A HISTORY OF THE ENGLISH PEOPLE
IN THE NINETEENTH CENTURY — VI

THE RULE OF DEMOCRACY

1905—1914

(BOOK II)

by

ELIE HALEVY

Translated from the French by
E. I. WATKIN

ERNEST BENN LIMITED
LONDON

First published in French 1932
First published in English 1934
Second (revised) Edition 1952

Publishers' Note

This is the second edition of the book originally published as *A History of the English People in the Nineteenth Century, Epilogue Vol. II*. The first edition was published as a single book but is now split into two; Book I containing Part I and the first two chapters of Part II and Book II the third chapter of Part II and Part III.

Published by Ernest Benn Limited
Bouverie House, Fleet Street, London.
Printed in Great Britain by
STAPLES PRINTERS LIMITED
at their Rochester, Kent, establishment

Contents

PART II

FOUR YEARS OF CRISIS

(continued)

CHAPTER III

From the Bosnian Crisis to the Crisis of Agadir

I THE AUSTRIAN ANNEXATION OF BOSNIA AND THE NAVAL SCARE OF 1909

I

THE passing of the new German law which hastened the speed at which old vessels should be replaced and ordered four large ironclads to be laid down every year until 1914 alarmed the British Government. And its alarm was the greater because the Reichstag had passed the new law amid scenes of enthusiasm, by an overwhelming majority and without debate. In 1900 the Government had with the utmost difficulty extorted the Reichstag's consent to its new programme of naval construction. Now on the contrary the party leaders had, it would seem, taken the initiative and forced the government departments to act. Have I said that the new naval law alarmed the British Government? It would perhaps be truer to say perplexed. For it left the Government embarrassed by the very success of that policy of *ententes* inaugurated in 1904 and persistently developed ever since. What in fact had the British Government in view when it embarked on this policy? Negatively, the Foreign Office sought to deter the German Government from its attempts to surround Britain with a cordon of hostile powers by proving how easily Britain could win over all those allies Germany hoped to array against her. But for the complete success of the policy, something more was necessary. It must achieve the *positive* result of awakening Germany to the dangers to which she was exposed in virtue of her Continental position, and making her pay more attention to her army and less to her navy, so that her statesmen would return to the principles which had governed German policy in the age of Bismarck, when exclusively occupied with Continental policy, Germany had abandoned to Great Britain, without a struggle, the empire of the seas. No such change of front was visible at present in Berlin. The German army estimates showed only a moderate increase. The naval estimates on the contrary rose by leaps and bounds and during the first year in which the re-modelled Liberal Cabinet was in office, the tension between the two navies and the two countries became greater than it had yet been.

In that remodelled Cabinet, indeed, the imperialists would seem to have gained ground at the expense of their opponents, since Asquith became Premier instead of Campbell-Bannerman and McKenna succeeded Lord Tweedmouth at the Admiralty with the avowed intention of speeding up naval construction. The spring and summer witnessed, in fact, a round of those visits from one ruler to another which had taken their place amongst the most important ceremonial of European diplomacy and could justly be claimed as a succession of triumphs, accessions of prestige, for the Foreign Office. In May, President Fallières came to London to be welcomed by the cheers of an enormous crowd. The pretext for his visit was the Franco-British exhibition opened a few days before and destined for the whole year to cement the new alliance between the two cultures. During the official speeches the English King spoke of 'a permanent *entente*', the French President of 'a closer *entente*'? between the two countries. More sensational was the King's visit next month to the Czar. It was the first time in history that a British sovereign had visited Russia. The two monarchs met on June 5 off Reval. The Czar recalled the agree-ment concluded the previous year between the two Govern-ments, by which questions equally important for both nations had been settled. The King mentioned other questions which might in future be settled by the same methods. What were they? Clearly the reforms which must be imposed upon the Sultan to secure the better government of Macedonia. And it would seem that the conversations between Sir Charles Hardinge who accom-panied the King and the Russian Foreign Minister, Isvolsky, did in fact achieve the feat of an Anglo-Russian agreement about the Balkans. Had not Sir Edward Grey during the negotiations which prepared the Anglo-Russian agreement of 1907 expressly de-clared his desire for such an understanding? From that meeting at Reval—followed in August by a visit of President Fallières to Petersburg—dates the expression Triple Entente[1] to denote the

---

[1] *National Review*, June 1908, vol. li, pp. 505–6: 'So far . . . there has been something wanting to complete and perfect the *entente cordiale*. So far as France's Russian ally and her British friend regard one another with suspicion . . . so long was the diplomatic position of all three Powers seriously complicated.' And the anonymous writer of the article con-

network of understandings between England and France, and England and Russia which, in the language of *The Times*, without being alliances 'may readily become the parents of alliances, should unjustifiable aggression by others ever render alliances necessary'.[1] Germany took alarm, and its extent was measured by the fall in the value of Government bonds on the Berlin Stock Exchange. And her fears were increased when on August 10, King Edward visited the Emperor of Austria at Ischl, after stopping *en route* at Cronberg just long enough for a short interview with William II.

Whatever the real subject of the conversations between Edward VII and Francis Joseph may have been, it is not surprising that this visit, the first paid by the English King to the Emperor of Austria, should have been interpreted by German opinion as the expression of a policy which aimed at breaking up the Triple Alliance after constructing the Triple Entente. But at this moment events occurred in eastern Europe—they had indeed already begun before the meeting at Ischl—which alarmed all the Foreign Offices, seemed at times to be bringing Europe to the brink of war, and which after a series of rapid vicissitudes finally enabled the German Government to achieve a striking diplomatic victory, and display to the entire world a strong Triple Alliance arrayed against a weak and disunited Triple Entente.

2

The first of these events was the Young-Turk revolution which broke out at Constantinople on July 23 after an insurrection which lasted three weeks. It was a military revolt led by a revolutionary committee whose headquarters were at Salonika. It was a movement whose causes were deep seated, so deep seated that they escaped the notice of superficial observers and the revolution took all the governments by surprise beginning with the diplomatic representatives of the Great Powers at Constantinople. But the occasion of the revolution, the incident which made it break

tinues under the heading 'A Triple Entente'. 'There is absolutely no reason whatsoever why Great Britain and Russia should not form as firm and faithful a friendship as Great Britain and France; and it is the duty of every patriotic Englishman to co-operate to that end. Once more King Edward has given the lead.' See also J. Ellis Barker 'The Triple Entente and the Triple Alliance' (*Nineteenth Century*, vol. lxiv, pp. 1, sqq.—July 1908); Ellis Barker throughout the article speaks of 'The Triple Entente'.

[1] *The Times*, June 11, 1908.

out at this precise date, July 1908, was undoubtedly the Reval meeting.

Let us recall the antecedents of that interview. Peace had been maintained in the East for ten years on the basis of a close understanding between Austria and Russia. Russia regarded the concession by the Porte in January 1908 of the Sandjak railway to the Austrian Prime Minister, Baron Aehrenthal, as a breach of this understanding. It was no doubt arguable that when she requested and obtained the concession Austria did not exceed her rights under the treaty of Berlin, but it was impossible to deny that at least it violated the spirit of the agreement between Austria and Russia. For Baron Von Aehrenthal's political aims were only too plain. By the construction of this railway, the Sandjak, a wedge of territory driven between Serbia and Montenegro, would become an Austrian zone of influence. Sooner or later the railway would be prolonged to Salonika and the old pan-German dream realized; Salonika would become a great German or Austro-German port. In Russia pan-Slavist opinion took alarm. Isvolsky, the architect of the agreement with England, sought to strengthen it by joint action of the two powers to force a system of reforms upon the Sultan. England by the mouth of Sir Edward Grey, demanded the setting up of a system of administrative autonomy in the Balkans under a governor chosen by an agreement between the Sultan and the Powers. Everyone believed and not without justification that at Reval Russia accepted the British proposal, possibly in return for certain concessions. What resource was left to the Turkish patriots? Could they count on Abdul Hamid to resist this first step towards the dismemberment of his empire? He was too weak and too corrupt. The malcontents rebelled, putting forward a programme at once democratic and patriotic. Compelling the Sultan to restore the constitution of 1876 they undertook the task of setting up in Turkey a system in which the Government was in the hands of a Chamber elected by the universal suffrage, not of all the Moslems alone, but of all the inhabitants of Turkey without distinction of race, language or creed. There would be no longer any reason to demand reforms, measures for protecting nationalities and faiths oppressed by the Turk. For there would no longer be oppressors and oppressed but fellow citizens on a footing of complete equality.

The immediate effect of this sensational revolution was

extremely favourable to England. Abdul Hamid's entire government had been in the pay of Germany. Within twenty-four hours all his pro-German counsellors were in prison and the German Ambassador, Baron Marschall, accustomed hitherto to use the language of a master, found himself beleaguered in his embassy by the hatred of the entire population. England, on the contrary, reaped an unexpected reward for the unpopularity she had incurred for so many years with the Sultan's Government by demanding a policy of reform. A new Ambassador, Sir Gerald Lowther, reached Constantinople on the very morrow of the revolution. He was embarrassed by the unrestrained enthusiasm with which he was greeted. Noel Buxton, the President of the Balkan Committee in London, and the unwearied champion of the peoples oppressed by the Turks, was equally disconcerted to find himself become overnight a Turkish national hero. Conservative and cautious Englishmen, not least the Ambassador himself, remained pessimistic and sceptical. How solid was the new system? And in any case what effect would the revolution produce in Egypt and India? But British opinion as a whole gave its confidence to the Young Turks and carried with it Sir Edward Grey, who thought that after all the best way to conciliate the Moslems of Egypt and India was to display openly and even advertise his sympathy with the experiment in reform on which the Moslems of Constantinople had embarked. Marschall consoled himself by reflecting that this new-born sympathy of the Turks for England was a 'natural' phenomenon, one of the infantile diseases of a nation adopting for the first time a Liberal constitution. Germany herself had suffered from the same malady before Bismarck cured her.[1]

Then a second event followed, a reply to the Young-Turk revolution, as that had been a reply to the meeting at Reval. On October 5 the Prince of Bulgaria declared himself the independent sovereign of Bulgaria and not only of Bulgaria in the strict sense, whose boundaries had been laid down by the Treaty of Berlin, but also of eastern Roumelia which after 1885 had remained nominally a Turkish province though the Prince of Bulgaria was its governor. And on October 7 the Austrian Government proclaimed the annexation of Bosnia and Herzegovina over which it

[1] Baron von Marschall to Prince von Bülow, September 4, 1908 (*Die Grosse Politik* . . . vol. xxv[11], pp. 622–3).

had exercised a protectorate since 1878. Though in either case no real change was effected and a status which had long existed in fact received the seal of official recognition, both acts involved a serious blow to the prestige of the new regime in Turkey, which Germany was reasonably suspected of having encouraged, if not actually engineered. The entire British Press without distinction of political allegiance expressed indignation and protested against this violation of international law. And naturally the indignation was still keener in Russia, which saw the policy of Mürzsteg violated more flagrantly, far more flagrantly than it had been in January by the Sandjak concession, since it was the treaty of Berlin itself which Austria was openly breaking. In Italy also, great indignation was felt and demonstrations hostile to Austria took place. An Austrian encroachment on the Adriatic coast was regarded as a violation of Italy's rights. And when that encroachment was effected without any previous understanding with a Power that was, or was supposed to be, Austria's ally, it must be regarded as a breach of the Triple Alliance. Was the Triple Entente not only to be knit closer but enlarged by the accession of Turkey and Italy? The event would prove far otherwise.

3

What did Russia claim? Compensation not for Turkey but for herself, particularly a free passage through the Dardanelles for her navy? What did England claim? Nothing for herself but compensation for Turkey whose honour had been seriously damaged. There was therefore no agreement between the policies of the two Powers, though both were indignant with Austria. It is true no doubt, that in 1907 Sir Edward Grey had informed the Russian Ambassador that the Foreign Office was no longer opposed in principle to the opening of the Dardanelles to Russian men-of-war. But the declaration had been confidential and by mutual consent the question of the Straits had been omitted both from the text of the agreement concluded in September 1907 and from the conversations at Reval in June 1908. Isvolsky however had not forgotten a declaration so invaluable for Russian foreign policy. Disclosures made by Baron Von Aehrenthal soon revealed that on the very morrow of Reval Isvolsky had approached him, and attempted to restore the Balkan *entente* between Austria and Russia on the following basis. Austria was to have full sovereignty over Bosnia and Herzegovina, Russia a free passage through the Dardanelles.[1] In Isvolsky's eyes Von Aehrenthal's crime was not the annexation of Bosnia and Herzegovina but that he had effected it so quickly that he had not had time to secure his part of the agreement. He was caught in the trap, compelled to admit that he had no objection to the annexation, and to beg from England the free passage of the Straits. But Sir Edward Grey was himself trapped, not daring either to refuse Russia what he had promised a year before to let her take, or to compel Young-Turkey to grant it.

We must add that Russia, which had no wish to abandon Bulgaria to the influence of Vienna, was quite willing to recognize her independence, even with the addition of Eastern Roumelia and to negotiate a direct agreement on the question between Ferdinand and the Porte. This, too, was unwelcome to England. But the Foreign Office had no desire to admit to the whole world that the policy of an understanding with Russia had broken down a year after the agreement, and three months after Reval. At Petersburg Sir Arthur Nicolson, without conceding to him what it was not in his power to concede, did his utmost to support Isvolsky against a hostile cabal. When in October Isvolsky visited London he had a splendid reception and Sir Edward Grey sought to find a formula by which he could make common cause with him against Von Aehrenthal. It would not be a revision of the Treaty of Berlin. This would have aroused too powerful appetites in Russia, too great alarm in England. It would be an unpretending conference of ambassadors which would sanction the double breach of the treaty by Bulgaria and by Austria, but would at the same time determine what recompense should be made to the Powers whose prestige or economic interests had suffered, Turkey and even Serbia.

This was little in comparison with Russia's desire. But it was too much for Austria and the Austrian Government soon perceived how strong a position it occupied. We must not imagine,

---

[1] See a private letter from the Baron Von Aehrenthal to Prince von Bülow, September 26, 1908: 'He (Isvolsky) assured me that he had not entered into any agreement with England on the question of the Straits. In showing myself ready to satisfy Russia's wishes on the point, I was influenced by the wider aim of detaching her from England' (*Österreich-Ungarns Aussenpolitik* . . . vol. i, pp. 99 sqq.).

as at the time Petersburg and all the capitals of Europe believed, that the Emperor William was behind the annexation of Bosnia. He was informed of Austria's decision only at the same time as the other Powers and in fact, owing to a mistake, not until twenty-four hours after the French President. At the moment he was extremely vexed by a step which bid fair to embroil him irretrievably with the Turks, and annoyed that Austria had failed to observe the decencies of behaviour between allies by consulting him first. And the German Press at first displayed annoyance. But Chancellor von Bülow, who was a more circumspect statesman and had moreover been informed in advance by the Austrian Government, decided to give Austria unreserved support and soon converted the Emperor and public opinion to his point of view. The struggle, therefore, quickly became a battle between Aehrenthal supported by the Emperor William and Isvolsky supported, though not without inevitable reservations, by Sir Edward Grey or, as they said in Vienna, by King Edward. For the King, if we may credit the gossip of court circles, was furious. Nothing had been said to him of the matter at Ischl. He had not been allowed to play on his return to England that part of European inquiry agent which he prided himself on filling so well.[1] The legend of 'King Edward's policy' made it easy to ascribe to his direct influence both the anti-Austrian attitude of the Foreign Office and the violent campaign in the British Press against the annexation of Bosnia. To the latter the Austrian Press replied with equal violence, and a coolness ensued between the two monarchs which lasted for months.[2] Before leaving Vienna in November for the embassy at Berlin, the English Ambassador, Sir Edward Goschen, received nothing short of a rating from the Austrian Prime Minister.[3] Such insolence would be inexplicable, if Aehrenthal had not already felt certain of victory.

Little by little the Young-Turk Government drew closer to the

[1] For the false reports which an Austrian journalist circulated in the German Press in August 1909 on the subject of Edward VII's attitude at Ischl, intended to excite German opinion against him, see Mensdorff's telegram from London, August 2, 1909, his report from London, August 19, 1909 and his private letters from London, November 12, 17, 1909 (Österreich-Ungarns Aussenpolitik ... vol. ii, pp. 424–448 and 531, 545). That summer, King Edward attempted in vain to secure an invitation from the Emperor of Austria.

[2] Von Tschirschky to Prince von Bülow, December 16, 1908 (Die Grosse Politik ... vol. xxvi, p. 340). Mensdorff—Despatch from London, November 3, 1908 (Österreich-Ungarns Aussenpolitik ... vol. i, p. 372).

[3] Sir Edward Goschen to Sir Edward Grey, November 5, 1908 (British Documents ... vol. v, pp. 484–5). Wickham Steed, Through Thirty Years, vol. i, p. 293.

Teutonic powers. The integrity of the Ottoman Empire had less to fear from them. Russia and England were still the enemy. At the beginning of October Marschall watched with amusement Sir Gerald Lowther silent, depressed, and extremely embarrassed to know how to repay the enthusiasm shown for him.[1] After all, Turkey could accept the loss of these two provinces, already three-quarters lost for the past forty years, the more easily because Austria had offered from the very first to renounce in return the rights over the Sandjak given her by the Treaty of Berlin. Was it not indeed the necessity of evacuating the Sandjak which decided Aehrenthal to give some compensation to the *amour-propre* of the military party by annexing the two provinces? Let Austria guarantee the Moslems of Bosnia and Herzegovina their possessions and religious liberty, pay the Turkish Government an indemnity to compensate her for the state lands Turkey had possessed in the annexed provinces, and promise to conclude a favourable commercial treaty and abolish the capitulations. On these terms Turkey, the power principally concerned, would undoubtedly be willing to separate herself from the other powers and recognize the annexation without waiting for the meeting of the Congress or Conference. She actually took this step on February 26, 1909. It was all very well for the British Press to dwell on the importance of the concessions made by Austria and explain them by the anxiety of Vienna to put an end to the Turkish boycott of Austrian goods. This was untrue, or at least only partially true. The truth was that at Constantinople Austrian or Austro-German diplomacy was once more gaining the advantage over British.

4

At the very moment when it secured this triumph in the Levant, Teutonic policy gained an equally decisive victory in Paris. At first the Young-Turk revolution had favoured French influence at Constantinople as much as British. The Salonika revolutionaries had served their political apprenticeship in Paris, French was more familiar to them than English, and their philosophy was the offspring of French democracy rather than of

[1] Baron von Marschall to the Minister for Foreign Affairs, October 11, 1908 (*Die Grosse Politik* . . . vol. xxvi[1], p. 152).

English Liberalism. But if the French Ambassador at Constantinople, Constans, a former Prime Minister, prepared to make good use of their friendly feelings, his manner of doing so was not entirely satisfactory to his British colleague. He pursued a policy of financial co-operation between France and Germany which ill sorted with the policy of the Franco-Russian alliance and the Franco-British *entente* and he expressed himself on the subject with a frankness anything but diplomatic. The new English Ambassador who came from Morocco, where for several years he had worked zealously to defend French interests against the claims of Germany, was disconcerted by the novel situation in which he found himself on the Dardanelles and expressed the wish to be 'rid of the Frenchman'.[1] But he was not rid of him, and it was Constans' policy which found favour for the moment with the French Government. During the months which followed— the last months of Clémenceau's ministry—French policy was more pro-Austrian and pro-German than at any other time during the years which led up to the War.

France deliberately adopted an attitude of conciliation. She declared her conviction that the best way to prevent the Bosnian crisis leading to war was to satisfy, as far as possible, the claims of Austria. Possibly the French Ambassador in Vienna when he advised this policy cherished the hope of detaching Austria from Germany, and there can be no doubt that this was the unavowed purpose of the new British Ambassador in Vienna, Sir Fairfax Cartwright, who would have been sent to Berlin instead of to Vienna, if Berlin had not refused to accept a man whose hatred of Germany was so well known. But the intention of the Quai d'Orsay in making this attempt to adapt its policy as far as possible to Austrian interests, was different. Beyond a *rapprochement* with Austria it had a *rapprochement* with Germany in view.[2]

[1] Sir Gerald Lowther to Sir Edward Grey, August 11, 1908. '. . . It will be interesting to see how the German Ambassador is treated on his return. All his friends are now locked up and his position will be difficult. I wish there were a possibility of getting rid of the Frenchman.' (*British Documents* . . . vol. v, p. 265.)

[2] For this *rapprochement* between France and Germany in the Near East and the part played in it by the journalist, André Tardieu, and the minister, Pichon, see the note from Stemrich to von Bülow, September 29, 1908 (*Die Grosse Politik* . . . vol. xxiv, p. 333). Baron von der Lancken to Prince von Bülow, December 19, 1908 (*Die Grosse Politik* . . . pp. 372–4). Von Schön to Prince von Bülow, October 10, 1908 (*Die Grosse Politik* . . . vol. xxvi, p. 145). A rumour, derived from a reliable source, was current in Vienna that Clémenceau himself at this moment had taken alarm at the prospect of finding himself involved, as a result of the policy favoured by Britain, in a war with Germany. (Private

During the forty years which followed the war of 1870 France pursued, if we neglect inevitable deviations, a fairly consistent policy. Squeezed between two powers of the first rank, England and Germany, she endeavoured to build up a colonial empire by the alternative favour of both. It was a difficult and a risky game to play but proved in the long run successful almost everywhere except in the Nile valley. In 1904 France had obtained from England a free hand in Morocco. At Tangier and Algeciras Germany had reminded her that this was not enough. French diplomacy was now trying to persuade Germany to acquiesce in, if not positively to favour, the extension of her influence in that country. On the spot where French and Germans were at loggerheads the difficulties were very great. But at Berlin the overtures of the Quai d'Orsay met with a more favourable reception. For on the one hand, the German Government was becoming every day more convinced that England would never allow her to gain a foothold on the coast of Morocco, and it would surely be worth while to save what could be saved of her influence and prestige in those regions by an agreement with France. And in the second place, there was an entire party in Germany who, from hatred for England rather than love of peace, entertained hopes of an eventual reconciliation with France. The Emperor was at the head of it and however odd the methods he employed at times, he had never lost sight of this goal.

Therefore, when during the last months of 1908 incidents occurred in Morocco which a few years before would have brought the West to the verge of war—Moulaï-Hafid's successful rising against the client of France, Abdul Aziz, and the episode of the six deserters from the Foreign Legion who took refuge at the German Consulate at Casablanca and were carried off from it by force, they were settled amicably. It was in vain that public opinion at Paris caught fire. And in vain that the British staff made plans for military operations to be undertaken in concert

Letter from Baron Von Aehrenthal to the Embassy at Berlin, December 15, 1908; *Österreich-Ungarns Aussenpolitik* . . . vol. i, pp. 602–03). See further on this point Baron Von Aehrenthal's earlier report of his interview with Isvolsky at Buchlau in September 1908 (*Österreich-Ungarns Aussenpolitik* . . . vol. i, pp. 91–92). In January 1909 Pichon suggested that common action should be taken by France, Germany, and England. Berlin rejected the suggestion. Stemrich's note for Von Schön, January 22, 1909 (*Die Grosse Politik* . . . vol. xxvi[11], pp. 191–92). Prince von Bülow to Von Tschirschky, February 6, 1909 (ibid., p. 197). Prince von Radolin to the Foreign Office February 18, 1909. (ibid. pp. 601–02). Prince von Radolin to the Foreign Office, February 19, 1909 (ibid., pp. 605–06.)

with France. Neither in Paris nor in Berlin was war desired by those in control of foreign policy, and the Casablanca incident had hardly been settled by referring it to The Hague Court of Arbitration when negotiations were begun and pushed forward with the utmost speed for an agreement between the two nations on the question of Morocco. It was signed on February 9, 1909. The French Government undertook 'not to put any obstacles in the way of German commercial and industrial interests' and the German Government in turn undertook not to stand in the way of 'the special political interests of France' and both Governments promised 'to give a share to each other's subjects in all undertakings for which a French or German firm might obtain a concession'.

By this recognition of her political interests in Morocco, France began to obtain her revenge not only for Tangier but also (though this was denied by the express wording of the agreement) for Algeciras. Alone among the powers of the Triple Entente, France reaped an advantage from the Bosnian crisis. In itself this was not calculated to give pleasure to Russia or England.[1] To cause anxiety to both was no doubt one of the objects the Wilhelmstrasse had in view in consenting to the agreement of February 9. But the English had further reasons for anxiety when they scrutinized the text of the agreement. For the real negotiations which had led up to its conclusion had taken place not between the two foreign offices but between the financiers and manufacturers of both countries. Between the lines of the text could be read an understanding in which Krupp and Schneider played an important part for a joint development not only of Morocco but the whole of North Africa, and joint action not only in North Africa but in Turkey. How could this be good news to the British finan-

[1] Sir Arthur Nicolson to Sir Edward Grey, March 1, 1909. 'French Ambassador communicated to-day fresh formula to Russian Minister for Foreign Affairs, which the French Government suggest should be communicated to Belgrade by the Powers. Minister for Foreign Affairs took exception to several points in it. . . . Every country had a right to have aspirations, and perhaps in the future Servia might wish to have some frontier rectifications with Turkey and would not tie her hands in the way suggested. These were the chief objections which occurred to him on a first hasty reading. Russian Minister for Foreign Affairs is being much irritated against the French Government.' Also Sir Louis Mallet's minute: 'It is very clumsy of the French to be so persistent. . . . Inform Sir A. Nicolson that you concur with Mr. Isvolsky in thinking the French proposal objectionable.' (*British Documents* . . . vol. v, p. 645.) The Same to the Same, March 24, 1909: 'Algeciras had to be revenged, the "ring" broken through, and the Triple Entente dissipated. The Franco-German agreement was the first step; and France is a quarter of the way towards a fuller understanding with Germany.' (*British Documents* . . . vol. v, p. 736.)

ciers and industrialists? Sir Francis Bertie informed Sir Edward Grey on February 8 that in Constantinople the group of French financiers had just broken with the English financiers and reached an understanding with a German group.[1] And London was further alarmed when the tariff committee in the French Chamber of Deputies proposed a general increase of tariffs likely to injure British export trade. In public the British Government might declare its unreserved satisfaction at a Franco-German agreement which was a further guarantee of European peace. In private, Sir Edward Grey and Sir Charles Hardinge informed the representatives of the French Government that it occasioned them no small anxiety. France must not allow herself to be duped by the German advances. Other questions besides that of Morocco divided the two countries. Nor must she forget those difficult days when she had been glad to rely on England's friendship in her struggle with Germany. On no account must the *entente* be dissolved.

5

On February 9 the King and Queen of England accompanied by the Colonial Secretary, Lord Crewe, Field-Marshal Lord Grenfell, and Sir Charles Hardinge, visited the German Emperor in his capital. It was King Edward's first visit to Berlin after eight years on the throne. The visit had been promised the summer before to counteract the bad impression produced in Germany by the two royal meetings at Reval and Ischl. It was more necessary than ever in February after the months of diplomatic tension which had followed. The King had become an old man, his bronchial tubes were affected, and he was suffering from the effects of influenza. But it would have been disastrous to cancel his visit. So he came, braving in the depths of winter the rigours of the North German climate. During his visit his health grew worse; he had an attack of coughing followed by a fainting fit which alarmed his entourage. But he conformed to the exacting ceremonial of a spectacular official reception with a courage universally recognized.

It was not a pleasant visit. Edward VII was unpopular in Berlin

---

[1] Sir Francis Bertie to Sir Edward Grey, February 18, 1909. (*British Documents* . . . vol. v, p. 605).

and the police feared hostile demonstrations. These indeed did not occur, but the public gave him a frigid welcome. The personal relations between the two monarchs were worse than ever in consequence of an incident which the previous October had astonished and amused the whole of Europe. The *Daily Telegraph* published the text of the German Emperor's conversation with an English friend. In the course of the conversation William II recalled all the services he had rendered to England during the Boer War—military advice by which the British staff had profited, and diplomatic assistance when he had thwarted the attempts of Russia and France to draw him into an anti-English alliance. And his friendly attitude towards England was the more meritorious because the feeling of his entire people was hostile to her. Why did she respond to such generosity with nothing but ingratitude?[1] It was strange language and aroused universal indignation in Germany. It was distasteful both to those Germans who disliked England and blamed the Emperor for humbling himself before the great rival power and those friends of peace who wished to see the relations between the two countries improve and found themselves represented as hating England. In England the effect was even worse. The account, partly true, of what the Emperor had done to help England during the Boer War had an insulting air of patronage. Moreover, all Englishmen were aware that his naval policy was directly aimed at their country and well-informed persons knew that at this very moment the American Government at the request of the British was preventing the publication of a particular number of a certain review in which another conversation of the Emperor's was reported which was

[1] *Daily Telegraph*, November 28, 1908. The article described conversations between William and an English host during his visit the previous autumn. Already on the very morrow of the visit the Emperor's loquacity had caused anxiety to his Government. A Manchester paper, the *Daily Despatch*, had published a conversation of the Kaiser's with 'a diplomat of high station'. The sole object of his navy, the Emperor had said, was to assist the commercial and colonial expansion of Germany by increasing her prestige at sea. Germany entertained no designs of conquest in the direction of Scandinavia, Holland, Belgium, Switzerland or the Baltic provinces which were completely Russian. And in regard to England the sole desire of German statesmen was to maintain friendly relations with her. The German Ambassador in London published a denial. The Manchester *Daily Despatch* replied by proving from documentary evidence that the text of the conversation had been revised and corrected at the Embassy. The Germans replied by another and more involved denial whose sole object was to clear the Emperor. The *Daily Despatch* once more published a triumphant reply. It must be added that though the Emperor's conduct was regarded as incorrect in Berlin, and the Ambassador was therefore compelled to deny it and though the incident revealed differences of opinion between William and his chancellor, it attracted very little public attention. (*The Times*, December 4–6, 1907.)

one long diatribe against the English. William was obliged to make his excuses publicly and promise to abstain in future from utterances not previously approved by his ministers. It was therefore a monarch out of humour with himself, out of humour with his ministers, out of humour with his people, and above all out of humour with the entire British people and their King who bade the latter welcome.

One thing alone was calculated to diminish his ill humour and soften his bitter feelings towards his Chancellor, von Bülow, whom he had loathed since November—the brilliant success the latter had just achieved for German diplomacy and indirectly for the Emperor himself. The Franco-German agreement was signed on the very day Edward VII reached Berlin. The negotiations had been hastened so that the signature should not be delayed beyond that day at latest.[1] Everyone knew that the agreement between Austria and Turkey would be shortly concluded and Turkey accept the annexation of Bosnia without any interference by the Powers. Russia was isolated and humbled, and indirectly England. At this meeting in Berlin in February 1909, the conqueror on the battlefield of diplomacy was welcoming the conquered.

Immediately after the royal visit to Berlin, Sir Arthur Nicolson wrote from Petersburg to Sir Edward Grey. 'M. Isvolsky is seriously alarmed at the *communiqué* which has been telegraphed from Berlin as to what passed at the recent meeting. *Communiqué* states that in the Near East there is a complete understanding

---

[1] The Emperor William had wanted the agreement signed before Edward VII's arrival, but Jules Cambon who brought it from Paris bearing the signatures of the French ministers only reached Berlin on the 9th and his train came in after King Edward's. Immediately, without losing an hour, Von Schön received Cambon in audience and the agreement was signed. (Baron von Schön *Erlebtes. Beitrage zur politischen Geschichte der neuesten Zeit*, 1921, pp. 87–88. French trans., pp. 120–22). Cf. Von Kiderlen-Wächter to an anonymous correspondent, March 7, 1909: 'You will of course have read that we have concluded the Morocco agreement which is, I think, a good thing. Between ourselves I may say that we have carried it through entirely by ourselves with the French Ambassador, M. Cambon. And it's been a tough job.' Kiderlen continues: 'Here, as at Constantinople, it is with the French Ambassador that I get on best. The French I'm convinced really want peace. Our English friends, faithful to their old principles, would be none too distressed if we slaughtered each other on the Continent while they remained in their island to sell to the entire world. . . . It would be really too idiotic if we had a European war and slew hundreds of thousands for the sake of those Serbian swine.' (Ernst Jaeckh Kiderlen-Wächter der Staatsmann und Mench. *Briefwecsel und Nachlass*, 1924, vol. ii, pp. 24–25.) Admiral von Tirpitz to the Minister of Marine, May 6, 1909. '. . . In this dispute between Austria and Serbia England has tried to push France and Russia on. But most characteristically France has united with Germany to pour oil on the troubled waters. In any case an "isolated" England has not dared to go to war over the question.' (*Politische Dokuments*, vol. i, p. 151.)

between Great Britain and Germany. He says this means Great Britain has joined Germany and Austria in Near Eastern policy. France has come into better relations with Germany and Russia has been isolated. Simultaneously with this he learns, from information from a good source, which is confirmed by the threatening attitude towards Serbia, adopted both by Austrian and Hungarian Press, that Austria intends to present shortly an ultimatum to Serbia, which, if not obeyed, will be probably followed by a punitive expedition, or execution, as it is termed.'[1] For it was already apparent and became more evident still at the end of February, that the conclusion of the agreement between Austria and Turkey and the annexation of Bosnia and Herzegovina had been directed not so much against Turkey as against Serbia, against the danger of a Bosnian insurrection, a possible echo of the Young-Turk revolution, perhaps fomented and certainly exploited by the pan-Serb agitators of Belgrade. Austria was arming, and the existence of a complete understanding between the Austrian and German Staffs was certain though the public did not know how far it had been actually carried. For at the proposal of the Austrian Field-Marshal, Conrad von Hötzendorf, a military convention had been concluded between the two staffs with the full approval of both Governments arranging for military assistance to be given to Austria, if a declaration of war by Austria upon Serbia were followed by a Russian declaration of war against Austria.[2] What would France do if Russia declared war? And what would England do if France were drawn into the war? All these possibilities were discussed at Berlin. For the first time, soldiers and diplomats saw rising above the horizon the storm-cloud of the world war.

British diplomacy sought to conjure this danger of war without damage to the prestige of England and the Triple Entente. Sir Edward Grey suggested joint action by the Powers at Vienna to discover what the demands of the Austrian Government were and transmit them to Belgrade, and accepting what he believed to be a proposal of the German Government, he proposed joint action

[1] Sir Arthur Nicolson to Sir Edward Grey, February 13, 1909 (British Documents . . . vol. v, p. 596).
[2] For the negotiation of this military convention between the two staffs see Field-Marshal Conrad von Hötzendorf's correspondence with Von Moltke (Feldmarschall Conrad von Hötzendorf, Aus meiner Dienstzeit, 1906–1918, vol. i, pp. 379 sqq., 631 sqq); Von Tschirschky to Prince von Bülow, December 17, 1908; and the editor's explanatory note. (Die Grosse Politik . . . vol. xxvii, pp. 342–44.)

at Belgrade to discover what concessions the Serbian Government was willing to make to Austria and to transmit them in turn to Vienna. He clung to the dream of ending the dispute by a conference which would give the settlement an international sanction. This was the very last thing Vienna or Berlin desired. They wanted Serbia isolated in face of Austria and yielding unconditionally to her demands. On March 22 the German Ambassador at Petersburg presented Isvolsky with what amounted to an ultimatum. He was called upon to give a plain reply to the question whether or not Russia recognized the annexation of Bosnia and Herzegovina. An ambiguous answer would be interpreted as a refusal, events would take their course (in other words Austria would declare war on Serbia) and Isvolsky would be responsible for the consequences. A council of ministers summoned in haste lasted for nine hours at the end of which Isvolsky, without delaying to inform Paris or London, submitted to the German ultimatum and agreed to recognize the annexation of the two provinces. Deserted even by Russia, Serbia capitulated. A separate agreement was concluded between Russia and Turkey, by which the Russian Government freed Bulgaria from her debts to Turkey by renouncing certain annual payments due from Turkey to herself. Another agreement was signed between Montenegro and Austria, which with the consent of England and Italy released Montenegro from certain military obligations imposed upon her by the Treaty of Berlin. In themselves these arrangements were not unfavourable to the maintenance of peace. To the advantage of Austria in Bosnia, of Bulgaria in Eastern Roumelia, of Turkey in the Sandjak, of Montenegro farther to the south, systems of divided sovereignty had been swept away which for many years past had exasperated the political situation in the Balkans. But the Yugoslav problem in Austria was not solved, had indeed been made more difficult by the annexation of Bosnia; and on the other hand the Austrian and German Governments had done everything to make the settlements actually reached appear not so much guarantees of peace as a flaunting assertion of the military power of the two Teutonic empires. The German Government was conscious of having gained a triumph exactly parallel to the victory it had won four years earlier. In 1905 after a year of the Anglo-French *entente*, it had compelled Delcassé's resignation. In 1909, less than two years after the Anglo-Russian agreement, it had humbled Isvolsky. He would indeed most probably have resigned, if his Government had not forbidden it, not wishing to give Austria and Germany the honour of a too striking victory and condemned him to endure for long months of helpless chafing the insolence of Viennese diplomacy. But sooner or later he would be obliged to retire. For it was in vain that he hunted about for a means of avenging his humiliation, engaging in further Balkan intrigues in concert with Italy. Everyone knew that he was in disgrace with his master, who had never liked England, and broken by a formidable opposition. Not only did the pan-Slavists refuse to forgive his final capitulation, but the reactionaries, the champions of an understanding with Germany, exploited his surrender to the disadvantage of the Liberal party, which supported the understanding with England.[1] And what was it that made possible these bloodless victories of Germany in the East and West alike? The fact that neither the French nor the Russian army counted for anything beside the German. The Russian army had been weakened and demoralized by two years of unsuccessful war followed by two years of revolution; the French by long years of political anarchy. The German army had no need of reinforcement. This masterpiece of military technique and discipline had, it would seem, been brought to the point of perfection by the contemporaries of Bismarck. Germany was free to devote every penny she could raise to the increase of her navy. It is not surprising that the struggle between the two navies, the English and the German, reached its apogee at the time of the diplomatic crisis provoked by the annexation of Bosnia and Herzegovina.

6

Still less shall we be surprised if we consider how intense that naval rivalry had become already during the years which preceded the crisis. We remember the anxiety which Germany's attitude at The Hague had caused the English pacifists. And we remember

[1] See Pourtalès' letter to Von Bülow written a year before, June 5, 1908. '. . . Herr Isvolsky remarked that he was the very last to underestimate the dangers of this campaign. But they must be looked for in domestic far more than in foreign politics. The outburst of jingoism and the unbridled language of the Press were symptoms that the revolution had not been completely suppressed. . . . The attack upon Germany was conducted almost exclusively by the radical organs. These advocated for domestic reasons a *rapprochement* with liberal England and a hostile attitude towards a Germany regarded as reactionary.' (*Die Grosse Politik* . . . vol. xxvi[11], pp. 445–46.)

the new naval law introduced immediately afterwards by the German Government and the plan of naval construction it laid down for the following four years, every year from 1908 to 1911 four large battleships—ironclads or armoured cruisers—of the latest type. We can imagine the excitement which the correspondence between Lord Tweedmouth and the Emperor produced at that moment of all others. And we can well understand how, in certain quarters, at once expert and interested, it was decided that this was the right moment to put pressure on the Liberal Cabinet to alter its programme of naval construction. And the opportunity seemed all the more favourable because Campbell-Bannerman's illness and retirement and the subsequent remodelling of the Cabinet encouraged hopes that the policy of the Government would take a new direction and the imperialists be in the saddle once more.

These interested experts were the large firms who manufactured guns, armour plate, and ironclads and directly suffered from the Admiralty's policy of economy. Five-sixths of the construction and equipment of the navy were in the hands of private firms—hence the enormous wealth of the industry. A witness, writing just before the War, estimated the total capital of the seven largest armament firms at £34,000,000. Among these seven Cammell, Laird & Co. had a capital of £4,000,000, Vickers a capital of £8,500,000, and Armstrong, Whitworth & Co. a capital of £9,500,000. Never since the beginning of the century had the dividends of the last two firms been less than 10 per cent. An entire group of publicists whose activities were the more embarrassing for the ministers because they belonged to their party, denounced the power of these firms.[1]

Consider the composition of the boards of directors in these large firms. Naval engineers and naval officers were constantly entering the service of shipbuilding firms where promotion was more rapid and far more lucrative. Elswick had taken Sir William White from the Admiralty, and when he went back to it Sir Philip Watts, also a formal naval officer, took his place. Vickers & Maxim had taken Trevor Dawson from the army, Dunn from the navy.

From the boards of directors let us turn to the shareholders in these large armament firms. From the information published by

---

[1] G. H. Perris, *The War Traders, an Exposure*, 1913. He quotes *The Economist* for April 26, 1913, H. N. Brailsford, *The War of Steel and Gold, a Study of the Armed Peace*, 1914. J. T. Walton Newbold, *How Europe armed for War*, 1916.

a provincial paper in 1909 it appears that the shareholders of Armstrong & Whitworth included sixty peers, fifteen baronets, twenty knights, twenty officers of the army or navy, eight Members of Parliament, and eight journalists. And in 1913 a pamphleteer called attention to the presence among these shareholders of two Cabinet ministers and two members of the Opposition Front Bench. In all this, we must bear in mind, there is no question of corruption in the strict sense. We have to do with a society so constituted that a large number of the ruling class have a personal interest in the prosperity of large firms which in turn depend for their prosperity on Government orders and are the more flourishing the more abundant they are. And the circle of those who had, to use Bentham's phrase, a 'sinister' interest in a policy of large armaments was wider, far wider, than this. Armstrong & Vickers employed 120,000 workers at Newcastle-on-Tyne, a third of the entire population—that is to say, a large town was living on war or the preparation for it. To reduce armaments would be to condemn a portion of these men to unemployment. In recent years government orders had even from time to time been increased to help the country to surmount a period of depression.[1] It was a dangerous expedient. For when the crisis had passed they dared not throw on to the street the men for whom work had been artificially provided. This in turn produced a permanent conflict between the economic interests of these men and the political ideals they usually held. They would elect a Unionist, the champion of a large navy. Or, if from habit they elected a Liberal or a member of their own class, he could hardly put up a stiff resistance to a policy of naval construction which supplied his electorate with wages: least of all when unemployment was rife and British industry was passing through a slump as at the beginning of 1908.

The Admiralty had one good reason for choosing to have its ships built by private firms—the competition between them. According to current belief competition favoured technical improvement while reducing prices. At the end of the nineteenth

---

[1] 'In 1884 began that sinister form of unemployment relief administered henceforward at regular intervals by the Government in the form of Admiralty extravagance. A careful study of the technical and trade literature of the early 'eighties makes quite evident the influence on armament policy of bad trade in the shipping and engineering branches of industry. It was this that made possible the success of the naval agitation which would otherwise have broken in vain against the Radicalism of such centres as Birmingham, Sheffield, Tyneside, and Clydeside.' (J. T. Walton Newbold, *How Europe armed for War*, p. 26.)

century the Admiralty patronized in turn Armstrong and Vickers. But it was in vain that England remained the citadel of competition, one of the European countries in which industrial unification met with the most powerful opposition. Here too the tendency to amalgamation made itself felt and, it would seem, its operation was particularly evident in the armament industry. Sometimes two rival firms amalgamated—for example, Vickers, Son & Co. and Maxim Nordenfeldt of Birmingham in 1896. Or one firm absorbed another. The Clydebank Shipbuilding and Engineering Co. was absorbed by John Brown & Co. in 1898, and Napier of Govan by William Beardmore & Co. of Parkhead in 1901. Or the absorption might be only partial, one firm becoming the dependency of another, a fate which befell Beardmore & Co. a year after it had bought up Napier. Vickers bought half the shares and by lending money to the firm enabled it to set up on the Clyde the largest shipyards England had known. Or again, without the avowed formation of a cartel of the German type the co-operation between leading armament firms became so close that it amounted to partnership. Such was the 'indefinable' bond which from the opening of the twentieth century united Armstrong-Whitworth with Vickers, Son & Maxim. Two firms long hostile were now reconciled and strengthened by the support of the Nobel Trust. Thus a solid block of firms was constituted, capable between them of building, equipping, and arming an entire squadron. This powerful combine however did not even now include all the firms engaged in naval construction. We notice the formation of an opposition combine (Charles Cammell, John Brown, Laird Brothers, Thomas Firth, Fairfield Shipbuilding Co., Coventry Ordnance Works). It might have served the public interest by competing with the former syndicate for Admiralty orders. The competition between the two groups did not however take this form. They asked for more orders, enough to satisfy both.

7

At the beginning of 1906, Mulliner, Chairman of the Coventry Ordnance Company, called the attention of the Admiralty to the alarming extension of the Essen works and tried to convince the department that its object was to intensify and accelerate naval construction. But the Admiralty refused to communicate these alarmist conjectures to the Cabinet. He then addressed himself with greater success to the Secretary for War, Haldane. But Haldane's insistence failed to overcome the opposition of his colleagues, who remained unmoved even by Tirpitz's statement in November that Germany was now building ships at a faster rate than England. Reduction of expenditure on preparations for war was one of the fundamental points of the programme on which the Liberals had been returned in 1906, and the ministers felt that to abandon it would amount to a surrender. But their hands were forced by an appeal to the leaders of the Opposition.[1]

On March 2, 1908, the Under-Secretary of State for the Admiralty, Edward Robertson, attempted to prove that a reduction of naval expenditure did not endanger the safety of the country and in particular did not involve the abandonment of the famous 'Two-Power Standard' to which appeal was always being made. Apart from ships of the pre-Dreadnought type (here the overwhelming numerical superiority of England was undisputed) England would possess in 1910 nine Dreadnoughts and three Cruisers of the Invincible type as against two French Dreadnoughts and Germany's four Dreadnoughts and two Invincibles —that is to say, a superiority of twelve to eight. Allowing for the possibility of accelerations in the German rate of construction, Germany might possess seven Dreadnoughts and three Invincibles by the end of 1910. If the two French vessels were added there would be twelve Dreadnoughts in the possession of the two powers to the English twelve. The Two-Power Standard would therefore be maintained. And the following week in reply to his critics, he proved that a year later England would once more have a positive advantage, would possess fourteen Dreadnoughts as against ten German and two French—that is to say, two large ironclads more than Germany and France combined. Then with the aid of facts supplied by Mulliner, Balfour, speaking after two or three Unionists of lesser importance, contested the official figures. Starting from the fact that the construction of the battleships laid down in the German programme began in June where-

---

[1] For the Mulliner episode see 'Mulliner's Diary' (*The Times*, January 3, 1910), also G. H. Perris, *The War Traders, an Exposure*, 1913, pp. 28 sqq.

as the construction of the British ships began six months later he sought to prove that though in January 1911 England would certainly possess twelve Dreadnoughts to Germany's nine, in the autumn of the same year, she would only possess twelve to Germany's thirteen. The Germans were building four Dreadnoughts a year, the British only two. 'Consequently the time is not only far distant, but imminent, when in regard to that particular type of vessel they will be, not our equal, but our superior.'[1] The Government, he said, was returning to the Two-Power Standard; it would be truer to say that it was being driven back to it by the attacks of the Opposition. In 1906 Campbell-Bannerman had attempted to escape from the onerous formula. Before applying it, he argued, we must consider which the other naval powers were, and after the Algeciras conference we were justified in doubting the likelihood of an alliance between France and Germany against England.[2] At once the Unionists were up in arms as though their own leaders the year before had not declared the standard obsolete. Nevertheless, the Prime Minister repeated his contention the following year: he was, he said, 'entirely in favour of the standard' but questioned whether it were still applicable supposing we were at any time to be in close alliance with the two Powers with the largest navies'.[3] In reply Balfour maintained not only that the British navy ought to be equal in number of ships to those 'of any other two powers' but further that it should have 'a margin of superiority' over the two.[4] A year later, when Campbell-Bannerman was already seriously ill, and Prime Minister in name alone, it was a modified form of Balfour's formula that Asquith defended when he asked for a navy strong enough to safeguard England 'against all contingencies that can reasonably enter into the calculations of statesmen'.[5] Eight months later, he allowed a Unionist speaker to draw from him the statement that England must possess 'a preponderance of 10 per cent over the combined strengths, in capital ships, of the two next

[1] H. of C., March 9, 1908 (*Parliamentary Debates*, 4th Series, vol. clxxxv, p. 1181).
[2] H. of C., July 27, 1906 (ibid., vol. cxlii, p. 116).
[3] H. of C., March 5, 1907 (ibid., vol. clxx, pp. 673–4).
[4] H. of C., March 5, 1907 (ibid., vol. clxx, p. 676). It was word for word the doctrine which Arthur Lee had preached the previous year. 'The Two-Power Standard has always meant that, in the matter of efficient first-class battleships, we should have a reasonable margin of superiority over the two next strongest Powers combined and even if those two Powers should happen, at any time, to be our two best friends, the formula would none the less apply.' (*National Review*, April 1906, vol. xlvii, p. 919.)
[5] H. of C., March 2, 1908 (*Parl. Deb.*, 4th Ser., vol. clxxxv, p. 377).

strongest powers'.[1] As he still refused to see any inconsistency between this formula and the formula he had previously defended he was urged to be more explicit. Did he mean 'the two next strongest powers, whatever they may be, and wherever they may be situated?' Yes, he replied, 'under existing conditions and under all foreseeable circumstances'.[2] There was always the same ambiguity, due to the fact that neither on the Government nor on the Opposition benches did speakers express plainly what was at the back of their minds.

When Opposition speakers asked whether in applying the Two-Power Standard all the Powers were taken into account, they were thinking of the United States. Does this mean that they contemplated the possibility of war against an alliance between Germany and America? Certainly not. They explicitly stated that an eventuality of this kind was not the ground on which they founded their demand for a navy at least equal to the combined navies of two other Powers. And when a speaker on the ministerial benches said that his party was content with a navy capable of facing any 'probable' combination of two Powers, he meant that he was excluding America from his calculations. Was he then thinking of Germany and France? Presumably. But Campbell-Bannerman never said so in plain terms and he had good reason to regard such a combination as improbable. The truth of the matter was that while everybody spoke of two Powers, everybody was thinking only of one. England had returned to the situation in which she had been placed half a century before when she regulated the size of her navy with reference to the strength of the French navy alone. But it was now a more formidable navy which caused her anxiety—the German. Those who wanted account taken of the American fleet in applying the Two-Power Standard did so because they knew that the American navy was more modern and increasing more rapidly than the French—that is to say, they were really demanding for the British navy a more marked superiority over the German. Those who on the contrary would take account of the French navy alone were those who were content with a lower margin of superiority. According to the most optimistic calculations England in 1910 would possess as many capital ships

---

[1] H. of C., November 12, 1908 (*Parliamentary Debates*, 4th Series, vol. cxc p. 560).
[2] H. of C., November 23, 1908 (ibid., pp. 1768–69).

as Germany and France together. But why? Because in 1910 France, if her programme of construction were carried out, would possess only two Dreadnoughts[1]—that is to say, this application of the Two-Power Standard would give England only two Dreadnoughts more than the German ten. That was not enough if England were to maintain her naval supremacy. What then did those want who wished to maintain this supremacy undisputed. Gradually, by a novel interpretation of the Two-Power Standard, they had come to demand no longer a navy equal (or superior by 10 per cent) to the two strongest foreign navies, but, what was a different thing altogether, a navy twice as strong in capital ships as the German. Or, employing a formula better calculated to impress the imagination of the public, they asked that for every Dreadnought Germany laid down, England should lay down two: 'two keels for one.'[2]

8

The great naval manœuvres held in the summer of 1908—the most formidable Europe had yet witnessed—were no doubt intended to reassure the public by bringing home to them the magnitude of England's provision for war. Two hundred and seventy ships took part with a total tonnage of 1,044,000 tons and close on 70,000 sailors. What in comparison were the sixty-two Ger-

---

[1] In point of fact France had no Dreadnoughts in 1910.

[2] 'Of course there is no question as to what John Bull will reply to this programme, be it little or big. He will say that he is sorry, but if it must be so he cannot help himself. . . . He wishes for nothing more than the maintenance of the *status quo*. He has no army to speak of; his only defence is his navy. The maintenance of its supremacy is for him a matter of life or death. . . . He simply says to himself: "What a bore ! The two foremost nations in the world might surely find something better to do with their money than spend it in a breakneck, beggar-my-neighbour competition in warships. But if Germany insists, what must be must be." He will not take much heed of programmes on paper, but the moment the challenger lays down the keels of a new Dreadnought, he will lay down the keels of two.' (W. T. Stead, *Review of Reviews*, vol. xxxvi, December 1907, p. 555)— 'It is recognized that command of the European Seas is an inflexible condition of our national security; how is this to be maintained? The "Two-Power Standard" is a good phrase, but it is by no means easy to define and exemplify in *material* and in *personnel*, in ships and guns and men. It is far easier, far clearer and infinitely more safe to adopt the simple standard, and avoiding "paper programmes" for every ship which our great rival builds, to build two of equal strength. Let Germany force the pace, but let England win the race. That is a pregnant phrase and a plain policy which every man of the British electorate can understand. Of any sound scheme of national or imperial defence, naval supremacy based upon the simple proportion of two to one is the vital essence.' (Lord Esher, *National Review*, May 1908. For the problem as it appeared at this date see Archibald Hurd, 'A British Two-Power Fleet,' *Nineteenth Century*, June 1908, vol. lxiii, pp. 485 sqq.

man ships which had just finished their annual manœuvres on the opposite coast of the North Sea? It was the first time that the recently formed Home Fleet had been mobilized and the trial proved successful without calling up the reserve or denuding the ports of the number of men required to carry on the ordinary work of naval bases. Sixty vessels were still left unused. It was in vain that to avoid wounding German susceptibilities the theme of the manœuvres was kept a strict secret. It was perfectly obvious that both in the Channel and in the North Sea the problem handled was to repel a foreign invasion or raid. One incident was the capture of Wick, the landing in that little town of a hostile force not to occupy it presumably but to obtain with the utmost possible speed all the information required and then to re-embark without interference. Inevitably public opinion, instead of being reassured by the magnitude of the British fleet, was alarmed by the success of the imaginary raid. And the alarm was increased a few weeks later when some local manœuvres off the mouth of the Tyne were interrupted by the appearance of a German torpedo boat. The Admiralty lavished explanations designed to calm the fears of the public. The torpedo boat was simply one of the vessels guarding the fishing fleet, it flew an international flag and had come only to take in a fresh supply of water. That was all very well. The peril of invasion was the staple topic of conversation all the same.

A weighty Conservative organ, the *Quarterly Review*, published an important article on the 'German Peril' couched in the language of panic,[1] which irritated the German Chancellor extremely. Such nervousness he considered unworthy of the British Press; it reminded him of France.[2] At the other end of the social scale in a

[1] *Quarterly Review*, July 1908 (vol. ccix, pp. 264 sqq.). See especially p. 291. 'We hold a quarter of the world. By what right do we hold it, if might be once invoked? White power can be the only solid basis of white dominion. If this be true, our huge pyramid is poised upon an apex. In the whole of the King's Dominions there are fewer white men than in Germany alone and we are increasing far more slowly than the Kaiser's subjects.' Also towards the end, p. 298 'Heedless Chauvinism will not avail us. Let us be quiet and prepare. Let us do nothing to hurry on a conflict. Let us not put ourselves in the wrong, as the French did in 1870. Above all, let us not despise our antagonists. The Germans, with all their faults, are a very great and patient people, formidable, not because of what is to be condemned in their modern characteristics, but because of what is excellent. Like them we must defend ourselves. Neither foreign alliances nor *ententes* will compensate in the end for any deficiency in our own strength.'

[2] Interview with Von Bülow by Sidney Whitman, *Standard*, September 14, 1908. See in the same number a leader which criticizes the interview. 'Prince Bülow affects to ignore them (the pan-German writers). He would do better if he could show that he is not, so far as the opportunity arises, playing, perhaps against his will and judgment, into their hand.'

Socialist weekly, the *Clarion*, a campaign on behalf of conscription conducted not only by Blatchford, whose patriotic attitude during the Boer War we have already noticed, but by Hyndman, the orthodox Marxist, caused a great stir. In all the leading papers a host of letters appeared denouncing the presence on the east coast of a host of German spies disguised as tourists or waiters.[1]

The question of accelerating the tempo of naval construction and the extent to which this should be done was the subject of heated debates in the Cabinet. In August Sir Edward Grey made a final desperate effort to persuade William II to build fewer ships so that England need not build so many. When King Edward on his way to Ischl paid a brief visit to the German Emperor at Cronberg, Grey gave the King two memoranda so drawn up that they could be handed directly to the Emperor. The King disliked the commission. He was aware that disarmament proposals made by a stronger to a weaker power are more likely to irritate than persuade. In the end he kept the memoranda in his pocket and the meeting passed off better because serious questions were avoided.[2] Edward VII confided the task of presenting the documents to Sir Charles Hardinge and his interview with the Emperor was stormy. The Kaiser disputed Sir Charles' figures, which, he said, were hardly consistent with the recent spectacle of 300 ships taking part in manœuvres. 'Cease to build or build more slowly,' Hardinge suggested. 'To do so', the Emperor answered, 'would be to defeat ourselves for this is a matter in which the national honour and prestige are at stake.' 'I looked him straight in the face', William wrote to the Chancellor in his account of the interview, 'and he blushed crimson. My frank language did not fail to produce its effect. That is the way in which we should speak to the English.'[3] But the Englishman on his side, writes in his report: 'I do not think it is to be regretted

[1] *The Times*, August 21, 1908, 'The Spy Mania.' The article protests against the scare which had assumed the proportions of an epidemic. See also *Contemporary Review*, January 1910: 'About German Spies,' vol. xcvii, p. 42. 'Such pernicious works of fiction have been positively pouring from the press for the last two years': 'The Invasion of 1910' —'The War Inevitable'—'The Swoop of the (Teutonic) Vulture'—'The Great Raid— 'How the Germans took London: Forewarned Forearmed'—'The Invaders'—'The Story of the Coming War'—'While Britain Slept'—'A Story of Invasion that will stir Britain to its Depths.'
[2] Sir Sidney Lee, *King Edward VII*, vol. ii, pp. 614 sqq.
[3] William II to Prince von Bülow, August 13, 1908 (*Die Grosse Politik* . . . vol. xxiv, pp. 127–8).

that a clear exposition of the views of the Government on the subject of naval armaments has been placed before the Emperor and the German Government, since their reply offers a complete justification to Parliament and to the world at large for any counter-measures that His Majesty's Government may decide upon taking in the near future. Although it is to be regretted that the German Government have assumed such an uncompromising attitude...it is as well to know the worst and be prepared for it.'[1]

That the Cronberg interview exercised a decisive influence on the Cabinet's naval policy there can be no doubt. But the country might not have supported the Government's new policy if it had not been aroused at the beginning of October by the Austrian annexation of Bosnia and Herzegovina and protracted the crisis which ensued. London thought Germany was behind the Austrian move. Vienna thought that England was plotting a naval demonstration in the Adriatic. Metternich retailed to his Government reports that General French and Sir John Fisher did not consider the moment unpropitious for a war between England and Germany,[2] and transmitted to Berlin an article from the *Standard* arguing in favour of a preventive war.[3] On November 23, Lord Roberts moved in the House of Lords a resolution calling upon the Government to adopt the military measures necessary to deter 'the most formidable foreign nation' from attempting to land an army on British soil and on the other hand 'in view of altered strategic conditions in the North Sea' to ask the Committee of Imperial Defence to re-examine the problem of possible invasion.[4] Two months later, a play of very mediocre quality called *An Englishman's Home*, enjoyed a long run at a London theatre. It

---

[1] Sir Charles Hardinge Memorandum of August 16, 1908 (*British Documents* . . . vol. vi, p. 188).

[2] Count Metternich to Prince von Bülow, December 1, 1908 (*Die Grosse Politik* . . . vol. xxvi[1]. p. 280).

[3] Prince von Bülow to Admiral von Tirpitz (*Politische Dokumente*, vol. i, p. 96). The article in question was probably the leader of November 18 which however did not say exactly what Metternich and Von Bülow read into it. We quote the most characteristic passage of this vigorous piece of writing: 'At this moment neither side dreams of using its navy in an aggressive attack on the other; but will that state of things continue? Will not keenness of competition develop into bitterness as the strain begins to tell; will not the temptation grow until it becomes overmastering, on one side or the other, to use the force that has been accumulated to strike the adversary a crushing blow?'

[4] H. of L., November 23, 1908 (*Parliamentary Debates*, 4th Series, vol. cxcvi, pp. 1679 sqq.). See especially in his speech pp. 1685–1696. The motion was carried but only when Lord Roberts had agreed to withdraw the second part which seemed too obviously aimed at Germany.

represented the house of a rich country gentleman in Essex where nothing was discussed except amusement and sport, or if politics were mentioned at all, it was only in reference to a general strike of Post Office employees which disagreeably affected all the members of the party. Suddenly the 'home' was surrounded by a strange army whose uniforms were taken at first for English. What army was it? The army of 'The Emperor of the North'. One of the heroes of the piece snatched a sporting rifle to defend himself and was shot on the spot for his breach of the laws of war. The Territorial Army came on the scene only to cover itself with ridicule. Finally, the regular army arrived and saved the situation but everyone knew that the ending was conventional and the dramatist's real attitude one of hopeless pessimism. At the same time a piece by Barrie was being acted in London, *What Every Woman Knows*. It became the current witticism to call the new play 'What Every German Knows'. It was an extremely effective piece of propaganda and yielded a host of recruits to the Territorial Army. The Government took it under its patronage and the Censor would not allow a parody to be put on the stage.

9

The primary object of this propaganda was to strengthen the army so as to provide against an invasion possible in spite of the fleet. But the nation's fundamental concern was still the navy. In March 1908 Asquith had expressly pledged himself to the construction in 1909 of a sufficient number of ships to prevent Germany having more Dreadnoughts than England at the end of 1911. In May the Cabinet at a secret meeting after violent debates in which the new First Lord of the Admiralty, McKenna, and Sir Edward Grey threatened to resign if their demands were not complied with, decided to lay down four Dreadnoughts in 1909 (as against two in 1908), and six if at the beginning of the year the situation were sufficiently grave to warrant that addition to the programme. The pessimists' predictions seemed justified in July when Krupp issued new bonds to the value of £2,000,000 and still more justified in November when it became known that orders were being given to the German shipyards six months before the publication of the naval estimates. The German Government through its Ambassador in London protested against these suspicions and Asquith himself took note in a speech of his protest.[1] But the British might well feel alarm. A nation which had twice taken Europe by surprise with her Dreadnoughts and Invincibles had reason to be afraid that Germany might retaliate in kind.

It was a day of triumph for Mulliner when on March 3, 1909, he was invited to lay his views before a meeting of the entire Cabinet. What action would the ministers take? Would they adopt the German plan, itself inspired by the system pursued in England at the close of the nineteenth century and commit Parliament for a term of years to a programme of naval construction? The Liberal Parliament was not in the humour for such committals. Would they have recourse to a loan to lighten the immediate burden of expenditure involved? The Radicals would have none of it. They wanted to make the taxpayer, the wealthy taxpayer in particular, feel the cost of a policy of armament. This was the explanation of the great Budget of 1909; on these terms, but only on these terms, would Lloyd George and Churchill and their followers agree to a more extensive programme of naval construction. How many Dreadnoughts then should be built? Four? Six? The Navy League and the entire Unionist party wanted eight. Their desire was gratified. It was decided to lay down four Dreadnoughts at once and four others later in the year if circumstances demanded it. Finally, Parliament sanctioned the construction of eight Dreadnoughts in two relays. All were to be launched and equipped by the end of March 1912. On both occasions less than a hundred members voted against the programme, Nationalists, Labour members, and a handful of Liberals. After three years of Radical Government the supporters of armament to the teeth had triumphed.[2]

The enemies of Liberal pacifism were to gain yet another victory. The Second Peace Conference held at The Hague in 1907 had at least reached one important decision. According to the established usage in wartime, the prize courts were national tribunals each applying its own rules and, as everything led one to suppose,

[1] H. of C., March 16, 1909 (*Parliamentary Debates*, Commons, 1909, 5th Series, vol. ii, p. 960).
[2] For the Naval Scare of 1909 see F. W. Hurst, *The Six Panics and other Essays*, 1913, pp. 62 sqq.

their judgments were determined by the interests of the nation to which the judges belonged. In future there would be an international prize court to decide all disputed cases in the event of war. But this international tribunal, which would it was hoped be supernational, must apply a definite code of naval warfare. An international naval conference sat in London from December 4, 1908, to February 26, 1909, and drew up a declaration known as the Declaration of London which seemed in many respects to constitute a notable improvement upon the Declaration of Paris of 1856. It was no slight gain that three lists were compiled of objects unconditionally contraband, objects which might be declared contraband under particular circumstances and objects which under no circumstances might be regarded as contraband.

It remained to ratify the declaration. This would be done by the King on his ministers' advice without any previous debate in Parliament. But on the one hand the Government had given it to be understood that if the House of Commons decided against the Declaration of London it would not advise the King to ratify it. On the other hand the declaration was bound up with the establishment of an International Prize Court, and English participation in the court would require an Act of Parliament. Lively debates took place in the House of Commons on April 7. Sir Edward Grey promised that the House should have entire liberty to discuss the Declaration of London. Which party would prevail in the debate? It was to England's interest as a neutral power that merchantmen should be protected against the seizure of their goods by belligerent vessels. But in the spring of 1909 who could believe that England would be neutral in the next war? It would no doubt be to England's advantage as a belligerent if neutral ships could maintain her food supply with impunity. But her real interest demanded that she should count for her food supply upon her enormous mercantile marine, protected by her huge navy, which would take the opportunity furnished by the war to bring the commerce of all other nations, belligerent or neutral, to a standstill. An entire session, crowded as we already know with other business, passed before the House of Commons was free to deal with the question. And the following year both matters, the Naval Prizes Bill and the Declaration of London, were allowed to drop. The Bill did not even reach a second reading. The party opposed to internationalizing the code of naval warfare and granting greater freedom to neutral commerce finally won the day.

The incidents which led a few months later to the fall of the First Sea Lord are more obscure and more difficult to interpret. In July 1908 the Press learnt that Admiral Lord Charles Beresford, Commander of the Channel Squadron, had given two of his ships orders which, it was alleged, would have produced a catastrophe if one of the officers had not taken it on himself to disobey them. Immediate publicity was given to the act of splendid insubordination for which Sir John Fisher accepted the responsibility. It was in vain that Lord Charles demanded an inquiry. Not only was the demand refused but he was informed that the period of his command would be reduced from three to two years. Retired from the service on March 24, 1909, he was received by a cheering crowd at Dover first, then in London and launched a savage campaign both in the Press and in Parliament against Fisher's policy.[1] He told stories and got his friends to tell stories of the measures to which Fisher resorted against any members of the high command whose ideas differed from his own.[2] He criticized the new methods of training officers. He denounced as a sham the pledge Fisher had given to Parliament to provide a stronger fleet with fewer men, fewer ships and at a lower cost. He condemned the Dreadnought policy which had played into the hands of Germany by leading England to concentrate her entire strength in home waters and neglect to build not only those light cruisers required to protect British commerce on the high seas but even the torpedo-boat destroyers without which her giant ironclads were exposed to the risk of sudden destruction. He protested against the absence of any plan of campaign. If war broke out were they to be at the mercy of the First Sea Lord or, even worse, left to the rival improvisations of the First Sea Lord

[1] Lord Charles Beresford's arguments will be found collected in the book he published at the beginning of 1912 entitled: *The Betrayal. Being a Record of Facts concerning Naval Policy and Administration from the Year 1902 to the Present Time*. The *Memories of Admiral Lord Charles Beresford Written by Himself*, 1914, contain a handsome acknowledgment of the improvements in naval methods effected by Fisher when in command of the Mediterranean squadron but are silent as to the quarrel between the two Admirals.

[2] For the Bacon episode see Sir George Armstrong's speech at the Constitutional Club on April 2, 1909 and the debates in the Commons, April 6, May 5, 19, 24 and 27, 1909 (*Parliamentary Debates*, Commons 1909, 5th Series, vol. iii, pp. 919, 1132; vol. iv, pp. 1032 sqq.; vol. v, pp. 383 sqq., 821 sqq., 1378) and in defence of Bacon his biography of Lord Fisher, vol. ii, pp. 111 sqq.

and the Commander of the Fleet? The navy should be provided with a general staff like that with which Haldane had equipped the army.

At a juncture when growing nervousness fostered every kind of scare, Lord Charles provoked a powerful outburst of popular feeling, and under its pressure the Government decided to hold an inquiry. A sub-committee of the Committee of Imperial Defence was formed, consisting of the Premier, Sir Edward Grey, Haldane, and Lord Morley. It reported in August. On the whole its conclusions were favourable to Fisher but not so unreservedly that he was satisfied with the report. The sub-committee regretted the absence of cordial relations between the Board of Admiralty and the Commander-in-Chief of the Channel Fleet without attributing the entire blame for this state of things either to Fisher or Beresford and like the malcontent Admiral it advised the establishment of a general staff for the navy.[1] The report could not therefore be regarded by Lord Charles Beresford as a defeat. At the end of October he returned to the charge with an attack upon the Board of Admiralty for cashiering two officers whose only fault was that they had given evidence in his favour before the sub-committee. Asquith protested against the publicity with which he brought his charges and the First Lord of the Admiralty attempted to disprove them. Notwithstanding, Lord Charles had reason to claim a victory when at the beginning of December the public learnt that Sir John Fisher had been replaced as First Sea Lord by Admiral Sir Arthur Knyvet Wilson.

A month later Sir John was raised, or rather banished, to the peerage.

Fisher's opponents in the navy were anything but pacifists and the Admiral's fall must, it would seem, be reckoned among the many incidents which in 1909 witnessed to the alarm the English felt at the thought of being insufficiently armed against the danger of a war with Germany. But the pacifists hated the ruinous policy of the Dreadnoughts, and detested the tactless remarks with which that genius or charlatan (or was he both at once?) had irritated Germany. His fall delighted Berlin and certainly helped to relax the tension between England and Germany when at the end of

---

[1] *Return to an Order of the Honourable the House of Commons, dated 12th August, 1909: or Report of the Sub-Committee of the Committee of Imperial Defence appointed to inquire into certain questions of Naval Policy raised by Lord Charles Beresford.*

1909 after the panic of the previous spring, relations between the two powers improved and a period of calm followed until another crisis arose.

II ATTEMPTS AT A RAPPROCHEMENT BETWEEN ENGLAND AND GERMANY

I

We must not imagine that all these incidents, the vote by the House of Commons of the necessary credits to lay down four additional Dreadnoughts, the abandonment of the Declaration of London, and Sir John Fisher's fall, produced a deep impression on the public. Its attention was turned elsewhere. The triumphal return at Croydon, in March, of a Unionist candidate on a programme of tariff reform and armaments must be regarded as the final episode of the 'naval scare' which had lasted so many months. After this the struggle over the Budget held the stage. Lloyd George and his friends were thus enabled to take their revenge upon the imperialists—Liberal as well as Unionist. Until the autumn of 1908 Lloyd George had waged a desperate struggle against them not only within the Cabinet but at public meetings. He had approached the German Ambassador, Metternich in the hope of finding some way of reconciling the two nations. When in August he visited Germany, it was not only to study on the spot the working of the insurance system but to discuss politic with journalists and statesmen, and if the interview with the Emperor which William would gladly have given, could not be arranged and the Chancellor refused to receive him, at least he had a long conversation with the Minister of the Interior, Bethmann-Hollweg.[1]

After this he had been swept off his feet by the current of anti German passion and had agreed to find the money to build the eight Dreadnoughts. But he soon recovered himself. He was delighted to see those who had demanded the Dreadnought

[1] Note by the Minister for Foreign Affairs to Von Schön August 7, 1908. Prince von Bülow to the Minister for Foreign Affairs, August 21, 1908. The journalist, August Stein to Prince von Bülow, August 22, 1908. (*Die Grosse Politik* . . . vol. xxv, pp. 119, 138, 142 Harold Spender, *The Prime Minister*, 1920, pp. 159–161.

refuse to pay the price, and launched an attack upon their selfishness and greed. When in December the moment came to dissolve Parliament and invite the country to choose between the supporters and opponents of the Budget it was in vain that the *Daily Mail* opened its columns to the Socialist patriot, Blatchford, and Balfour in the speech in which he unfolded his programme insisted upon the German peril. It is safe to say that the gains, such as they were, of the Unionist party at the January Election were due not so much to the fear of Germany as to a revolt against the Radicals' fiscal policy. Nor did they wrest the Parliamentary majority from the Liberals, Labour members, and Nationalists, and the Liberal opponents of militarism could flatter themselves with the hope that now the panic of the previous winter had passed they would fulfil the promises made in 1906 and keep the imperialists in check, as they had done until the Second Peace Conference.

They were encouraged by the embarrassment which the attitude of the imperialists betrayed. There was nothing which resembled that bellicose and aggressive enthusiasm which ten years before had led England to conquer South Africa. Since the end of the Boer War England had not added a square inch to her Empire. In Asia she was making terms with Russian imperialism, in Africa assisting French imperialism. Why all this prudence, all these concessions? Because the dominant sentiment in England was fear of the power of Germany. The policy of the Foreign Office was not precisely to isolate Germany; at the beginning indeed it had been an attempt to prevent Germany from isolating England, but to form a species of alliance between England, France, and Russia as a counterpoise to the Triple Alliance, thus applying the doctrine of the European balance of power. But if this aim was openly avowed in the diplomatic despatches of the leading British diplomatists, Sir Charles Hardinge or Sir Nicolas O'Connor, the Prime Minister and the Minister for Foreign Affairs, though sharing their ideas, were careful not to express them so frankly. They disclaimed the too bellicose design of arraying one group of powers against another. If their public statements were to be trusted, the *entente* with France and Russia did not imply hostility towards Germany. And they taxed their ingenuity to state the policy of the European balance of power in the language of the European concert—that is, in the pacifist terminology current with a nation which, if it feared Germany, feared her just because it entertained an increasing horror of war.

2

But when we speak of the terminology of pacifism we must be clear as to our meaning. For there are two pacifisms speaking two languages. There is a Socialist pacifism, and there is a pacifism which is the reverse of the Socialist. Socialist pacifism sees in capitalism the source of war as of all the other evils which afflict modern society. And in obedience to the materialist philosophy of history it looks for an economic cause of war which it states as follows. The structure of industrial society is such that the production of a great civilized nation cannot be absorbed by the national market. For this to be possible the wages of the working class would have to be such as to enable it to purchase the entire produce of its labour. But in that case what would become of the employer's profit? The employer is therefore compelled to look for foreign markets for his goods when the home market has been glutted. These markets he finds at first in the other civilized countries but they become industrialized in their turn. A new glut occurs and the industrial countries are compelled to pour the goods they manufacture into all the non-European and uncivilized portions of the globe. Hence the 'scramble for Africa' and the railway battle in Asia Minor and China. The world had become too small to satisfy the greed of European capitalism. If, therefore, a market was to be found for goods, colonies must be conquered, and the ground occupied by other conquering nations contested, for 'trade follows the flag'. And the competition was the keener because the nations of Europe possessed a surplus not only of manufactured articles but of capital. England, France, and Germany sought abroad a double source of profit, for their manufacturers in the first place, then for their investors. In the trenchant language of an English Socialist: 'Capital, like labour, has its periods of unemployment, and its favourite method of meeting them is emigration. . . . Imperialism is simply the political manifestation of the growing tendency of capital accumulated in the more civilized industrial countries to export itself to the less civilized and the less settled.'[1] Imperialism therefore meant in the first place war against the uncivilized peoples, then war between the civilized peoples for the defence or extension of their colonial possessions. Because the modern world was becoming industrialized, it was hastening towards an inevitable war, unless that war were anticipated by a revolution which, by overthrowing capitalism, would destroy the evil at its roots.

This doctrine had its English defenders during the opening years of the twentieth century. But serious flaws can be detected in their argument. It is true that there were soldiers and sailors in great Britain, Germany, and elsewhere who attributed the conflict between England and Germany exclusively to economic causes, as though eager to saddle the merchants with the responsibility for the war they were preparing.[2] But there is no proportion between the sufferings involved by an economic crisis and the vast toll of sacrifice war exacts from the combatants. Surely there were many expedients which industry might employ before having recourse to so desperate a remedy. Moreover, the Tariff Reformers tried to create alarm by pointing to the continual encroachment of German trade. But the majority of the nation turned a deaf ear to their propaganda, and by associating their cause with militarism they rather damaged the latter than advanced the former and made free-traders incredulous of the imminent possibility of war. Conditions had indeed been more favourable to their propaganda at the close of the nineteenth century when a depression in trade gave birth to Williams's slogan—

[1] H. N. Brailsford, *The War of Steel and Gold. A Study of Armed Peace*, 1914, p. 79.

[2] 'Commerce is the leading idea and first interest of the modern state and so soon as a government is faced by the alternative of seeing some millions of workers lose their livelihood through unemployment or of losing a few thousand lives in battle, it will quickly know how to decide.' (General Sir Ian Hamilton, *Compulsory Service* . . . 1911, pp. 46–7.) Admiral von Tirpitz to Prince von Bülow, February 28, 1907: 'It is incontestable that the political friction between Great Britain and ourselves is due predominantly to our economic success and the more extensive demands of a growing population. The City of London is well aware of the increasing importance of German commerce and industry. Since British policy is almost wholly determined by the interests of the city the decision between war and peace depends in the last resort on the attitude of the great commercial magnates.' (*Die Grosse Politik* . . . vol. xxiii[11], p. 35.) Cf. General Jacobi's report to William II, February 29, 1908, of a conversation with the Russian general Roedinger. (*Die Grosse Politik* . . . vol. xxv[11], p. 342), also an article by Marschall von Schlieffen. *Der Kreig in der Gegenwart* (*Deutsche Revue*, January 1909; *Gesammelte Schriften*, vol. i, pp. 20–1). See on the other hand the brochure, entitled *England und Deutschland* in which in 1908 Schultze-Gävernitz explains the rivalry between England and Germany which is leading them to an inevitable war exclusively by economic causes. Schultze-Gävernitz was not a soldier. But it would not, we think, be easy to find a single economist or representative of commercial circles in England who expressed this point of view.

Made in Germany—yet it was then that England had contemplated an alliance with her most formidable competitor in the world market. Now, on the contrary, trade was prosperous. After a slight setback in 1907 it once more advanced rapidly both in England and in Germany—and in England perhaps even more rapidly than in Germany.[1] Between 1909 and 1913 though the population of Germany was much larger and was increasing more quickly than the British, British imports rose by £144,000,000, German by £91,000,000, British exports by £147,000,000 (£165,000,000 if we include re-exports), German only by £152,000,000. In Europe, German trade was growing at the expense of British. But within the Empire British trade was more than making up the lost ground and everywhere else an equal balance was maintained between the two countries which were advancing at the same rate. Was this the moment to raise the alarm?

In support of their thesis the Socialists appealed to the policy of armaments. But their argument on this point should perhaps be regarded as a particularly unfortunate application of their fundamental thesis. To argue that capitalism is the source of war because it has an interest in the wholesale manufacture of guns and ironclads is to view the question from a very restricted angle. Even if this particular contention were correct, it applied only to the iron and steel manufacture. Surely the cotton, woollen, coal, and in so far as the mercantile marine was concerned, the shipbuilding industries had other interests. Nowhere in England had Germany more friends than in Lancashire. It was on the coast of the North Sea where a bombardment or the landing of an armed force was feared that Germany was an object of alarm and her commercial agents were dreaded, not because they damaged British industry but because they were regarded as officers in disguise. And even in the steel industry we do not observe any very profound hatred of Germany. Sheffield fraternized with Essen and every year Krupp visited England to discuss business with his Yorkshire friends. The position was not different on the Continent where at the beginning of 1909 Essen entered into an agreement with Le Creusot for the joint exploitation of the mineral wealth of Northern Africa. The agreement, it is true, proved abortive but this was because it was wrecked by the opposition,

[1] Bernadotte E. Schmitt, *England and Germany 1740–1914*, 1916, pp. 96 sqq.

sentimental not economic, of French patriotism and Socialism. Is it really true that capitalism spells war? Would it not be nearer the truth to borrow another formula from Socialist ideology irreconcilable with the thesis we are discussing and say that capitalism has no nationality? And may we not draw the conclusion that it is a force which makes for peace?[1]

3

This precisely was the contention of a small book more lucid than profound but captivatingly written by an English man of business who like so many business men before him was an amateur economist. It was first published just before the Election of January 1910 under the title *Europe's Optical Illusion* and a second edition which appeared a year later bore the slightly altered title which became famous, *The Great Illusion*.[2] The arguments of its author, Norman Angell, based on a study of banking rather than industrial capitalism and on the machinery of exchange and credit rather than on the machinery of production, led to the conclusion that the 'optical illusion' from which Europe was suffering, the 'great illusion' was the belief that war could ever be a source of profit. This might have been possible when one man could become another man's property and the victorious state could enslave the citizens of the defeated state and make them work for it. But the position had completely changed since the only normal economic relation between individuals and nations had become one of exchange. Suppose the victorious country annexed the conquered. Then the individual inhabitants of that country would become more dangerous competitors than before of the citizens of the victorious country because no longer

---

[1] Count von Metternich to Prince von Bülow, May 4, 1906: 'It is a consoling sign that in the very quarter where competition might have been expected to have produced a natural hostility the wish for friendly relations is strongest. In the course of the winter I have often come into contact with prominent representatives of British industry and commerce and have always found a genuine wish that Germany and England might remain on excellent terms with each other.' (*Die Grosse Politik . . .* vol. xxi[11], p. 425.) 'It was the great commercial centres of Great Britain that were most pacific and least anti-German up to the very outbreak of the Great War.' (Viscount Grey of Fallodon, *Twenty-five Years, 1892–1916*, vol. i, p. 134.)

[2] *Europe's Optical Illusion*, November 1909, reprinted in April and June 1910—*The Great Illusion. A Study of the Relation of Military Power in Nations to their Economic and Social Advantages*, November, 1910.

divided from them by a political frontier. Suppose the conqueror were content with imposing an indemnity upon the conquered people. The consequent influx of gold into the victorious country would produce a general rise in prices, and thus render more formidable the economic competition of the defeated country which paid the indemnity. Would it be argued that the causes of war were not economic but movements of feeling inaccessible to financial considerations? History proved that societies of the military type had been steadily losing their ascendancy, that as mankind becomes civilized it becomes commercialized, and that, like wars of religion or duelling, wars between nations are being rendered obsolete by the growth of enlightenment.

The success which *The Great Illusion* enjoyed throughout the entire world is well known. Within a year of publication, it had been translated into eleven languages. In England, with which alone we are here concerned, it made a profound impression. Nothing short of a school grew up around it, among the Cambridge undergraduates first, then in commercial circles at Manchester, then at all the universities and in all the industrial centres of the United Kingdom. Finally, there were no less than forty study circles centred round an institution called from the name of the patron who financed it: The Garton Foundation for Promoting the Study of International Policy.[1] And indeed, apart from the intrinsic merits of the book, its success is not difficult to explain. For that other ideology which explained war as due to the economic structure of the modern world was at once too revolutionary and too pessimistic to appeal to the British public. Since it represented war as one of the evils inherent in a capitalist Society it left only the choice between war and a revolt of the working class, and Englishmen, even Englishmen of Socialist sympathies, disliked both. And it conflicted with the deep-seated conviction of business men who, whatever might be said in Germany, knew that they desired not war but peace. Norman Angell's philosophy, on the contrary, suited perfectly the Radical free traders who, threatened after their victory at the 1906 Election by

---

[1] Lord Esher '*La Guerre et La Paix quelques facteurs nouveaux de la politique internationale*, a speech delivered at the Sorbonne, March 27, 1914. (*The Influence of King Edward and other Essays*, 1915, pp. 229 sqq.; see especially pp. 237–8.) Norman Angell the *Foundation of International Policy*, 1914, pp. 194 sqq., 220 sqq. King Edward who was not much of a reader read Norman Angell's book and was attracted by his brilliant and clear reasoning (*Lord Esher*, iv, p. 55).

the double counter-offensive of the militarists and the tariff reformers, were delighted to meet with a popular book which justified their belief in free trade and their hatred of a policy of armaments. Moreover, at the same moment Lloyd George's great Budget had brought home to the wealthy class which constituted the shock troops of the Unionist party the heavy cost not only of war but even of preparation for it. Even Sir Edward Grey's imperialist convictions would seem to have been shaken. Anxious for the fate of European civilization 'if this tremendous expenditure goes on' we find him in 1911 refusing to believe war possible: 'I think it is much more likely that the burden will be dissipated by internal revolution, by the revolt of the masses of men against taxation.'[1]

4

This pacifist movement, and the movement inseparable from it in favour of a better understanding with Germany which came to birth after the Tangier episode—and had never altogether ceased—was now gaining a new strength, marked by the foundation of societies, the publication of magazines, and the exchange of visits between British and German members of Protestant religious bodies, British and German journalists, and the municipalities of large towns in Great Britain and Germany. But had it struck deep roots? In the first place, among the leaders of the movement we notice a disquietingly large proportion of German or German Jewish names. Sir Max Waechter was advocating a European federation against America which would include England and Germany.[2] Lucien Wolf urged as a reply to the raising of the French tariff the conclusion of a commercial treaty between England and Germany. Sir John Brunner of the great chemical firm, Mond-Brunner, was President of the National Liberal Federation. Sir Alfred Mond of the same firm directed the *Westminster Gazette*. Sir Edgar Speyer, who controlled the underground railways of London, was intimate both with Asquith

[1] H. of C., March 13, 1911 (*Parliamentary Debates*, Commons 1911, vol. xxii, p. 1985).
[2] Sir Max Waechter, *European Federation. A Lecture delivered at the London Institution on the 25th February, 1909*. See also on Sir Max Waechter's project an article in the *Economist* for October 12, 1907; Sir Max Waechter was one of the Vice-Presidents of the Tariff Reform League—also *Contemporary Review*, November 1912 (vol. cii, pp. 621 sqq.). Sir Max Waechter 'The Federation of Europe: Is it Possible?' (an article in which the writer tones down the anti-American colour of his original project).

and the German Chancellor.[1] Lord Rothschild in London and the banker Schwabach in Berlin worked hand in hand to improve relations between the two countries.[2] Sir Ernest Cassel founded an Anglo-German Institute to assist young Englishmen who settled in Germany and young Germans who settled in England.[3] Whenever a meeting was to be arranged between the rulers of England and Germany, we find Sir Ernest Cassel, the great London financier, in communication with Albert Ballin, the great Hamburg shipbuilder. Both were Jews and Germans by birth. Ballin had remained faithful to his native creed and country, Cassel had been nationalized an Englishman and converted to Catholicism. Ballin was an intimate friend of William II, Cassel both the friend and banker of Edward VII who, when in London, wound up every afternoon at his whist table.[4] All these men brought to the cause of peace the far from negligible support of their influence and brains. But they can hardly be regarded as representative of English society.

Other influences played their part in the movement for peace, of which the most important were the activities of those humanitarian groups, religious and intellectual, which found a willing and eloquent mouthpiece in Lloyd George. But even under a Liberal Government we must not exaggerate their power. They had indeed succeeded in compelling a reform in the administration of the Belgian Congo. But that was because the agitation served important financial interests and was supported by all the commercial magnates of Liverpool, who were eager to destroy the monopoly of a foreign country. And their violent hostility towards Russia, which found expression in loud protests when the King of England went to Reval and again the following year when the Czar visited the King at Cowes, was a source of considerable embarrassment to the Government. But when all is said their opposition effected nothing. The friendship between England and Russia had more dangerous enemies in the imperialist camp and when it was a matter of attacking the new Russian policy of the Foreign Office Arthur Ponsonby found his ally in Lord

[1] Prince von Bülow to Count von Metternich, December 25, 1908; Von Bethman-Hollweg to Count von Metternich, February 3, 1911 (*Die Grosse Politik* . . . vol. xxviii, p. 37; vol. xxvii[11], p. 668).
[2] For the details of their correspondence see Paul H. von Schwabach, *Aus meiner Akten*, 1927.
[3] *The Times*, August 17, 1911.
[4] For Sir Ernest Cassel see Sir Sidney Lee, *King Edward VII*, pp. 60 sqq. *et passim*.

Curzon. When, on the other hand, it was a question of attacking directly the policy of armaments, we have already seen the weakness of the pacifist opposition. The general staffs of the British and French armies were making joint preparations for an eventual war with Germany. Can it be said that Parliament seriously attempted to exercise its right of control by demanding full information on the subject?[1] The pacifists clung to the belief that the advent of a Liberal Government would inaugurate an era of disarmament and international peace. What had they done to prevent the Admiralty building Dreadnoughts in constantly increasing numbers, eight now at once? Did it mean that the instinct of 'pugnacity', denounced by Norman Angell as a survival of barbarism, was still powerful even among the sincerest friends of peace? In a powerful novel, H. G. Wells showed how 'a war in the air' threatened European civilization with ruin.[2] But he played at soldiers with his two little boys and invented new military games for their amusement.[3] W. T. Stead was the most vociferous and the most theatrical representative of British pacifism. But he was also one of the protagonists of the formula: two keels to one: two English Dreadnoughts to one German. In the Cabinet Lord Loreburn was a convinced opponent of Sir Edward Grey's foreign policy, but he did not object to Lady Loreburn's christening a Dreadnought.[4] And in a book written a little later, one of

---

[1] 'We hear that we are under a formal obligation to assist the French armies with an expeditionary force which would land in France in the event of an attack on France by Germany. This open secret is the property of all in the three countries concerned who pretend to be well informed. It has been set in black and white by the "*Temps*"; it has passed uncontradicted in the French Chamber; it has received publicity on German platforms from an authority so competent as Herr Bassermann, the leader of the Natiohal Liberals. It is only our own House of Commons which shows no curiosity to have it affirmed or denied.' (The *Nation*, March 12, 1910, p. 903).

[2] *The War in the Air and particularly how Mr. Bert Smallways fared while it lasted*, 1908. For a general statement of H. G. Wells' pre-war opinions see vol. xx of the Atlantic Edition of his works entitled: *The War in the Air and other War Forebodings*.

[3] *Little Wars. A Game for Boys from Twelve Years of Age to One Hundred and Fifty and for the more Intelligent Sort of Girls who like Boys' Games and Books. With an Appendix on Kriegspiel*, 1913. The book, it is true, concludes on a pacifist note. 'Great War is at present, I am convinced, not only the most expensive game in the universe, but it is a game out of all proportion. Not only are the masses of men and material and suffering and inconvenience too monstrously big for reason but—the available heads we have for it are too small (p. 100). But this does not alter the fact that Wells played the general for the entertainment of himself, his children and his readers.

[4] *The Times*, October 28, 1909. Cf. John Viscount Morley, *Memorandum on Resignation, August 1914*, 1928, p. 19: 'With a fleet of overwhelming power, a disinterestedness beyond suspicion, a foreign minister of proved ability, truthfulness and self-control, when the smoke of battlefields has cleared from our European sky, England might have expected an influence not to be acquired by a hundred of her little Expeditionary Forces.'

the most forcible and sincere impeachments by an Englishman'
pen of his country's policy during the years which led up to the
War, it is amusing to read such an unconscious relevation as the
following remark: 'So long as he (the author) lives he will
remember the thrill of admiration and something akin to pride
that he experienced when he viewed the Grand Fleet at Spithead
in July 1914. It was a mighty monument to the sciences and crafts-
manship of Britain.'[1]

5

Nevertheless, the British public was thoroughly convinced that it
wanted peace, even if perhaps it did not always want its indispensable conditions. Even during the naval scare attempts were made to
pour oil on the troubled waters. In September 1908 a leading
review, the *Fortnightly*, published an important article, unsigned
whose anonymous author urged that an attempt should be made
to effect an Anglo-German *entente*. 'Beyond question the British
and the Germans are the two races most fitted to advance the
orderly, competent administration of the world. In fact, if they
could only divide up between them the troubled portions of the
globe there would be a good chance of firm, steady government

[1] J. T. Walton Newbold, *How Europe Armed for War (1871–1914)*, 1916, p. 76. The
author adds: 'It was a tragedy of steel cunningly designed and admirably wedded to the
fulfilment of the misdirected genius of a nation.' But these words are double-edged and
what matters is the thrill of admiration and pride which runs through them. And it is
perhaps among the revolutionary writers that the most striking expressions of England's
pride in her navy are to be found. The syndicalist, Stephen Reynolds, in the preface to a
book he published in 1912 entitled, *The Lower Deck. The Navy and the Nation* writes a
follows: 'Of all our great public institutions I confess to being proudest of the Navy. For
it does seem to me that, whatever its faults, the Navy is the outward and visible sign of
that which is best in the British seafaring spirit. Armaments, no doubt, are an appalling
piece of international pigheadedness, a frightful waste of human lives and national resources; yet I imagine that men of the future will look back on us and say: "Out of that barbar-
ous foolishness they created, on an heroic scale, one thing that was splendid in spite of it
defects—their Navy"—And I fancy that our naval history will make their blood run
faster as it makes mine. An economic waste may be in other ways a gain.' (p. vii.) Notice
also the perplexity felt by young Keeling, who was indeed a Fabian, not a syndicalist, but
also a convinced friend of Germany. '. . . I see as clearly as anything that aggressiveness
and quarrelsomeness is no earthly good—it has done me no good and won't do anyone
else any good. Tolstoy taken literally is absurd . . . I am a Big Navy Man. But the spiri
of Tolstoy and Shaw or Voltaire (each at his best) is the only tolerable outlook on life one
sees and feels.' (To Miss Townshend, June 3, 1914); *Keeling Letters and Recollections*, 1918
p. 173. '. . . I am hesitating on the brink of taking part in Liberal politics. I think I shall;
don't see what else I can do usefully in politics. I am decidedly anti-revolutionist, and
don't believe in most of the doctrines which distinguish the I.L.P. from the Liberals—
the right to work, extreme anti-militarism, Little-Navy, and Little-Englandism.' (To the
Same, June 14, 1914; ibid., p. 175.)

replacing flabbiness and chaos in all quarters which cause anxiety from time to time.'[1] The crisis which immediately followed the annexation of Bosnia did not prevent the Liberal Press in London and Manchester expressing its desire to see the question settled by the joint arbitration of England and Germany. It was, to be sure, an empty wish, for it ran directly counter to the deliberate policy of the German Government. But the crisis had barely been brought to an end by Isvolsky's surrender when another important review, the *Nineteenth Century*, published the answers obtained by a journalist who had sounded several Germans in high position with a view to discovering a basis for an *entente* between the two countries.[2] Their answers cannot be called encouraging. The writer's desire for an *entente* is obviously far stronger than that of his German interlocutors. Nevertheless, there existed in Germany and even in government circles a party which began to feel alarm at the dangers in which their country might be involved by the naval policy pursued during the last few years.

For we must not imagine that the diplomatic victory which Von Bülow gained in 1909 over Isvolsky was such an unmitigated triumph as his victory over Delcassé in 1905. His stroke at Tangier had set the seal on his reputation for statesmanship. The episode of Bosnia was the prelude to his downfall. He had arranged the

---

[1] 'Why not an Anglo-German *entente*?' (*Fortnightly Review*, September 1908, pp. 394 sqq. and 401). For the real or supposed affinities between the two peoples cf. Basil Williams, 'Anglo-German Relations' (*Edinburgh Review*, October 1909, No. 430, pp. 447 sqq.). See especially p. 447: 'Nowhere on foreign soil have English writers and thinkers found a readier hearing than in Germany, or those in Germany than with us. Such close connections are but natural: for we are of the same blood, and in the main of the same religion, while in fundamental characteristics no two nations resemble one another more closely than the English and the Germans.' See also a little later Sir Henry H. Johnston, 'German Views of an Anglo-German Understanding' (*Nineteenth Century and After*, December 1910, vol. lxviii, pp. 978 sqq.). 'The Need for an Anglo-German Understanding' (ibid., January 1911, vol. lxix, pp. 82 sqq.). See especially vol. lxviii, p. 978: 'Any person of average intelligence and over, who has been enabled to visit the German Empire at the present time, even cursorily, must be aware of the enormous progress made by the German people in science, art, social legislation, internal communications, commerce, and the amenities of life. And even a tourist of no quick apprehension—in fact, for this purpose the stupider the better—must feel that in travelling about Germany he is more at home, made to feel more at home, than in any other country outside the British Dominions and the United States, for the reason that nowhere outside the lands where English is the national speech is our tongue more widely spoken than in Germany; with no race in the world have we so frequently inter-married than with the Germans.' And conversely on the psychological paradox of the Anglo-French *Entente* see Whelpley, *The Trade of the World*, 1913, p. 99. We have called attention to all these passages to bring home to the reader on the one hand how sincere were the sentiments they express, on the other hand for how little they counted on August 4, 1914.

[2] Aeneas O'Neill, 'Six German Opinions on the Naval Situation' (*Nineteenth Century and After*, No. 339, May 1909, vol. lxv, pp. 725 sqq.).

former in complete harmony with his sovereign. The latter left them at loggerheads. The *Daily Telegraph* incident was the occasion of the quarrel, but its causes lay deeper. The uneasiness with which the Chancellor regarded the anti-English naval policy pursued by William II and Von Tirpitz was the greater because it was so costly and the problem of raising the money was more difficult for the German than for the British Government. For in Germany there were no direct taxes which could be increased whenever more money was needed. In consequence of the still incomplete unification of the Empire the sources of revenue at the disposition of the Government were inadequate. To increase them it would be necessary to reform the entire system of taxation and such a reform must, according to the method adopted, offend the rich or the poor, alternatives equally formidable. Von Bülow, therefore, at the end of 1908, was pressing prudence upon the German Admiralty. Could they not build fewer ironclads and more torpedo boats and submarines? Or without abandoning the programme of 1909 as regards the number of ships to be built, could they not build them more slowly?[1]

To statesmen trained in the old school of Bismarck the position seemed nothing short of scandalous. The war to which they must look forward would not be a continental struggle which might lead later to English intervention. Thanks to Tirpitz and William II—so the malcontents alleged—the threat of a naval war with England hung over Germany. The general staff of the army which had always looked askance at the constantly increasing prestige of the Admiralty regarded as madness a war which must be carried on by a navy which as was known and admitted beforehand could never equal the British. What should the army do in that case? While the British army apprehended a German landing on the coast of Norfolk, the German army found itself compelled to form very different plans. In the event of war with England the Chief of Staff would be obliged 'to ask the Emperor to declare war on France at the same time'.[2]

---

[1] Prince von Bülow to Admiral von Tirpitz, December 23, 1908; The Same to the Same, January 11, 1909 (*Die Grosse Politik* . . . vol. xxviii, pp. 39, 61).

[2] 'Protocol by the Head of the Ministry of Marine, Vice-Admiral von Müller, reporting a meeting held at the Chancery on June 3, 1909, from half-past four to half-past eight.' (A. von Tirpitz, *Politische Dokumente*, vol. i, p. 160.) It is interesting to notice the forecasts made by several Germans a year earlier about the time of the Reval meeting. The German economist Schultze-Gävernitz after predicting that England would declare war on Germany continues: 'England's naval victories would perhaps be compensated by the defeat

But before adopting such extreme measures, might not Germany take advantage of the favourable opportunity presented by her recent successes in the Balkans, and her agreement with France about Morocco to make new proposals to England such as would not be derogatory to German prestige? Von Bülow summoned the Ambassador Metternich to a Cabinet council held on June 3 to meet Tirpitz, Von Moltke, Von Schön, Bethmann-Hollweg, and Von Müller. He sketched an entire programme of reconciliation, a colonial agreement, a pact of neutrality with England, and an abatement of the naval competition. He fell from power, overthrown, for the first time in the history of the German Empire, by a majority in the Reichstag. He was replaced by Bethmann-Hollweg who immediately adopted his predecessor's policy. Negotiations were begun between the two Governments and dragged on very slowly for two years. The Emperor, though extremely sceptical, indeed almost hostile, did not refuse his consent.[1]

of France on land. An unsuccessful naval war would necessarily force Germany to adopt Napoleon's policy which is far from her present intention'—and he adds: 'Would it be possible to strike England a blow on land—for example by allying ourselves with the Moslem world? In any event such a war (between Germany and England) which many of our jingoes regard as a naval war easily despatched would usher in a period of general and long-drawn conflict.' (Dr. von Schultze-Gävernitz, *England und Deutschland. Zweite erweiterte Auflage der Festschrift zur Geburtstag Seiner Königlichen Hoheit des Grossherzog von Baden. am 9 Juli, 1907*, 1908.) And the head of the Admiralty von Müller wrote to von Tirpitz on August 31, 1908: 'It is easy to say, "better a world war than dishonourable peace". But what aspect will this world war assume? What main objectives will it pursue? Will it spread from France to England, or will its theatre be the East? Have we sufficient naval strength, our leaders being the men they are, even to contemplate tasks of such a Napoleonic magnitude, not to speak of achieving them? To answer such questions is a very serious responsibility.' (A. von Tirpitz, *Politische Dokumente*, vol. i, p. 85.) Is it credible that no echo of these speculations, reached England? As early as 1907 Austin Harrison wrote: 'All the loose talk of war amounts, in fact, to this: if ever we have friction with Germany, France will be made to foot the bill. The French know it; all German diplomacy is based upon it. In the event of hostilities, Germany will invade France within a few hours of the declaration of war, directly through Belgium. Nor can there be any question that all her military plans of invasion are drawn up with that intention. The British Fleet, Germans say, may destroy our Navy—if they can get at it—but we shall be in Paris in a short time; and the price of peace will be some £750,000,000 and the entire French Navy, to say nothing of ports, and forts, another useful accessory.' (*England and Germany*, p. 169.)

[1] For these negotiations see *British Documents* . . . vol. vi, pp. 283 sqq.; and *Die Grosse Politik* . . . vol. xxviii, pp. 199 sqq.

The ultimate and avowed object of these negotiations was to put an end to the naval competition which threatened to ruin both nations without benefiting either. But as soon as the position was stated in these terms it was England's turn to make demands. Either she simply asked for an assurance that the German Naval Law of 1900 would not be reinforced by a further law before 1920 when the entire programme would be completed—for example, in 1912, the critical year after which, if the law of 1900 were strictly carried out, Germany would lay down only two Dreadnoughts a year instead of four. Or she suggested ingenious devices by which Germany could reduce her naval expenditure without violating the provisions of the law of 1900, for example, by building more slowly or by building smaller vessels.

To these proposals the German negotiators returned an evasive answer. The fleet for whose construction within twenty years the law of 1900 made provision was not specially directed against England. It was regarded by the German Admiralty as strictly proportionate to the present position of German commerce and the strength of her mercantile marine. If the German Government were to accept a smaller navy, it must be in return for some adequate compensation—for example, the conclusion of a 'political agreement' between the two Powers. It was this request for an agreement which Bethmann-Hollweg, on this point obeying the Emperor's express wish, persisted in pushing to the front, whereas the British kept the limitation of armaments in the foreground. Already when Bülow was Chancellor three alternative proposals had been prepared by the German Foreign Office, a proposal for a regular alliance, a proposal for a pact of neutrality, and a vaguer proposal for an *entente*. At the close of 1909 it was the pact of neutrality that was suggested. England was to promise 'benevolent neutrality' towards Germany, and Germany reciprocally towards England whatever the conflict in which either power might engage. Sir Edward Grey, and this no doubt was what William II intended, found the proposal extremely embarrassing.

How indeed could he admit that the *entente* with France made any alliance or quasi-alliance with Germany impossible? And how could he conclude even a pact of neutrality when the General Staffs of England and France were concocting the best means to

protect the North of France in the event of a German invasion?
He evaded the issue by replying that neither the Anglo-French nor
the Anglo-Russian *entente* contained such a guarantee of neutrality, comprised indeed no provisions other than those by which the
powers concerned—England and France, England and Russia—
settled amicably individual questions in dispute between them.
Why not therefore conclude a simple colonial agreement between
England and Germany? On the question of Bagdad and the Persian railways a settlement could surely be reached. To this the
German Government raised no objection: before his fall, von
Bülow had contemplated such a colonial agreement. But it insisted on the primary importance of a political pact. Sir Edward
Grey was not prepared to meet this repeated demand by a blunt
refusal but sought to find a formula which would satisfy Germany
without losing the friendship of France and Russia. What could
it be? He explained his views on the matter to the colonial delegates when in May 1911 the Imperial Conference once more met
in London. 'The *entente* must be public.' It must not 'put us back
into the old bad relations with France and Russia'. And it must be
of such a nature that 'there is no chance of a disturbance of the
peace between Germany and France or Germany and Russia'.[1]
In short, it was to be such an understanding as the temper of the
Continental powers made impossible. Did not Sir Edward know
this? In May 1911 the conversations had already been suspended
for several months.

The conversations had been secret, as also was Sir Edward
Grey's statement to the Imperial Conference. Nevertheless, the
mere fact that they were begun and continued so long is a proof
that the feeling of the public towards Germany was not so hostile
as it had been during the diplomatic crisis which followed the
annexation of Bosnia. The struggle over the Budget, and the conflict between the Upper and Lower Houses of Parliament had
contributed largely to this change of feeling. Public attention

---

[1] H. H. Asquith, *The Genesis of War*, 1923, p. 124. Cf. Sir Edward Grey to Sir E.
Goschen, September 1, 1909: 'There is nothing in our agreements with France and Russia
which is directed against Germany and therefore nothing to bar a friendly arrangement
with Germany.... I want a good understanding with Germany, but it must be one
which will not impoverish those which we have with France and Russia—I should have
thought some formula could be found to which they also could be parties; that would be
the best and most reassuring solution, though I see that the French could not be a party to
anything which looked like confirming the loss of Alsace and Lorraine.' (*British Documents
. . vol. v, pp. 803–4.)

was elsewhere. And other circumstances favoured if not an *entente* it least a relaxation of tension between England and Germany.

7

In the first place there was King Edward's death. His influence upon British foreign policy, as we have already emphasized, was slight. It could have been as important as it is sometimes represented, there could have existed that 'policy of King Edward' which legend depicts, only if the King had been a greater man than he was, and he would have found himself compelled to override the opposition of public opinion as expressed by the Press by his Parliament, by his ministers and by the civil service.[1] There were, however, two—and only two—occasions on which up to a point he had insisted on having his own way. When he decided to visit Paris in 1903 he had to overcome the scruples of his ministers who were afraid that it might be the occasion for hostile manifestations which might imperil the understanding with France they were trying to achieve. And when he decided to visit Reval in 1908 he was obliged to defy the noisy opposition of the Radicals who thought it disgraceful that the King of England, by visiting the Czar for the first time in history, should appear to condone the sanguinary repression of the revolution. But on both occasions the policy which these visits furthered was the policy of the Foreign Office, the Admiralty, and the War Office and a policy supported by the great bulk of the Press. These and all the other visits he made, accompanied by Sir Charles Hardinge, were simply the visits of an ambassador more mobile and more splen-

[1] 'The popular idea, outside the British Isles, that King Edward moulded the foreign policy of his country, is of course pure illusion. Once or twice in a century, the policy of a great nation is determined by the throne or by the action of a statesman. Such men were Cavour and Bismarck. But as a rule the force that drives one nation toward unity, another towards revolution and another towards expansion, comes from the necessity of the people influenced by the conditions under which it is striving for existence (Lord Esher, *The Influence of King Edward and Essays on other Subjects*, 1915, p. 50.) Lord Esher who held an important position at court had been one of the most active agents in bringing about the *rapprochement* between England and France. In the article from which the passage just quoted has been taken and which appeared shortly after the death of Edward VII in the *Deutsche Revue*—and which was probably submitted to King George before publication—it is also of interest to notice a passage in which Lord Esher expressed the wish that the Anglo-French *entente* might be transformed into a triple *entente* between England, Germany, and France (ibid., p. 53). See further on the influence exercised by King Edward on foreign policy the judicious remarks of Jacques Bardoux 'Victoria I, Edouard VII, Georges V,' pp. 230 sqq.

did than the rest but also perhaps more anxious to obey exactly the instructions of his Foreign Minister. Nor were these Royal journeys so consistently anti-German as they are often represented. The visit to Cronberg was not a deliberate slight on William II though the latter chose to regard it as such. And the visit to Berlin in January 1909 six months after Cronberg and three months after the *Daily Telegraph* incident, was an advance made to the German nation as well as to its Emperor. It would seem that on the occasion of this visit William II had the satisfaction of hearing his uncle express approval of his policy of naval construction and disavow the campaign the British Press was conducting against it.[1] On the other hand, we must remember that these visits—an innovation in British diplomacy—gave the policy of the Foreign Office such a dramatic embodiment that the growth of the legend is easy to understand. And it is not surprising that William II in particular should have regarded them as hostile acts or rather as encroachments upon his own province. For he had been the creator of the part. For a long time his journeys had focused the attention of the world. But now accounts of the comings and goings of another monarch filled the European Press. The King of the great rival nation visited all the rulers in Europe including the one whom William was not allowed to visit.

It was intolerable, and Edward VII's death relieved the Emperor's vanity, so often hurt on a particularly tender spot since his uncle's accession to the British throne. Moreover, he came to London for the King's funeral and the emotion he displayed was not a mere formality. The son of an English woman, England was, after all, in many respects his second fatherland. At Windsor—at Buckingham Palace, memories of childhood and youth thronged thick about him. He was delighted to witness among a people whom the German Press had depicted as consumed by the fever of revolution the grave bearing, the respect, and the genuine sorrow with which tens of thousands of his subjects watched the funeral of their monarch. And since the London crowd transferred to him something of the emotion it felt in the presence of King Edward's coffin, before he left England something not unlike a reconciliation had been effected between the British people and the German Emperor.

[1] Szögyény. Despatch from Berlin, February 17, 1909 (*Österreich-Ungarns Aussenpolitik* . . . vol. i, p. 835).

The new King was a more pronounced Conservative than his father and, as we should expect from an old sailor, more directly concerned at the growth of the German fleet than the clubman he succeeded.

But, on the other hand, he can hardly have failed to entertain towards imperial Germany those mingled sentiments of esteem and dislike felt by the entire British aristocracy and by all the officers in high command, and the English ruling class had come to the conclusion that for the moment at least their esteem was greater than their dislike. The naval attaché at Berlin whose reports were believed to have embittered the relations between England and Germany was replaced by another charged to create a more friendly atmosphere. Admiral Jellicoe visited Germany and made himself pleasant and popular. In England the domestic situation had become too serious for the Conservatives even to think of attempting to divert the voter's attention by reviving the German peril when in December they were again summoned to the poll. And two months later both McKenna and Sir Edward Grey speaking in the House of Commons on the navy estimates used language calculated to give satisfaction to German opinion.

8

McKenna, as First Lord of the Admiralty, discovered that England had exaggerated the speed of German naval construction. The German Government had spoken the truth when it made diplomatic protests against the miscalculations of the British Admiralty. It had been given out that by March 1911 Germany would possess nine Dreadnoughts as against England's twelve. In fact, she possessed only five. Did that mean that all the recent expenditure on Dreadnoughts, eight in 1909, five in 1910, and this year five more, had been money wasted? Not at all: for even at this rate of construction, to look a few years ahead, the Two-Power Standard could not be maintained. Liberal ministers began once more to give the formula a more moderate interpretation. McKenna asked for a fleet that was 'Supreme as against any foreign navy, and as against any reasonable probable combination which we might have to meet single-handed', and Sir Edward Grey also declared in so many words that the American navy must not be taken into account, and that he would be satisfied with 'a fleet sufficient to hold the sea against any reasonably probable combination'.[1] It was an empty formula at a time when England had no coalition of hostile navies to fear. It meant, in fact, a fleet superior to the German fleet by itself. And what degree of superiority would suffice? The special effort now being made would give England in 1913 thirty large ironclads to twenty-one German. Not 'two keels to one' but almost three keels to two. It was the formula which in 1908 Lloyd George had championed against the formula of the party in favour of large armaments[2] and the Wilhelmstrasse interpreted Sir Edward Grey's speech as a surrender. 'If four years ago', the Emperor remarked, 'we had taken the advice of Metternich and von Bülow and ceased to build, we should be Copenhagened now ! You see how our determination is respected and how they are obliged to submit to hard facts. Let us go on then quietly building.'[3]

In May, William II paid another visit to London. The occasion of his visit, which was a family affair (Sir Edward Grey seems to have eluded all his attempts to discuss politics)[4] was the opening of the monument to Queen Victoria, grandmother both of the German Emperor and the English King. The spectacle Europe presented to his eyes was calculated to flatter his pride. He saw England stripped of the bulwark the Upper House had presented against the demands of the pacifists, labour, and the Irish. He saw anarchy spreading in France: a strike of post office employees had been followed by a strike of railwaymen, and the strike of vine dressers which had assumed such formidable proportions in the South two years before was prolonged in Champagne by disorders in which German *agents provocateurs* had a hand. In 1909 Russia had shown the world how weak she had been left by the combined disasters of the war and revolution, and the two Emperors were drawn together by their common fear of popular insurrection. William did not want war. Never had the ruler of a powerful state while employing so freely the language of war,

[1] H. of C., March 13, 1911 (*Parliamentary Debates*, 1911 Commons, 5th Series, vol. xxii, pp. 1916, 1979).

[2] Prince von Metternich to Chancellor von Bülow, August 1, 1908 (*Die Grosse Politik* ... vol. xxiv, pp. 113–14).

[3] Note to a despatch from the naval attaché in London to the German Admiralty, March 14, 1911 (von Tirpitz, *Politische Dokumente*, vol. i, p. 189).

[4] Szögyény's despatch from Berlin, January 19, 1912 (*Österreich-Ungarns Aussenpolitik* ... vol. iii, p. 778).

so dreaded its reality. He disapproved of the pan-German agitation which was becoming increasingly vocal. Though in the bottom of his heart he may have sympathized with its aims, he found fault with its impatience. He cherished the hope that the day would come when his navy would intimidate England as the German army had intimidated France since 1871. When it arrived a German statesman might perhaps risk the decisive venture.[1] But this was nothing more than a vague dream whose accomplishment he was glad to believe would be remote. The speeches delivered in March by Sir Edward Grey and McKenna, the cordial welcome he received when he visited London unofficially with his wife and two of his sons, and the information he received from all quarters confirmed him in his belief—and he was delighted to have it confirmed—that peace was secure.

If peace was secure, the moment was perhaps favourable to make England a gesture of friendship. Not indeed of the kind dear to humanitarian Liberalism. When the American Government invited the three Governments of England, France, and Germany to conclude general treaties of arbitration, the proposal, gladly accepted by the French and British Governments, had been rejected by William, and to any protests that might be raised he was in a position to reply that at that very moment the House of Lords, after much procrastination, was rejecting the Declaration of London, thereby nullifying all the work accomplished at the Second Hague Conference. If however peace were really assured how could the negotiations begun in 1909 between Grey and Bethmann-Hollweg, be allowed to break down finally? In the matter of a reduction of armaments which Germany could not accept, and in the matter of a pact of neutrality which England

[1] See a curious article in the *Allgemeine Evangelische Lutherische Kirchenzeitung* written in November 1908 to justify the interview published by the *Daily Telegraph* and which probably expresses the views current in the Emperor's immediate entourage: 'The Emperor is doing his best to secure the friendship of Great Britain. This is not very honourable for us but is *necessary so long as we are obliged to avoid war with England* because we are not yet sufficiently strong to risk it. It is only a short time since the German people understood our need of an adequate navy. And we must go on improving it and competing with England until if she still possesses three times as many vessels as we she will be unable to find the sailors to man them. Until that day to agitate for war is sheer lunacy. The mischief of which our Press has been guilty in this connection, the *Emperor is striving to undo*.' (Quoted by Ed. Bernstein, *Die Englische Gefahr und das deutsche Volk*, 1911, p. 20.) For the dreams of a naval war in which the Kaiser liked to indulge see the report of interviews given in Berlin between February 22 and 25, 1910 by William II and The Chancellor, Bethmann-Hollweg. Abbazia March 6, 1910 (*Österreich-Ungarns Aussenpolitik . . .* vol. ii, pp. 724 sqq.).

ould not accept, agreement was impossible. But Sir Edward
rey had again put forward the suggestion of an exchange of
formation between the respective Admiralties. In both coun-
ies competition had been increased by mutual suspicion of bad
ith; the statements made to their respective Parliaments by the
ritish and German ministers as to the actual state of naval con-
ruction were regarded in the other country as mendacious.
Jould it not be possible to allow the naval attachés under certain
efinite conditions to visit the dockyards and see for themselves
e exact number, size, and equipment of the vessels being built?
o a British note of June 1, Bethmann-Hollweg returned a favour-
le reply on the 27th. For the first time he communicated to
irpitz the conversations between the two countries, and asked
m to prepare for negotiations with the technical experts of the
ritish Admiralty. But the German note of June 27 received no
ply.[1] For on July 1 England, while still plunged in domestic
rife, found herself taken unawares by a new Moroccan crisis,
anco-German and Anglo-German, more serious than any pre-
ding crisis had been.

9

When the summer of 1911 opened, it was evident that the
Moroccan agreement concluded between France and Germany
February 1909 was doomed to remain ineffective. It met with
o much opposition in Morocco itself, where the French and
ermans refused to be reconciled, in France, where it was un-
opular alike with the Socialists and the Nationalists and in
ngland, where it interfered with too many private interests.[2]
Moreover its phraseology was ambiguous. It was very quickly
scovered that in many spheres, the railways for example, any
rmula of economic collaboration which did not involve some
dministrative or political condominium was not easy to discover.
or was it easy to apply an instrument which recognized that
ance possessed 'special political interests' throughout the whole
Morocco and at the same time maintained the inviolability of
e Algeciras pact which denied that any European power, least

British Documents . . . vol. vii, pp. 636 sqq. *Die Grosse Politik* . . . vol. xxviii, pp. 402
.
André Tardieu, *Le Mystère d'Agadir*, p. 79.

of all France, possessed special political rights in Morocco.
May the French Government made use of this German recogn
tion of her privileged position to despatch a punitive expeditic
to Fez. The Spanish Government, anxious to safeguard the secr
clauses of the 1904 agreement, occupied El-Ksar which w
situated within the territory which they assigned to her. Th
German Government which had protested from the first again
the despatch of the French expedition to Fez as a violation of tl
pact of Algeciras now regarded it as definitively condemne
While conversations were in progress between the German ar
French Governments as to the possibility of permitting a Frenc
occupation of the country in return for adequate compensatior
the German Government despatched on July 1 a small warshi
the *Panther*, which was followed shortly by a larger vessel, to tl
port of Agadir in Southern Morocco. The pretext for the step w
the protection of German interests in the district. The true moti
was to compel negotiations between the three powers—Franc
Germany, and England—for a new settlement of the Morocc
question on the ruins of the Algeciras pact.[1]

The German step was calculated to annoy the British Gover
ment, thus deliberately ignored. But it was embarrassed l
domestic difficulties. The coronation had brought about a tru
in the struggle between the Commons and the Lords. In a fe
days the conflict would be resumed. And it had not even effectec
truce in an even more serious social struggle, a general strike
seamen and dockers which, aggravated by outbreaks of riotin
had since June brought the work of all the ports to a standstill.
France, the political situation was more chaotic than ever. Sin
Clémenceau's fall and the election of 1910 the disintegration
parties and the instability of cabinets had reached a climax. On
a week before the Germans despatched the battleship to Agad
a new cabinet had confronted the Chamber. Of the Prime Min
ter, Joseph Caillaux, who had never before been President of t
Council, nothing was known except that as Minister of Finan
he had pursued for several months with but slight success a poli

[1] For the Agadir crisis see *Die Grosse Politik* . . . vol. xxix, pp. 137 sqq. *British Docum*
. . . vol. vii, pp. 173 sqq. *Le Mystère d'Agadir* by André Tardieu though the work of a pa
san and deprived to a certain extent of its documentary value by subsequent publicati
is still worth consulting. We must however add that on the question with which we
specially concerned, England's attitude during the second half of 1911, the author is cc
pletely silent.

of economic *rapprochement* with Germany. At the Foreign Office, de Selves was a political tiro who was not only for the first time Minister for Foreign Affairs but for the first time a Cabinet minister. There could be no doubt that the German Government hoped to take advantage of the obvious weakness of both Governments to punish France for the audacity of her expedition to Fez and England for having made common cause with France for several years. But what exactly was her aim? By making a landing at Agadir to drive England and France into war? Or simply to occupy Southern Morocco and defy France and England to treat the occupation as a *casus belli*? Or to compel France by the threat of occupying part of Morocco to make territorial concessions elsewhere? And were these concessions to be extensive and humiliating for France? Or on the contrary so moderate that they would satisfy France and eventually detach her from England? If that were Germany's intention, her stroke at Agadir was the worst possible inauguration of such a policy. It aroused too much anger in France, too much greed in Germany. It is however probable that the German Government, at variance with itself, was not clear as to its own aims. It simply intended to derive whatever advantage it could from its action at Agadir now that the step had been taken, committing itself and Europe to the mercy of events.

10

Without loss of time the Quai d'Orsay charged its ambassador in London to propose a joint naval demonstration by France and England in reply to the German, and at first before he had consulted his colleagues, Sir Edward Grey favoured the suggestion. But at a meeting held on July 4, the Cabinet refused to consider the immediate despatch of a British man-of-war to Agadir,[1] and was content to demand that England should be kept informed of the negotiations which should not, as Germany proposed, be confined to three powers, France, Spain and herself. Four powers,

---

[1] Is there any reason to think that King George exercised his personal influence in the same direction? See Metternich to Bethmann-Hollweg, September 25, 1911 (report of a conversation with the King at Balmoral) 'The King, while lamenting the position, observed that as a result of the grouping of the Powers (which he dislikes intensely) England was obliged to support France. But he had at least prevented the despatch of a British man-of-war to Agadir which would probably have led to war.' (*Die Grosse Politik . . .* vol. xxix, p. 245.)

France, Germany, Spain and England must take part in any settlement. On July 6 Asquith, speaking in the House of Commons, simply stated in general terms but in accents of gravity that as regards the question which had just arisen in Morocco and for which he hoped diplomacy would discover a peaceful solution, England in the possible event of future developments affecting her interests more directly would adopt the attitude dictated by a 'due regard to the protection of those interests and to the fulfilment of our treaty obligations to France'.[1] As for the French Government, the very day on which the British Cabinet refused to send a battleship to Morocco Joseph Caillaux, temporarily in charge of the Foreign Office, energetically opposed the despatch of a French man-of-war. On this point, therefore, he was in agreement with Sir Edward Grey. But there the agreement ended. For Caillaux proposed to Berlin that negotiations should take place not between three powers as Germany had originally suggested, or between four as England demanded, but between two alone, France and Germany, for the amicable settlement of all questions in dispute between the two countries outside Europe. But he refused to put forward any definite proposals, waiting for Germany to make them.

They were made about the middle of July. Kiderlen-Wächter, the German Foreign Minister, offered France a free hand in Morocco and was even willing to consider the cession of Togo, if in return France would hand over to Germany her entire colony in the Congo. These proposals were revealed to the public by an article which appeared in the *Matin*, followed on July 20 by an article in *The Times*. It was easy to exploit these revelations against Germany. For, on the one hand, when England seven years earlier had given France a free hand in Morocco, she had asked for no territory in return but simply for the abandonment of certain rights. On the other hand, a right of pre-emption on the Belgian Congo was attached to the French colony. Would Germany receive this as well? Finally, though detailed information was lacking, the whole world knew of the agreement concluded twelve or thirteen years before between England and Germany by which the latter was given certain rather indefinite rights over the Portuguese colonies to the south of the Belgian Congo. It was evident that Germany intended to build up a vast

[1] *Parliamentary Debates*, Commons 1911, 5th Series, vol. xxvii, p. 1341.

colonial empire in equatorial Africa. France was to give her what she wanted, and England to abstain from interference. Otherwise Germany would land troops at Agadir. And the British Government had been kept in complete ignorance of these proposals; the only information it had received had come from the Press. On July 21 Lloyd George, the guest of honour at a banquet of city financiers, speaking as the mouthpiece of the Cabinet made a formal protest against the attitude of the German Government. 'If a situation were to be forced upon us in which peace could only be preserved by the surrender of the great and beneficent position Britain has won by centuries of heroism and achievement, by allowing Britain to be treated where her interests were vitally affected as if she were of no account in the Cabinet of Nations, then I say emphatically that peace at that price could be a humiliation, intolerable for a great country like ours to endure. National honour is no party question.'[1]

II

Thus the great demagogue, the arch-enemy of a costly programme of naval expenditure, and the leading champion of a *rapprochement* between England and Germany, came forward in opposition to Germany as the mouthpiece of British patriotism and imperialism. On the Continent the speech made a profound impression. But its first effect in Germany was to irritate rather than intimidate. On the 25th the Ambassador, Metternich, made strong representations to Sir Edward Grey about a speech which violated the accepted code of diplomatic procedure. He assured

[1] Speech at the Mansion House—Sir A. Nicolson to Sir F. Cartwright, July 24, 1911: The speech of Lloyd George which, they tell you, was no sudden inspiration but a carefully thought-out one.' (*British Documents* . . . vol. vii, p. 396.) To what extent was Lloyd George the mouthpiece of his colleagues? The question has never been cleared up. According to Churchill (*The World Crisis*, pp. 46–7) he submitted the draft of his speech to Churchill, Asquith, and Grey in turn. So far as Grey is concerned, the statement has been confirmed by himself. (*Twenty-five Years 1892–1916*, vol. i, pp. 224–5.) Grey however states that he suggested no change in the wording but approved the speech as it stood. On the other hand what weight should we attach to a story which the Austrian Ambassador in Berlin heard from the Emperor, who in turn heard it from a Hamburg commercial magnate, who was his intimate friend (probably Ballin)? According to this story Lloyd George in the course of a conversation with the Emperor's informant excused himself by ascribing the entire responsibility for the invidious passage to his colleagues. Himself a stranger to foreign politics he had simply read the text put into his hands by Asquith and Grey. (Szögyény despatch from Berlin, December 19, 1911: *Österreich-Ungarns Aussenpolitik*, vol. iii, pp. 698–9.)

the British Government that his Government had no intention of establishing itself in Morocco. But when Sir Edward proposed an international congress to resettle the Moroccan question he replied by demanding the simple restoration of the *status quo*,[1] which would do nothing to obviate the risks of an armed conflict between the French and the Germans. Already, the day before Lloyd George's speech, the English and French General Staffs had concerted the emergency measures to be taken.[2] On the 26th the newspapers informed the public that the Atlantic Squadron, instead of starting for its manœuvres in Norwegian waters, had received orders to concentrate at Portsmouth, and in spite of a reassuring official denial the conclusion was universally drawn that the Admiralty, foreseeing a rupture between France and Germany, was preparing for war.[3] On the 27th the Premier, speaking in the House of Commons, explained the attitude of the Government. Though it hoped that the conversations between France and Germany might lead to an agreement honourable and satisfactory to both parties, it could not remain passive if they broke down. England would be obliged to intervene because she was a party to the Pact of Algeciras, because she had made an agreement with France in 1904, and because her interests were affected. Balfour, the Unionist leader, gave the Prime Minister, as we should expect, his hearty support, and even Ramsay MacDonald, the Labour leader, felt himself obliged to introduce into the peroration of a pacifist speech a patriotic utterance. 'I do pray that no European nation will assume for a single moment that party divisions in this country will weaken the national spirit or national union.'[4]

If the immediate effect of Lloyd George's speech at Berlin had been an outburst of anger, after ten days of strain the conversations between France and Germany became at the beginning of August a piece of bargaining. And the Germans drove a hard

---

[1] Count von Metternich to von Kiderlen-Wächter, London, July 25, 1911. (*Die Grosse Politik* . . . vol. xxxix, p. 213.)

[2] Memorandum of Meeting held on July 20, 1911 between General Dubail and General Wilson. August 11, 1911 (*British Documents* . . . vol. vii, pp. 629 sqq.).

[3] In his memoirs General Macready adds a curious detail. 'So acute was the tension that on the 28th of July a subordinate officer in an access of nervous enthusiasm despatched telegrams to all record offices to the effect that clerks were to remain on duty night and day, in case mobilization should be suddenly ordered. Happily the *faux pas* was discovered and rectified before it became public property.' (*Annals of an Active Life*, vol. i, p. 161.)

[4] H. of C., July 27, 1911 (*Parliamentary Debates*, Commons 1911, 5th Series, vol. xxvii, p. 1831).

bargain: for if they abandoned their claim to the whole of the French Congo, they persisted in demanding, in spite of French opposition, an extension on the Atlantic Coast of their territory in the Cameroons and above all means of access to the Congo and Ubangi. While the French Foreign Minister was negotiating directly with the German Minister for Foreign Affairs through the French Ambassador at Berlin, the Prime Minister, Caillaux, was secretly conducting parallel negotiations through an unofficial channel. And the bargaining was complicated by the growing excitement of the patriotic Press in both countries which made it increasingly difficult to reach a compromise mutually acceptable. Throughout the negotiations Sir Edward Grey, regularly informed of their progress by the French, acted as a moderating influence. It was in vain that the Quai d'Orsay attempted to arouse his opposition to some particular German demand. He maintained that every demand for territorial compensation should be considered whether it were in Morocco itself, or in Equatorial Africa or, as it was suggested at one moment, in the Indian Ocean or the Pacific. The one thing that mattered was to prevent a rupture of the negotiations which would involve war—a war in which England would be obliged to participate—and not allow the French Foreign Office to make the British responsible for the rejection of any German claim. And the anxiety of the Foreign Office reached a climax when towards the middle of August the French Government became convinced, on evidence which it believed to be reliable, that the German Government was bent on war and communicated its fears to the British Government at a juncture when circumstances rendered the prospect particularly formidable for both countries.

For the diplomatic situation was unfavourable. Since Isvolsky's fall the Anglo-Russian *entente* seemed to be in process of dissolution. In Persia the English and Russians were at loggerheads almost as openly as the Germans and French in Morocco. And though the official declarations of the Russian Ambassadors in Paris and London were reassuring and the French and Russian staffs maintained close contact, indeed that very August a military convention was concluded between the two Powers, the Russian Government made a gesture whose meaning could not be doubted. It published on August 19 the agreement of Potsdam by which Russia consented to support the German construction of the Bagdad railway on condition it were not extended into the zone of Persia assigned to Russia by the agreement of 1907. It was a deliberate reply to the Franco-German agreement of February 9, 1909, concluded when the Bosnian crisis was at its height. Then France had betrayed Russia. Now Russia betrayed France.

The domestic situation was also unsatisfactory. The struggle between the two Houses had indeed reached its conclusion on August 3. But though the final debates had been stormy the attention of the public was elsewhere, concentrated on the series of strikes, which after a temporary interruption about the beginning of July, broke out afresh with a violence hitherto unexperienced, in the port of London first, then at Liverpool. The workmen rioted, the troops were called out, there were shootings and deaths. And now the agitation spread to the railwaymen. 'War has begun', declared the Secretary of their Union:[1] not war between England and Germany, but the class war under the form of a general strike on the railways. It seemed a revival of the Englishman's Home acted by the entire nation.

12

On August 18 the morning papers prepared their readers for the imminent rupture of the Franco-German negotiations. The same day at the request of the general staff of the army and contrary to established usage, the House of Commons passed without debate the second and third readings of an Official Secrets Act which reinforced the powers of censorship possessed by the Government in the event of war.[2] The same day the Russian

[1] Keeling to Mrs. Townshend, August 18, 1911: 'The Strike is magnificent. Nothing else really matters' (Keeling, *Letters and Recollections*, p. 92).

[2] An Act to re-enact the Official Secrets Act, 1889 with amendments (*Official Secrets Act* 1911). The first reading of the Bill had been passed the day before. Only one division had been taken, in which the Opposition mustered only ten votes as against 107. Among these seven besides Keir Hardie we notice the names of Lansbury, Henderson, MacDonald, and Snowden. But the division was concerned only with a point of detail. In substance the Bill was passed unanimously. (*Parliamentary Debates*, Commons 1911, 5th Series, vol. xxix, pp. 2251 sqq.). For the pressure brought to bear upon the Speaker by all the members and even from the Labour benches to induce him to accept this radical breach with constitutional custom see Major-General the Right Honourable J. E. B. Seely, *Adventure* p. 144. In his reminiscences the Speaker passes over these difficulties with a majestic silence and mentions only the strike 'Just at this moment there was a general railway strike which mightily inconvenienced all holiday traffic and postponed for some days the adjournment but the strike being temporarily settled, we rose for the autumn recess on the 22nd of August to meet again on the 24th of October. In the autumn I went to Scotland for some

Ambassadors in Paris and London informed the Governments to whom they were accredited that the Potsdam agreement would be made public on the following day. That same day the Cabinet made a desperate effort to prevent the general strike on the railways. Lloyd George took the railway directors and the trade-union officials into his confidence, and begged them in the national interest at a moment when the country was on the verge of war to effect a settlement. He was successful. The strike did not take place. And the menace of war also vanished. On the 22nd, Parliament was prorogued until October but on the following day, August 23, the Cabinet decided to call a meeting of the Committee of Imperial Defence to discuss the general military situation in the event of war. The high command was very pessimistic about the Russian army. But it was optimistic, too optimistic some of the members of the Committee thought, as to the capacity of the French army to resist a German invasion with the help of a British expeditionary force. But what the Government chiefly wished to ascertain was whether the Admiralty and the War Office were working in harmony. In point of fact there was no co-operation or common policy.

As the result of a series of conversations begun in 1906, detailed arrangements had been made for joint action by the staffs of the British and French armies. But during these five years no communications had passed between the two Admiralties. How many soldiers should be sent to France, at which ports they should be embarked and disembarked and at what points they should be concentrated—on all these matters agreement had been reached on both sides of the Channel. But the crossing itself must be protected and not only had the Admiralty made no plans for this, it did not even wish to make any. For the British navy was opposed to the rapid despatch of an expeditionary force to the French front. It wanted complete freedom during the requisite period of weeks or months to seek out the German fleet and destroy it in a great battle which would be the twentieth century Trafalgar. This once accomplished and England once more mistress of the seas, the Admiralty had no objection to the despatch of a British

stalking and shooting' (Lord Ullswater, *A Speaker's Commentaries*, vol. i, p. 117). Keir Hardie in his account of the railway strike (*Killing no Murder! The Government and the Railway Strike*) makes no allusion to the danger of war. Lord Askwith (*Industrial Problems and Disputes*, p. 166) mentions it but gives us to understand that it was perhaps only a scare engineered by Lloyd George to make the companies and men come to terms.

force to the Continent. But it did not want the troops to be sent to France where the British army would help the French to win French victories. It wanted them sent to German territory, and landed on the coast of Hanover to win victories which would be exclusively English.[1] Thus the revelations published in the Paris Press on the occasion of the Tangier incident which had made a considerable sensation on the Continent were proved true. Sir Arthur Wilson, the First Sea Lord, explained the Admiralty's views to the Committee. McKenna defended the standpoint of the Navy. But this divergence of policy could not be permitted to continue without grave—possibly immediate—danger. Haldane pointed this out to his colleagues. Long weary of the War Office, where in his opinion there was nothing more for him to do, he had already attempted when the Cabinet was remodelled after Campbell-Bannerman's death to exchange it for the Exchequer. He had failed owing to the opposition of the Gladstonians in the Cabinet.[2] Now he asked for the Admiralty—and was faced no doubt by the same opposition.[3] But it was clear that McKenna was doomed, as Lord Tweedmouth had been doomed in 1908. Ten months later Churchill left the Home Office, where he was no longer a success, and took his place.

Once again at the beginning of September, war was believed to be imminent. The French Government, before deciding what territorial concessions it would be willing to make in Equatorial Africa, wanted to know what freedom of action Germany would concede in Morocco. A draft convention was laid before the German Government which replied by putting forward an agreement of a very different tenor. The German document proposed to set up an economic condominium throughout Morocco like that whose failure had brought the French army to Fez and the German fleet to Agadir, and which in the Sous district round Agadir would be a literal condominium, political as well as

---

[1] Winston S. Churchill, *The World Crisis 1911–14*, 1923, pp. 58–9. See also Lord Haldane's remarks reported by J. H. Morgan. 'The Riddle of Lord Haldane' (*Quarterly Review*, January 1929, vol. cdxc, p. 185). See also F. W. Roch, *Mr. Lloyd George and the War*, 1920, p. 47. Cf. Sir John Fisher to Lord Esher: 'The regular Army (as distinguished from the Home Army and the Indian Army) should be a projectile to be fired by the Navy' (Admiral Bacon, *Life of Lord Fisher*, vol. i, p. 206). The Same to the Same, September 20, 1911: 'I simply tremble at the consequences if the British Red Coats are to be planted on the Vosges Frontier' (Lord Fisher, *Memories*, p. 206).

[2] John Morgan, *John Viscount Morley, an Appreciation and Some Reminiscences*, 1924, p. 48.

[3] See F. W. Rich, *Lloyd George and the War*, 1920, p. 50. J. H. Morgan, 'The Riddle of Lord Haldane' (*Quarterly Review*, No. 499, January 1929, vol. cclxii, p. 185).

economic. The agreement was not acceptable either to France or to England; the negotiations reached a deadlock, and a final rupture; a German landing at Agadir and war were in sight. Germany and France made preparations for the event of war: Belgium mobilized. In London panic prevailed in naval circles when the Admiralty's scouts one day lost sight of the German fleet on the high seas. Would the German navy repeat on a large scale the blow of Chemulpo, by destroying one by one the vessels of the three British squadrons scattered to the south, east and north of Great Britain? In the utmost secrecy the War Office recalled officers and soldiers on leave and assembled the officers of the Territorial Army.[1] But for the third time the storm dispersed.

13

During forty years of European peace the nations had ceased to contemplate war as a serious possibility. Before their attitude could be so changed that war once more became a genuine likelihood, more years of nerve-wrecking tension were required and the equilibrium of Europe must be more profoundly disturbed. A financial crisis broke out in Germany at the beginning of September. It was due primarily to economic causes, but it was aggravated by the prospect of war and when the Bank of France forbade all export of gold it became evident to the whole world how solid still was the old structure of French capitalism, how weak the new structure of German industrialism. The advocates of peace once more gained the upper hand in Germany. They were assisted by the personal action of the Emperor William who had long opposed a naval demonstration in Moroccan waters, at the end had yielded with reluctance to his ministers' decision, and was delighted to be able to resume what a contemporary termed his 'fantastic dream of a *rapprochement* between France and Ger-

[1] See Captain Faber's revelations in a speech at Andover, November 9, 1911 (*Daily Telegraph*, November 20, 1911). According to another account the episode was even more dramatic. A British cruiser had encountered in British waters off the coast of Scotland the German high seas fleet drawn up in battle formation and preceded by its scouting vessels and torpedo-boat-destroyers. The German fleet had then been lost sight of and for this grave dereliction of duty two officers in high command had been dismissed from the Service. (W. Morgan Shuster, *The Strangling of Persia, a record of European Diplomacy*, 1912, p. 222.)

many'.[1] He was encouraged by the fact that the French Prime Minister thoroughly distrusted the Franco-British *entente*, was a convinced advocate of friendly relations with Germany, and ever since the end of August had been corresponding directly with the French Ambassador at Berlin over the head of his Foreign Minister. In September and October it was Caillaux, not de Selves, who was in charge of the negotiations.

In England the domestic situation improved. For the moment no strike on a large scale occurred. In October, however, the Commons reassembled to pass the National Insurance Bill and the debates on its clauses were sufficiently heated to fill the columns of the Press. On the other hand, at the end of September an Italian army suddenly invaded the Tripolitana and transferred the attention of journalists from Fez to Tripoli, and the war between Italy and Turkey involved the diplomatists of all the Great Powers in a labyrinth of new problems connected with the Mediterranean and the Balkans, in which they were slow to find their way. This enabled the conversations between France and Germany to be conducted more quietly unwatched by the public, and the French representatives went on gaining ground at the expense of the German. Instead of the entire French possessions in Equatorial Africa—though France it is true abandoned her claim to Togo—Germany obtained only some 63,000 square miles of territory, an enclave within the French colonies with two 'punctures' opening into the Ubanghi and Congo, through which France kept a right of transport. Moreover, she accepted a slight rectification of the frontier in favour of France in the region of Lake Chad. On the other hand, she gave France complete freedom 'to help the Government of Morocco to introduce the administrative, judicial, economic, fiscal, and military reforms necessary for the good government of the empire.' The purpose of this concession was, in the language of the official text, to 'carry out in the general interest the work of pacification and progress contemplated by the pact of Algeciras'. In reality, the convention departed from the provisions of that instrument of internationalization, as is clear from an explanatory letter Kiderlen appended to the document which stated 'that if ever the French Government should see fit to declare a protectorate of Morocco the Imperial Government would raise no objection'.

[1] Lieutenant-Colonel Pellé to M. Messimy, Minister for War, December 16, 1911. (*Documents diplomatiques français, 1871–1914*, 3rd Series, 1911–14, vol. i, p. 346.).

We can well imagine the feelings with which Germany received the agreement of November 4. The despatch of the *Panther* to Agadir in July had been an imprudent step because of the hopes it had inevitably aroused. The German public were confident that their country would claim her share in Morocco and was strong, enough to obtain it or in default of a portion of Morocco would receive elsewhere concessions so important that in the eyes of the world they would represent a striking diplomatic success. As we have seen, these expectations were disappointed. The minister for the colonies resigned rather than put his signature to an agreement he regarded as treason to his country's interests. The Emperor, always suspected with good reason of favouring a policy of *rapprochement* with France, found himself attacked by a clique at court of which the Crown Prince put himself at the head and by a large section of the Press and public. An epidemic of Anglophobia and Gallophobia traversed Germany.

What is more surprising, the agreement was equally unpopular in France. What, the public asked, was the meaning of these two outlets pushed forward to the Ubanghi and Congo by the new German territory? Were they only fragments of what Germany had hoped to receive and had renounced or were they stakes planted for a future claim? Had Germany even abandoned all claim to a pre-emption on the Belgian Congo? An ambiguous clause of the agreement left the point doubtful. Finally, the publication of the secret clauses of the Franco-British *entente* of 1904 respecting Morocco revealed that in return for the territory she renounced on the Congo France was to receive not the whole of Morocco but Morocco without the Riff, which was assigned to Spain. Nor was it simply on these points of detail that complaints were raised. The public took offence at the very idea of territorial compensation. Accustomed by now to the *entente cordiale* and encouraged, if not by the British Government, at least by an entire group of English diplomatists and journalists, French public opinion considered that England was under an obligation to help France to obtain everything she had promised her in 1904 and that with England's aid she was strong enough to secure it. Moreover, the despatch of the *Panther* to the harbour of Agadir had produced the same bad effect in Paris as in Berlin; since July every territorial concession made by France was regarded as extorted from the weaker by the more powerful nation. The negotiations

had been conducted during the recess of the Chambers, a circum-
stance which had considerably facilitated the negotiators' task.
The position changed when the Chambers reassembled and were
invited to ratify the agreements. Popular feeling displays surprising changes of front. Six years before, the Chambers had overthrown Delcassé because he had committed France too far to the
entente cordiale, which they regarded as dangerous and Rouvier,
the champion of a *rapprochement* with Germany, had been victorious. Now Caillaux was pursuing the same policy as Rouvier
then. And he was employing the same method of secret negotiations behind the back of his Foreign Minister. Moreover, he had
been more successful than Rouvier had been, for the Imperial
Government had conceded to him what it had refused to Rouvier
as well as to Delcassé and liberated France from the shackles
imposed upon her action in Morocco by the pact of Algeciras.
Nevertheless, it was upon his head, as then upon Delcassé's that
the Chambers discharged the vials of their wrath. In January he
would be driven from office and with his fall French foreign
policy would change its attitude once more.

14

Thus the agreement of November 4, far from improving the
relations between France and Germany, made them worse.
English opinion in turn took fire and as in Germany and France
retrospectively, when a series of sensational revelations informed
the country that on two or three occasions during the previous
summer it had been on the brink of war. Without its knowledge
was the bitter comment of advanced Liberal critics, and not to
defend any British interest but simply to give France another
colony. They severely censured Sir Edward Grey's policy. They
depicted England as a nation sacrificed to the superstition of the
European balance of power—a catspaw serving everywhere the
interests of foreign nations, in the Near East betrayed by Russian
imperialism, in the West drawn by French nationalism further
than she desired to go. Arthur Ponsonby, a democrat of noble
birth and a violent opponent of the *entente* with Russia, published
a pamphlet which made a stir by demanding that foreign policy

should be subject at every step to popular control.[1] These Liberal critics of the Government were not a large group but they were zealous propagandists and their arguments produced an obvious effect upon the entire party. Even certain Conservatives, burdened by taxation and alarmed by the spread of labour unrest, began to ask themselves whether Grey's policy were not in certain respects imprudent and whether it was wise to surrender the foreign policy of the country blindly into his hands. The *Standard*, an organ of orthodox Toryism and until the middle of November extremely hostile to Germany, suddenly changed its tone about that date and began a campaign in favour of a *rapprochement* with Berlin.[2] While approving the policy pursued by the Foreign Office, Bonar Law, the new leader of the Unionist party in the Commons, and Lord Lansdowne, the leader of the Opposition in the Lords, made the same criticism of the Government. Both blamed Grey for having on July 26th left it to Lloyd George to state the British attitude in the Moroccan dispute. They hinted that the interference of a demagogue had been prejudicial to the cause of peace.[3]

Unquestionably, these attacks upon the policy pursued by the Foreign Office and these expressions of a desire for a *rapprochement* with Germany were sincere. But it is equally certain that taken as a whole they were deliberately or unconsciously ambiguous.

'We were not aware', the malcontents complained, 'that we were so near war. The Government deceived and betrayed us.' Was this true? Lloyd George's speech in July was certainly the reverse of secret diplomacy and the naval preparations which followed were published in the Press. On the other hand, not a syllable had appeared in the Press about the panic of August or the true nature of the ministerial intervention which ended the railway strike. Neither had a syllable appeared about the panic in September and the military measures adopted at that time. But is it credible that all those in the confidence of the Government—

---

[1] *Democracy and the Control of Foreign Affairs*, 1912. This pamphlet of thirty pages may be regarded as the source from which were derived both the title and programme of the Union of Democratic Control formed in November 1914 to protest against the war with Germany whose leaders would play such an important part in British policy after the war when German naval power had been destroyed.

[2] Cf. in the November number of the *Fortnightly Review* the article entitled 'Sir Edward Grey's Stewardship' and Sir Sidney Low's article 'An Anglo-French Alliance'. (New Series, vol. xc, pp. 963 sqq., 999 sqq.).

[3] H. of C., November 27, 1911 (*Parliamentary Debates*, Commons 1911, 5th Series, vol. xxxii, pp. 70 sqq.) H. of L., November 28, 1911 (*Parl. Deb.*, Lords 1911, 5th Ser., vol. x, pp. 392 sqq.).

in September there were a host of them—kept such strict silence that not a single newspaper was informed? The silence of the entire Press—Radical as well as Unionist—a deliberate silence, inspired by the patriotic wish not to embarrass the Government. The country did not know because it refused to know. There is an ignorance whose true name is connivance.

'Yes,' Grey's critics replied, 'we refused to know because on the particular issue we were bound to France by the agreement of 1904. But the question of Morocco, the only question on which we pledged ourselves to her, has now been settled in her favour. In future, whatever dispute may arise between France and Germany our liberty is complete. We are perfectly free, if we wish, to remain neutral or even side with Germany.' Here again we must ask: Was it true? Was it really the conflict between France and Germany in Morocco which divided England and Germany, and opposed the British to the German navy? On the contrary, if England, instead of disputing the possession of Morocco with France, as she would have done had Germany remained a nation without a navy, decided to abandon Morocco to her, was it not in order to protect herself against the new danger presented by the appearance on the high seas of a powerful German fleet? And was that danger less after Agadir than before Tangier? Would Germany desist from building giant ironclads because the Moroccan question had been settled to her disadvantage? The important speech Sir Edward Grey delivered in the House of Commons on November 27 to defend his policy contained only a single sentence dealing with the naval problem, but it is the key to the entire speech. It was impossible, he pointed out, to return to the policy of 'splendid isolation'. It would ally all the powers of Europe against England. 'In the course of a few years, we should be building warships not against a Two-Power Standard, but probably against the united navies of Europe.' The Foreign Office therefore continued unmoved the policy it had pursued for the last six years, in the certainty that it represented the fundamental interest and the genuine will of the British people. But at the same time it took account of the fact that the policy of the Triple Entente aroused in the country misgivings by no means devoid of foundation and that in the years to come that policy would have to be pursued under stormier skies and in more difficult circumstances than hitherto.

PART III

ON THE BRINK OF THE CATASTROPHE

CHAPTER I

Domestic Anarchy

I THE SYNDICALIST REVOLT

I

NOW that the Parliament Bill had been passed, what use would the Government make of it? Which Bill would it choose to carry for the first time in 1912, for the second in 1913, if the House of Lords threw it out in 1912, and if again the Lords opposed their veto, for the third time in 1914, then however definitely and without appeal? A Home Rule Bill was introduced, as everyone expected. For the hour had come to pay for the support which since January 1910 the eighty or so Irish Nationalists had unswervingly given the Government, and it was this Bill as everyone equally expected, that would prove the storm centre on which the party struggle would concentrate its force. A Welsh Disestablishment Bill was introduced at the same time. The thirty Welsh Radicals whose leader Lloyd George had been before he became the great popular leader and prominent statesman of the entire country, like the Irish Nationalists wanted their reward and the disestablishment of the State Church in their little principality was the symbol of their desire for devolution. For the Welsh Nonconformists constituted three-quarters of the Welsh people and regarded the Welsh Anglicans as representatives of an alien Church forced upon Wales from without. Once already in 1909 the Liberal Government had introduced a Bill to abolish the privileges of the Anglican Church in Wales, but there had been no time to discuss it. Now the path was free. The Bill of 1912 provided that the four Welsh dioceses should no longer form part of the province of Canterbury, the Welsh Bishops should no longer sit in the House of Lords, all ecclesiastical jurisdiction should be abolished and the laws of the Anglican Church should be held binding in Wales only in virtue of the tacit consent of the Welsh Anglicans, who would, moreover, be free to hold synods and set up a representative body to govern their Church. These measures of disestablishment were accompanied by measures of disendowment. The church buildings and all gifts made to the Church since 1662 were left in her hands. Of the remaining endowments a quarter would be given to the University of Wales, three-quarters to the County Councils to be spent on public services and particularly on poor relief. The Bill was bitterly attacked by the Unionist party, which was the accredited defender of the Church of England and witnessed with alarm the Church in process of dismemberment. But the country as a whole took no interest in the question. It was quite clear that the Bill, which the Lords threw out in two successive sessions, would become law at the time fixed by the Parliament Act, if the Liberal Government remained in office so long.

Both Bills be it noticed—the important Bill to grant Home Rule to Ireland and the minor Bill to disestablish the Church in Wales—were intended to satisfy local sections of the United Kingdom, neither of which was in the true sense English. Was nothing to be done for England herself, or for the United Kingdom as a whole? To begin with the Government might fulfil the promise contained in the preamble to the Parliament Bill and reform the House of Lords after restricting its powers. But it was content with repeating the promise and never kept it. Neither party really desired the reform in question and the country did not demand it. Instead a Franchise and Registration Bill was introduced to effect such a reform of the franchise that England should be at last what France had been since 1848 and the German Empire since its creation in 1871, a country of universal suffrage. For even now universal suffrage did not exist in England. In 1910 out of twelve million adult males in the United Kingdom only some seven million seven hundred were voters.[1] This left over

[1] *Parliamentary Constituencies (Electors, etc.) (United Kingdom)—Return showing with regard to each parliamentary constituency in the United Kingdom, the total number and, as far as possible, the number of each class of electors on the Register for the year 1910; and also showing the population and inhabited houses of each constituency, 1910*—For an estimate of the number of adults who did not possess the vote, which the nature of the British franchise makes it extremely difficult to calculate, see the very different results reached by contemporaries: H. of C., February 12, 1908. The Attorney-General's speech. There were 7,250,000 on the register as opposed to the 10,000,000 who should be there, if, as would be the case under a system of adult male suffrage, a quarter of the population possessed the franchise. (*Parliamentary Debates*, 4th Series, vol. clxxxiv, p. 143.) H. of C., January 23, 1913, Asquith's speech: an electorate of 7,500,000 to 8,000,000; 2,000,000 or 2,500,000 adult males without a vote (*Parl. Deb.*, Commons, 1913, 5th Ser., vol. xlvii, p. 653). Cf. A. Lawrence Lowell, *The Government of England*, 1908, vol. i, p. 213. Price Collier, *England and the English*, 1909. (Popular edition 1911, p. 288) gives the figure of 700,000 adult males without the franchise, a gross underestimate. L. G. Chiozza Money (*Things that Matter . . . 1914*, pp. 189 sqq.), taking into account the plural vote and the lodgers who did not take the trouble to have their names placed on the register, estimated at 38.6 per cent the proportion of adult males not on the register.

four million adult males without the vote. And those four million comprised not only lunatics, prisoners, and men deprived of the franchise for offences at common law, but also paupers in the technical sense, that is to say all in receipt of poor relief. They also included other categories which the motley and complicated franchise established by the successive Reform Bills of the nineteenth century had left without a vote. A man-servant who lived in his master's house, a son who lived with his father had no vote, though a gardener or gamekeeper had because he had a separate lodging. A lodger, who paid for his lodging a rent not below ten pounds, could vote. But was the workman who sublet a room from a lodger himself a lodger within the meaning of the law? On this point legal decisions conflicted, so that the British franchise was not only limited but also uncertain.[1] Moreover the registers were revised only once a year: an official whose promotion was rapid, a labourer obliged to change his place of abode frequently to obtain work, were therefore often unable to claim a vote. In consequence, moreover, of the plural vote the franchise operated unfairly in favour of the rich. Anyone who possessed several places of residence, business premises and a dwelling-house or a town and a country house had a vote for each of these. There were, it was calculated, over half a million plural voters in the United Kingdom. They were particularly numerous in the London district, where their vote had, in January 1910, it was estimated, cost seven or eight Liberal candidates their seat.[2] We have already noticed the Government's attempt to correct the anomaly in 1907. It had been defeated by the opposition of the Lords.

When in 1908 Asquith became Prime Minister, he seems to have thought of making a general reform of the franchise the battlefield between the two Houses.[3] Lloyd George and Churchill

---

[1] The registers were compiled, so far as 'the lodgers' franchise' was concerned, by Revising Barristers, subject to no control except the check exercised by the party agents, who could appeal to the Court of King's Bench. See Michael MacDonagh 'The Making of Parliament' (*Nineteenth Century and After*, No. 347, January 1906, vol. lix, p. 31). On this and many other points the impartiality of the judge who had to decide the validity or invalidity of an election was not always above suspicion. See the incident of the Yarmouth Election Petition and Judge Grantham's decision, May 4, 1906. The public after a little grumbling accepted it. But the matter was re-opened when in January 1911 Grantham violating every precedent attempted to justify his decision by maintaining that his colleague Judge Channell who had differed from his opinion was suffering from an enfeeblement of his mental powers. Asquith protested. H. of C., February 8, 1911. (*Parl. Deb.*, Commons, 1911, 5th Ser., vol. xxi, p. 291.)

[2] Ramsay Muir, *Peers and Bureaucrats*, 1900, p. 122.

[3] Speech at the Reform Club, May 21, 1908.

disagreed and he gave way. That their opposition was justified was shown by what happened four years later when the Cabinet decided, now that the House of Lords had been reduced to impotence, to take up the matter afresh. The Franchise and Registration Bill of 1912 set up a uniform franchise, based exclusively on residence, which in turn was defined by occupation, reduced to six months the interval between the revisions of the register and abolished the plural vote.[1] But the Bill which, without actually establishing universal suffrage, would, it was estimated, extend the franchise to some two million five hundred thousand new electors was dropped amid universal indifference. The debates which began in July in the Commons with a scanty attendance were soon broken off. 'Once or twice in the course of the debate', wrote a journalist ironically, 'quotations from Bright or Disraeli served to remind us that there had been a time when great men were interested in a Bill for parliamentary reform.'[2]

2

How are we to explain this indifference? In the first place, those who were deprived of the vote were not in a position to form a body of malcontents. They were in part the dregs of the population, below the social stratum which produced conscious revolutionaries. And in part, owing to the anomalies of the existing franchise, they were a medley of scattered individuals who formed neither an economic class nor a political party. Neither the Liberals nor the Unionists had a strong interest in effecting a final extension of the franchise. The Liberal agents did indeed want the plural vote abolished, but that was too restricted a reform to arouse the enthusiasm of the masses. Even the trade unions were not particularly dissatisfied with the existing franchise. The events which had occurred since 1906 had proved how powerful already, even without an extension of the suffrage, was the pressure they could exercise upon Parliament. Even those workers for whom the measures of social legislation passed during the last five years were not enough did not blame an insufficiently democratic

[1] For the details of the Government Bill see H. of C., June 17, 1912—J. A. Pease's speech (*Parliamentary Debates*, Commons, 1912, 5th Series, vol. xxxix, pp. 1325 sqq.).
[2] *The Times*, July 19, 1912.

franchise; they attacked the system of representative government and parliamentary democracy. At the opening of the century the British workers had believed that the attack made upon them by a judicature in alliance with the employers could not be met by the direct action of the trade unions alone, and that political action was required. They had therefore listened to the appeal of the Socialists and formed a Labour party to defend their interests in Parliament. After ten years many of them, particularly among the younger men, were dissatisfied with the results obtained by this method.

The Socialists had hoped to defeat the bourgeois policy pursued by the secretaries of the great unions, which dominated the annual meeting of the Trade Union Congress. But the union officials were a very powerful body and the new Labour party had been obliged to place them in control of its organization. The Labour party in the Commons consisted therefore, as we have seen, entirely or almost entirely of trade union leaders, whose attitude now that they were provided with the political labour ticket remained what it had been before the party had been created. They were the very opposite of revolutionaries, sharing on all questions of foreign policy and general politics the opinions of the advanced Radicals and differing from the Radicals of bourgeois origin only by their more professional and therefore more conservative spirit. Unable to find in their own ranks a man with the stature of a party leader (Keir Hardie was a dreamer and they were seeking a pretext to shelve him), they finally turned to the only or almost the only man in their ranks who had not been a manual labourer. But Ramsay MacDonald was not the man to give the impression either in the House of Commons or in the country that the advent of the Labour party meant the birth of a new world. He had few friends and few enemies, was in fact nothing more than a prominent Member of Parliament who was appointed in 1912 to sit on an important commission of inquiry into the government of British India and who, if report were correct, was plotting a coalition with the Radical left wing. In that coalition Lloyd George, not he, would have been the outstanding figure.

Nevertheless, all the important measures of social reform which had been passed, had been passed, it seemed, under pressure from the Labour vote. The Conservative and Liberal Members of Parliament were equally afraid of seeing the Labour party win seats at their expense if they did not pass such measures. But what-

ever benefit the workers derived from these Statutes they did no
make the Labour party more popular with the masses. To carry
them out an entire bureaucracy had to be called into existence. To
fill the posts thus created the Government had not instituted a
system of examinations like that which protected the other
branches of the Civil Service against favouritism in every form
The Cabinet appointed its nominees. What sort of people had
hastened to apply for all these new appointments? They were no
solely, nor even principally, Liberal politicians. The ministers had
considered themselves justified in utilizing the practical experience
of labour possessed by the trade union officials. It was also a clever
move to conciliate by this largess the favour of the Labour party
The Trade Board Acts had necessitated the creation of 800 post
whose salaries reached in some cases £1,000 a year. There was a
deluge of applications.[1]

Richard Bell, the Secretary of the Railwaymen's Union, who
had been dismissed by his union in disgrace, was appointed super-
intendent of the Labour Exchanges at a salary of £400 a year. In
1910 Churchill created at the Home Office two new posts of
Labour Advisers, one of which he gave to an old official of the
Textile Workers' Union, Shackleton, the other to the Welsh
miner, T. Richards, and thirty posts of sub-inspectors of mines
and quarries, to be reserved for miners and quarrymen.[2] In 1911
the passing of the National Insurance Bill brought with it another
batch of official posts to satisfy the hunger of trade union officials.

---

[1] H. of C., September 28, 1909, Churchill's speech: '... The staff of all grades ... will
be somewhat over 800. ... Probably only about a quarter or a third will be appointed
during the present financial year' (*Parliamentary Debates*, Commons 1909, 5th Series, vol
xi, pp. 1075–76). September 27, 1909: 'A great mass of applicants are coming in daily
Altogether nearly 4,000 have been received and they are coming in at about the rate of 200
a day. I have had to organize a small staff for the simple purpose of docketting, filing, and
answering the applicants' (ibid., p. 921). Cf. 5th *Report* of H.M.'s Civil Service Commissioners with Appendices, 1911, p. 11—Old civil servants were afraid that these newcomer
would be promoted over their heads. (H. of C., October 8, 1909, Sir William Bull's
question; *Parl. Deb.*, Commons 1909, 5th Ser., vol. xl, p. 2461.) Cf. *Standard*, October 8
1907, *Nation*, July 15, 1911, p. 576.

[2] *The Times*, November 12, 13, 1910.

[3] *Royal Commission on Civil Service. Fourth Report of Commissioners*, 1914, p. 25: 'This
system of appointment has recently been adopted to some extent for the purpose of recruiting officials under the National Health Insurance Act. It claims—and herein lies its essential
character—to determine the comparative fitness of candidates by an appraisement
through personal interview, supplemented by testimonials, of their qualities of education
and intelligence. Examination is often dispensed with, or, if used at all, is used only as
qualifying test. Substantially, the system of appointment is selection by patronage, the
abuses of patronage, being, it is claimed, precluded by the substitution of a Board or
Committee of Selection for the Patron. It makes a new departure in recruitment for the
Civil Service, which calls for the most careful examination.'

At the beginning of 1912 Bonar Law charged the Liberal Government with having created within five or six years some four to five thousand new administrative posts to be filled, in the majority of cases, without competitive examination and having thus organized a political spoils system which already resembled that of the United States.[1] A year later labour statistics proved that in the last six years places had been found at the Board of Trade for 117 active union workers at a total salary of £25,240 a year, for 124 in the National Insurance Departments at a total salary of £33,700, for forty-eight at the Home Office at a total salary of £13,600, and for eighty-five in other branches of the Civil Service at a total salary of £34,800.

Worse still, since the judgment of the courts in the Osborne case had precluded the trade unions from employing part of their funds for political purposes and in particular from paying their Parliamentary representatives a salary on which to live while in the service of the House, the Cabinet in compensation abandoned the principle that the representatives of the nation should be unpaid and passed a resolution in accordance with which the House voted every member of the Commons an annual salary of £400.[2] In 1912[3] a new Statute expressly conferred on the trade unions the right to spend their funds for political objects with the reservation —destined to remain a dead letter—that the political fund of a union should be a special fund, to which individual members should be free to refuse their subscription. The Members of Parliament kept their salary all the same. The union official would perhaps no longer be so completely the servant of his union, kept in the strictest tutelage as he had been hitherto. Henceforward a path of escape was open and the ambitious workman could promise himself after some years of toil and bondage, a fixed salary—of which his class could not deprive him, at least for the

---

[1] Speech at the Albert Hall, January 26, 1912.

[2] H. of C., August 10, 1911 (*Parliamentary Debates*, Commons 1911, vol. xxix, pp. 1365 sqq.). The first session under the Liberal Government had hardly opened in 1906 when the members of the majority urged that Election expenses should be defrayed by the State and not by the candidate, that members' letters should be franked and that they should receive a salary of £300 (H. of C., March 1, 1906). J. N. Barnes' question. March 6, 1906, J. Rowlands' motion, March 7, 1906, H. Lever's motion (*Parl. Deb.*, 4th Ser., vol. clii, p. 1310; vol. cliii, pp. 388 sqq.; pp. 522 sqq.). Both motions had been passed by the Commons and the ministers had declared themselves favourable in principle to the proposals, simply asking for the necessary time to give effect to the vote of the majority. Actually, nothing was done until 1912.

[3] 2 & 3 Geo. V., Cap. 30: An Act to amend the Law with respect to the objects and powers of Trade Unions (*Trade Union Act*, 1913).

life of one Parliament if he got into the House of Commons—for life, if having forfeited the approval of his union or failed to secure re-election he had contrived to obtain a post at the Board of Trade or Home Office. All this is sufficient to explain on the part of all those active workers in the cause of labour who had secure berths in the Civil Service, and of those masses of trade unionists whose sole ambition was to improve the conditions of their labour, a growing distrust and contempt for 'politics'.[1]

Even the material advantages the workers derived from the new legislation aroused no feelings of gratitude. The little they obtained merely encouraged them to demand far more. They observed that of all the measures passed up to 1911, only one, the Act of 1909 on Trade Boards, dealt with the question of wages, and it was a very timid measure, and the last of the series, the National Insurance Act, imposed a compulsory payment out of wages. But it was the question of wages which in the economic situation of the country interested the working class more than any other. We must once more insist on the extraordinary industrial prosperity of the years immediately preceding the war. The crisis of 1908 had been overcome. Imports had risen from £542,600,000 in 1903 (the year in which Chamberlain opened his campaign in favour of tariff reform) to £592,933,000 in 1908, and exports during the same period from £360,374,000 to £456,728,000. Neither the revolutionary Budget of 1909 nor two years of constitutional conflict, nor the cloud which twice

[1] For the bad effects of the Government's policy on the organization of the tutorial classes (for these classes see Book I, p. 88-90) see Albert Mansbridge, *University Tutorial Classes: A Study in the Development of Higher Education among Working Men and Women*, 1913, p. 56: 'The actual number of students who have accepted appointments as Labour Exchange Officials or in connection with the Insurance Act is not to hand, but the effect is considerable. Several classes have, in this way, lost secretaries and replaced them by, to say the least of it, less efficient men.' And Mansbridge without actually condemning a system of recruitment which presents its advantages and is often necessary expresses the wish that 'as few students in tutorial classes as possible should obtain appointments in the public service by virtue of their having been in such classes'. Cf. A. P. Orage, *National Guilds*, 1914, pp. 217–18: 'It is not generally realized how successfully the present Government has sterilized the Socialist and Labour Movement by enlisting in the ranks of the bureaucracy energetic young Fabians as well as prominent political Socialists and Labour leaders. Large posts in London, smaller posts in the provinces. . . . The accession to the ranks of the Civil Service of a certain number of men alleged to be democrats has, of course, in no way democratized Downing Street and its purlieus. Classification still rules, appointments to the first class still being the perquisite of the universities. In this way the bureaucratic organization is securely linked to the governing classes; they worship the same God; their tone, manners, and ambition derive from the same source. It is not, therefore, surprising that the British bureaucracy is regarded by the bulk of the working population as an element of oppression.'

overhung international relations, had prevented the country growing more prosperous. Imports had risen to £624,705,000 in 1909, £678,257,000 in 1910 and £680,158,000 in 1911, exports to £469,525,000 in 1909, £534,146,000 in 1910 and £556,878,000 in 1911. In 1912, in spite of a serious social conflict at home and the outbreak in the Balkans of a war which threatened to become universal, imports reached £744,641,000, exports £598,961,000. It was no use for the Tariff Reformers to argue that the favourable impression produced by these figures was illusory and that when prices were continually rising an increase in the value of exports did not mean an increase in the amount of goods exported. The calculations of the free traders proved that exports had increased not only in value but in amount. But if there seemed little to justify the claims of the Tariff Reformers, it was very different with the claims of the Socialists, or to use a less theoretical term, of Labour.

The workers were justified in pointing out that the employers profited more than themselves by this rise in prices. It is true their wages rose but not in proportion to the rise in the cost of food and other necessities of life; or, to speak more strictly, the rise in wages always lagged behind the increased cost of living.[1] And how did the workers obtain the increase in their wages, such as it was? Political action obviously effected nothing. The workers must bring direct pressure to bear on the employers. An important Statute had been passed in 1906, snatched by fear from the politicians of the older parties. It was the Act which had legalized peaceful picketing and freed the unions from all financial liability. After years of restricted action, the working class was once more free to wield against the employers the only efficacious weapon at its disposal, not the vote but the strike.

The movement of discontent among the working class was inevitably accompanied by the revival of an extremist policy among the Socialist leaders. Its first symptom had been the elec-

[1] For the fall in real wages see *Abstract of Labour Statistics, Board of Trade (Labour Department) Fifteenth Abstract of Labour Statistics in the United Kingdom*, 1912, pp. 70, 152. According to this calculation wages rose between 1895 and 1910 from 88.23 to 99.70 while the retail price of articles of food in London rose from 93.2 to 109.9. L. G. Chiozza Money, *Things that Matter. Papers upon Subjects which are or ought to be under Discussion*, 1912, Chap. i: 'The Recent Fall in Real Wages,' also Chap. xxiii: 'The Rise in the Poverty Line' (pp. i, sqq.; 252 sqq.) gives reasons for believing that the fall in real wages in England was probably greater than one would gather from the official figures. See also for the more restricted sphere of the railways Charles Watney and James A. Little (*Industrial Warfare, The Aims and Claims of Capital and Labour*, 1912, pp. 50 sqq.).

tion of Victor Grayson to Parliament in 1907. After this the extremists seemed to have lost ground, a phenomenon to which the depression which followed the economic crisis of 1908 and the effect produced by the policy of social reform favoured by Lloyd George and Churchill undoubtedly contributed. But it soon became evident that this was no more than a truce. When British Socialism at last acquired a daily newspaper, the *Daily Herald*,[1] it was an organ of the left wing, to which the official party in vain opposed a rival organ, the *Daily Citizen*. At the universities and in certain public schools it became fashionable for an increasing number of young men, readers of Bernard Shaw and Wells, to call themselves Socialists. Under the auspices of Hyndman's Social Democratic Federation, now the 'Social Democratic Party', after the policy of co-operation with the official Labour party had been given up, a Socialist Representation Committee was formed in 1909 and at a Socialist Unity Conference, held on September 30 and October 1, it was decided to found a British Socialist party which would combine the old adherents of Social Democracy with the youthful left wing of the Labour party.[2] The new party of doctrinaires was founded with a great flourish of trumpets but the enthusiasm was somewhat artificial. For what after all did Hyndman propose? To found yet another political group. But if history taught any lesson, did it not prove that the new party would inevitably go the same way as the Labour party, already to all appearance discredited? The men who were the life and soul of the new left wing were disciples of a different school opposed to all political action and therefore in harmony with the present attitude of the working class, a school not like Marxian Socialism of German origin but hailing from France.

3

To understand the origins of this new doctrine we must go back to the time when in 1870 two opposing groups contested the control of the First International, the respective supporters of the German, Karl Marx, and of the Russian, Bakunin. To Marx's

---

[1] For the beginnings of the *Daily Herald* see George Lansbury, *My Life*, 1928.
[2] A. W. Humphrey, *A History of Labour Representation*, 1912, pp. 182 sqq. M. Beer, *Geschichte des Sozialismus in England*, 1913, pp. 496 sqq.

authoritarian Communism which looked to a centralized State to expropriate the capitalist class, the latter opposed a freer and, they argued, more flexible doctrine to which amongst others they gave the name of 'anarchism'. Bakunin's movement, for a time very powerful in the Latin countries, finally failed, and the 'anarchist' groups disintegrated into a number of isolated individuals who, renouncing collective action of any kind, confined themselves to individual propaganda, by book, newspaper, and also— to use their own phrase—'by deed'—that is to say, by assassination. Nevertheless, they soon became more numerous. In France they made their way into the *Bourses de Travail*—through the *Bourses* into the trade unions which originally Jules Guesde had affiliated to his orthodox Marxian party. They finally built up out of the unions an organization based on what they termed 'revolutionary syndicalism'.[1] According to them parliamentary politics demoralized the representatives of labour, made them lose their class consciousness, and distracted their attention to religious, national, and constitutional questions which had nothing to do with the sole question in which the workers had an interest—the social question. Militant Socialists therefore should not enter the Chamber or hold any official post except the post of secretary to a trade union, in which capacity they should organize in the factories 'direct action' against the employers, passing from dispute to dispute, from strike to strike, at every step strengthening the workers' control and reducing the profits of capital until the day when a universal revolutionary strike should complete the expropriation of the capitalists and the body of workers organized in the *Confederation Generale du Travail* set up, by their unaided efforts and without any help from the State, the free republic of producers.

From France the doctrine spread to Spain and Italy, then crossed the frontiers of the Latin countries to reach Holland, Scandinavia, and the English-speaking world: In the United States it became the creed of the organization entitled 'The Industrial Workers of the World'.[2] In the States the proletariat was itself divided into two classes. On the one hand, there was a class of highly-paid workers, the aristocracy of the proletariat, strongly organized in trade unions who by amicable agreements periodically concluded

[1] [From the French syndicat=Trade Union. Trs. Note.]
[2] For the Industrial Workers of the World see the extremely erudite study by Paul Frederick Brissenden, *The I.W.W. A Study of American Syndicalism*, 1917 (for the French influence which however Mr. Brissenden is inclined to underestimate see pp. 272 sqq.).

had concluded a species of alliance between capital and labour. On the other hand there was a class of unskilled labourers usually consisting of American citizens not of Teutonic race, which was shamelessly exploited by the employers with the connivance of the more fortunate workers. The Industrial Workers of the World incited the latter to form revolutionary organizations or rather a single organization, one big union, which could launch a frontal attack on the employers and effect the social revolution by a universal strike. The American workers were in constant touch with Ireland and an Irishman named Connolly, attracted by a doctrine calculated to appeal to a turbulent race, brought back to his native country the theories of the Industrial Workers of the World.[1]

Meanwhile these doctrines spread in Australia where a powerful Labour party existed, which already controlled the great cities, held office in many of the States, and hoped to gain possession of the Commonwealth Government. Owing to its very success it had ceased to be a revolutionary party, had found itself compelled to subordinate the class interests of the proletariat to the interests of Australian society as a whole, and even to repress strikes. Here therefore the soil was favourable to the growth of syndicalist ideas. Parliamentary government, State action, were shams, and the strikers betrayed by the politicians naturally came to regard the strike as the only efficacious lawful instrument of liberation. Here the Industrial Workers of the World came into contact with some Englishmen, jetsam of abortive Socialist agitations who were stranded in Australia. There were champions of the Social Democratic Federation; there were Ben Tillett and Tom Mann, the former originally a transport worker, the latter from the engineering trade, who in 1889 had both taken an active part in revolutionary strikes in London. Tillett and Mann had then been in their way important men. Forgotten now, they were attracted by the prospect of making their reappearance in England armed with the doctrine they had discovered at the antipodes. In turn they came back to Europe. An English militant, by name Guy Bowman, in close contact with the French Revolutionaries, who had translated a book by Gustave Herve and was trying to introduce the syndicalist agitation into England, sent them to Paris to receive orders from the leaders of the movement. So quickly in

[1] See his book, *Socialism Made Easy*, 1909 also his biography by Desmond Ryan, *James Connolly, His Life, Work and Writings* with a preface by H. W. Nevinson, 1924.

the twentieth century do ideas encircle the globe.[1] On November 26, 1910, at Manchester 200 delegates representing some seventy groups, sixteen trade councils, and 60,000 workers, founded the Manchester Syndicalist Education League which immediately launched a campaign of propaganda by lectures, pamphlets, and books. The Central Labour College which Dennis Hird had founded in London in opposition to Ruskin College, which was regarded as too moderate, provided the propaganda with the necessary centre. Among the intelligentsia syndicalism gained as many converts as among the manual workers. Young men of letters, attracted to Socialism by its promise of emancipation but repelled by its bureaucracy and pedantry, thought they had found in syndicalism a way out of the impasse. They read Georges Sorel, the theorist who by adapting Bergson's philosophy gave revolutionary syndicalism a metaphysical foundation. They claimed for the workers and for themselves the right to be liberated without being civilized and made bourgeois. In their interpretation revolutionary syndicalism expressed, in opposition to democratic nationalism, a revolt of the *élan vital*, the obscure forces of instinct.[2]

In 1910 the situation favoured their propaganda.[3] The strike movement, which had been fostered by the action of the Liberals in 1906 and the passing of the Trade Disputes Bill, had been checked by the crisis of 1908. It was in 1910 that it first seriously alarmed the wealthy classes. Important strikes broke out in the coalfields of northern England and Wales, among the cotton spinners of Lancashire and Cheshire, and in the Clyde dockyards.

[1] Tom Mann, *From Single Tax to Syndicalism*, 1913. Charles Watney and James A. Little, *Industrial Warfare*, 1912, pp. 30–34. There is very little in Ben Tillett's *Memories and Reflections*, 1931.

[2] Stephen Reynolds, *A Poor Man's House*, 1909. *Seems So! A Working-Class View of Politics*, also his correspondence published by Harold Wright, 1923. Fabian Ware, *The Worker and the Country*, 1912.

[3] For the Labour agitation in England on the eve of the Great War see in the first place the official documents and the figures published (particularly for the great strikes of 1911 and 1912) in: *Strikes and Lock-Outs*. Board of Trade (*Department of Labour Statistics*) *Report on—and on Conciliation and Arbitration Boards in the United Kingdom in 1910 with comparative Statistics*, 1912, pp. 21 sqq.—*in 1912 with comparative Statistics*, 1913, pp. xxi, sqq. See also the excellent contemporary work by Charles Watney and James A. Little, *Industrial Warfare. The Aims and Claims of Capital and Labour*, 1912, Lord Askwith, *Industrial Problems and Disputes*, 1920, pp. 148 sqq. (The personal reminiscences of a man who at this time was the chief arbitrator at the Board of Trade.) See also G. D. H. Cole, *A Short History of the British Working-Class Movement, 1789–1929*, vol. iii, *1900–1927*, Chaps. v and vi, pp. 63 sqq., also Sidney and Breatice Webb, *The History of Trade Unionism* (revised edition extended to 1920) 1920, Chaps. ix and x *passim*. W. H. Cook, *The General Strike. A Study of Labour's Tragic Weapon in Theory and Practice*, 1931, says very little about the agitation in England at the date with which we are concerned.

The number of strikers was the highest registered since 1893. And it was remarked that 30 per cent of the strikers had downed tools to protest against the use of non-union labour—in other words, to defend the supremacy of the unions.[1] But it was also noteworthy that in many instances the strike broke out spontaneously without orders from headquarters, sometimes even against the wish of the union officials. It was therefore a revolt not only against the authority of capital but against the discipline of trade unionism. And the abuse made by the miners on strike in South Wales of the right of picketing conferred by the Act of 1906 caused general consternation. The strike became a lawless revolt when on the evening of November 8 the strikers looted the village of Tony-pandy.[2] Should we also mention an incident which took place in London two months later? At Stepney two Russian anarchists suspected of having committed political murders were besieged in the house where they lived. The troops were called out, there was shooting and cannon fire, and the Home Secretary, Churchill, came in person to take charge of the operations until finally both anarchists perished in the burning building. In fact, this dramatic scene was not English. It was an incident of the Russian revolution enacted on British soil. But the *Industrial Syndicalist*, Tom Mann's monthly organ, made use of it for his propaganda. He offered a prize of two guineas for an essay of 3,000 words on the following problem. 'If two men can keep 2,000 men employed and hold them at bay in one street, how many men would be required to defeat two or three million men, spread over the area of Great Britain?'[3]

4

What bodies of workmen would Ben Tillett and Tom Mann on their arrival from Australia select as the field of this propaganda? As we might have expected, Ben Tillett, a former dock labourer,

[1] *Strikes and Lock-Outs. Board of Trade (Labour Department) Report on*, 1911, pp. 2–3. Letter from G. R. Askwith. The number of workers directly involved in strikes had been 56,380 in 1904, 67,653 in 1905. It rose in 1906 to 157,872, fell to 100,728 in 1907, rose again to 223,909 in 1908, and fell to 170,258 in 1909. The movement of rapid increase began in 1910 with a total of 385,085 (p. 14). If we add to the number directly involved in the strike, those obliged to cease work on account of the strike of other workers, we obtain a total of more than half a million.

[2] 'An orgy of naked anarchy' (*The Times*, November 9, 1910). For these disorders see General the Rt. Hon. Sir Nevil Macready, *Annals of an Active Life*, vol. i, pp. 136 sqq.

[3] *The Industrial Syndicalist*, vol. i, No. 6.

and leader of the great strike at the London docks in 1889, turned his attention first to the dockers. In 1889 they had won a great victory and had considerably improved their conditions of labour. Since then however they had lost ground. There were always three times as many men wanting work as those in employment, and the dockers were moreover divided among thirteen rival organizations and hampered by the competition of a host of yellow and black workers, the scum of Asia and Africa. Ben Tillett set himself to revive the old Dock, Wharf, Riverside, and General Workers' Union, the child of the strike of 1889.[1] A strike which broke out at Newport in Wales drew public attention for the first time to the dockers' grievances. The arbitration of the Board of Trade was accepted by the officials of the union but the men refused to accept the award. It was propitious soil for the syndicalist propaganda, a rising of the workers against their leaders' moderate policy. Another organization in the ports provided a field of operations for the other leader of syndicalism after the French pattern, Tom Mann. In collaboration with the Secretary of the Seamen's Union, J. Havelock Wilson,[2] he went from port to port to gather recruits for this still youthful organization. Their programme, drawn up in July 1910 was to form a National Conciliation Board which should fix a uniform standard of wages, the minimum wage to be £4 10s. a month and reform the methods of recruiting labour—in short, draw up an entire code of corporate labour. In spite of pressure from the Board of Trade the Shipbuilders' Federation refused to negotiate with the Union's representatives. War was declared.

The struggle quickly assumed international proportions. For in France among the seamen from Marseilles to Dunkirk, strikes were endemic, and citizeness Sorgue, an unwearied agitator, acted as a link between the workers of both countries. At a congress held in Copenhagen in August, the International Federation of Transport Workers, in spite of some opposition from the German dele-

[1] Ben Tillett, *Dock, Wharf and General Workers' Union. Commemorating the 1889 Dockers' strike*, September 1910. *Sub finem*: 'Our Union is stronger, richer and more useful now than ever, and its future is with you, brothers and comrades, in a great battle that must only end with the workers being masters of their destinies and that of their respective countries. We must not rest until the cause of poverty is removed, and the abolition of the capitalist system is complete.'

[2] Joseph Havelock Wilson's autobiography, *My Stormy Voyage through Life*. Vol. i, 1925 relates only the first part of his career, and volume ii has not been published. Moreover the book was written by Wilson when in his old age he had become a professed patriot and conservative.

gates, decided in favour of an international strike of seamen. It
was to be a general strike not only of the sailors in the mercantile marine but of all who played any part whatever in handling
merchandise at the ports. Tillett and Mann won their crowning
victory when in November a National Transport Workers'
Federation was formed in England comprising thirty-six unions,
unions of seamen, dockers, and carters of every description.[1]

The signal for the international strike of seamen was given on
June 14, 1911. On the Continent it went unheeded but in England
nothing short of a revolutionary outbreak followed. Here we
meet again those labour disorders with which we have become
acquainted already as intervening so strangely in the Agadir crisis.
They took everybody by surprise, 'It is a revolution,' an employer
told a high official at the Board of Trade, 'the men have new
leaders, unknown before; and we don't know how to deal with
them.' And a Labour member told the same official that he could
not understand what was happening. 'Every one seems to have
lost their heads.'[2] The strike was marked by a violence to which
England was unaccustomed and which terrified the middle classes.
At Hull, Manchester, and Cardiff there were cases of arson and
looting and riots between the crowd and the police in which a
large number were wounded. Finally, about the first of August a
settlement seemed to have been reached, though the employers
found themselves obliged to treat not only with the transport
workers but with several other unions. The strikers' official programme was a 'national' programme including the regulation of
the conditions of labour throughout the whole of the United
Kingdom. But the issue was soon narrowed down to the question
of wages and everywhere the employers were striving to save
what they could. Everywhere the men obtained an increase of
wages equal or almost equal to what they had asked, and often
secured in addition the recognition of their union.

But the struggle broke out again almost at once. The port of

[1] The International Socialist Congress held at Stuttgart in 1907 had spent much time
debating a motion put forward by Gustave Hervé calling upon the citizens of every
country to reply to a declaration of war from whatever quarter it might come by a military strike and an insurrection. At the next congress held at Copenhagen between August
28 and September 3, 1910, Keir Hardie, in Hervé's absence advocated the general strike
in a more restricted form characteristic of the tendencies prevalent at the moment in the
British unions, a general strike in all industries which provided the implements of war,
arms, munitions, and transport.

[2] Lord Askwith, *Industrial Problems and Disputes*, 1920, p. 149.

London had escaped the troubles of June and July since the authorities had made haste to negotiate with the dockers and a settlement had been reached on July 27. But the settlement itself created a new grievance. The wages of the dockers in the port of London had been raised to the level of the wages received by dockers in the employment of certain private companies. The latter then demanded an increase of wages, and this in turn led the dockers who had accepted the agreement of July 27 to demand a corresponding increase in their wages. Ben Tillett formed a strike committee. A strike actually broke out which in the end affected 77,000 men.[1] The conflagration had been rekindled. It was aggravated when another organization intervened.

5

In spite of its title the Federation did not contain all the transport workers in the widest sense of the term transport. The four unions of railway servants remained outside it. But among railwaymen a discontent prevailed which the settlement of 1907, far from allaying, had intensified, and which made them the natural allies of the dockers and seamen. They complained of the composition of the conciliation boards, from which the secretaries of the unions were excluded. They were dissatisfied with the poor results secured by the new method, an increase of wages insufficient to cover the rise in the cost of living and rendered worthless by a host of devices to which the companies had recourse and against which they were powerless to defend themselves. They also complained that the procedure of the conciliation boards was slow, complicated and expensive, and became ruinous when no settlement was reached and arbitration became necessary. In 1910 the General Secretary of the Amalgamated Society of Railway Servants calculated that the operation of the agreement of 1907 had cost the Society £25,000 in three years, to which must be added the cost of the Osborne case.

Moreover, as the result of the Osborne decision the railwaymen turned towards advisers who opposed political action. Richard

---

[1] For the strike in the port of London see Ben Tillett, *History of the London Transport Strike*, 1911 (with a preface by H. Quelch). It is however a confused and not very informative account. See further the works quoted above, p. 453 *n*.

Bell, responsible for the agreement of 1907, had been replaced as General Secretary of the Society by a man of more pugnacious temper, J. E. Williams, who was provided with an 'assistant secretary' destined to become famous and like Williams a Welshman, the supple J. H. Thomas. But what could they do? The conditions of labour had been fixed for six years: until 1914 the unions' hands were tied. Their officers could not fight unless they were pushed into war by a revolt of their troops. This revolt had begun in July 1910 when, in consequence of the dismissal of a platelayer at Newcastle which they considered unjustified, 3,000 railwaymen had gone on strike dislocating for three days all the communications of that important industrial centre. The companies had won. But the unrest had continued. Here, as among the seamen, the French example was contagious. In October a general strike on the French railways had created a sensation. The French Government had broken it by militarizing the railway service and mobilizing all the railwaymen. If a general strike broke out on the British railways, the Government could not employ this weapon.

At the beginning of August 1911 a general strike seemed very near. In many places serious local strikes occurred, in which the railwaymen revolted against the Conciliation Board and attempted to obtain by direct action an increase of wages and a reduction of hours. A thousand men went on strike at Liverpool. The dockers' strike which had ended ten days before broke out once more in sympathy with the railwaymen. The employers launched a counter-offensive and declared a lock-out of the entire union comprising 48,000 workers. In Liverpool Mann, like Tillett in London, took charge of operations.

The situation became serious. In England's two greatest ports the population was threatened with famine or at least was at the mercy of two proletarian dictators, Ben Tillett and Tom Mann. In the wealthy quarters the price of meat doubled. To supply children and the hospital patients with milk the vans which delivered it were obliged to obtain passes signed by Tillett or Mann. Alternatively a military convoy must be obtained. It was freely granted to anyone who asked for it. Churchill, a former soldier who had gone over to pacifism, became once more a militarist when, as Home Secretary, he lent his services to the Admiralty at a moment of diplomatic tension to organize in the ports a hunt for German spies and borrowed troops from the War Office to patrol the streets of London and Liverpool. This military intervention was not always successful. If in London the dispute was peaceably settled by an agreement concluded on August 11, it was not the same at Liverpool where the presence of the Irish element no doubt gave the strike a particularly violent character. One day the offices of the Shipping Federation were burnt down. Another day the soldiers used their rifles and there were casualties. They were to be sure local disturbances. But by the indignation they aroused throughout the working class they provoked or came within an ace of provoking another social crisis of a more formidable character.

On August 15 at Liverpool, the day after the affray with the troops, the secretaries of the four railwaymen's unions acting in concert, after protesting against the massacre declared that in conformity with 'the almost universal demand' of the workers they gave the Companies twenty-four hours in which to open negotiations for a new settlement of the questions outstanding between themselves and their employees. Otherwise there would be a general strike. On the 16th the Prime Minister summoned to London the four signatories of the manifesto. On the 17th he had an interview with the Companies' official representative, as a result of which the latter considered themselves entitled to inform the Press that in reliance upon the assurances of protection they had received from the Government they were prepared to guarantee an efficient though reduced service even in the event of a general strike. Asquith then had an interview with the secretaries of the four unions in which he offered to appoint a royal commission to examine the men's grievances impartially and accompanied his offer by a threat as to the consequences of a refusal.[1] To this the men replied by giving the order for a strike which was immediately obeyed everywhere. On Friday morning, August 18, the dislocation of the railway services began.

6

Asquith was in favour of firm resistance. And Churchill was despatching troops in all directions without even waiting for the local authorities to ask for them. It was at this juncture that

[1] On this point see the resolutions of the President of the Amalgamated Society of Railway Servants in the *Nottingham Guardian* for August 28.

Lloyd George who had already spoken in conciliatory terms in the House of Commons[1] wrested from his colleagues authority to open negotiations. He informed the representatives of the companies and the railwaymen in confidence of the danger of war and urged the bad effect which in the existing situation would be produced by a general strike. The same evening a compromise was reached.[2] The men agreed that the dispute should be referred to a Commission. But on the other hand the Companies undertook to reinstate all the strikers in the positions they held before the strike, and promised that, before the question was referred to the Commission, the directors should meet the secretaries of the unions, which might well seem a first step towards recognizing the latter. Lloyd George indeed evidently encouraged the secretaries to believe that the recognition was only a question of weeks. If the railwaymen's complaints of the Conciliation Boards were justified the Commission could not fail to recommend a system of collective agreements concluded directly with the unions, and the Companies would be obliged to accept on the decision of an impartial umpire what they had refused in August to the pressure of the unions.[3]

The Labour Crisis of 1911 was reaching its end. Disorders in-

[1] H. of C., August 16, 1911. Lloyd George denied the promises alleged to have been made to the Companies by the Prime Minister in a document read to the House by the Labour member Wardle: 'It is a very misleading thing to put down. I object to it very much in the interest of the railway companies, the men, and the community, because it is so important that the Government's position of strict impartiality should be preserved. (*Parliamentary Debates*, Commons 1911, 5th Series, vol. xxix, pp. 2045 sqq.). H. of C. August 17, 1911. Lloyd George did not want the relegation of the dispute to a Commission to be regarded as the Government's device to evade responsibility. 'The Government of course cannot abrogate its responsibility and cannot accept the report of any Commission without investigation. The responsibility, of course, must be, in the first instance, the responsibility of the Government and then finally of the House of Commons. . . . I hope it will be possible, at any rate during the next few hours, to conduct negotiations without any exasperating intervention, either inside or outside the House.' (*Parl. Deb.*, Commons 1911, 5th Ser., vol. xxix, pp. 2196, 2198.) See the equally conciliatory words spoken by Ramsay MacDonald (*Parl. Deb.*, Commons 1911, 5th Ser., vol. xxix, pp. 2193 sqq.).

[2] *Railway Workers—United Kingdom. Terms of Settlement 19th August, 1911.* (*Strikes and Lock-Outs. Board of Trade [Labour Department] Report on*, 1911, pp. 168 sqq.).

[3] For the railway strike see, besides the various works mentioned above p. 453 n. 1, Keir Hardie, *Killing no Murder! The Government and the Railway Strike. What Caused the recent Railway Strike? Who Settled it? For what Purposes were the Troops Called out?* (no date)—the interesting evidence given by J. H. Thomas before the Industrial Council November 27, 1912 (*Inquiry into Industrial Agreements, Minutes of Evidence*, pp. 428–9, Rowland Kenney, *Men and Rails*, 1913. G. W. Alcock, *Fifty Years of Railway Trade Unionism*, 1925 pp. 424 sqq. Charlotte Leubuscher, *Der Arbeitskampf der Englischen Eisenbahner im Jahre*, 1911. *Mit einem einleitentenden Überblick über der allgemeine Entwicklungstendenz in der heutigen englischen Arbeiterbewegung*, 1913 (in the *Staats und Sozialwissenschaftliche Forschungen* by G. Schmoller and Max Sering. Heft, 174). An excellent history prefaced by a general picture of the British labour movement about this date.

deed continued in Wales, where a fight took place between the troops and railwaymen on Friday the 19th which cost seven victims, and Jewish shops were looted in the village of Tredegar. But order was soon restored. The Railway Commission reported on October 18. The report disappointed the railwaymen. It recommended, it is true, that the procedure of the Conciliation Boards should be expedited in the first place by abolishing the right of appeal, but the competence of each board was to be strictly confined to disputes which concerned a particular section of the men, so that it would be impossible to submit claims involving the entire staff. It suggested that their jurisdiction instead of being confined to wage disputes should be extended to all questions concerning the conditions of labour but that questions of discipline should remain outside their competence. It recommended that the secretaries of the unions should sit on the boards, but it did not recommend that the recognition of the unions, the fundamental demand of the railwaymen since 1907, should be granted. The union officials spoke of recommencing the strike. It was in vain. The men's spirit had been broken. One of the four unions, the engineers' and firemen's, stood aloof and the three others thought it prudent instead of ordering a strike to take a referendum on the question. To this the Companies replied by an adroit move cleverly calculated to conciliate the body of the workers. In agreement with the Government which authorized them in turn to raise their rates they decided to grant a general increase of wages.[1] The referendum went in favour of striking but the

[1] In fulfilment of a promise given in August (Railway Workers)—United Kingdom Terms of Settlement 19th August 1911 (*Strikes and Lock-Outs Board of Trade* [*Department of Labour Statistics*] *Report on*, 1912, p. 169). The promise was kept by an Act not passed until the opening of 1913: 2 & 3 Geo. V., Cap. 29: An Act to amend Section One of the Railway and Canal Traffic Act, 1894 with respect to increases or rates or charges made for the purpose of meeting a rise in the cost of working a railway due to improved labour conditions (*Railway and Land Traffic Act*, 1913). In 1907 as compensation for the concessions made to the railwaymen the Government had authorized the companies to pursue freely their policy of amalgamation. The men had protested. For since the effect of this policy would be to diminish the staff required it would involve many dismissals. The protests were obviously unjustified. Can any corporation be forced in the interest of its employees to employ more men than it needs? And, in fact, when the demand for labour was so great were many men thrown out of work as a result of this policy? In 1911 the Government empowered the railway companies to raise their rates to compensate for an increase in wages. The port of London authorities did the same after the August strike. It amounted to making society as a whole instead of a group of capitalists, pay for the concessions made by the latter to their employees; from the Socialist standpoint an extremely questionable solution. The Labour members protested and as their cause was that of the entire public making use of the railways they carried an amendment restricting the operation of the Act to five years. But the House of Lords rejected it and the Commons yielded. See

men had obviously voted only for form's sake. When it was held, the Companies had already decided in obedience to a final command by the House of Commons[1] to meet the union secretaries in conference. A few slight modifications of the Commission's proposals sufficed to satisfy the latter.[2] The men did not strike but accepted the agreement.

7

The railway question was thus settled for the time. But the Labour unrest continued. In December there was a strike of dockers and carters at Dundee, and at the end of the same month a strike of the weavers in north-east Lancashire. In January a general strike broke out at Glasgow. Then in March after the general strikes of transport workers, and the abortive general strike on the railways there followed a general strike in the mines. It had almost broken out in 1909 and though a settlement was reached at the eleventh hour the hostility felt by the miners towards the alterations in the time-table which had followed the introduction of the eight-hours' day persisted. The syndicalist propaganda therefore found favourable soil in the mining districts, particularly in South Wales, where Dennis Hird's Central Labour College organized a course of Socialist lectures; two young miners, Stanton and Vernon Hartshorn, without breaking with the Labour party kept in touch with the revolutionaries, and at the beginning of 1912 the most sensational of the purely syndicalist manifestoes which had appeared in England was published under the title 'The Miners' Next Step'. The issue upon which the conflict centred was the new question of what were known as 'abnormal places'. Was it just that the miner who was paid by the piece should receive less when the lesser output of his labour was due not to the smaller amount of work done, but to the greater difficulty of extracting the coal? The dispute began in a district of the Welsh coalfield, where 10,000 miners remained on

the debates H. of C., January 30, February 11, 12, 1913. H. of L., February 19, 1913 (*Parliamentary Debates*, Commons 1912, 5th Series, vol. xlvii, pp. 1571 sqq., vol. xlix, pp. 756 sqq., 1333 sqq. Lords 1912–13, 5th Ser., vol. xiii, pp. 1448 sqq.).

[1] H. of C., November 22, 1911 (*Parl. Deb.*, Commons 1911, vol. xxxi, pp. 1209 sqq.)

[2] Railway Conference Agreement, December 11, 1911. (*Strikes and Lock-Outs. Board of Trade [Labour Department] Report on*, pp. 169 sqq.).

strike from September 1910 to September 1911 to be defeated in the end. But at the very moment when they surrendered, the British National Federation of Miners decided to take up the question and demand on behalf of the entire federation special wages for men working in 'abnormal places'. They had attempted to discuss the matter with the Mining Association which contained all the mine owners in the kingdom. Such a recognition of national bargaining would however have been a step towards the unification perhaps the eventual nationalization of the mines. The owners therefore proposed regional negotiations and the miners accepted their demands, but proceeded to raise the issue of the minimum wage. The question of abnormal places would be settled by implication if it were agreed that throughout Great Britain, however unproductive the seam, the miners' wage should not fall below a certain minimum. In this way the suggestion for the equalization of wages throughout the country was again brought forward. If the mine owners refused the miners' terms there would be a strike. And a strike we may observe in breach of contract. For the Welsh miners were bound by contract for more than two years, the Scottish for more than one. The union officials though themselves in favour of moderate courses were swept away by the wave of syndicalism.[1]

Throughout the greater part of the country the mine owners accepted the miners' terms, but in Scotland, South Wales, Northumberland, and Durham they refused, and on January 18 the miners by 445,800 to 115,300 votes decided in favour of striking. The solidarity of the workers was now such that half of them who had no direct interest at stake came to the help of the other half. Moreover, a new set of demands was now put forward by the Miners' Federation. It demanded, under pain of a strike, a general tariff of wages drawn up for each district, no wage to be less than five shillings for adults, two shillings for children.

The Government intervened. Four Cabinet Ministers—the Prime Minister, Sir Edward Grey, Lloyd George, and Sydney Buxton—met the representatives both of the mine owners and the miners. Asquith submitted his proposals to both parties. The principle of a minimum wage was recognized. In each district special agreements would be necessary to fix that minimum which

[1] For the miners' strike see in addition to the works mentioned above p. 453 *n*. Maurice Alfassa, *La Grève noire et l'Evolution des Syndicats*, 1913.

would differ in different districts. In each district a joint conference might be set up on which the Government would be represented, and if it failed to reach an agreement, the representatives
of the Government would act as umpire. As in November, the
mine owners were divided, though the miners were already asking more than in November, not only the acceptance of the
abstract principle of a minimum wage but that it should be legally
fixed. The men unanimously rejected Asquith's proposals. The
strike began, affecting directly a million men, indirectly a further
million—the railwaymen, for instance, and the iron workers. It
lasted a month and in contrast to the labour troubles of 1911 was
conducted peaceably. Not a single sanguinary incident occurred.
Tom Mann was imprisoned for inciting the soldiers to make
common cause with the workers against the Government; but
there was no collision between the troops and the strikers. The
calm however was itself formidable. Finally, to escape the *impasse*,
the Government carried a Bill establishing a minimum wage in
the mines. It provided that it should be fixed under conditions
prescribed in detail and varying with each class of worker, by
twenty-three joint district boards with independent chairmen.
Introduced on the 19th of March it was passed on the 29th. The
Conservative Opposition refrained from embarrassing the
Government by obstruction and allowed the Bill to pass, merely
expressing the hope that once it had become law the Government
would show itself sufficiently firm to make the working class
accept it.

For this was the critical issue. The new Act embodied the
proposals made by Asquith in February, not the claims of the
miners: it contained no clause fixing a national minimum wage.
What would be the attitude of the union officials now the Act
had been passed? They evaded the difficulty by taking another
referendum of the union, and though a majority voted in favour
of continuing the strike it was so small that the officials overruled
the decision on the ground that two-thirds of the miners had not
voted for the strike. And soon they decided to raise a pæan of
victory. It was surely an event of historic importance that so soon
after the excitement aroused by the dispute between the two
Houses, Parliament, instead of discussing such political questions
as Home Rule or Welsh Disestablishment had devoted its time
for two entire months to the Labour question. And if the miners

had not obtained everything they had asked for, they had obtained for the first time in the history of labour legislation recognition of the principle of the minimum wage, not as in 1909 for certain classes of workers incapable of self defence, but for the most powerful union in the United Kingdom and in consequence of its victorious action. 'The solidarity of the workers', Vernon Hartshorn declared on March 28, 'has become so firm that in less than a week, by the stoppage of the railways and other means of transport, we can paralyse the nation, bring the government to its knees and make it beg us to resume work on harder conditions than those that it would have declared inacceptable at the outset.'

8

This labour unrest, which at times verged on anarchy, was embarrassing to the Government and the more so since it no longer possessed the hold over the working class it once exercised through the channel of those Members of Parliament who claimed to be their accredited representatives. We can picture the great demagogue of the Cabinet, Lloyd George, struggling with difficult problems of parliamentary tactics. After the important series of measures, from the Trade Disputes Act of 1906 to the National Insurance Act of 1911, whose only result seemed to have been to increase the discontent of the industrial proletariat, what further step could he take in the same direction? Must he content himself with using his diplomatic ability to intervene in the labour disputes which were following in rapid succession? We have seen the brilliant success with which in August 1911 he had taken the Prime Minister's place and prevented the railway crisis from issuing in disaster. In March 1912, a witness depicts him, while arbitrating in company with three of his colleagues on the coalminers' strike, 'keeping conspicuously quiet and possibly keeping himself in reserve for a crisis'.[1] He must find some new slogan, turn the attention of the public to some other question and place himself once more in the limelight. And the need became the more pressing the more enemies he made in the course of his stormy career. Once already he had been libelled by a journalist; but he had prosecuted the libeller, who had made an abject apology

[1] Lord Askwith, *Industrial Problems and Disputes*, 1920, p. 210.

and he had emerged victorious. It was very different when at the end of 1912 after attacking so many people he found himself the object of attack, defamed by a group of bitter foes.

They did not belong to the syndicalist group. Nevertheless, they were fighting as free-lances on what may be termed the right wing of the movement. The two Chesterton brothers and Hilaire Belloc had constructed a philosophical and social system which they defended by a lavish supply of paradoxes. The philosophical foundation was Catholic. The two Chestertons were or would soon be Catholics, Belloc was a born Catholic, and they emphasized the negative aspects of their Catholicism, an equally fanatical hatred of Protestantism and the Jews. In their eyes Protestantism and Jewry stood for the bourgeois spirit, the spirit of big business, and it was in their criticism of bourgeois civilization that they joined hands with the syndicalists. Belloc had provided the latter with useful formulas by his denunciations of the 'Servile System', the 'Selfridge System' in which he enveloped in a common condemnation Capitalist and Collectivist industrialism. What difference did it make to the individual whether he was the slave of a private employer of a democratic state; earned his wage as the employee of a large company or of the Government?[1] Belloc and his friends wanted to return to the old system of small property, home industries, and trade guilds and they could justify their Catholic sympathies by the fact that it was in Catholic Europe, Ireland, and the South and West of the Continent that large-scale industry had made least progress. They published a new weekly, *The New Witness*, which aggravated the prevalent intellectual chaos. Belloc attacked Lord Murray, who administered the Liberal party funds, two Jewish members of the Cabinet, and Lloyd George himself.

The great inventor, Marconi, had founded a company in England to exploit his inventions and had offered to conclude an agreement with the British Government for the sole right to set up official wireless stations throughout the Empire. The Government was in a hurry to conclude the agreement at a time when like all the other European Governments it was making prepara-

---

[1] Hilaire Belloc, *The Servile State*, 1912, with its device: 'If we do not restore the Institution of Property we cannot escape the Institution of Slavery; there is no third course.' See also G. K. Chesterton's fantastic Utopia inspired by the same spirit, *The Napoleon of Notting Hill*, 1909 and for the controversy with orthodox collectivism, *Socialism and the Servile State. A Debate between Messrs. Hilaire Belloc and Ramsay MacDonald, M.P.*, 1911.

tions for a war possibly imminent. It was accused of being too hasty and there was talk of corruption. The men just mentioned were accused, the two Jews being Sir Rufus Isaacs, the Attorney-General, who was brother of Godfrey Isaacs, Chairman of the British Marconi Company, and Herbert Samuel, the Postmaster-General, who in the eyes of his detractors was guilty of the double offence of signing the agreement and being a Jew. We shall not enter into the details of the Marconi affair which dragged out for several months. It is enough to say that it provoked debates in the House, and was submitted to a Parliamentary Committee of Inquiry and that, if as the result of the investigation Samuel was proved completely innocent, the others were proved to have been guilty, if not of corruption in the strict sense, at least of incorrect financial dealings.[1] The affair, once politically settled, hung fire. A new agreement was made with the Marconi Company more favourable to the State than the former had been. The campaign against Lloyd George and his friends had not therefore been fruitless. After this the country was obviously of the opinion that it was in bad taste to continue to attack them. The London Press refused to imitate methods of political warfare only too fashionable, as Lloyd George himself observed 'on the other side of the Channel'.[2] When a few months later Sir Rufus Isaacs was promoted to one of the highest judicial positions in the kingdom the public does not seem to have protested. Nevertheless, Lloyd George smarted from the attacks made upon him. For we cannot deny that his detractors had laid a brutal finger on a sore place in the system of democratic government. Men of the humblest origin rise to political power on a programme of war against the rule of wealth and, if they become ministers, receive as such a salary which enables them to take their place in a society based on the inequality of wealth which they denounce. But if ever they

[1] See the debates H. of C., October 11, 1912; appointment of a Committee of Inquiry (*Parliamentary Debates*, Commons 1912, 5th Series, vol. xlii, pp. 667 sqq.); June 18–19, 1913, Cave's motion of censure on the three politicians incriminated (ibid., 1913, 5th Ser., vol. liv, pp. 391 sqq., 542 sqq.). Cf. Asquith, *Memories and Reflections*, vol. i, pp. 207, 212. For a good account of the Marconi affair see the article entitled 'Ministers and the Stock Exchange', in the number of the *Round Table* for June 1913 (vol. iii, pp. 425 sqq.). The case of Lord Murray of Elibank was the object of a special inquiry by the House of Lords (H. of L., March 9, 1914, *Parl. Deb.*, Lords 1914, 5th Ser., vol. xv, pp. 412 sqq.). Without hypocrisy the Unionist opposition could scarcely have pushed the matter to extremes against Lloyd George. In 1900 Rufus Isaacs had defended Arthur Chamberlain when he was accused during the Boer War of similar offences in connection with army supplies.
[2] Speech at the National Liberal Club, July 1, 1913.

should cease to be ministers how will they maintain their position? This is the trap laid for a statesman of plebeian origin by a society democratic in form, but plutocratic in fact. And this moral weakness of popular leaders who have become wealthy afforded a welcome argument to the syndicalists, eager as they were to proclaim the bankruptcy of politics.

9

What revenge could the Welsh country solicitor, convicted of having become in his turn a capitalist, and moreover of having made use of his political position for that purpose, take upon those plutocrats who so often wounded by his denunciations, had at last found an opportunity to make their enemy suffer? At the close of 1911 when the railway crisis was approaching its end an 'Industrial Council' composed half of representatives of the employers and half of representatives of the unions had been formed by the Government to arbitrate in labour disputes and try to devise some regular method of effecting their peaceful settlement. It was invited in June 1912 to hold an inquiry on the latter question and reported a year later.[1] Lloyd George had promised to give effect to its recommendations[2] but he let the matter drop. The danger of the great strikes had for the moment been averted and the idea was not calculated to arouse popular enthusiasm. He would seem rather to have thought of raising the question of nationalizing the railways and it was probably at his request that a Royal Commission was appointed to examine the question.[3] But without waiting for its report and deciding whether it might be good policy to place the question in the forefront of the Government's programme, he launched a campaign against the monopoly of the great landlords. He had indeed made preparations for an attack, heralded by certain clauses in the Budget of 1909, before

[1] *The Industrial Council. Report of Inquiry into Industrial Agreements 1913* and *Minutes of Evidence taken before the Industrial Council in connection with their Inquiry into Industrial Agreements 1913.* (The answers of a hundred witnesses afford an excellent picture of the relations between employers and men in England on the eve of the war.)

[2] H. of C., July 23, 1912 (*Parliamentary Debates*, Commons 1912, 5th Series, vol. xli., pp. 1116–17).

[3] *A Royal Commission to inquire into the relationship between the railway companies of Great Britain and the State in respect of matters other than safety of working and conditions of employment and to report what changes, if any, are desirable in that relationship.* (Appointed October 1913 with Lord Loreburn as chairman.)

the Marconi scandal broke out. And he never desisted from it throughout his long career. On this point at least a statesman, so often charged with tergiverzation, showed a persistence carried almost to the point of obstinacy.

He began, as Chamberlain began his campaign for tariff reform, by forming a Committee, the Land Inquiry Committee, to collect for the use of himself and his supporters all the necessary information about the situation of British agriculture. On the other hand, after lengthy discussions which occupied the greater part of 1913 he obtained the support of the Cabinet as Chamberlain had failed to do ten years earlier when he tried to commit the official Unionist party to his protectionist campaign, and he unfolded his agrarian programme in two important speeches delivered, the first at Bedford on October 11, the second at Swindon on October 22—the day on which the first volume of the Land Inquiry Committee's report was published. What were its recommendations? To understand it we must go back a quarter of a century and seek in the experiments made in Ireland by both the great historic parties the origin of the two programmes of agrarian reform which confronted each other in 1913. The first possible method of assisting the small farmers was to allow tenants to purchase their farms with financial aid from the State and become owners themselves. The Unionists had employed it in Ireland, tentatively at first (Lord Ashbourne's Acts) then on a large scale by the Land Law of 1903, which sought to parcel out the entire arable area of the country into small independent holdings. But even before the Unionists tackled the question in Ireland, the Liberals, when Gladstone was Prime Minister, had tried a different method, not making the tenants smallholders, but regulating by law their relations with their landlords, fixing the amount of rent payable and protecting them against unjustifiable evictions. The method had been extended almost immediately to the small tenants of the Scottish Highlands who were called crofters and whose condition closely resembled that of the Irish cottiers. The Liberal party had been faithful to this second method when in 1911 it repaired its defeat of 1907 and passed a Scottish Land Act, which extended the provisions of the Crofters' Act to all the small farmers of Scotland. And at present while the Unionists to stem the depopulation of the country districts advocated an agrarian policy which would settle on the land the largest possible number of small freeholders,[1] the Liberals, affected by the increasing influence of Socialism, rejected this programme of peasant individualism. If the land was to be purchased it must be for the benefit of the entire community. Lloyd George proposed to give the farmer the same legal protection that the new social legislation had given the worker in the towns, and as he proposed to give it to the agricultural labourer by fixing a legal wage. The execution and development of the new legislation would be the task of a Ministry of Land which Lloyd George proposed to create and which besides a host of other functions would take over the work of the Board of Agriculture. This new department would complete the revision of the land survey ordered by the Budget of 1909 and of which two-thirds had already been accomplished, acquire uncultivated land, plant trees, drain it and fit it for cultivation, and regulate the relations between the landlord and the farmer, between the farmer and the agricultural labourer and even more generally the relations between landlord and tenant in the town as well as in the country. For all the land in the United Kingdom urban as well as rural would be under the jurisdiction of this important department intended by Lloyd George to regenerate Britain by methods which had nothing in common with those of Socialist industrialism, by reviving and repopulating the countryside.[2]

Was this campaign likely to succeed? As we know, the world war prevented its development. We can therefore only guess the answer. But the prospects of success would not seem to have been hopeful. In the first place, conditions were less favourable than ten years earlier. The farmers' economic position had greatly improved in the interval. The prices of foodstuffs had risen, in the first place for the same reason that prices in general had risen—the increase in the amount of gold in circulation—and secondly because of the decline in the American supply since the United

[1] For the agrarian policy of the Unionist party see Lord Lansdowne, speech at the Westminster Palace Hotel, July 24, 1912; speech at Matlock Bath, July 21, 1913—and the propaganda pamphlet entitled: *A Unionist Agricultural Policy, by a Group of Unionists*, 1913.

[2] *The Land. The Report of the Land Inquiry Committee*, vol. i Rural, 1913; vol. ii Urban, 1914. For the question of rural estates see further the two speeches delivered by Lloyd George at Bedford on October 11 and at Swindon on October 22, 1913 (the second outlines his complete programme); for urban estates see his reply at the Treasury on October 30 to a deputation of urban tenants and his speech at the Holloway Empire on November 29 and for the application of his programme to Scotland his speech at Glasgow on February 4, 1914.

States had begun to absorb its agricultural produce.[1] In the second place, if Lloyd George wanted to ally the farmer and the farm labourer he had a difficult problem to solve. He must find some means of identifying their interests. But the first thing which struck the farmer in Lloyd George's scheme was the legal guarantee of a higher wage for his hands, and this was sufficient to throw him into the arms of the landlord. In the third place, Lloyd George might indeed win the support of a large section of the public— both of the working and the middle class—by denouncing the abuses of the landlords' monopoly in the great cities: he had already brought the subject into prominence when he introduced his Budget of 1909. But the problems of urban and rural landed property were so different that it was not easy to combine their solution in a single scheme of reform. And finally, what was his aim? Was it in truth to repopulate the countryside by bringing the town labourers back to the land? A Utopia. As well attempt to turn back the course of a river.[2] The utmost that could be hoped was to check the depopulation of the countryside. To succeed, Lloyd George must win the agricultural labourers. But this dull and ignorant class, incapable of organizing except by fits and starts,[3] could not be relied upon to save itself or even to assist

[1] The yearly average price of wheat which had fallen to about 26 shillings a quarter during the period 1899–1901 then rose, not again to fall below 30 shillings during the years which followed 1907. It was above 43s. in July 1909, above 38s. in July 1912 (*Commerce and Industry. Tables and Statistics for the British Empire from 1815* edited by William Page, p. 217). For the fluctuations in the price of wheat see William Sutherland, *Rural Regeneration in England. A Short Discussion of Some of the Outstanding Features of the Rural Land Question and of the Principal Proposals for Reform*, 1913, pp. 13–16.

[2] 'Attached to both the old-established political parties there is an army of open-air speakers and other so-called "workers". . . . It fell to my lot at that time' (about 1914) 'to supervise the work of a group of them in London. . . . It appeared that the smallholdings, the growth of cabbages and potatoes, and Wat Tyler's Rebellion, figured prominently in their harangues. They were quite pained when I pointed out to them in the frankest possible terms that the electors of industrial London were not likely to become enthusiastic supporters of any political party that had nothing more serviceable to offer.' (Christopher Addison, *Politics from Within*, vol. i, pp. 31–2.)

[3] See the remarks by the American, Price Collier (*England and the English*, 1909, Pop. Ed. 1911, p. 289), on the dullness which he finds incredible of the British rustic: 'This appeals to the stranger, the American stranger at least, because he knows no such types among those of his own race at home. When he meets with stupidity and political disability, it is among the lower classes of foreigners, but here are families who have lived side by side perhaps for centuries, the one in the squire's house, the other in the labourer's cottage, yet the difference between them mentally and politically is as great as was the difference between the southern planter and the hands in his cotton fields. . . . The Englishman of this type is uneducated, inarticulate, inaudible and grotesquely awkward, both mentally and physically. But he has his small political value, for he is always and unalterably for no change !' With this quotation we may compare a description whose agreement with the former is the more striking because it comes from a very different source. It is an English Socialist who writes: 'The English labourer is the worst used and the least bold

actively those who tried to save it. Let us even suppose the impossible, that they joined their voices to the powerful chorus of discontent heard from the urban proletariat. The outcry of a class, scattered and constantly diminishing in numbers, would scarcely be audible above the syndicalist uproar. For it was here that the real problem lay and we must resume the history and define the character of the syndicalist revolt as it developed after a series of Labour triumphs had brought to an end the great campaign of strikes among the seamen, transport workers, railwaymen, and miners which had lasted almost a year from June 1911 to May 1912.

10

Two social crises, two episodes of the class war, two great strikes obviously syndicalist and revolutionary filled the papers for a considerable time. Neither indeed took place in Great Britain. But it was a remarkable fact that both broke out in parts of the British Empire where everyone believed racial animosity to be too intense to leave room for class hatred;[1] and yet even there the class war raged. In South Africa there arose in opposition to a South African party in whose ranks the most prominent of the Boer leaders in the late war fraternized with their conquerors, a new 'Labour party' which mustered the workers without distinction of race—English, Russian Jews, poor Boers from the country absorbed by the Rand proletariat—against the capitalist tyranny. But if the whole truth is to be told, the movement was inspired by stronger racial passions than it was willing to admit.

peasant in Europe. . . . It is futile to assert that the French peasant on his own land is poorer and works harder than the English agricultural labourer. Though the French peasant may be in the hands of moneylenders and though the English smallholder may be robbed by market salesmen and railway companies, each possesses a dignity, a glimpse of freedom unvisioned by the agricultural labourer.' (F. E. Green, The Tyranny of the Countryside, 1913, p. 253.)

[1] Tom Mann, Memoirs, 1915, p. 321: 'Early in 1914 . . . I was sent to South Africa to endeavour to weld the working classes together, and was enthusiastically received by the miners, the railwaymen, and others. To my pleasurable surprise the foremost contingent in a procession of 10,000 people who met me at Johannesburg Station, was a couple of hundred young Dutchmen, with their trade union banner. This was a great advance on anything I had seen when in the same district in 1910. At that date, very few of the Dutch Afrikanders were working in the mines, and those few would have no truck with the Britishers. In the interval between my two visits, economic pressure and fraternization had brought the young Dutchmen into the industrial field, and they had learned the necessity for industrial reorganization.

The South African labour agitation was no clearer as to its character and aims than the agitation in England five or six years before against the employment of Chinese labour in the Rand mines. The workers of the South African Labour party were protesting against the competition of native labour, and the party's real name should have been not the Labour but the White Labour party. Nevertheless this did not alter the fact that two parties faced each other, in each of which representatives of the two white races, the English and Boer, worked side by side, and the strength of the new Labour movement was suddenly revealed in the summer of 1913 when a mining company attempted to increase the hours of work and its employees replied by a strike which quickly became a general strike of all the miners. There were enough Russian Jews on the Rand to spread in this favourable environment the current doctrines of European revolution. And the disturbance assumed such serious proportions that troops had to be sent to Johannesburg. On July 4 shooting took place, nineteen persons were killed, and a hundred wounded. In reply, the offices of an important paper and the railway station were sacked, and the central electric power station seized by the rioters so that when night fell disorder reigned in a city totally deprived of light.[1] A truce followed but in the following January the civil war broke out anew. The South African railways were owned by the State. The Government attempted to reduce the staff of railwaymen, and the latter declared a general strike. The Government took vigorous action, arrested the leaders before they had time to concert measures with the Federation of Trade Unions, and when the Federation declared a general strike of all the unions, took the necessary steps to break it. But the situation remained uncertain. Not only did the new Labour party win a majority of seats on the Transvaal Provincial Council, but at the same time a Boer stalwart named Hertzog, uniting Nationalist propaganda with the Socialist propaganda of the Labour party, accused the two leaders of the South African party, Botha and Smuts, of betraying their race and selling themselves to British capitalism. Nine South African trade unionists deported by Smuts without trial received an enthusiastic welcome in London and no less enthusiastic was the

[1] For the Rand Strike see the excellent accounts in the *Round Table*, September 1913, No. 12, vol. iii, pp. 750 sqq.; December 1913, vol. iv, No. 13, pp. 170 sqq.

welcome Tom Mann received from the South African workers when he returned in June.[1]

At England's very door Ireland presented the same spectacle. It was at Belfast in 1907 that there occurred for the first time one of those great revolutionary strikes of which England would be the theatre a few years later. A strike of a limited number of men was followed by a sympathetic strike of other workers. The employers replied by a lock-out which threw still more men out of work and this in turn was followed by a general strike of all the workers of the city. For an entire month the work of the port was at a complete standstill; 10,000 soldiers policed Belfast, men were killed and wounded. These disturbances made practically no impression in England. Disorder was chronic in Ireland. Moreover, the movement failed. The Catholic and Protestant workers were divided too deeply to remain long united in a common programme of Socialist action.[2] But the Belfast disturbances produced a man who during the next few years would be the great leader of Irish trade unionism. James Larkin, known to the Irish crowds, more familiarly as 'Jim', the local secretary of the dockers' union, was a fanatic of irreproachable morals[3] who fascinated the strikers of Belfast by his eloquence and strange appearance. He wore long black hair, a heavy drooping moustache, a large, broad-brimmed black hat, and a kind of black toga. After the conclusion of the Belfast strike he broke with the British dockers' union and founded an Irish Transport Workers' Union. At the same time he entered into relations with the thinker who provided him with a creed—James Connolly, who in 1896 had attempted to found an Irish Socialist Republican party had since gone to America, where, as we have already said, he learned the doctrines of syndicalism from the Industrial Workers of the World. Settling

[1] The South African Strike (*Round Table*, March 1914, No. 14, vol. iv, pp. 231 sqq.). An interesting measure in the history of strike legislation is an Act passed in 1912 by the South African Parliament (*Railway and Harbours Service Act, 1912*) which provided that railway servants who went on strike should be liable not only to dismissal with loss of their right to promotion, but also to penalties not exceeding a fine of £50 and six months' imprisonment. But even in 1914 no attempt was made to enforce it.

[2] For the Belfast Strike see Lord Askwith, *Industrial Problems and Disputes*, pp. 115 sqq. See also the evidence, very incoherent however, given by J. Larkin before the Industrial Council (*Inquiry into Industrial Agreements*) July 30, 1912, *Minutes of Evidence*, pp. 243 sqq.

[3] He was, it is true, at the beginning of his career as a trade unionist sentenced to twelve months' imprisonment for misappropriation of funds. But the witness who made this statement in 1916 before the *Royal Commission on the Rebellion in Ireland* (*Report 1916*, Q. 1657) adds that he was released by Lord Aberdeen at the end of the three months and that 'from that moment dates the influence exercised by Larkin upon Irish administration'.

n Dublin, Larkin and Connolly worked together to bring into
he Transport Workers' Union all the men, particularly the un-
killed labourers, who were unwilling or unable to join the exist-
ng unions, and thus to found in Ireland the one big union by
vhose instrumentality in the United States the Industrial Workers
of the World hoped one day to achieve their revolution. They
published their paper, the *Irish Worker*, a weekly which soon
possessed a circulation of 15,000. Their headquarters was Liberty
Hall, from which they issued their marching orders. Their plan of
campaign, intended to gain immediate successes, and at the same
ime to impress public opinion and make recruits, was to launch
a succession of sudden strikes, every time forcing the employers
o yield the more speedily as they were taken the more completely
by surprise.

On August 25, 1913, Larkin having brought the fury of the
bourgeoisie to a climax by provoking a strike of the Dublin tram-
ways was arrested with four other leaders on a charge of 'criminal
conspiracy'. He was indeed immediately released with a caution,
but his arrest nevertheless gave rise to riots brutally repressed by
the police and troops (one person was killed) in the course of
which he was again arrested. Then the Dublin employers decided
o meet the attack by a counter-attack. While professing their
respect for the legitimate forms of trade unionism they refused
o keep in their employment any member of the Irish Transport
Workers' Union since its aims were revolutionary and its methods
made regular work in Dublin impossible. To the amazement of
the British public at a juncture when the question of Home Rule
had reached a crisis Unionists and Nationalists combined against
Larkin's agitation. The leader of the Opposition was Murphy, a
wealthy capitalist, chairman of a tramway company, and director
of an important Nationalist organ, the *Irish Independent*. Both in
Ireland and in South Africa Socialism seemed to be outstripping
Nationalism.

The struggle lasted four months, months of pauperisation and
disorder.[1] Larkin was sentenced to seven months' imprisonment,
on the charge not of conspiracy for which the penalty was more
severe but simply of seditious language, then liberated for fear of

[1] For the Dublin Strike see G. D. H. Cole, *A Short History of the British Working Class
Movement 1789–1927*, pp. 103 sqq.; 'Larkinism, The New Force in Ireland' (*New States-
man*, September 13, 1913, p. 711); and T. M. Kettle 'The Agony of Dublin' (*Irish Review*,
November 1913. Vol. iii, pp. 441 sqq.).

an insurrection of the working class, not only in Ireland but perhaps in Great Britain as well. For Larkin, monarch of the Dublin
proletariat, crossed St. George's Channel and entering into relations with the English syndicalists attempted to rouse the Parliamentary Committee of the Trades Union Congress from it
slumbers and bring about the declaration of a general strike in
England in aid of the Irish general strike or, if that were impossible, at least a refusal by the British transport workers and
railwaymen to handle goods coming from Ireland. With what
success? He was warmly applauded at a number of public meetings, and his influence provoked sporadic outbreaks of striking in
several ports on the west coast of England. But he failed to persuade the Congress to issue the orders he desired and the Irish
strike, after all attempts at arbitration had failed, came to an end
at the beginning of January. There was good reason to think that
four months conflict had done more to spread the syndicalis
creed than the final defeat to discredit it.

II

All these manifestations which occupied public attention wer
not, it must be recognized, in the true sense English. In the Ran
the general strike was the work of a cosmopolitan proletariat,
seed plot for the ideas and passions of the Continental Revolution
In Dublin, Irish disorder gave the movement a distinctive colour
And in Great Britain two years before, where had the most violen
disturbances occurred? In Celtic Wales and in Liverpool wher
there was a host of Irish workers. We must therefore be clear a
to the nature of the obstacles which strictly English society, eve
when affected by this uprising of labour, opposed to its threat o
anarchy.

We have already seen how many strikes from 1910 onward
were anarchist in the sense that they were revolts of the workin
masses instigated by unofficial agitators against agreements pre
viously concluded between the employers and the union official
To read the lamentations of the middle class one might believ
that the structure of 'social peace' based on reciprocal concessior
freely accepted, hitherto the boast of British society, was a thin
of the past. In reality nothing could be more untrue. If the numbe

of strikes in breach of contract was increasing, the number of collective contracts was increasing even more rapidly. And these anarchist breaches of contract were often due to the fact that the original contract had been badly drawn, couched in ambiguous terms, or did not cover all the members of the union. Sir George Askwith, the official arbitrator at the Board of Trade, made it his business to see that each of these disputes resulted in the conclusion of a more satisfactory contract and therefore strengthened the operation in England of the system of collective bargaining and conciliation boards at the very time when it was widely believed to be in jeopardy.[1] And in this respect the policy of the Board of Trade would seem to have been successful. Such at any rate was the conclusion reached by the extensive inquiry conducted by the Industrial Council of which we have spoken above.[2] According to an official report, at the end of 1911 293 Conciliation Boards had been set up under the Conciliation Act of 1896. A year later there were 297 and at the end of 1913 325.[3] On these figures, discouraging from his point of view, a young syndicalist commented bitterly: 'There is a good deal', he wrote, 'to be said for the view that we have too much conciliation, and that a big increase in the number of strikes would do us no harm.'[4]

Moreover, the syndicalist doctrine was opposed to the regulation of industry by the State. State interference with the unions was acceptable only if confined to a unilateral guarantee of advantages to the working class. There was no objection to the Acts establishing an eight-hour day and a minimum wage in the mining industry, and the latter was the direct result of an agitation conducted by the unions. But what had syndicalism to say of the National Insurance Act which compelled the workers to contribute? At that very time a French law dealing with old age pensions and based like the British on the model of Bismarck's legislation was defeated by the obstinate resistance of both classes directly affected—the employers and the workmen—assisted by the hostility of the judges. Would not the same thing happen in England and must not the Government expect very strong oppo-

[1] Lord Askwith, *Industrial Problems and Disputes*, p. 129.
[2] *The Industrial Council, Report on Inquiry into Industrial Agreements*, 1913, p. 4.
[3] *Conciliation (Trade Disputes) Act, 1896. Ninth Report by the Board of Trade of proceedings under the Conciliation (Trade Disputes) Act, 1896*, 1912, p. 11. *Tenth Report*, 1913, p. 13. *Eleventh Report*, 1914, p. 10.
[4] G. D. H. Cole, *The World of Labour*, 1913, p. 316.

sition to a measure which if duly put into operation would take fourpence a week from the pockets of 14,000,000 wage earners and sums varying from £1,000 to £10,000 from the pockets of employers? It had the pleasant surprise of finding the opposition less than it had anticipated. Why? No doubt it was partly due to the zeal and skill displayed by the talented officials Lloyd George had selected to help him in applying the Statute, but chiefly to the almost universal docility shown by all classes of the population. There were indeed some attempts at 'passive resistance' by small employers, but the example of scrupulous obedience given by the heads of the great firms was soon followed. The principle of workmen's contributions was naturally unpopular with the masses, and their ill humour on this account explains, at least in part, several defeats of Liberal candidates at by-elections after 1912. But though the Labour party and the Trades Union Congress protested against contribution by the workers neither advised them to disobey the law and employees everywhere, if they did it with a grumble, paid their weekly contribution.

The payment of contributions began on July 15, 1912. By October 15,250,000 wage earners were paying their contributions,[1] a proof that the law was being fully carried out. On January 15, 1913, the day arrived when drugs and medical treatment were given for the first time to those entitled to them by the Act. This involved the active co-operation of the doctors, and the medical profession, which constituted a species of bourgeois trade union, was in revolt against the National Insurance Act. But Lloyd George had made concessions which satisfied the majority of doctors, particularly country districts and in January 1913 the British Medical Association, while continuing to protest in principle against a measure 'which touched upon the honour of the profession and was harmful to the public interest', declined to strike against it. Meanwhile the system of insurance against unemployment was working with the utmost smoothness. Since

---

[1] Lloyd George's speech at the Hotel Cecil, October 12, 1912. In 1913, 3,600,000 persons received sickness benefit; 44,000 the special treatment provided by the Act for tuberculosis. The total cost of benefit per week was £283,600—that is to say, for the entire year 1913, £14,224,500. (*National Insurance Benefit, Return to an Order of the Honourable the House of Commons dated 1 July, 1914; for Return showing approximately: a. The Number of Insured Persons who received each week 1, Medical Benefit, 2, Sickness Benefit, 3, Maternity Benefit. b. The Average Weekly Cost of such Benefit. c. The Aggregate Cost of each Benefit per Person, ending 11th day of January 1914 and d. The Number of insured Persons who have received one or more of these Benefits in the period ending the 11th day of January, 1914*).

the boom continued more money was being collected than spent: when the next slump arrived, and it was scarcely to be expected for the next two or three years, there would be an ample reserve with which to face it.[1] We may add that by providing for the treatment of consumptives and setting up new institutions called schools for mothers, State aid increased every year with the most beneficial effects on public health.[2] But beneficial or not these undertakings were so many triumphs of State action.

Would these victories of State intervention check the growth of the friendly societies and trade unions? On the contrary. The State invited both to help in administering the Insurance Act. The passing and enforcement of the Act fostered both. The friendly societies, so powerful already, increased their membership. And it was the same with the trade unions. At the end of 1910 the membership of the unions in the United Kingdom was a little less than 2,500,000, at the end of 1911 it was a little above 3,000,000, an increase which was no doubt due to the syndicalist propaganda. But in 1913 the number of members almost attained 4,000,000 and in this case it is not easy to say how far the increase was due to the progress of revolutionary syndicalism, how far to the desire of a large number of workers to share in administering the National Insurance Act through a union. We are driven to the paradoxical conclusion that during those very years in which revolutionary syndicalism was so vocal, co-operation between the trade unions and the Government became closer than before.

12

A little book had been published in 1906 entitled *The Restoration of the Gild System* whose author, Arthur J. Penty, does not appear to have been influenced by Continental syndicalism. Indeed the term syndicalism is absent from his book. He was a

---

[1] *Unemployment Insurance. First Report on the proceedings of the Board of Trade under Part II of the National Insurance Act, 1911, with Appendices, 1913* (by W. H. Beveridge).

[2] For these new developments see Christopher Addison, *Politics from Within, 1911–18,* 1924, vol. i, p. 29. Two Statutes were passed amending the National Insurance Act of 1911. 1, 3 & 4 Geo. V, Cap. 37: An Act to amend Parts I and III of the National Insurance Act, 1911 (*National Insurance Act 1913*). 2, 4 & 5 Geo. V, Cap. 57: An Act to amend Part II of the National Insurance Act (*National Insurance Act [Part II Amendment] Act, 1914*). But neither the first of these which increased the sickness benefit nor the second which modified in certain details the machinery of the unemployment insurance represented any change of principle.

disciple of Ruskin and William Morris. The enemy whose mis-
deeds he denounces is 'collectivism', by which he means more
particularly that administrative socialism of which the Webbs
were the protagonists. According to him the evil which afflicts
modern society is not competition, which would be an excellent
thing if it meant a rivalry in putting goods of better quality on
the market, but commercialism whose object is to increase the
producers' profit by putting on the market as large a number as
possible of manufactured articles and thus supplying the largest
possible number of consumers at a cheap price. To save the community, therefore, we must devise an industrial system which
would substitute the control of the artisan for the control of the
financier and a social structure in which the producers' point of
view prevails over the consumers'. It would be in some respects
a return to the system of the mediæval guilds. It was a conservative
Socialism, of restoration rather than revolution, but it agreed
with syndicalism in its hostility to all political action and the
supremacy of the bureaucratic State. When therefore about 1910
syndicalism was imported from France and began to make disciples the *New Age*, a pioneer weekly which defended the ideas
of Penty and his group, perceived at once the advantage to be
derived from the new labour creed. In its columns a new form of
Socialism took shape called 'Guild Socialism'. The complicated
plan was worked out of a society in which capitalism and profit
would be eliminated but not by transforming all producers into
wage slaves of the democratic State. They would be free servants
of the guilds, independent corporations represented by a single
co-operative assembly which would allot work and settle disputes. The democratic State, however, also had its place, perform-
ing all the non-economic functions of society, political, military,
and judicial and also, according to some Guild Socialists, guaranteeing the consumers as such against exploitation by a combination of producers.[1] The derivation of these ideas has been sought in
the teaching of the German jurist Gierke, presented to the British
public by Maitland the great historian of law.[2] Gierke refused to

---

[1] G. D. H. Cole, *The World of Labour. A Discussion of the Present and Future of Trade
Unionism, 1913.* A. R. Orage, *National Guilds. An Inquiry into the Wage System and the
Way out,* 1914.

[2] *Political Theories of the Middle Ages* by Dr. Otto Gierke Professor of Law in the University of Berlin. Translated with an Introduction by Frederic William Maitland, LL.D.,
D.C.L. Darwin Professor of the Laws of England in the University of Cambridge, 1900.

attribute to the State an absolute sovereignty which made the rights of subordinate associations depend upon its sufferance. According to him society was composed not of individuals but of associations which were not obliged to justify their existence to an omnipotent and jealous state. The State was simply one association amongst others whose functions must be prescribed and limited in relation to the latter. But there is no need to look to Germany for the origin of a point of view so essentially English. The Roman conception of sovereignty has never been popular in England. Did not this Guild Socialism simply restate in another form the liberal and anti-authoritarian doctrine of the division of powers which for two centuries the English had become accustomed to regard as the most essential feature of their political constitution?[1] And did it not express in the form of a modified syndicalism that old spirit of self-government, of voluntary discipline, of which the English had once been so proud and which was still strong enough to counterbalance alike the excesses of popular anarchy and the abuses of governmental authority?

13

Nevertheless, the British middle class did not recover from the alarm inspired by the labour troubles. Besides the events in South Africa and in Ireland and their repercussion in England other incidents attracted the attention of the Press. Another strike of the London dockers broke out in the summer of 1912 though it was a rash and ill-advised attempt which enabled the employers to avenge their defeat of the previous summer.[2] In the autumn a lightning strike of 6,000 railwaymen broke out on one of the main lines in sympathy with a comrade's dismissal for drunkenness off duty. The Conservative Press called it the strike for the right to get drunk.[3] And finally there was the general lock-out

[1] Cf. Arthur J. Penty, *The Restoration of the Gild System*, pp. 70–1: 'As to the form which the government of the future will take, it is not improbable that the division of function between the Upper and the Lower Chambers will continue, with this difference that whereas the Lower Chamber would be elected by the people in their private capacity, the members of the Upper Chamber would be nominated by the Gilds . . . the principle of authority on a popular basis would be thereby established, while a balance of power between the various interests in the State would be automatically maintained.'
[2] For a good account of this strike and its failure see Charles Watney and James A. Little, *Industrial Warfare and the Aims and Claims of Capital and Labour*, 1912, pp. 89 sqq.
[3] G. D. H. Cole, *A Short History of the British Working-Class Movement 1789–1927*, vol. iii, pp. 92–3. G. W. Alcock, *Fifty Years of Railway Trade Unionism*, p. 459.

in the building trade proclaimed by the contractors in January 1914 to put an end to a succession of minor irresponsible strikes and transformed in June into a national lock-out, which was still in progress on August 1st. There were indeed no disputes comparable in gravity to those which had marked the summer of 1911 and the following winter. But the figures for 1913 showed a greater number of strikes than ever before and a larger number of men affected than at any time before 1911[1]: and a still more disquieting feature was the reorganization of the unions which was being achieved in the background. England was not perhaps on the brink of a revolution as understood on the Continent. British labour did not revolt against patriotism in the name of class loyalty nor did it seek to abolish the state or even capitalism. But in the pursuit of more restricted objectives—recognition of the unions, increase of wages, reduction of hours it was making preparations by the employment of a new strategy to involve England in a class war on a scale in excess of anything previously witnessed.

Imagine—to make our ideas clearer we will take a concrete instance—that on a railway the platelayers, the engine drivers, the firemen, the guards, the porters, the men employed in the clerical departments, and every other branch of the company's service possess separate unions and that one of these separate unions finding itself unable to obtain its demands by friendly negotiation decide to strike. Not only will the men employed in other branches be unwilling to join it, it may even be impossible for them to do so because they are bound by agreements made with the company which have not yet expired. Therefore, instead of leaving the workers to form as many minor unions as they please—each confined to a special branch—and therefore unable to undertake more than futile skirmishes, in every industry all these unions must be amalgamated into a single union covering the entire industry and in a position to fight pitched battles with the employers. This was the strategy advocated in France by the *Conféderation Générale du Travail*. In England it appealed to many young trade unionists and was perhaps the most attractive feature of the French movement. These men did not call themselves 'revolutionary syndicalists' but simply syndicalists, adopting the

[1] 1,497 strikes; 516,037 workers directly affected; 688,925 workers directly or indirectly affected. (*Strikes and Lock-Outs. Board of Trade [Department of Labour Statistics] Report on* p. x.)

French name without its adjective, or Industrial Unionists in opposition to the Craft Unionists, since they advocated unions embracing an entire industry not some special branch like the unions of the old style.[1]

There were legal obstacles to the amalgamation of several unions in a single body, for it was necessary to secure the consent of two-thirds of their members.[2] Many unions therefore unable to amalgamate were content with the looser bond of federation which, while preserving the financial independence of the unions entering the federation, united them in a common front defensive or offensive against the employers. We have already seen how the foundation of the Federation of Transport Workers by Tom Mann in 1910 marked a turning-point in the history of trade unionism and paved the way for the syndicalist offensive of 1911. The Federation of British Miners, founded in 1888, did not embrace all the miners, since it did not include Durham, Northumberland, Cumberland, Wales or the South of England. Nevertheless, it possessed a numerical strength, a prestige and an organization which enabled it to conduct the general strike of 1912 on behalf of the entire body of miners. But trade unionism was not content with federation. It aimed at the constitution of large militant unions by amalgamating many small unions. In 1911 and again in 1912 the Trades Union Congress declared in favour of this policy of amalgamation. Already in May 1912 forty-seven unions with a total membership of 403,000 workers were attempting to reduce their number to five by amalgamation.[3] In the case of the railwaymen this aim was achieved, or almost achieved, when in January 1913 J. H. Thomas succeeded in uniting in a single union, the National Union of Railwaymen, three out of the four unions of railway servants, the engine drivers alone refusing to join it.

---

[1] G. D. H. Cole and W. Mellor, *The Greater Unionism. With special Reference to Mining, Building, Engineering and Shipbuilding, Transport and General Labour and to the position of the General Federation of Trade Unions*, 1913.

[2] 39 & 40 Vict., Cap. 22: An Act to amend the Trade Union Act, 1871 (*Trade Union Act, Amendment Act*) 1876, Sec. 12.

[3] Ironmoulders and Ironfounders: six unions with 30,000 members. Tailors and Garment Workers: thirteen unions with 30,000 members. Iron and Steel Workers: eight unions with 53,000 members. Building Trades: seventeen unions with 180,000 members. Railway Workers: four unions with 110,000 members. (*The Times*, May 14, 1912.) In this as in every other sphere Germany provided a model. In Germany, where trade unionism was strongly organized, there were only a hundred unions as against more than 1,000 in England.

The French unions were not content with advocating the amalgamation of all the workers in a particular industry into one militant force. They wanted to make all these federations in turn corps of a single army commanded by a single general staff. The *Conféderation Générale du Travail* was the entire body of workers preparing a general strike not in particular industries but in all at the same time for the final and complete overthrow of capitalism. And, as we have seen, the American syndicalists dreamt of one big union mobilizing all the workers without exception for revolutionary action. In Dublin, Connolly and Larkin imitated this strategy. In England the trade unions were too solidly organized for even the most visionary of revolutionaries to contemplate for a moment such a Utopia. But might it not be possible to make use, if not of the Trades Union Congress, at least of the General Federation of Trade Unions whose very name resembled that of the French *Conféderation* by transforming it into a species of executive body with authority to draw up lists of claims and if the employers refused them to declare strikes? Certain syndicalists entertained the idea.[1] But if the Federation had flourished for the last year or two it was as an 'approved society' for the administration of the National Insurance Act. And if it attracted to its ranks many unskilled labourers who had not hitherto shown any desire to enter the unions affiliated to the Congress, the attraction was not the hope of imminent revolution but its double function of collecting contributions and distributing sickness benefit. But at this point a project struck root in the minds of certain active Labour leaders, typically British in character though suggested by the formulas of French syndicalism, and destined soon to draw widespread attention.

In November 1911 when the railwaymen, dissatisfied with the report of the Commission of Inquiry, were speaking of reopening

[1] Tom Mann 'Prepare for Action' (*The Industrial Syndicalist*, vol. i, No. 1, July 1910, p. 18). G. D. H. Cole and W. Mellor, *The Greater Unionism 1913*, p. 18: 'The close touch now existing between the Unions of General Labour and the General Federation of Trade Unions is a hopeful sign and points the way to the realization of this central control. All the Unions must come into the General Federation, the T.U.C. must become its mouthpiece and the Parliamentary Committee must become a committee of the General Federation.' Cf. Articles by the same writers 'The Sympathetic Strike. Labour's New Weapon and the Way to use it' (*Daily Herald*, May 5, 1914). 'The Real Solidarity of Labour' (*Daily Herald*, June 23, 1914).

the strike, the miners suggested to them a species of alliance, an agreement to strike in concert and achieve their respective aims at the same time. So long as the dispute continued, negotiations were carried on.[1] But the railwaymen did not strike after all, and the miners fought alone. Two years later in October 1913 the miners at their annual congress at Scarborough did not get beyond vague suggestions of a general strike, but in December when a 'special congress' of the trade unions met to discuss the help to be given to the Dublin strikers, the miners' leader, Smillie, proposed on behalf of his union a formal alliance of the miners, railwaymen, and transport workers for common action. These three bodies— the miners, railwaymen, and transport workers had been the three militant bodies in 1911 and 1912. Though they did not constitute a majority of the British proletariat, they were never-theless a most formidable host. They numbered more than 2,000,000 workers, of whom 1,300,000 were union members. And since their work was of such a nature that if in obedience to the word of command they declared war on the employers, the whole of industry would be deprived of coal, and the entire country of food. As a weapon of intimidation a strike of these three bodies would be equivalent to a general strike.

The suggestion was taken up instantly. The reasons for its success are plain. In the first place it enabled the masses to imitate the action taken in South Africa and above all in Ireland. And at the same time it satisfied the desire of certain leaders, more moder-ate in the sense that they were more methodical, to guide the agitation of the extremists into a practicable channel. The infec-tion of the Dublin strike had produced a number of sporadic strikes, costly and barren. Could not these be prevented by put-ting before the stalwarts the hope of a struggle on a grander scale and more decisive?[2] Moreover, some of the railwaymen's leaders,

---

[1] M. Alfassa. *La Grève noire et l'évolution des syndicats en Angleterre*, p. 25.

[2] To understand the views which prevailed among the officials of the Triple Alliance see J. Havelock Wilson's reply to a revolutionary manifesto issued by J. Larkin, November 22, 1913: 'Over two years the Sailors' and Firemen's Union—i.e., the Dublin branch—has been subject absolutely to the control of James Larkin. We have been involved contin-uously in disputes without any reference to or consultation of the governing body of our union, and I have personally entered many protests against the way in which the business has been conducted'; also J. H. Thomas' speech to a meeting of railwaymen on November 23: 'Because of what the British trade union movement had done, and was prepared to do, in defence of the basic principle of combination, it was not to be assumed that the leaders in England were to be stampeded into a certain course of action. . . . While they insisted on the companies observing agreements, the men must observe the same code of honour' (*The Times*, November 24, 1913).

J. H. Thomas among them, even more prudent than the former, merely hoped that when the existing agreement expired it would be renewed on terms more acceptable to the workers if they hung over the directors' heads the threat of a general strike of the three bodies. However that may be, sixty-one delegates representing 300,000 railwaymen, 800,000 miners, and 250,000 transport workers met in London and appointed a Sub-Committee to draw up a scheme. It was submitted on June 4 to the governing bodies of the three groups for their examination. It proposed to set up a common Advisory Council for the three bodies with authority to formulate their demands so that if they were not accepted three strikes would be declared simultaneously. All agreements as to wages and conditions of labour were to be for short periods and to terminate on the same date so as to make a simultaneous strike possible. And in face of hostile action by the employers or Parliament the three bodies should be ready to take concerted measures. This did not amount to a regular constitution in the strict sense of the term—it was merely a draft scheme for discussion by the three organizations. But the fact remained that the Triple Industrial Alliance, as it would soon be called, had been founded and that if on December 1 the railwaymen did not obtain from the Companies the concessions for which they were asking, the country was faced with the prospect of a strike of 2,000,000 allied workmen in a position to involve its entire industry in stagnation and chaos. On July 17, 1914, Lloyd George, addressing an audience of city financiers and merchants, admitted the gravity of the threat which hung over the nation. He would have liked to express his confidence that the crisis would be overcome like so many others in the past. If however the insurrection of labour should unhappily coincide with the Irish rebellion which as we shall see every one feared, 'the situation will be the gravest with which any government has had to deal for centuries'.

II THE FEMINIST REVOLT

I

We have given one explanation of the fact that five years after the Liberal victory of 1906 the British franchise had not yet been rendered fully democratic and there seemed little prospect of the

486

reform in the near future. It was the indifference of the proletariat which did not seek in political action the weapon it required to achieve its purposes. But this was not the only reason. The Liberal Cabinet found other obstacles in its path when it attempted to carry a measure extending the franchise. Granted it had the boldness to introduce universal suffrage was it to be confined to one sex alone? The restriction was already opposed by a sufficient number of Members of Parliament to obstruct any measure which ignored the political claims of women. Some of our readers may be surprised that among the problems which embarrassed the Liberal Government during the years immediately preceding 1914 we attach such importance to the question of female suffrage. They have evidently forgotten the strange agitation carried on twenty years ago by English women to compel their enfranchisement. These women refused to regard as a genuine democracy a form of government which reserved to the male sex the double privilege of electing and being elected to Parliament. Against this masculine tyranny they organized a revolutionary agitation without parallel in any other European country. Therefore, while in the syndicalist movement something of French and Latin anarchism invaded England, there sprang up a distinctive form of anarchy, specifically English. If however this suffragist movement, as it was termed, broke out suddenly at this juncture, the way had been paved by a long campaign for the emancipation of women. We must briefly relate its history and describe its character, since at this point it enters the main stream of British political history.

Why did women demand emancipation? And why in England more than in any other country? The philosophy of historical materialism, as formulated by Marx, suggests an answer plausible at first sight. Capitalism had flung a host of women and children into the new factories of northern England. Its motive was simply the accumulation of wealth. Women were more amenable to discipline and their labour was cheaper. Nevertheless, automatically and unconsciously it was promoting their emancipation. It was breaking down the exclusive and rigid principles of the traditional patriarchalism and enfranchising women, in as much as it took them from the domestic hearth and incorporated them in a wider group, which in the long run would prove less oppressive to its members when the machine had been placed at the service of the workers instead of the capitalists who exploited them.

Nevertheless, it is doubtful whether the industrial revolution and the factory system played the important part in the history of modern feminism which Marx ascribed to them. We must not imagine that these English girls, whom the official reports depict working long hours almost naked, mingled promiscuously with their male fellow workers in the hot and humid atmosphere of the cotton mills or in the darkness of the mines, were therefore at least emancipated from the control of their parents or husbands. To the latter they represented extra wages and only too often were compelled to take the hardest labour off the men's shoulders. When women were forbidden by law to work in mines, whole families of miners emigrated in search of an industry where the labourer could make his wife and children wage earners. When the law was content with limiting women's hours of work the male workers accepted the restriction only as the one lever they could employ to shorten their own hours. In either case the new legislation was possible at a period when the dominant Liberalism was bitterly hostile to any legal regulation of adult labour, only because it was supported by a public opinion which regarded the woman as physically and intellectually man's inferior and entitled for that reason alone to the protection of the law which placed her in the same category as the child, treated her as a minor, and sought to bring her back from the factory to the home.[1] In 1844

[1] H. of C., March 15, 1844, Lord Ashley's speech: 'The females not only perform the labour but occupy the places of men; they are forming various clubs and associations and gradually acquiring all those privileges which are held to be the proper portion of the male sex. . . . What is the ground on which the woman says that she will pay no attention to her duties, nor give the obedience which is owing to her husband? Because on her devolves the labour which ought to fall to his share.' (*Parliamentary Debates*, 3rd Series, vol lxxiii, p. 1096). It has been pointed out that the proportion of women to men employed in the textile industry before the industrial revolution was the same as after it. Even if this is the case, as a result of the enormously rapid growth of the industry the actual if not the relative number of women employed increased at a rate equally rapid. It has also been pointed out that the opponents of the factory system seriously exaggerated the number of married women employed in the Lancashire mills, that the miners sent only their daughters into the factory, and that in principle women left it on marriage. Possibly but the mistake figured nevertheless among the arguments, by which the philanthropist persuaded Parliament, and moreover it was not only married women but young girl whom the middle-class Utopians wished to remove from the factories. For the reservation we have just discussed see Ivy Pinchbeck's excellent book, *Women Workers and the Industrial Revolution 1750–1850*, 1930—for British Factory legislation in so far as it affected women see *Women under the Factory Acts*, Part I, *Position of the Employer*. Part II, *Position of the Employed* by Nora Vynne and Helen Blackburn. With the assistance of H. W. Allason, M.A., Solicitor on certain Technical Points of Law 1903. For the effect of the legislation on the number of women employed in industry and the nature of their work see *A Study of the Factors which have operated in the Past and those which are operating now to determine the distribution of Women in Industry. Presented by the Secretary of State for the Home Department by Command of His Majesty. December 1929*. 1930.

Lord Brougham, arguing against the legal regulation of women's work in factories, appealed to the principles of Liberal orthodoxy: 'Cannot a woman make a bargain? Cannot a woman look after her own interests? Is not a woman a being capable of understanding those interests, of saying whether or not she has stamina and strength to work?'[1] Thirty years later these arguments had by no means lost their power to convince British Members of Parliament. During the 'seventies, at first under Gladstone's Liberal Cabinet, then under the Conservative administration of Lord Beaconsfield, the opposition of the orthodox Liberals prevented reinforcement of the legislation protecting the labour of women in factories and mines and its extension to domestic industries, and this successful opposition came from the pioneers of English 'feminism'[2] who objected to a system of legal protection as degrading to their sex.[3] The years passed by; we have reached the threshold of the twentieth century, the old Liberalism is on its deathbed and the feminists have accepted Socialism of a more or

[1] H. of L., May 20, 1844 (*Parliamentary Debates*, 3rd Series, vol. lxxiv, p. 1315).

[2] The term of course had not yet been invented. Indeed it is a curious fact that if the theory is older in England than on the Continent the name is of French origin, in current use since 1895. That year a '*Revue Féministe*' appeared for the first time in Paris (Mme Avril de Sainte-Croix, *Le Féminisme 1907*, p. 137) and a Belgian quarterly already in existence for three years, *La Ligue, Organe belge du Droit des Femmes* devoted a final paragraph in each number to the '*Mouvement Féministe*'. In 1901 the *New English Dictionary* contains indeed the two words 'Feminism' and 'Feminist' (the latter is labelled rare) but with meanings very different from those we attach to them. We have not come across the word in the columns of *The Times* before 1908 (*The Times*, June 3, 1908) and then in connection with the feminist movement in France. As late as May 7, 1910 *The Times* uses the form 'Femininism'.

[3] [Barbara Leigh Smith] *A Brief Summary in plain Language of the most important Laws concerning Women together with a few Observations thereon, 1854*, p. 13: 'Philosophical thinkers have generally come to the conclusion that the tendency of progress is gradually to dispense with law—that is to say, as each individual man becomes unto himself a law, less external restraint is necessary and women, more than any other members of the community, suffer from over legislation.'—*Factory and Workshops Acts' Commission. Report o the Commissioners appointed to enquire into the working of the Factory and Workshops Acts, with a view to their Consolidation and Amendment; together with the Minutes of Evidence Appendix and Index*, vol. i, *Minutes of Evidence*, pp. 337 sqq.: Resolutions passed at a meeting of women: 'That this meeting fully recognizing the hardships endured by many women engaged in laborious and unsuitable occupations is nevertheless of opinion that legislative enactments placing restrictions on their employment, though they in some instances apparently palliate, do not overcome the evils they intend to remedy, but rather tend to perpetuate them and it therefore advocates the entire removal of all existing restrictions.' See Professor Fawcett's speeches in the House of Commons, H. of C., May 6, June 11, June 23, 1874 (*Parl. Deb.*, 3rd Ser., vol. ccxviii, pp. 1801–2; vol. ccxix, pp. 1421 sqq.; vol. ccxx, pp. 314 sqq.). February 21, 1878 (ibid., vol. ccxxxviii, pp. 106 sqq., 115, 124 sqq., 308, 311, 548, 596, 603, 610–11, 612). See also for this opposition of the pioneers of feminism to legislation regulating female labour Ray Strachey *The Cause . . . 1928*, pp. 234–6. Beatrice Potter 'The Lords and the Sweating System' (*Nineteenth Century*, June 1890, vol. xxvii, pp. 899). G. D. H. Cole, *A Short History of the British Working Class Movement 1789–1927*, vol. ii, pp. 126–7.

less Radical description. But 'protests are still raised against any legislation which does not place men and women on a footing of absolute equality, whether it is a question of restricting the labour of women in laundries and dressmaking,[1] or making their employment on the surface work of mines illegal as well as their employment in the mine itself. In 1908 John Burns attempted to carry the latter reform but was defeated by the opposition of women.[2] The history of British Factory Legislation therefore presents an air of paradox. In the middle of the nineteenth century those who were seeking to regulate the conditions of male labour in the factories adopted a circuitous route and proposed the regulation of women's labour alone. Now when the exploitation of women in certain branches of industry presented a spectacle too glaringly scandalous to be tolerated and the law was compelled to intervene, Parliament could protect the women only by protecting at the same time the workers of both sexes, as was exemplified by the Trade Boards Act of 1909.

2

The paradox however is a proof that feminism owed its birth to influences not directly connected with the industrial revolution. The historian of feminism must not depict women driven against their will into the factories by the greed of manufacturers and then emancipated in their employers' despite as a result of the common conditions which the factory system enforced on both sexes. The majority of trade unions contained no women, and where women were members, as in the cotton industry, they neither secured nor demanded access to the executive.[3] There were no feminine trade unions, or if one or two had come into being their existence was artificial and precarious. Advanced ideas of eighteenth century enlightenment, the philosophy of the French revolution, the revival of these ideas and this philosophy

[1] Jessie Boucherett, Helen Blackburn, and some Others, *The Condition of Working Women and the Factory Acts*, 1896, p. 50.

[2] Ibid., p. 53. Annie Kenney, *Memories of a Militant*, pp. 130 sqq.

[3] H. of C., July 12, 1910, Winston Churchill's speech: 'The Amalgamated Association of Card-Room and Blowing-Room Operatives have a membership of 45,000. Of these 35,200 are women and 9,800 men. The association has an executive of 10 members. Not a single woman had been elected at the time I refer to, to serve on the executive' (*Parliamentary Debates*, Commons 1910, 5th Series, vol. xix, p. 222).

in the great individualist and liberal movement which after years of stagnation marked the years around 1860—these are the sources from which was derived the impulse which drove women to claim equality with men in the factory and the office, in the liberal professions and in public life. The origin of the movement was intellectual not economic, bourgeois not proletarian.

The first important legislative victory won by the champions of the emancipation of women was the passing in 1857 of the Matrimonial Causes Act, in the teeth of a bitter opposition from the Church of England of which Gladstone made himself the mouthpiece and thanks to Palmerston's support.[1] According to the law as it existed previously not only was the married woman enslaved to her husband or rather, to use Blackstone's words, 'absorbed, incorporated' into his person, but it was in principle impossible for her to regain her freedom by divorce. The marriage bond could indeed be partially or completely broken in two ways. But neither of these amounted to divorce in the modern sense of the term. Both the partial and the complete rupture were determined by the Canon Law and were pronounced by the ecclesiastical courts. The former was divorce *a mensa et toro* (from bed and board), what we now call separation of person and property— though the separation of property was not as complete as one might have expected. The latter a divorce *a vinculo matrimonii* was a declaration of nullity. The marriage was not dissolved but declared after inquiry 'null and void from the beginning'. For, as Blackstone explains 'the canon law, which the common law follows in this case, deems so highly and with such mysterious reverence of the nuptial tie, that it will not allow it to be unloosed for any cause whatever, that comes after the union is made'.[2] The rule admitted only one exception. It had been devised by husbands of the governing class, galled as they were by the fetters of a matrimonial code which if strictly applied did not permit them to divorce even an unfaithful wife. The British Parliament made use of its sovereignty to override the prohibitions of Canon Law and by a 'private' Bill—that is to say, a measure applicable only

---

[1] 20 & 21 Vict., Cap. 85: An Act to amend the Law relating to Divorce and Matrimonial Causes in England. To which must be added a Statute passed the following year (1858): 21 & 22 Vict., Cap. 108: An Act to amend the Act of the Twentieth and Twenty-first Victoria, Cap. Eighty-five.

[2] I Comm., 441.

to the individual case—passed in due form by both Houses,[1] declare a particular marriage dissolved and the parties free to remarry. But the procedure was extremely costly. Only the very wealthy could obtain a Divorce Bill.[2] All this was altered by the Act of 1857.

The Act transferred matrimonial causes from the Church Courts to a new civil court composed of the Lord Chancellor, one of the Chief Justices, and an ecclesiastical judge. This court would decide whether it should grant what the old canon law called divorce *a mensa et toro* and which would be called in future a judicial separation or what was now called simply divorce, not a declaration of nullity but the dissolution of the marriage bond for acts committed subsequent to marriage. In the case of the wife adultery would be a sufficient ground. In the case of the husband incest, rape, bigamy with a married woman, an unnatural offence, or adultery accompanied by cruelty or desertion was required. A clause which forbade a wife divorced for adultery to marry her lover was subsequently repealed. A wife who had obtained a judicial separation was placed for the first time in the position of a *feme sole*—that is to say, was given full enjoyment of her civil rights, the right to enter into contracts and bring civil actions, and a deserted wife might under certain circumstances be placed in the same position.

The mere fact that the jurisdiction in 'matrimonial causes' was transferred from an ecclesiastical to a civil court possessed a momentous significance. It meant that marriage had lost that quality of semi-religious 'mystery' of which Blackstone spoke. In future it would be a mere civil contract. Could it then like other civil contracts be dissolved at the pleasure of the contracting parties? Far from it. For in the first place it was only in a small number of cases strictly defined by law that the new judges could after due investigation dissolve the marriage contract and in the second place, the Act of 1857 did not place the two contracting parties on an equal footing; simple adultery which gave the hus-

---

[1] In reality by the Lords alone. When the Bill was sent down to the House of Commons from the Upper House in which it had been first introduced it was regularly passed without debate.

[2] The husband must take the following steps. 1. He must bring a suit at the Assizes against his wife and her lover for what English law called 'criminal conversation'. 2. If he won his suit he must obtain a decree of separation from an ecclesiastical court. 3. The decree secured, he must obtain from the House of Lords the private Bill which would effectively set him free.

band the right to a divorce did not give it to the wife. The new legislation had, it is true, made divorce less aristocratic, for it had made it cheaper. It no longer cost £200 and often far more to obtain as in the days when a private Bill was required. In future it would not cost more than £60 at most, often £40 or even £30 and legal aid might be given to a poor suitor.[1] But there was only one tribunal competent to grant divorces, and it was fixed in London. How enormously therefore the cost was increased when the suitor lived in a remote district and in addition to the ordinary costs must defray the expense of travel to London, and lodging there, not to speak of the cost of bringing up witnesses! If divorce was no longer the exclusive privilege of the enormously wealthy, it was reserved for the rich and for the inhabitants of London and the home counties.

We might therefore have expected that under the pressure of the same moral forces which had led to the Act of 1857 the legislation concerning divorce would have undergone important modifications during the next half century. In fact, hardly any alteration was made. In 1878 a husband's aggravated assault upon his wife was declared a ground for judicial separation.[2] But this was all. A lavish use of simple separations summarily pronounced by the Justices of the Peace was the expedient by which the unaltered rigour of the divorce law was rendered more tolerable. But it was an expedient which presented serious drawbacks. Countless homes among the poorer classes were legally broken up with no possibility of replacing them by new. A host of illegitimate unions was the inevitable result of a code which made divorce too difficult, particularly for the poor, and separation on the other hand perhaps too easy. Complaints were raised. A society was founded to secure a reform of the divorce law. It demanded and obtained—though not until 1909—the appointment of a Royal Commission of inquiry. The Commission held seventy-one sittings, fifty-six of which were devoted to taking evidence and 246 witnesses were heard. It unanimously reported in favour of making the grounds of divorce the same for the wife as for the husband and a large increase in the grounds of nullity.

[1] *Royal Commission on Divorce and Matrimonial Causes*, February 25, 1910. Mr. Musgrave's evidence. (*Minutes of Evidence*, vol. i, pp. 10 sqq.), also John Galsworthy, *A Commentary*, pp. 243 sqq.
[2] 41 Vict., Cap. 19: An Act to amend the Matrimonial Causes Act. (*Matrimonial Causes Act, 1878*.)

With equal unanimity it recommended that the high court should be empowered to appoint deputies to bring divorce within the reach of the poor in every part of the country, and that restrictions should be placed upon the publicity of proceedings and their publication in the Press. The majority further recommended that the grounds for divorce should be enlarged, and besides adultery should include prolonged desertion, cruelty, madness, habitual drunkenness, and imprisonment for life in commutation of a death sentence.[1] But neither the Government nor Parliament had time to take these proposals into consideration. The British divorce law remained what it was when the twentieth century opened. The movement for the emancipation of women followed other paths.

3

To facilitate the dissolution of the marriage bond was to emancipate the woman in as much as it made it easier for her to escape from a union in which she played the part of prisoner or slave. But could not her freedom also be secured by improving her legal position in marriage itself? To give effect to the principle that the husband and wife are legally a single person and the personality of the woman incorporated into her husband's, English common law almost wholly denied a married woman the right to hold property. Her personal estate became the husband's property by the fact of marriage. And even over her real estate he possessed a large number of rights and he enjoyed an unrestricted right to the income derived from it. If injured by a third party the wife could bring an action only with her husband's consent and in his name as well as her own. In the latter half of the nineteenth century such provisions necessarily seemed anomalous. They had in fact survived so long only because a number of expedients had effected a compromise between the rigour of the law and the demands of real life. The father who shrank from surrendering his daughter's fortune—his own after all—to the caprice of a son-in-law could make in her favour what the English law called a settlement, drawn up according to the rules of 'equity' to

[1] *Royal Commission on Divorce and Matrimonial Causes Report*, November 2, 1912, *Minutes of Evidence*, 3 vols. and *Appendices* 1912.

correct the 'common law'.[1] Nevertheless, since the system had been devised not so much to protect the wife as her patrimony it involved a host of complications which did not make for her pecuniary independence. And even so it was expensive and out of the reach of people of small means. When the latter by the pressure they exercised upon the wealthy classes obtained successive and considerable extensions of the franchise, how could Parliament avoid taking action to give poorer women something analogous to what the jurisprudence of equity had secured for their wealthier sisters?

It was in fact a reform which the champions of the emancipation of women had pressed upon Parliament even before the Matrimonial Causes Act was passed in 1857. The passing of that Act proved at first detrimental to their cause. What reason was there to commiserate the lot of the married woman when, if her case really deserved pity, it had been made easier for her to obtain her freedom? Nevertheless, the anomaly remained flagrant and too obviously out of harmony with the ethics of the period. The consumers' co-operative societies, it was noticed, paid their dividends to married women of the working class as if they were the private property of the latter and the public opinion of the proletariat accepted a practice which had no legal justification. Custom also allowed a married woman to conduct a business as if, in spite of her marriage, she possessed an independent juridical personality. If she became bankrupt were not her creditors defrauded by a law which declared her financially irresponsible unless it could be proved that she had been her husband's 'agent' acting under his orders?[2] A succession of Married Women's Property Acts were passed which within a few years profoundly transformed English law.

An Act passed in 1870,[3] and completed by an Act passed four years later[4] gave a married woman a right of property in any

[1] The courts of equity could even compel the husband if he claimed a property in his wife's name to settle part of it on her, provided the property in question was not worth less than £200. (B. L. Smith, *Brief Summary*, p. 6.)

[2] For the problem to be solved see the interesting debates in both Houses during the session of 1869; H. of C., April 14, July 21, 1869, H. of L., July 30, 1869 (*Parliamentary Debates*, 3rd Series, vol. cxcv, pp. 760 sqq., vol. cxcviii, pp. 402 sqq., 979).

[3] 33 & 34 Vict., Cap. 93: An Act to amend the law relating to the Property of Married Women (*Married Women's Property Act*, 1870).

[4] 37 & 38 Vict., Cap. 50: An Act to amend the Married Women's Property Act, 1870 (*Married Women's Property Act* [1870] *Amendment Act*, 1874). The Scottish law was reformed on similar lines by two Statutes 40 & 41 Vict., Cap. 29: An Act for the Protection

personal gain made since marriage, investments made with the produce of her work, and all bequests. In respect of the property thus declared her separate estate she could take legal action in her own name. The Act of 1882[1] was at once a Statute of consolidation which united in a single measure the two Acts of 1870 and 1874, and a new measure which extended the application of the principles laid down by the Act of 1870. The latter Statute had been in fact that remnant of a far more radical Bill passed by the Commons but mutilated by the Lords. Twelve years later, the House of Lords passed without debate a Statute which enacted that the entire property of a married woman, both that which she possessed at the time of marriage and that which she obtained from any source after marriage, should be as much her property as if it had been settled upon her. Her liberty was restricted on one point alone, and the restriction was in her own interest. Settlements were respected by the new Act and those who made them were entitled to protect a married woman against her own weakness and make it impossible for her to alienate under pressure from her husband the capital settled upon her. This fundamental Statute of 1882 has been completed in more or less important respects by four Statutes, passed respectively in 1884,[2] 1893,[3] 1907[4] and 1908.[5] But by 1882 a legal development may be regarded as in its main features complete which for speed is probably unequalled outside periods of violent revolution. Before 1870 a married woman in England, in the poorer classes at least, was subject to a legal tutelage of almost iron rigour. Twelve years later separate property had become the normal condition of married people and a wife enjoyed a freedom unknown in any other country. In this respect English law amazed, we might almost say, shocked the jurists of the Continent.[6]

of the Property of Married Women in Scotland (*Married Women's Property [Scotland] Act*, 1877) and 44 & 45 Vict., Cap. 21: An Act for the Amendment of the Law regarding Property of Married Women in Scotland (*Married Women's Property [Scotland] Act*, 1881).
[1] 45 & 46 Vict., Cap. 75: An Act to consolidate and amend the Acts relating to the Property of Married Women (*Married Women's Property Act*, 1882).
[2] 47 Vict., Cap. 14: An Act to amend the sixteenth section of the Married Women's Property Act, 1882 (*Married Women's Property Act*, 1884).
[3] 56 & 57 Vict., Cap. 63: An Act to amend the Married Women's Property Act, 1882 (*Married Women's Property Act*, 1893).
[4] 7 Edw. 7, Cap. 18: An Act to amend the Married Women's Property Act, 1882 (*Married Women's Property Act*, 1907).
[5] 8 Edw. 7, Cap. 27: An Act to render Married Women with a separate Estate liable for the support of their Parents (*Married Women's Property Act*, 1908).
[6] For this legislation see Emile Boutmy, *Essai d'une Psychologie politique du Peuple*,

The English matrimonial code underwent further modifications during the half century which preceded the Great War. The wife's refusal to return to her home was no longer regarded as an offence punishable with imprisonment,[1] and the law deprived the husband of his right to confine a wife who refused to live with him.[2] The husband was no longer permitted to deprive his wife by testament of the guardianship of her children.[3] The procedure by which a deserted wife could obtain alimony was made easier.[4] And we may mention in passing the permission at last granted in 1907 to marry a deceased wife's sister.[5] What is extraordinary is the survival to that late date of the old prohibition of canon law and the opposition to the reform organized by the Anglican High Church party under the leadership of Lord Salisbury's two sons, Lord Robert and Lord Hugh Cecil. It is of greater interest to notice that the Labour members introduced into the Workmen's Compensation Act an amendment providing that an increase of pension might be claimed for support of illegitimate children by their maternal parents or grandparents as though the relationship in question arose out of a lawful marriage.[6] Thus proletarian morals demanded a sort of indirect legalization of the free union.

anglais au XIXe siècle 1901, pp. 311–2. A. V. Dicey, Lectures on the Relation between Law and Public Opinion in England during the nineteenth century, 1905, pp. 369 sqq. Ray Strachey, The Cause: A short History of the Women's Movement in Great Britain, 1928, pp. 73, 76, 272 sqq. The feminists however were not satisfied. They demanded that part of the husband's income should be regarded as belonging to the wife as a wage for the work she performed in the home. See the eighth of the nine Bills drafted by Lady Maclaren under the common title of 'The Women's Charter' and introduced in the House of Commons by Sir Charles Maclaren on March 14, 1910.

[1] 47 & 48 Vict., Cap. 68: An Act to amend the Matrimonial Causes Acts (Matrimonial Causes Act, 1884).

[2] High Court of Justice Queen's Bench Division: ex parte Emily Jackson for a suit of Habeas Corpus, March 16, 1891. Supreme Court of Judicature. Court of Appeal. The same suit, March 17, 19, 1891.

[3] 49 & 50 Vict., Cap. 27: An Act to amend the Law relating to the Guardianship and Custody of Infants (Guardianship and Custody of Infants Act, 1886).

[4] 49 & 50 Vict., Cap. 52: An Act to amend the Law relating to the Maintenance of Married Women who shall have been deserted by their Husbands (Married Women Maintenance in case of Desertion Act, 1886). The Act was repealed in 1895 and its very brief provisions were incorporated into a more complete Act: 58 & 59 Vict., Cap. 39: An Act to amend the Law relating to the Summary Jurisdiction of Magistrates in reference to Married Women. (Summary Jurisdiction [Married Women] Act, 1895).

[5] 7 Edw. 7, Cap. 47: An Act to amend the Law relating to Marriage with a Deceased Wife's Sister (Deceased Wife's Sister Marriage Act, 1907).

[6] 6 Edw. 7, Cap. 58: Workmen's Compensation Act, 1906, Section 13. In 1911 Keir Hardie attempted by an amendment to the National Insurance Bill to give the unmarried mother an equal right with a married woman to receive Maternity as well as Sickness Benefit. But the Government did not accept his amendment which after a lively debate was rejected by 207 to 95 votes. (H. of C., July 17, 1911; Parliamentary Debates, Commons 1911, 5th Series, vol. xxviii, p. 806.)

But at the same time the insurgent women were turning their efforts in another direction and conducting a campaign peculiar, if not to England, at least to the Anglo-Saxon world. European sex morality rests on the complementary pillars of marriage and prostitution. The latter was the field on which the defenders of women's right won a brilliant victory.

4

The Napoleonic system in France made prostitution a profession, dishonourable, no doubt, but sanctioned and regulated by law. It expressed the attitude of a soldier who, since he condemned a vast number of young men to compulsory celibacy and therefore to irregular forms of sexual union, deemed it his duty both to them and to the country to protect them against the danger of venereal disease. The innovation was calculated to appeal to soldiers of other nations. About 1860 the British high command introduced in India for the use of the soldiers the system of regulated prostitution. Measures entitled Contagious Diseases Acts were passed in 1864, 1866, 1868, and 1869 empowering the police in certain urban centres to classify women on the denunciation of their agents as common prostitutes, liable to imprisonment if they refused to submit to a periodical medical examination, and the system spread rapidly in the seaports and garrison towns.

Public opinion rose in revolt. It was not a question of abolishing a long-established institution which had become an abuse because it was antiquated, but of protecting England against a foreign importation, an 'infection' from the Continent and, what was worse, Napoleonic and French. And had the system of legalized prostitution really reduced venereal disease? On this point statistics were uncertain and susceptible of conflicting interpretation. Too uncertain in any case, contended the opponents of the Contagious Diseases Acts, to justify condemning a woman on the mere denunciation of a policeman to be for the rest of her life a species of slave and pariah. And assuredly too uncertain to warrant the introduction of this servitude into a country whose proud boast it was that for the past two centuries it had been the protagonist of freedom. The movement was led by a woman of the middle class, the wife of a man who occupied an important place in the scholastic profession, the admirable Josephine Butler.[1] A ministerial candidate, shortly before Governor of Malta, where he had introduced the system of licensed houses, stood for Colchester. Josephine Butler and an entire group of women fired by her enthusiasm conducted a campaign against him. They braved the ordeal of public discussions, open-air meetings, abuse and violence from the mob, and they won the victory. A Royal Commission was appointed to examine the question and after an inquiry, in the course of which John Stuart Mill gave evidence, reported in favour of abolishing licensed prostitution and raising the age of consent from twelve to fourteen.[2] But it required twelve years' propaganda, religious preaching one is tempted to call it rather than political agitation, before the Government, acting on a resolution of the House of Commons,[3] suspended the operation of the Contagious Diseases Acts, and it was not until three years later that they were formally repealed. As regards the Commission's other recommendation that the age of consent should be raised, it was again Josephine Butler who led the way. She passed her cause on to the great journalist, a blend of crusader and charlatan, W. T. Stead. He was converted and a sensational campaign in the Press, not devoid of scandal, led in a few months to the passing of the Criminal Law Amendment Act of 1885, which raised the age of consent not to fourteen but sixteen, made procuration a crime, and an attempt to violate a girl under thirteen punishable by flogging or penal servitude.[4] The adoption of these measures, reinforced by further legislation passed from time to time until the eve of the War,[5] was not simply a victory for the women who were their passive beneficiaries. It was a victory for

[1] For this campaign see Josephine Butler, *An Autobiographical Memoir*. Edited by G. M. and L. A. Johnson, 1909, 3rd Edition, revised and enlarged 1928; also an excellent chapter in Ray Strachey *The Cause*, 1928, pp. 187 sqq.
[2] Report of Royal Commission upon the Administration and Operation of the Contagious Diseases Act, 1871, pp. 19–20.
[3] H. of C., April 20, 1883, Stansfield's motion. (*Parliamentary Debates*, 3rd Series, vol. cclxxviii, pp. 749 sqq.).
[4] 48 & 49 Vict., Cap. 69: An Act to make further provision for the Protection of Women and Girls, the suppression of Brothels and other Purposes (*Criminal Law Amendment Act*, 1885).
[5] 61 & 62 Vict., Cap. 39: An Act to amend the Vagrancy Act, 1824 (*Vagrancy Act*, 1898). Its first section is directed against the bullies. The measure was extended to Scotland by 2 Edw. 7, Cap. 11: An Act to make further provision for the Punishment of Persons Trading in Prostitution in Scotland (*Immoral Traffic (Scotland) Act*, 1902)—2 & 3 Geo. 5, Cap. 20: An Act to amend the Criminal Law Amendment Act, 1885, the Vagrancy Act, 1889 and the Immoral Traffic (Scotland) Act, 1902 (*Criminal Law Amendment Act*, 1912) which on several points of detail tightens up the previous legislation.

women in another sense in as much as they were the result of an agitation conducted by women, and by methods hitherto the monopoly of the male sex. With this double agitation against the legalization of prostitution and the white-slave traffic, the revolt of women in England began.

5

We must not however imagine that these two campaigns represent the entire history of the movement for the emancipation of women during the concluding years of the nineteenth century. They were accompanied by another agitation which was not the less important because it scarcely engaged the attention of Parliament. Women claimed the right to perform on an equal footing with men the same social functions. By degrees they secured their object. But though success followed success, in 1914 they had not yet won along the entire front. Nor is their victory complete[1] even now.

It had always been admitted that women as well as men could be teachers. The concession was, in fact, founded on the belief in an unalterable difference between the sexes which made it inadvisable for girls to be taught by men. Elementary schools for poor girls, and private schools for the daughters of the middle class had no difficulty in procuring a cheap supply of women teachers, and it was an easy matter for wealthier middle-class parents to obtain governesses to give their daughters at home a very sketchy education which imparted more social accomplishments than intellectual training. And everyone agreed that for little children a mistress was better than a master. Accordingly, professional statistics show from the opening of the nineteenth century an enormous majority of female over male teachers. The growth of education produced a constant increase in the number of women teachers— 70,000 in 1851, 172,000 in 1901[2] and according to a ratio a little higher than the increase in the number of male teachers.[3] Another

---

[1] [1932. Translators note].

[2] In England and Wales 69,340 in 1851; 80,057 in 1861; 94,229 in 1871; 123,995 in 1881; 114,393 in 1891; 171,670 in 1901.

[3] In 1861 72.5 per cent of the teachers were women, in 1871 74.1 per cent, in 1881 72.7 per cent, in 1891 74 per cent, in 1901 74.5 per cent (*Census of England and Wales, 1901*. General Report with Appendices, 1904, p. 86). Between 1901 and 1911 the increase seems to have

effect was a continuous improvement in the quality of their teaching. Governesses received a better training. A new type of private school for girls, far superior to the old, came into existence. In the history of these schools the year 1865 was a decisive date for it was then that after a campaign extending over years Cambridge admitted girls to its local examinations, thereby putting the secondary education of girls as regards the examinations by which it was regulated on an equality with the secondary education of boys. The era of the school boards followed and the schools under their authority in the case of girls as well as boys tended to exceed the standard of primary education. To educate mistresses for a teaching of better quality than before, training schools became necessary and in turn teachers for the training schools. Could the latter be refused the advantages of a university education? If not, why should they not be thrown open at the same time to young girls of good family whose brothers were undergraduates of Oxford or Cambridge? The conquest of the universities was one of the great objectives pursued by women during the last third of the nineteenth century.

It was not easy. The agitators were faced by a double opposition, from the universities—two clubs of conservative old bachelors—and from parents alarmed at the prospect of mixing the sexes at adolescence. The first step was to found by subscriptions raised for the purpose, a college for women twenty-five miles from Cambridge. Enthusiastic Fellows accepted the fatigue of the journey to and fro to give lectures to the students. Then the college was transferred to a distance of two miles. Finally the plunge was taken and another women's college opened in the town itself. At Oxford two were founded. But every precaution was taken against scandal. The girl students could not go out unaccompanied and attended the lectures in groups in charge of a chaperon. Nor were they admitted from the outset to the same examinations as the young men. The first concession, made by the University of Cambridge, was to communicate the subjects of an examination to friendly professors who held an unofficial examination of the women students parallel to that which the men were taking at the

been greater among the men than the women. But the *Census of England and Wales, 1911* (vol. x, *Occupations and Industries*, Part I, p. xxi) explains this semblance. 'In order to obtain a better measure of the increase in the teaching profession, the numbers of ages twenty years and upward at the two censuses may be compared, and these show an increase of 30.4 per cent among males and of 33.6 per cent among females.'

same time. But the movement which was equipping the great cities with universities enabled the women to win at a single stroke an important victory in this field. A Statute of 1875 had expressly authorized these new universities to confer their degrees on women. When in 1878 the University of London became a teaching-university it immediately made use of the right. It laid down the principle of absolute equality between the sexes. All degrees and positions in the teaching body were thrown open to women students. The Victoria University followed suit in 1880, the University of Wales in 1893, Durham College in 1895. Oxford and Cambridge could not refuse to make concessions. In 1881 and in 1884 Cambridge first, then Oxford admitted women students to the same examinations as men, though they refused to confer degrees on the successful candidates.[1]

It is surprising that the claim of women to practise medicine met with stronger opposition than their claim to teach. For it had always been admitted that there was nothing incompatible with a woman's nature in the professions of midwife and sick nurse. Moreover, if it was more suitable that women should teach women, why did not the same principle apply to medical treatment? Nevertheless, the opposition was formidable and determined. It was, it would seem, a question of professional interest. The doctors who were powerfully organized and regarded medicine as a commercial profession were defending a lucrative monopoly.

The great battle was fought simultaneously with the battle to force an entrance into the universities. Often both fronts were combined and the victory was, at least apparently, won on both at the same time. It was about 1870 that three young girls attempted to storm the medical faculty at Edinburgh University, braving the coarse jests of their male comrades and what were nothing short of riots among the students encouraged by the professors. They succeeded in securing admission to the lectures and in passing some examinations but in the end the Senate of the University refused them the right to practice. The women adopted other manœuvres. They attempted to enter the medical profession by way of the corporation of apothecaries—by taking a midwife's diploma or obtaining the degree of doctor of medicine

[1] Ray Strachey, *The Cause*, pp. 141 sqq., 255 sqq. Barbara Stephen, *Emily Davies and Girton College*, 1927.

on the Continent where in most countries it was open to women. These attempts were always baffled. They founded in London a medical school for women. The girls who had attended it were not admitted to a single hospital in the metropolis. At last victory seemed assured when in 1875 an Act was passed permitting universities to confer degrees on women and another forbidding the Royal College of Surgeons to exclude them.[1] Even before the University of London in 1878 had laid down the principle of complete sex equality, the two Irish Colleges of Physicians had admitted women and one of the London hospitals had accepted students from the Women's Medical School. The decennial census returns enable us to follow this invasion. In the census of 1881 lady doctors made their appearance for the first time—twenty-five in England and Wales. In 1891 there were a hundred, 212 in 1901, 477 in 1911. Nevertheless, in these years before 1914 they were still faced with insurmountable difficulties. The new national services indeed offered them an increasing number of openings, the management of schools for mothers, infant welfare centres and crèches and inspectorships under the Ministry of Health. But they were very rarely admitted to study in the hospitals and women medical students were usually obliged to seek better facilities at Vienna or in America. Nor would the hospitals accept women doctors. Certain bodies, for instance the Ophthalmological Society and the Society for the Study of Infantile Diseases, refused to admit them to membership. We even hear of a medical journal which refused to accept articles signed by women.[2]

6

The old universities of Oxford and Cambridge continued to refuse to admit women to the examinations in medicine, theology, and law. As regards medicine this was of no consequence since women could now obtain a doctorate at all the other universities of the kingdom. As regards theology, it might be argued that by excluding women Oxford and Cambridge shared the opinion

[1] 38 & 39 Vict., Cap. 43: An Act to amend the Medical Acts so far as relates to the Royal College of Surgeons of England (*Royal College of Surgeons Act*, 1875) Section 2.
[2] Ray Strachey *The Cause*, pp. 166 sqq., 251 sqq. Dr. Flora Murray, The Position of Women in Medicine and Surgery (*New Statesman*, November 1, 1913, *Special Supplement*, pp. xvi-xvii).

universal throughout Christendom that a woman could not be a priest or a minister. What was the use of giving her a degree when she could not become a teacher? But the Salvation Army had made the innovation of giving women an equal place with men among their officers[1] and therefore, in so far as a religious body without sacraments and therefore without ordination may be regarded as a church, it was a church in which women violated the principle laid down by St. Paul that women should not 'teach' but 'keep silence'. The movement spread to the other religious bodies. In 1874 the Wesleyan Conference allowed a woman elected by one of the synods to take part in its deliberations.[2] The Anglican Church allowed a woman to become a deaconess and to sit on the parish councils.[3] Militant feminists cherished the hope that the day was near when, if not the Established Church, at least the sects would consent to ordain women.[4] Finally, as regards the law, the exclusion maintained by Oxford and Cambridge corresponded to the unyielding determination of the legal profession. Could the Inns of Court lawfully admit women? Some maintained that they could; but it would be a very long time before they made use of the right, if it existed. Should the word 'person' in the Solicitors' Act of 1843 be interpreted as meaning man or woman? The courts replied in the negative.[5] But could England much longer lag behind the United States where 20,000 women practised as lawyers, several of the Colonies,

[1] By a decision taken in 1875 (Ray Strachey, The Cause, p. 214). Some innovators appealed to another text of St. Paul, where he permits women to prophesy, 1 Cor. xi, 5, 6, also to Acts ii 17–18, xxi 9–10, to prove that the prohibition was not absolute. (The Dean of Wells, 'Ought Women to Preach? 1. The Ministry of Women', Contemporary Review, January–June 1884, vol. xlv, pp. 43 sqq.).

[2] A committee appointed by the Conference to examine the question reported the following year in favour of admitting women, and if the report was rejected by the Conference it was by a very narrow majority.

[3] In virtue of a decision taken in July 1914, by the Representative Council of the Anglican Church. The voting proves that the Bishops were more favourable to the proposal than the priests, the priests more favourable than the laity.

[4] And even the Establishment: Flora Murray, 'The Position of Women and Surgery' (New Statesman, November 1, 1913, Special Supplement, p. xvii), 'It must be recognized that a university education—even for women—leads directly to the door of the Bar, the Church and the Medical Profession, and that the admission to these fields of learning and enterprise and remuneration is only a question of time.' So far as the sects are concerned the forecast has been realized. See the decision of the Wesleyan Conference of 1925. Cf. Albert Peel, The Free Churches 1903-1926, 1927, p. 444: 'Another way in which the outlook has been broadened is seen in the fuller and freer acceptance of the service of women, who now not only do the work they have done so well before, but are trained as ministers, elected as deacons and officers, and called to equal service with men.'

[5] Bebb v. Law Society (Supreme Court of Judicature. Chancery Division. July 2, 1913, Court of Appeal, December 9, 10, 1913).

and France? A Bill was about to be introduced into the Commons to enable women to become solicitors and the Lord Chancellor and the Prime Minister promised to support it.[1] The final struggle was at hand.

Though women could not become barristers or solicitors they were not totally debarred from the purlieus of the law. They entered lawyers' offices as clerks, shorthand writers, and typists.[2] Simultaneously, they invaded the world of business.[3] They were indeed prevented by the rules of these bodies from becoming outside or inside brokers, or sitting on the governing body of the Stock Exchange or Bank. But here too, as throughout the hierarchy of commerce and industry, they could occupy positions which, if subordinate, were nevertheless positions of trust and in which their punctuality and prompt obedience gave complete satisfaction to their employers. For the first time women were making their appearance as insurance agents and commercial travellers. In the 'seventies when the great struggle for university degrees was raging, there was not a woman in the City. Twenty years later they were still few and attracted attention. Now they were a multitude and you jostled past them without taking notice.

At the same time, they entered the public services. Here and especially in the Post Office it was nothing short of an invasion. The number of persons employed by the central government or local authorities was estimated by the census of 1911 at some 300,000, of whom 249,000 were men, 51,000 women. Comparison with the figures of 1901 shows a total increase of 46 per cent representing an increase of 42.3 per cent for men, 69.4 per cent for women.[4] Nor was the new invasion of the same nature as the

[1] Lord Haldane's reply to a deputation from *The Committee for the Admission of Women to the Solicitors' Profession*, March 27, 1914.

[2] The census of 1871 enumerates 51 women 'connected with law', the census of 1881, 100 'law clerks and others connected with law'. In 1891 there were 166 'clerks', in 1901 367. The progress becomes striking during the following decade. The number of 'law clerks' of both sexes which had increased by a quarter during the previous decade increased only by a twentieth. But whereas the number of male clerks showed an insignificant increase, from 34,066 to 34,106 the number of women rose from 367 to 2,159.

[3] The number of women employed as commercial and business clerks rose from 7,749 in 1881 to 23,050 in 1891, 74,620 in 1901 and 153,973 in 1911. In other words it had increased twentyfold while the entire number of employees of both sexes had merely doubled: 212,067 in 1881, 420,538 in 1911.

[4] *Census of England and Wales, 1911*, 1914, vol. x, p. xiii. We must however bear in mind that the vast majority of these women were employed in the Post Office. See *Royal Commission on Civil Service, 4th Report* 1914, p. 22. 'The Board of Education has, since 1898, recruited some female clerks (of whom about twenty are now employed) by means of the examination held to fill the Women Clerkships in the General Post Office, and a

invasion of the factories by women a century earlier. The women had been driven into the factories by the necessity of earning a livelihood and their presence was not in itself a triumph of feminism. It rendered the champions of women's rights no other service than to furnish them with an argument against their opponents. 'You want, you say, to keep women at home, why then do you set them to the forced labour of your factories?' Now, however, women entered offices of their free will and to find freedom.

7

The young girl who leads a young man's life adopts his manners. She no longer curtsies on entering a drawing-room nor awaits her elders' invitation to be seated. She talks with her back against the mantelpiece puffing at her cigarette. All these gestures are signals of independence. They proclaim that she is in no hurry to get married and that when she does marry she is determined to maintain her independence in face of her husband and, if need be, in opposition to him. What Blackstone termed with such unction 'the mysterious reverence of the nuptial tie', is a thing of the past. An entire literature has come into being which urges women to revolt. Grant Allen was the first to invite English girls to imitate The Woman who Did, the woman who refuses to consecrate by legal wedlock her union with the man she loves. In her ponderous and grotesque novel *The Heavenly Twins* Sarah Grand branded masculine immorality and advised her women readers to refuse to consummate legal marriage with a dissolute husband and thus shake off the yoke of the male when he was unworthy. Among the rebels the outstanding figures were Ibsen, Shaw, and H. G. Wells, who had their disciples and fanatics. One young

few more of this class have been taken into the office of the Registrar General, in addition to the considerable force of women which has on several occasions been employed temporarily in that department on work connected with the decennial census. The office staff of the Public Trustee is a mixed male and female one, and female clerks have been introduced into the centres of the Labour Exchange offices, but these situations are at present on a temporary basis. With these exceptions and excluding female typists who are employed in many departments in increasing numbers, but form a class by themselves, it remains true at the present time that women have not procured admission to the clerical service of the State. They are, however, in growing, though still small, numbers, employed with advantage to the community as inspectors under various departments, where they discharge useful functions in connection with women and children. Their employment under the Local Education Authorities as teachers in the Public Elementary and Secondary Schools lies outside the scope of our inquiry.'

woman would say 'I will be Norah' and for no serious reason leave a husband who in her opinion was attempting to treat her as a doll: Another 'I will be Vivian Warren,' quit the home of an unworthy mother and refuse a fortune amassed by immoral methods. But for a logical Socialist what capital has been acquired in a manner less infamous than Mrs. Warren's money? 'I will be Ann Veronica': 'I will be Isabel Rivers.' In 1909 H. G. Wells published his *Ann Veronica*, in 1911 his *New Macchiavelli*, in 1913 his *Passionate Friends*, three novels, two of which are autobiographical. He advocates a system in which the woman alone will be responsible to society for her children, and receive a bounty from the State for every child she bears and brings up. The men with whom she entertains free relations will be conscious of no bond with her children beyond sentiments of free affection. It is with a smile that we hear Hugh Price Hughes at the opening of the century congratulate himself on the fact that the Protestantism, the Puritanism of the sects had imparted to British feminism a moral austerity which had preserved it from the immorality that tainted the movement in some foreign countries.[1] Nevertheless, on further reflection we become aware of a survival of Puritanism —certainly one of which Price Hughes never thought—at work in these defiances of traditional morality. These bold young girls flung themselves into free love not so much at the urge of sexual passion as to perform a duty, to prove to the world and to themselves that they had learned the lessons of Shaw and Wells. They wrestled with the reluctance of blushing young men until they bent them to their cold determination. 'I've had a biological training,' declared Ann Veronica. 'I'm a hard young woman.'[2]

It is not without hesitation that I approach such a difficult subject. How deep did this movement for the emancipation of women go, and what in fact did it signify?

There was an industrial proletariat where the morals of the young people were very free and custom simply required a young man to marry the girl whom he had made pregnant. And there was a rural proletariat where it even allowed young men to enter into trial unions. They did not marry until they were certain the

[1] *Life of Hugh Price Hughes* by his daughter, pp. 254–5.
[2] *Ann Veronica*, chap. xiv. Cf. John Stuart Mill, *On the Subjection of Women*, p. 123: 'An Oriental thinks that women are by nature peculiarly voluptuous: see the violent abuse of them on this ground in Hindoo writings. An Englishman usually thinks that they are by nature cold.'

girl was not barren. Once married the stern law of poverty and labour sufficed to compel husband and wife to fidelity. And there was an aristocracy, an aristocracy of birth and an aristocracy of wealth—where leisure engenders laxity and laxity inconstancy, in which men and women become accustomed to live above the level of ordinary morals and enjoy themselves on the produce of other people's morality. It was only in the middle class—whose boundaries above and below were not easy to draw but whose character was very definite—in which those habits prevailed of self-imposed discipline and voluntary obedience to the law of work and the law of marital fidelity which are the essence of morality. But the feature of the feminist revolt of the early twentieth century which seemed so disquieting was that it arose in this very middle class which, it appeared, was beginning to doubt itself. In England more than in any other country the middle class had succeeded in imposing its culture upon society and exacting from the classes above and below it at least an outward respect for its moral prejudices. Now England was ceasing to be middle class.

If, however, we view the situation from another angle and consider the relations between the sexes without respect to class we may perhaps be disposed to adopt a different interpretation of the change which was in process while fully admitting its far-reaching character. To maintain that the woman differs from the man is not to maintain that she is his inferior. It means that she is different and that her distinctive qualities though of equal or, if you will, higher social value than his give her activities a different direction. It is a striking and a significant fact that in all the commercial or administrative careers now being opened to women the latter were content to occupy subordinate positions. In the government departments all the higher positions carrying with them authority remained closed to women. And their salaries remained lower than men's.[1] In countless instances a rule was in force that a woman must leave her post on marriage and return to the home.[2] Was

[1] See on this point the unsuccessful efforts made in 1872 by Miss Davies and Mrs. Garrett Anderson. (Ray Strachey, *The Cause*, p. 227) and the criticisms of the anti-feminist, Sir Almroth Wright, in a letter to *The Times* (March 1912). See also on the eve of the War the debates at the annual conference of the National Union of Teachers, April 14, 1914. A motion brought forward by women demanding equal salaries was rejected by a majority of 58,483 to 11,017 votes.

[2] See for instances the debates at meetings of the London County Council on April 8, and July 28, 1914. Margaret Wynne Nevinson can still write in 1923: 'We have had many examples lately of how municipal authorities hamper and restrict married women in their work; a woman doctor was lately dismissed in a London borough for the crime of mar-

this simply a survival from the period when man ruled over woman and, the period of transition once passed, would a system soon exist which made no differentiation between the sexes? We cannot forget the admission implied in the complaint made by an uncompromising feminist in 1913 that, in the world of business, women 'are not sufficiently ambitious', and that 'they seem too often content with the poorly-paid routine posts and too little inclined to venture anything on their own account'.[1] The question forces itself upon us whether the two sexes are not so distinguished by the law of their natures that the man is prone to command, the woman to self devotion, so that when a man claims rights it is to increase his power, when a woman claims them it is on the contrary to have further opportunity of service. We cannot fail to be struck by the large number of women who at the very moment when they came boldly into the open to urge their claims professed conservative political opinions. The others very seldom professed themselves Liberals but went straight to the Socialist camp. Was this the sign of a passionate nature which loves extremes? It would seem on the contrary that they were attracted by Socialism not as a more revolutionary form of Liberalism, a movement for complete emancipation, but because they saw it as in many respects a reaction against the Liberalism which had originally demanded the emancipation of women. Its appeal was its policy of a grandmotherly legislation which did not shrink from interference with every detail of private life to ensure the welfare of the weak and which treated society as a magnified home.[2] We are therefore compelled to ask how far the women's

riage; and Education Committees have always discouraged and in some places forbidden women to continue teaching after marriage though many experts maintain that women who are mothers have more sympathy and skill in the management of small children than the single' (*The Legal Wrongs of Married Women*, p. 6). And in 1926 the custom was formally sanctioned by a regulation of the London County Council (Standing Order 395). For the problem of married women's labour as it presents itself in private business see Clémentine Black's interesting study, *Married Women's Work. Being the Report of an Inquiry undertaken by the Women's Industrial Council*, 1915.

[1] Mrs. W. L. Courtney, 'New Types of Subordinate Women Brain-Workers' (*New Statesman*, November 1, 1913, *Special Supplement*, p. xix).

[2] This was one of the reasons for which Herbert Spencer, the thorough-going opponent of Socialism, was equally hostile to woman suffrage. 'It would aid and stimulate all parts of State administration, the great mass of which are necessarily antagonistic to personal freedom. Men in their political actions are far too much swayed by proximate evils and benefits; and women would be thus swayed far more. Given some kind of social suffering to be cured or some boon to be got, and only the quite exceptional woman would be able to appreciate detrimental reactions that would be entailed by legislative action. Political foresight of this kind, uncommon enough in men, is extremely rare in women' (Letter to

revolt must be interpreted as an attempt to achieve equality with men or on the contrary as an attempt to reform society according to the ideal of their sex, to make themselves masculine or society feminine. This doubt must be borne in mind when we study, as we now must, the last of the feminist claims—the right to vote and be elected to Parliament, and to be admitted to executive office—the claim which may truly be said to have absorbed the entire energies of the feminists of both sexes during the years immediately preceding the War. Whatever the purpose, libertarian or conservative, which in the last resort inspired these

John Stuart Mill, August 9, 1867). Mrs. Ramsay MacDonald, one of the pioneers of British neo-Socialism, considered the essential function of Socialism to be the protection of the home. J. Ramsay MacDonald writes (*Margaret Ethel MacDonald*, p. 233): 'She once defined Socialism as "The State of Homes"' and he himself stated in 1908: 'Socialism is essential to family life . . . the idea of divorce is foreign to the Socialist state' (Haslemere, May 11, 1908; *Labour Leader*, May 15, 1908). Cf. the interesting biological and sociological observations presented by Walter Heape in a book entitled *Sex Antagonism*, 1913. According to him the male sex is essentially individualistic, whereas the female sex represents the subordination of the individual to the species. The feminists protested against these statements. But often they unintentionally confirmed them. See Beatrice Webb, *My Apprenticeship*, p. 276: 'It is no use shifting one's eyes from the facts that there is an increasing number of women to whom a matrimonial career is shut and who seek a masculine reward for masculine qualities. . . . I think these strong women have a great future before them in the solution of social questions. They are not just inferior men; they may have masculine faculty, but they have the woman's temperament and the stronger they are the more distinctly feminine they are in this.' You may perhaps reply that Mrs. Webb has never been more than a very moderate feminist and was not a feminist at all when she wrote these lines in November 1885. Consider then the admission implied in an article by Lady Betty Balfour, indeed in its very title, 'Motherhood and the State' (*New Statesman*, November 1, 1913, p. xii) 'In the working of the modern state there is more of [this] spirit of motherhood than has probably ever been exhibited before throughout the historic ages. . . . It is significant of the new spirit of social service that the undergraduates at the Universities now discuss practical, social, and economic problems where formerly they would have discussed theology or literature. Symptoms of this spirit are yearly more apparent in our national legislation and in the subjects discussed at international gatherings . . . symptoms of the same thing, the awakening of a spirit of motherhood in the State.' Cf. the anonymous article entitled 'Women in Industry. Character and Organization,' *The Times*, April 29, 1913: '. . . The women who are the outstanding figures in the Labour movement prefer Socialism and probably the ablest of the younger generation whom they have trained have strong Socialistic leanings; but their socialism is assuredly not of a revolutionary type. *It might almost be said to be domestic.*' Lucien Romier (*Promotion de la Femme*, 1930, p. 60) explains the success of the feminist movement in English-speaking countries by the fact that there women differ less from men than elsewhere, though the men are more feminine, not the women more masculine. 'By nature women dislike the abstract, speculative analysis, the thrust and parry of logical argument, the criticism which questions everything before it attempts to construct, all of which are native characteristics of the Mediterranean race and opposed to the Nordic mentality. You will bore the average Englishman and a woman of any country if you speak of the ideal constitution of a State, but the same topic will arouse the passionate interest of a docker at the Piræus, a grocer of Toulouse, and a professor of Salamanca. Without denying the historical effects of chance, we shall perceive that the supremacy at present enjoyed by the Anglo-Saxon and Nordic peoples over the Mediterranean and Oriental races represents in the last resort the triumph of this feminine type of mentality which apprehends and pursues a practical aim without worrying about barren logic.'

women, the methods they employed to attain their object and give their cause the advertisement of scandal were undoubtedly anarchic.[1]

8

Bentham had claimed equality of political rights for both sexes but his disciple James Mill had parted company with him on this point and the Chartists after preliminary hesitations finally decided against his programme. They were content with asking for the universal suffrage of men, manhood suffrage. When however John Stuart Mill in his *Representative Government* and *Subjection of Women* returned to Bentham's doctrine the time seemed at last to have arrived for it to bear fruit. More even than these two books the important speech Mill delivered in the House of Commons pleading that woman suffrage should be introduced into the Reform Bill passed that year forced the matter upon the attention of the Press and public.[2] The amendment was of course rejected but Mill and his friends convinced themselves that the reform would be effected before many years had passed and would precede and facilitate all the other reforms—the grant to married women of the right to own property, the abolition of State-regulated prostitution to which the efforts of the feminists were directed at the time.[3] As we know, the exact contrary hap-

[1] For the strictly political emancipation of women see *History of Women Suffrage* in 6 volumes (vol. i, *1848–1861*, 1881; vol. ii, *1861–1876*, 1887; vol. iii, *1876–1885*, 1887; vol. iv, *1885–1900*, 1902; vols. v and vi, *1900–1920*, 1922). The first three volumes were written by Elizabeth Lady Stanton, Susan B. Anthony and Mathilda Joslyn Gap, the fourth by Susan B. Anthony and Ida Husted Harper, the fifth and sixth by Ida Husted Harper. It is a monumental American compilation chiefly concerned with the United States, containing chapters which deal with England and the British Colonies. A. E. Metcalfe, *Women's Effort. A Chronicle of British Women's Fifty Years' Struggle for Citizenship (1865–1914) with an Introduction by Lawrence Housman*, 1917. Margaret Wynne Nevinson, *Five Years' Struggle for Freedom. A History of the Suffrage Movement from 1908 to 1912*, 1913. See further the work already mentioned by Ray Strachey, *The Cause, passim* and for the 'suffragette' movement the works quoted later in a note to p. 307.
[2] H. of C., May 20, 1867 (*Parliamentary Debates*, 3rd Series, vol. clxxxvii, pp. 817 sqq.). For Mill's intervention see the remarks of the *Annual Register* for the year, p. 72: 'The next Amendment was of rather a singular character; it was moved by Mr. J. S. Mill, the object being to enable women to vote. The discussion assumed a somewhat jocular character; but the proposition was advocated with serious earnestness by Mr. Mill.'
[3] John Stuart Mill to Florence Nightingale, December 31, 1867: '. . . What, however, constitutes an even more pressing and practical reason for endeavouring to obtain the political enfranchisement of women, instead of endeavouring to sweep away any or all of their social grievances, is, that I believe it will be positively easier to attain this reform than to attain any single one of all the others, all of which must inevitably follow from it. To prefer to sweep away any of these others first, is as though we were to prefer to cut

pened. Whereas these reforms were extorted by the action outside Parliament of women who had no vote, the question of their
political rights continued to hang fire.

Between Mill's death and the year 1906 the House of Commons
had voted on four occasions in favour of woman suffrage. But in
every instance it had been simply a declaration of principle and
the majority, always a mixed majority of Liberals and Conservatives, were perfectly well aware that no Cabinet, Liberal or Conservative, would make woman suffrage a government measure.
At first sight it surprises us to find such a persistent opposition to
the women's claim, to which the latter would reply by a fanaticism
equal to their opponents' obstinacy. To allow women to become
professors and doctors, to invade the offices of lawyers and men
of business was nothing less than to revolutionize their life and in
consequence the state of society as a whole. But would the social
order be greatly perturbed if every six years old maids, young
girls, even married women, silently dropped their vote in the
ballot box? Did not husbands allow their wives to take an active
part in their electoral campaigns? Had not women been permitted
ever since 1834 to vote for the Boards of Guardians who administered the Poor Law? Had they not possessed since 1869 the municipal vote and since 1870 the power to elect and be elected to the
School Boards? In 1888 they had obtained the right to vote for
the new County Councils. And had not the Local Government
Act of 1894 when it set up district and parish councils granted
women the right not only to vote for these bodies but to sit on
them and in addition to sit on the Boards of Guardians?[1] Never-

---

away branch after branch: giving more labour to each branch than we need do to the
trunk of the tree.' (*The Letters of John Stuart Mill*, vol. ii, pp. 102–3.) To Sir Charles Dilke,
May 28, 1870: 'I am in great spirits about our prospects and think we are almost within
as many years of victory as I formerly thought of decades' (ibid., vol. ii, p. 254).

[1] The following is an attempt to summarize the extremely confused and illogical
English legislation in respect of women's civic rights as it existed at the end of the nineteenth century. The *Poor Law Amendment Act* of 1834 (4 & 5 Will. IV, Cap. 76 S. 34) gave
the right to vote for the boards of guardians which it set up to the ratepayers. But among
these ratepayers were women and they made use of the right attached to their payment of
rates. On the other hand, the Act of 1835 on 'municipal corporations' (5 & 6 Will. IV,
Cap. 76 sec. 9) reserved the right to vote to 'every male person of full age' who fulfilled
certain conditions. It was only in 1869 (32 & 33 Vict., Cap. 55: An Act to shorten the
Time of Residence required as a Qualification for the Municipal Franchise and to make
provision for other purposes, sec. 9) that the 'feminists' of the period secured an amendment providing that all the words in the Act 'implying the male sex' should be regarded
as applicable to women 'in so far as concerns the right to vote'. The following year when
the *Education Act* of 1870 (33 & 34 Vict., Cap. 75 sec. 29) set up to administer the new law
school boards very similar in constitution to the boards of guardians set up by the Poor

theless there must have been a deep-seated reason for this stubborn opposition which was by no means confined to England. And in all probability it was this.

There is one right which women have never claimed in the West,[1] to serve in the army as privates or officers.[2] But from time immemorial the performance of political functions has been associated with the performance of military. It is on those who defend the country that the office of governing it devolves. It was no doubt this military conception of government which consciously or unconsciously inspired the opposition of public opinion to the political claims of feminism when it became increasingly tolerant of the rest. Certainly women might have a share in dealing with

Law of 1834 the Statute was deliberately drafted, as the Government declared (H. of C., June 16, 1870; *Parliamentary Debates*, 3rd Series, vol. ccii, p. 259) in such terms as to enable women to vote for the new boards and be elected to them. Could it be concluded from this that the Act of 1869 which gave women the right to vote for municipal councillors also permitted their election? In fact, no women made the experiment and when an important consolidating Act was passed in 1882 dealing with the municipal councils (45 & 46 Vict., Cap. 50) a clause in the Statute declared in the very terms of the Act of 1869, that a woman was put on an equal footing with a man 'so far as the right to vote' is concerned and for the rest kept silence. When, therefore, the *Local Government Act* (51 & 52 Vict., Cap. 41) which set up the County Councils was passed in 1888 and two women were elected to the London County Council the courts pronounced the election illegal on the ground that the Act as regards the conditions of election referred to the Act of 1882 which in turn coming after the Act of 1869 must be regarded as excluding women from the right to be elected. (Beresford-Hope v. Lady Sandhurst, Supreme Court of Judicature, Queen's Bench Division, March 18, April 14, 1889; Court of Appeal, May 8, 15, 16, 1889.) It was in fact expressly laid down the same year by the *Local Government (Scotland) Act*, 1889 (52 & 53 Vict., Cap. 50 sec. 9) that no woman could be elected a county councillor. We may add that in 1894 the feminists won an important victory when the *Local Government Act* of that year (56 & 57 Vict., Cap. 73) gave both sexes an equal right to vote for the parish councils and boards of guardians, and be elected to them and provided that marriage should not deprive a woman of the civic rights she had hitherto enjoyed. But very little progress in this direction was made during the years which followed. If the *Poor Law Guardians (Ireland) (Women) Act* of 1896 (58 & 59 Vict., Cap. 5) gave the women the same right to be elected to the Boards of Guardians as they already possessed in England and the *Local Government (Ireland) Act* of 1898 (61 & 62 Vict., Cap. 37) which set up County Councils in Ireland gave women as in England the right to vote but not to be elected, women were not entitled to sit on the Borough Councils set up in London by the *London Government Act* of 1899 (62 & 63 Vict., Cap. 14) though they had always possessed the right to sit on the vestries which the Act abolished and the *Education Act* of 1902 (2 Edw. 7, Cap. 42) by abolishing the school boards on which a large number of women had seats and transferring their functions to the County Councils for which women were ineligible constituted in this respect a serious setback to the cause of feminism.

[1] Mrs. Pember Reeves certainly writes as follows (*New Statesman*, November 1, 1913, *Special Supplement*, p. xxiv): 'To say with seriousness that women should be eligible for positions in the army . . . provokes both horror and ridicule. But that does not prevent the statement being true.' But see how she justifies her assertion. She continues: 'Hundreds of women . . . would make able officials in the commissariat and other departments of the army and the navy. Florence Nightingale revolutionized certain aspects of the British army.' Evidently what Mrs. Pember Reeves is claiming for women is access to the nonmilitary departments of the army.

[2] Written 1932, Editor's note.

questions of poor relief, education, and the provision and maintenance of roads. These were domestic questions. And when the women who opposed female suffrage founded an anti-suffragist league of which Mrs. Humphry Ward was President they were careful to state expressly that all these problems are within the competence of women. But on the other hand these municipal elections had little interest for the public. Only a small minority of the voters took the trouble to record their votes. But it was the great consultations of the people which were milestones in the history of the nation. If more insistently every year women were pressing their claim to share in these it was not simply to defend the distinctive interests of their sex. They had won many victories by other means and the trade unionists were discovering that to secure the immediate satisfaction of their demands the strike was a more powerful weapon than the ballot box. What women claimed was the right to perform the highest duty of citizenship in the interest of the entire community.

9

After the period of successful agitation which had marked the years when Gladstone and Disraeli guided the destinies of the nation, the close of the nineteenth century had marked a halt in the progress of feminism as in that of other democratic ideas. But when a Liberal revival followed the Boer War the question of the political emancipation of women, as we should expect, came again to the forefront. In 1904 a motion in the House of Commons in favour of women's suffrage was passed by a majority of 114, the largest it had yet obtained.[1] Its champions could point out that on this point England now lagged behind the rest of the English-speaking world. New Zealand had possessed women suffrage since 1893, South Australia since 1894, Western Australia since 1899, New South Wales since 1902, the Australian Commonwealth from its foundation that very year. Tasmania adopted it in 1903 and Queensland would adopt it in 1905. In the United States of America four Western States had admitted women to the suffrage, Wyoming in 1869, Colorado in 1893, Utah in 1895,

[1] H. of C., March 16, 1904. Sir Charles Maclaren's motion (*Parliamentary Debates*, 4th Series, vol. cxxxi, pp. 1331 sqq.).

Idaho in 1896, and its extension to the entire country seemed inevitable.[1] And in Europe itself, almost at England's door, in 1901 two years after the extension of the suffrage to all male citizens, Norway had granted the franchise to about half the women above twenty-five years of age.[2] The moment was near when the Liberal party would be once more in office. It was professedly the party of reform. Every champion of reform believed himself to have a claim upon it. Feminist propaganda redoubled and concentrated its efforts on securing political rights for women.

There was an old society of women 'suffragists' founded under the auspices of Mill in 1867. In that year the London National Society for Women's Suffrage was formed which, working in close co-operation with a number of similar societies in the provinces, employed all the methods of legal propaganda current in England and brought peaceful pressure to bear on Members of Parliament. In 1888 it had been embarrassed by an attempt of its Liberal members to introduce their party organizations into the society and gradually to annex it to the Liberal party. The attempt gave rise to quarrels and a split which weakened the Society. But about the beginning of the new century the two rival groups became reconciled and united to form the National Union of Women's Suffrage Societies. How long would it be before the Union's patient methods were victorious? Meanwhile its members abandoned themselves to the pleasure which English people enjoy so keenly of founding groups, gathering recruits—they began to come in in large numbers—drawing up rules, electing presidents, secretaries, and treasurers, and organizing public meetings in the customary style.[3] But side by side with the National Union a new society came into existence of a very different

[1] For the progress of women suffrage in the United States about this period see Frank Foxcroft 'Women Suffrage in the United States of America' (*Nineteenth Century*, November 1909, vol. lvi, pp. 833 sqq.) who however points out that since 1898 the movement seemed to have come to a sudden halt owing to the obvious indifference of the women.

[2] Marie Blehr Schlytter, 'The Women's Movement in Norway' (*New Statesman*, February 7, 1914, pp. 554–6).

[3] Ray Strachey, *The Cause*, p. 309: 'Within a year or two they had evolved a technique of democracy inside their own ranks *which became in itself an absorbing interest.*' Cf. ibid., p. 105. The writer is speaking of the formation of the first suffragist committee in 1867: 'For a fortnight the little committee worked, delighted with the distinguished and respectable signatures which came in and *enjoying themselves to the full*'; and a little later (pp. 118–119), speaking of the first public meetings held by the women: '*Delightful* as the actual occasion was . . . the new style of meeting did not escape unfriendly comment. . . . It was undoubtedly very hard work for those first speakers and very agitating work too. . . On the other hand it must have been much more *entertaining* than public meetings have since become, *more full of novelty and excitement and of the sense of real adventure*.'

character, founded in 1903, the Women's Social and Political Union. Its founders, Mrs. Pankhurst and her daughter Christabel, women of a middle-class family which for years had devoted itself body and soul to Socialist propaganda, would appear to have desired at first to give the new feminist organization a distinctively Socialist character. They would have liked to make it the feminine section of the Labour Representation Committee which was being formed at the time. Then the political beliefs of its foundresses changed. By degrees they transferred their allegiance from Socialism to the Conservative party. It was its violent methods which distinguished the Women's Social and Political Union from the National Union. And as the years passed these methods dictated an original form of constitution. The Union possessed no written constitution, no rule which might hamper its leaders' decisions. Anyone willing to subscribe, subscribed as much as he wished and the zealots who led the organization made whatever use of the funds they pleased.[1] The 'suffragettes' as the militants of the new movement[2] soon came to be called to distinguish them from the 'suffragists' of the old National Union had no control over the central organization whose orders they blindly obeyed.

In 1897 in the course of the debates in the House of Commons on a feminist Bill introduced that year, a member speaking in support of the Bill had pointed out the obstacles with which women were faced when they attempted to urge their claims. 'It is contrary', he said, 'to the nature of women to take part in those formidable demonstrations which from time to time mark the activity of political enthusiasm among men.'[3] Mrs. Pankhurst was to prove his psychology false by showing that women could organize demonstrations which, if they were of a different charac-

[1] For this new agitation see E. Sylvia Pankhurst, *The Suffragette. The History of the Women's Militant Suffrage Movement, 1905–1910*, 1911 and especially her excellent work, far more thorough in its treatment than the former, *The Suffragette Movement. An Intimate Account of Persons and Ideals*, 1931. Also Annie Kenney's entertaining *Memoirs of a Militant*, 1924.

[2] The word makes its appearance between inverted commas in the *Daily Mail* at the beginning of 1906 (January 10, February 12) and it is to this paper that Sylvia Pankhurst ascribes its invention. (*The Suffragette*, p. 62 n.) Two years later it is in current use. See A. L. Lowell, *The Government of England*, vol. i, p. 216; (The preface is dated April 1908): 'Many women are agitating for it very vigorously, and the most enthusiastic of them have sought martyrdom by refusing to pay taxes, by creating a disturbance in the ladies' gallery of the House of Commons, and by getting arrested for speech-making in Palace Yard. They are known as Suffragettes.'

[3] H. of C., February 3, 1897, Atherley-Jones' speech (*Parliamentary Debates*, 4th Series, vol. xlv, p. 1182).

ter from the riots in which the male sex had indulged in the past, were no less formidable. On October 13, 1905, Sir Edward Grey took the chair at a great Liberal meeting held in the Free Trade Hall, Manchester. Everyone knew that a general election was imminent and that the Liberal party must decide upon its programme. A number of women, members of the Social and Political Union, waving small flags which bore the words Votes for Women and interrupting at every turn the speech of the principal speaker, succeeded in seriously holding up the meeting until at last they were roughly ejected, taken in charge by the police, and finally sentenced to a fine and imprisonment if it were not paid. They chose imprisonment. They were Christabel Pankhurst, Mrs. Pankhurst's daughter, and Annie Kenney, a young Lancashire mill girl whom the Pankhursts had discovered, converted, and adopted. At last the cause possessed its martyrs.

The militants continued their campaign throughout the entire Election. After its victory what would the Liberal Cabinet do? We must examine the difficulties which confronted them, if they wished to give the feminists any satisfaction.

10

The Government might adopt the plan put forward by Mill in 1867, and propose to give women the vote on the same terms as men possessed it under the existing franchise. This course presented the advantage that the reform would be extremely moderate. Only a small number of women would receive the vote, spinsters, widows, and married women who carried on some species of trade. 500,000 women it was estimated would be enfranchised,[1] as against a male electorate of over 7,000,000. And it would be extremely undemocratic. Almost all the new women voters would belong to the wealthier classes, and only a handful of working women would obtain the vote. Mill was prepared to accept this result. 'If only one woman in 20,000 used the suffrage, to be declared capable of it would be a boon to all women. Even that theoretical enfranchisement would remove a weight from the expansion of their faculties, the real mischief of which is much

[1] H. of C., February 3, 1897. Faithfull Begg's speech (*Parliamentary Debates*, 4th Series, vol. xlv, p. 117).

greater than the apparent.'[1] But it was not acceptable to all the Liberal politicians. In the case of the boards of guardians, the school boards, and the county, district, and borough councils a reform on these lines might be tolerable. We have seen how little interest the country took in these elections. But it would be dangerous to extend it to parliamentary elections and when an important national decision was at stake to grant the vote to a minority of women suspected of Conservative sympathies. And the danger would be the greater because a considerable section of the Unionist opposition under the guidance of its most eminent leaders had declared in favour of women suffrage. The Liberal members of the House of Commons were indeed the readier to vote in favour of the principle because they knew that their leaders were divided on the question and its settlement remote.

Or another method might be chosen and women suffrage incorporated into a Bill effecting a general reform of the franchise. After the reform of 1884 only one more step remained to be taken and England would possess an unqualified system of universal suffrage. Why not enact that every adult Englishman should possess the vote but only a single vote and every Englishwoman as well? But how long must the women wait before such a reform could be effected? If the House of Commons and even the House of Lords was prepared at a stretch to take this final step on the road to universal suffrage by granting the vote to the minority of adult males which was still unenfranchised, it would be a long time before a majority could be found to risk a reform which by establishing universal suffrage for both sexes would more than double the electorate at a single stroke. To link the two questions of universal and women suffrage was, the feminists suspected, nothing more than a device for shelving the second question. In 1907 a motion in favour of women suffrage was, the Speaker reluctantly decided, 'blocked' by a previous motion in favour of adult suffrage for both sexes alike.[2] Had not the latter motion been deliberately introduced to prevent the discussion of the former? When a month earlier the annual congress of the Labour party wished to settle the question of women suffrage by passing a motion in favour of equal adult suffrage the chairman, Keir Hardie, a fanatical feminist, had threatened to resign from the

[1] H. of C., May 20, 1869 (*Parliamentary Debates*, 3rd Series, vol. clxxxvii, p. 824).
[2] H. of C., March 25, 1907 (ibid., 4th Ser., vol. clxxi, pp. 1525–1526).

party rather than associate himself with tactics which in his opinion were intended to postpone the issue.

II

After the Liberal victory at the polls the members of the different groups of women working for the suffrage, the National Union and the Social and Political Union, in spite of the serious difficulties in the way of common action demanded and obtained a joint interview with the new Premier. On May 19 Sir Henry Campbell-Bannerman received the deputation at Downing Street and stated that he was personally in agreement with their claim, which he regarded as based upon 'conclusive and irrefutable' arguments. But he reminded them that on this subject his party and the Cabinet itself were divided and that they would have many difficulties to overcome. He concluded by giving them two pieces of advice: 'to go on pestering', and exercise 'the virtue of patience'. The suffragists followed the second and their patience was in fact put to a severe test. During the first two sessions of the Liberal Government they were obliged to be satisfied with two Acts passed simultaneously which permitted women to sit on County Councils and Borough Councils in England and on County Councils and Town Councils in Scotland.[1] And it was provided that if a woman were elected chairman of a County Council or mayor of a borough she could not exercise the functions of a justice of the peace which, had she been a man, would have been attached automatically to the office. The 'suffragettes' followed Sir Henry's first piece of advice and continued to 'pester'

[1] 7 Edw. 7, Cap. 33: An Act to amend the Law relating to the capacity of women to be elected and act as Members of County or Borough Councils (*Qualification of Women [County and Borough Councils] Act*, 1907). 7 Edw. 7, Cap. 48: An Act to amend the law relating to the capacity of women to be elected and act as Members of County or Town Councils in Scotland (*Qualification of Women County and Town Councils [Scotland] Act*, 1907). The same rights were extended to women in Ireland by 1 & 2 Geo. V, Cap. 35: An Act to enable women to be elected and act as Members of County and Borough Councils in Ireland (*Local Authorities [Ireland] Qualification of Women Act*, 1911). For the real unimportance of this reform see H. of L., May 5, 1914, speech by the Bishop of London: '. . . It is true that women have since 1907 been made eligible for County Councils, but as I have already pointed out, on so narrow a qualification that very few indeed can serve, and the number of women who are now administering our Education Act and giving a service which no one can contest is a valuable one has gone down to hundreds when it used to be thousands' (*Parliamentary Debates*, Lords 1914, 5th Series, vol. xvi, p. 52).

the Liberal statesmen by an unceasing series of demonstrations. And their anger increased when Campbell-Bannerman who was in favour of their cause was succeeded as Prime Minister by an opponent of women suffrage who had hardly entered on his new office when he took an opportunity to state his position. A Women's Enfranchisement Bill had just passed its second reading in the House of Commons.[1] Asquith stated that it would be impossible during the present session to provide the necessary time for its further discussion. The only prospect he held out was that before the dissolution of the Parliament elected in 1906—in other words, within the next four years, the Government would introduce a Bill to reform the male franchise and the supporters of women suffrage would be at liberty to propose whatever amendments they desired to give effect to their views.[2]

The women organized monster processions through the London streets which often mingled with the columns of unemployed. They besieged the Houses of Parliament, the government offices, the Ministers' private houses, lying in wait for prominent politicians, tormenting them with the monotonous repetition of their demands, haunting them with their presence. They never ceased harassing Liberal public meetings until Lloyd George, against whom their persecution was chiefly directed, announced his intention not to speak at meetings from which all women had not been excluded. They rose in the women's gallery of the House of Commons and interrupted the debates, whatever their subject, by screaming at the top of their voices 'Votes for Women'. One day two suffragettes chained themselves to the grille which enclosed the gallery and while they continued to bawl and hold up the debate workmen had to be summoned to remove the grille and the women with it. The women's gallery was then closed until the day not long afterwards when male feminists made the same scenes in the men's gallery which had in turn to be closed. The suffragettes exploited the weakness of their sex, its proneness to hysteria. The men were cowards if they allowed them to behave in this way, cowards if they used force to repress their disorders.

[1] H. of C., February 28, 1908. Stranger's motion (*Parliamentary Debates*, 4th Series, vol. clxxxv, pp. 212 sqq.).

[2] May 20, 1908. Reply to a deputation of 60 Liberal Members of Parliament, supporters of women suffrage also H. of C., May 28, 1908 reply to Alfred Hutton (ibid., vol. clxxxiv, p. 962).

A Public Meetings Bill[1] hastily passed by both Houses in December 1908 which provided special penalties for those who disturbed public meetings completely failed to achieve the purpose which the guardians of order should have kept in view. What they had to avoid as far as possible was the odium of imprisoning the suffragettes. An order was given to the metropolitan police to arrest them but release them before they were brought into court. They then adopted new tactics to force the authorities' hands. Assaults on policemen and breaking windows were typical offences which they committed in cold blood in order to get themselves imprisoned. They were duly imprisoned, went on hunger strike and by their violent struggles made forcible feeding impossible. Ill, almost at death's door, they were released. As soon as they had recovered their health, they committed a new outrage. What could be done with them except send them back to prison? But what purpose did it serve? A feminist of noble family, Lady Constance Lytton, was imprisoned but immediately sent to the infirmary on account of her ill health and soon released. She persuaded herself that she owed this leniency to her social position. She got herself arrested a second time under a false name and was subjected to the ordinary treatment, refused all nourishment and fell so seriously ill that though released she never recovered her health. A new chapter had opened in the history of feminism and its martyrs.

12

The picture we drew of the struggle between the two parties between 1909 and 1911 on the double question of Lloyd George's Budget and the restriction of the rights of the House of Lords was not therefore complete. We must also picture the Liberal party tormented without respite under the mocking gaze of their Unionist opponents by a swarm of buzzing and stinging gnats. The persecution was interrupted only by a brief truce of six months when on the accession of George V all parties agreed to allow the new monarch to make his first essays in sovereignty amidst a universal peace. A group of Members of Parliament formed a

[1] 8 Edw. 7, Cap. 66: An Act to prevent Disturbances of Public Meetings (*Public Meetings Act*, 1908). It had been introduced in the Commons by Lord Robert Cecil (H. of C., December 17, 19, 1908; *Parliamentary Debates*, 4th Series, vol. cxcviii, pp. 2168 sqq., 2328 sqq.).

committee which entitled itself the Conciliation Committee to draw up a Women's Enfranchisement Bill sufficiently moderate to reassure the Unionist supporters of women suffrage and sufficiently comprehensive to overcome the opposition of those Liberals who considered the Suffrage Bills hitherto presented too undemocratic. Stanger's Bill, which had been debated in the House of Commons in 1908, was open to the objection that it multiplied the grounds qualifying for a vote and therefore aggravated the abuse of the plural vote to the profit of the wealthy classes: as a property owner, lodger, university graduate, the rich woman could by arrangement with her husband secure two or three additional votes for the family. Moreover, the Bill permitted a married woman to claim a distinct vote when the rent paid for the domicile exceeded £20, another privilege for the wealthy. The Conciliation Bill introduced in June 1910 by a Labour member, Shackleton, was not open to these objections.

The franchise it proposed to give women would be based not on the complicated qualifications hitherto prescribed but simply on 'occupation' of a domicile. All women who were householders would possess the vote, all that is to say, who occupied a house or part of a house, even if it were only a single room, provided it was in their own name, or occupied a shop or office whose rental was not less than £10. Not many however would come under the latter category. Not more than 5 per cent, Shackleton estimated. In this way the danger, real or imaginary, on which the Liberals harped, of artificially multiplying votes to the benefit of the rich, would be avoided. Shackleton moreover considered that the number of women who would benefit by a measure of this description had been under-estimated. They would amount he maintained to about a million and he claimed that by methodical investigations it had been proved that 75 to 80 per cent of the women enfranchised would belong to the working class.[1]

The Bill passed its second reading on July 12 by 299 to 190 votes. Asquith had spoken against it, also Lloyd George and Churchill. The latter were not indeed intransigent opponents of women suffrage. At bottom Lloyd George was in favour of the reform. But they had been exasperated by the attacks of the suffragettes.

[1] H. of C., June 14, 1910. Shackleton's motion, and the passage of the first reading of the Bill. July 11–12 the Bill passes its second reading (*Parliamentary Debates*, Commons 1911 5th Series, vol. xvii, pp. 1202 sqq., vol. xiv, pp. 41 sqq.). For the character of the Bill see H. N. Brailsford, *Woman Suffrage. The Conciliation Bill. An Explanation and Defence*, 1910

Lloyd George was the victim of an unremitting persecution. Churchill had been assaulted in the street by a fanatical suffragette armed with a whip. Moreover, Lloyd George's objection was not without foundation. While he was prepared to vote in favour of the principle of women suffrage, he wanted the Bill, which he regarded as insufficiently democratic, drawn up in such terms that it could be amended in course of debate and completed by clauses extending the franchise to all classes of men.[1] This was done by the Second Conciliation Bill introduced in the Commons on May 5, 1911, by Sir George Kemp, which passed its second reading by 255 to 88 votes. What would happen during the session of 1912? Lloyd George, speaking apparently in the name of the Government, promised the necessary time to debate the clauses and pass the third reading of the Bill. Asquith did not dissent but replying on November 9 to a deputation which waited on him to plead the cause of universal suffrage he promised a Bill to reform the franchise on the lines they desired into which the supporters of women suffrage would be allowed but not encouraged by the Government to introduce any amendments they could get the House to accept.

On March 28, 1912, the Conciliation Bill came up once more in the Commons. In the previous session it had been passed by a majority of 167. It was now defeated by a majority of fourteen, 222 to 208 votes. Is this change of front on the part of the majority to be explained by the exasperation aroused by the suffragettes' extravagant behaviour? Or was it rather due to the pressure which Asquith and his friends brought to bear on certain members of the Liberal majority, the Irish Nationalists in particular, to vote against the Bill or abstain from voting? In any case the way was now free for Asquith to introduce his general measure of franchise reform into which, indeed, a feminist amendment might, he said, be introduced though he was counting on the House of Commons not to stultify itself and by going back on its decision of March 28 commit what he termed a 'national mistake'. The Government's Franchise Bill which passed its second reading on July 12 by 290 to 218 votes came up for its third reading on January 24, 1913, at the end of an interminable session whose work, held up by the Irish question which now occupied the

[1] H. of C., July 12, 1910 (*Parliamentary Debates*, Commons 1910, 5th Series, vol. xix, p. 305).

front of the stage, had not been completed by December 31. The Government did not indeed propose to introduce universal suffrage. But by suppressing the plural vote and the representation of the universities, and by a radical alteration of the method by which the register was compiled, the Bill practically amounted to a universal suffrage Bill. It would moreover confer a more or less extensive franchise on women, if one or other of four amendments accepted by the Prime Minister were embodied in it. But at this juncture a dramatic blow fell. Some days before the debate opened Bonar Law, the Leader of the Opposition, had asked the Speaker, referring to a precedent of Parliamentary procedure, whether such a radical alteration of the Bill as amendments of this kind would involve was not unconstitutional. He had requested a few days in which 'to consider the question'.[1] On the 27th he decided in favour of Bonar Law's objection and refused to allow any of the amendments to be discussed. Asquith was obliged to drop the Bill. On the other hand, he could not bring it forward again with one of the feminist amendments embodied in the original text, for he himself and many others of his Cabinet and party were hostile to them. All he could do was to promise that if a Bill on similar lines to that which Sir George Kemp had introduced in May 1912 were again brought forward, the Government without sponsoring it would set apart as much time for its discussion as though it were a Government Bill. This was to return to the promise made by Lloyd George in 1911 which had resulted in the adverse vote of March 28, 1912. Always the same vicious circle.

13

Indignation in the feminist camp was at its height. For several years the moderates of the National Union had given their confidence to Asquith and his party. They now broke with the Liberals and decided to support the Labour party, the only one of the three which had made women suffrage a part of its official programme.

---

[1] H. of C., January 23, 1913 (*Parliamentary Debates*, Commons 1913, 5th Series, vol. xlvii, pp. 643 sqq.). Lord Ullswater's account (*A Speaker's Commentaries*, vol. i, pp. 136–7) is not quite accurate in as much as he gives us to understand that on the 22nd and 25th everything took place in private conversations between Bonar Law, Asquith and himself. The Tories had already raised the difficulty a year earlier but had admitted a few days later that it could be overcome. (E. Sylvia Pankhurst, *The Suffragette Movement*, p. 371.)

The leaders of the party accepted their support without enthusiasm, for it condemned the party to an attitude of uncompromising hostility to the Liberals, which it had no desire to adopt. But the women had the money the party lacked and so profitable an alliance could not be refused. Throughout the country at by-elections Labour candidates came forward who secured the defeat of the Liberal candidate either to their own advantage or the advantage of the Conservative candidate. And the suffragettes who fought under the Pankhursts' banner redoubled the number and violence of their outrages.

Their agitation assumed new forms. Banished from the gallery of the House of Commons they turned their persecution against a more highly placed victim. In the theatre, at church, even at Buckingham Palace the King was roughly addressed by unknown women who rose to denounce him as 'Czar' and 'torturer'. Corrosives were placed in letter boxes to destroy the correspondence. Pictures were defaced in Museums. Buildings were set on fire whether they belonged to notorious opponents of feminism or were simply adjacent to a house where a Liberal meeting was being held. Shots were fired at trains. Then the suffragettes attacked churches, in which they placed bombs which did considerable damage. Two old country churches were burnt down.

Friends of law and order consoled themselves by the reflection that these extremists were injuring the cause they professed to serve. In 1913 and 1914 the only result achieved by the feminist agitation seemed to have been to torpedo the Government's Bill to extend the franchise. The Cabinet resigned itself to introducing, as in 1907, a Bill to abolish the plural vote which, twice thrown out by the House of Lords, was waiting for the session of 1915 to receive the royal assent without passing the Upper House. Meanwhile a Bill in favour of women suffrage was rejected by the Lords in 1914 after debates interesting indeed, but as academic as they could have been in the lifetime of Campbell-Bannerman.[1] Moreover, the Conservatives had the satisfaction of observing that the violent methods employed by the Social and Political Union were alarming an increasing number of its members. There had been a split in 1908 when Mrs. Despard founded a separate group, the Women's Freedom League. A more serious split

[1] H. of L., May 5, 6, 1914 (*Parliamentary Debates*, Lords 1914, 5th Series, vol. xvi, pp. 7 sqq., 66 sqq.).

occurred when in 1912 Mr. and Mrs. Pethick Lawrence, a couple of feminists with Socialist sympathies, retired from the Union, withdrawing their paper, *The Common Cause*, from the influence of the extremists. And there was a further split in 1914 when Sylvia Pankhurst, the founder of the East End federation, broke with her mother and Christabel. But it could not be denied that those who remained were, like Gideon's soldiers, though fewer, more formidable.

What could be done? The Government hastily passed in April 1913 an Act which empowered the courts to order the discharge from prison of a woman whose health was endangered as the result of a hunger strike, subject to her reimprisonment without further trial when her health had been restored.[1] It became known as the cat and mouse Bill. Its authors hoped that the women after their first experience of prison and the hunger strike would shrink from a second. This was true of some but not of the majority or the more ardent. Mrs. Pankhurst, held responsible, as Chairman of the Social and Political Union, for one of the first cases of feminist incendiarism, had been sentenced to nine years' imprisonment and it was to prove that the sentence was intended to be a reality from which she could not escape by a fortnight's hunger strike that the cat and mouse Bill had been passed. But the only result was that for a whole year the mouse played with the cat rather than the cat with the mouse. Once more what was to be done? Pass a measure making all the subscribers to the Social and Political Union civilly liable for the damage committed? Could anyone believe that the prospect of trials by the hundred would act as a deterrent? Pass a Bill in one clause absolving the prison authorities from all responsibility for the lives of prisoners who refused to take nourishment? Was it certain that any of the prisoners would recoil from sacrificing her life? On Derby Day in 1913 they had seen a suffragette adopt a new form of propaganda by action, throw herself beneath the feet of the horses and die from the wounds received. In the case of Miss Davidson on Derby Day 1913 feminist fanaticism was still confined to voluntary martyrdom. But when the suffragettes placed a bomb in a church, set fire to a house or fired at a train in motion, though

---

[1] 3 Geo. 5, Cap. 4: An Act to provide for the Temporary Discharge of Prisoners whose further detention in prison is undesirable on account of the condition of their health. (*Prisons [Temporary Discharge for Ill Health] Act*, 1913.)

they took care that the church or house was empty, and the train a goods train, they were playing a dangerous game. Who could be certain that some zealot might not soon commit a murder? At the annual congress of the Union of Teachers in April 1914 when it refused to pass a motion in favour of women suffrage Miss Hewitt of East Ham declared amidst uproar that 'the power of tyranny' was 'tempered by assassination'.[1] A painful conflict was in process between British toleration and the fanaticism of the suffragettes. Not to have prevented the latter was a defeat for the former. And now what could be done to avoid further defeats? Yield and grant the franchise to women as though the methods employed by its supporters had been legal? That would be to capitulate to violence, to pay tribute to revolutionary fanaticism. Repel violence by violence. Even if successful would that be a victory? Would it not rather be a defeat, an admission that the Russian not the British methods of government were the right ones? Wait and by employing a minimum of repression attempt to exhaust by patience this strange frenzy, unprecedented in the history of modern England? Was it certain that it would be exhausted? The evil certainly showed no sign of diminution in July 1914. Never had acts of violence and incendiarism been more frequent.

III   THE IRISH REVOLT

I

When the summer of 1914 opened, the threat of a general strike called by the Triple Alliance of the miners', railwaymen's, and transport workers' unions weighed on England. But the alarm felt was due to memory of the disorders which had occurred in 1911. For the moment the labour unrest was certainly less grave than it had been three years before. The suffragist agitation on the contrary was more irritating, more pestering than ever. But if it contributed to the general unrest, and if the changes of which it was apparently the symptom were perhaps the most profound which society was undergoing, these disorders were a source of embarrassment rather than a serious threat to the Government. It was in Ireland that the general anarchy was on the point of

[1] *The Times*, April 17, 1914.

degenerating, had indeed begun to degenerate, into civil war. To understand the origin of the crisis there is no need, as in the case of the feminist agitation, to delve into past history. For this was not an agitation which sprang suddenly upon the world of politics. How many times already had Irish history, while remaining obstinately apart from the current of English, hampered and poisoned the latter? We have already related the course of events to the day when the Liberal Government shortly before Campbell-Bannerman's death had been confronted on the one hand with the defeat of its Irish Council Bill, on the other with the failure at least partial of the attempt made by the late Unionist Government in 1903 to transfer gradually and peaceably the entire soil of Ireland to the native tenants.

During the years which followed, the Nationalist party remained faithful to its policy of alliance with the Liberals, awaiting a favourable opportunity to summon the latter to honour a long standing pledge and grant Home Rule to Ireland. We have told the story of the crisis which followed the rejection of Lloyd George's great Budget by the House of Lords and pointed out that the two General Elections of January and December 1910 had apparently made the Irish masters of the situation. When the session of 1912 opened, the Government was free to pass the Home Rule Bill through the House of Commons by the disciplined combination of Liberals, Labour members, and Nationalists and this once done could defy a House of Lords now rendered powerless. But to understand the details of the crisis which ensued we must discover what authority John Redmond and his party possessed in Ireland at a moment when their influence in the British Parliament was in the ascendant.

The first enemies with whom Redmond had to contend were the moderates led by William O'Brien who had helped Gerald Balfour and after him George Wyndham to pursue, while the Unionists were in office, their policy of 'devolution'. But O'Brien's party had been weakened by the invincible hostility the Ulster Protestants displayed towards the attempts at conciliation made by the Tory Cabinet and still further by the Liberal victory at the Election of 1906. Once more hopes were kindled in Ireland of concessions which would far exceed the offers made by certain English Conservatives and would not stop short of complete autonomy. It was in vain that O'Brien attempted to exploit against Redmond the defeat of the Irish Council Bill and his acquiescence in the failure which had befallen the Land Act of 1903. Instead of accepting with an ill-concealed delight the defeat of a measure which he continued to defend warmly and persisting in its claims for immediate and complete Home Rule the Nationalists, he maintained, should have accepted the Irish Council Bill and in return have demanded that the English taxpayer should provide the funds necessary to bring back into operation the Land Act of 1903. As we have already seen he had been finally compelled to surrender to Redmond. But was the surrender unconditional? The terms of 'reconciliation' contained a clause, the second, which laid down that 'it was the duty of the Nationalist representatives of Ireland, while striving incessantly for Home Rule, to devote themselves earnestly to working for every measure of practical amelioration which it might be possible to obtain for her people from either English party, or from both,' and it could be interpreted as a concession to O'Brien's opportunism. The clause enumerated among the most urgent reforms, a settlement of the University question satisfactory to Catholics, measures to hasten the expropriation of the landlords, and a reduction of taxation. If Redmond and his followers, having torpedoed the Irish Council Bill, failed to obtain satisfaction on any of these points, it would be a proof that their method was the wrong one and O'Brien's more effective.

For the moment the third question did not come before Parliament. As we shall shortly see, its aspect had been completely changed by the passing of the important measures of social reform in 1908 and 1911. But this was not the case with the two former, particularly the University question, and it was a triumph for the reunited Nationalist party, a defeat therefore for O'Brien, when in 1908 the Government introduced a Bill calculated to give final satisfaction both to the Irish Protestants and the Irish Catholics. The question had first been tackled by Bryce, who had submitted it to the examination of a Committee of nine, which by a majority of six to three proposed to incorporate all the existing Irish colleges in a single University. It was a solution unacceptable either to Trinity College, the citadel of Protestantism in Dublin which was not prepared to surrender its independence, or to the Catholic Bishops who wanted a College of their own in the capital on an equal footing with the Protestant. The new Bill which Birrell explained in the House of Commons on March 31, 1908, abolished the 'Royal University' of Ireland, made the Belfast College which had formed part of it hitherto, a separate university, set up a new college in Dublin on an equality with Trinity and completely distinct from it, and incorporated this new college and the colleges of Cork and Galway into a single University. To receive State assistance these two new universities, Dublin and Belfast, must be undenominational. Nor could the State grant be employed to support a building where any form of worship would be carried on or any theological teaching given. But Trinity College was undenominational in theory and in practice Protestant. It was equally certain that the University of Belfast would be Presbyterian and the new Dublin University Catholic, both in the composition of its professorial staff and in the spirit of its teaching. The sole guarantee of religious neutrality contained in the Bill was a provision that the senates of the two universities, during the first few years at least, should be appointed by the Government. And the Government took care to appoint one Catholic among the thirty-five members of the Belfast Senate, seven Protestants among the thirty-six members of the Dublin Senate. The Irish Bishops had the wisdom to accept a compromise which gave them in substance what they wanted. In London Liberals and Unionists agreed in approving the Bill and in a few months the British Parliament rid itself of a problem which for many years had appeared insoluble.

2

The question of the Land Act was tackled at the same time.[1] It was impossible to postpone it any longer. The continuous fall in the value of consols made the Act of 1903 increasingly costly to operate both to the British Treasury and the Irish ratepayer. The Government at first adopted a circuitous route and its attitude appeared to show a determination not to modify but to reinforce the agrarian legislation begun in 1903. A phrase in the King's speech of January 1908, as interpreted by the then Chancellor of the Exchequer, Asquith, promised a measure to expedite the division of the pasture land into small holdings. The Congested Dis-

[1] For a bibliography see Book 1, p. 54 n.

tricts Acts had already dealt with the problem, but they were applicable only within narrow limits and were moreover permissive. The principle of compulsory purchase of the grazing land would be laid down. But almost immediately the Committee appointed to inquire into the working of the Land Act of 1903[1] reported and the report pointed out that the public finances demanded a complete remodelling of its provisions. The Committee proposed in substance that to pay for purchases already made which could not be undone a limited amount of Land Stock should continue to be issued, the landlord whose land was being purchased having the right to be paid in Land Stock at a rate of £92 for every nominal £100. For future purchase it proposed a new type of stock at 3 per cent, and since the 3 per cent was at par, it was hoped to avoid difficulties arising from an eventual depreciation in value. Moreover, to be on the safe side and make further provision against this risk the report recommended that the new shares should never be issued below par, and if it should become impossible to maintain this restriction, the landowner who wanted to sell should have the right to be paid in shares bearing 3 per cent interest on their face value. The bounty payable to the purchaser must also be reduced. This should be effected by establishing a sliding scale by which the cheaper the landlord sold, the higher the bounty he received. On the other hand, the annuities to be paid by the tenant purchaser must be raised from $3\frac{1}{4}$ to $3\frac{5}{8}$ per cent of the cost of purchase. A Bill was accordingly introduced by the Government in November. It contained a number of provisions giving effect to the Committee's recommendations[2] and others besides. The Treasury would be made responsible for the costs hitherto chargeable to the Irish ratepayers in virtue of a clause in the Act of 1903 whose application had caused such discontent. The relief thus given to the ratepayer was estimated at £7,000,000. The Bill further made the Congested Districts Board a body possessed of a legal personality, a 'corporation' invested with more extensive powers[3]

---

[1] *Irish Land Purchase Finance. Report of the Departmental Committee appointed to inquire into Irish Land Purchase Finance in Connection with the provision of Funds required for the Purposes of the Irish Land Act, 1903, February 18, 1908.*

[2] With certain modifications. For example the annuities payable by the purchasers were raised from $3\frac{1}{4}$ to $3\frac{1}{2}$ (not $3\frac{5}{8}$).

[3] For further details of these innovations which became law in 1909 see W. L. Micks, *An Account of the Constitution, Administration and Dissolution of the Congested Districts Board for Ireland from 1891 to 1923*, 1925, pp. 120 sqq.

and gave the Estates Commissioners the right to effect under certain definite conditions a compulsory purchase of land.

In November 1908 it was too late for the Bill to be debated seriously before the end of the autumn session. But it was reintroduced with hardly any alterations at the beginning of the following session. The two clauses which relieved the Irish ratepayer and established the principle of compulsory purchase enabled Redmond to support a measure which proclaimed the partial failure of that Act of 1903 of which he had been a hearty supporter. For John Dillon, who had always been hostile to the Act of 1903, the new Statute was a triumph. By accepting the Bill of 1903 Redmond had surrendered to O'Brien. By accepting the Bill of 1909 he surrendered to Dillon. The Bill passed after debates spread over considerable intervals and never heated.[1] The battle over Lloyd George's Budget had opened, attention was elsewhere. O'Brien however did not resign himself to the failure of a measure which he regarded as in a sense his own work. The Committee's report had scarcely been published when he called a meeting at Dublin of the parliamentary party to demand a mixed conference between representatives of the party and representatives of the landlords at which an attempt would be made to devise, in opposition to the Government's solution, a solution more favourable to Irish interests. Defeated by forty-two votes to fifteen he attempted to do alone what he had failed to do in collaboration with the entire parliamentary group, and called for on August 5, 1908, a large meeting of representatives of the tenants and the landlords, who appointed a joint deputation to lay before the English Government the grievances of those Irishmen who wished to maintain the essential provisions of the Land Act of 1903. The deputation obtained nothing. O'Brien was howled down at a National Convention held in Dublin on Feburary 9, 1909, and feeling himself irretrievably defeated he shortly afterwards resigned his membership of the party and of Parliament. But it was not long before he returned to his favourite strategy of setting up an organization in opposition to the Nationalists and he founded an All for Ireland League to oppose his old foundation, the United Irish League, of which Devlin had taken possession. He found a valuable helper in a leading business man of Dublin,

---

[1] 9 Edw. 7, Cap. 8: An Act to amend the Law relating to the Occupation and Ownership of Land in Ireland and for other purposes relating thereto (*Irish Land Act*, 1909).

W. M. Murphy, who had quarrelled with the Nationalist leaders and had founded in opposition to their *Freeman's Journal*, a rival paper, the *Irish Independent*, which had already become a serious rival to the former. He found another in Tim Healy, an inveterate schismatic, who after leading an ultra-Catholic group had for some years past been drawing closer to O'Brien's moderates. He denounced the bad faith of Dillon whom not without good reason he regarded as the author of the new policy pursued at present by the official party. If Dillon accepted the Land Act of 1909 it was not astonishing. Had he not always hated the Land Act of 1903? Had he not done his utmost in his county of Mayo to prevent it from being successfully worked?[1] With greater success O'Brien exploited against Redmond and Dillon the unpopularity of the 1909 Budget. Not only was Ireland, as we have seen, protectionist and on this point in agreement with the English Unionists, but the increase in the duty on spirits aroused strong opposition throughout the towns and country districts of Ireland. At the General Election he won an initial triumph by securing the return of eleven members in County Cork on his programme of political conciliation and economic reform.

According to O'Brien and his followers the most urgent reform was not political separation from Great Britain but the transformation of the rural proletariat into a population of small peasant holders and the Land Act of 1909 would, he contended, have the effect, perhaps designed by its authors, of bringing to a standstill the great movement of land purchase in process since 1903. Was his contention borne out by the facts? The statistics are not easy to interpret.[2] For in 1908 and 1909 when everyone expected a measure which would make land purchase less profitable to vendor and buyer alike there had been such a rush to purchase land on the terms laid down by the doomed Statute of 1903 that in any case a reaction during the next few years was inevitable; and it was certainly no small measure of success for the land purchase scheme that when the War broke out two-thirds of the arable land had already changed hands. In any case after this slight success at the Election of January 1910 O'Brien's influence steadily declined.

[1] Captain D. D. Sheeham, *Ireland since Parnell*, pp. 188–9.
[2] See the divergent conclusions reached by Erskine Childers, *The Framework of Home Rule*, p. 314. Justin Phillips, The New Peasant Ireland. 1. 'Land Purchase' (*The Irish Review*; a monthly magazine of Irish Literature, Art, and Science*, February 1913, vol. ii, pp. 635 sqq.). *The Land Purchase Deadlock* (March 12, 1913; vol. iii, pp. 81 sqq.).

In a Parliament in which the Unionist and Liberal forces were evenly balanced the seventy-three official Nationalists were masters of the situation, the true victors of the Election and we have seen how during the ensuing months Redmond's authority steadily increased. He dominated the debates in the House of Commons, and brought about the failure of the joint Liberal and Unionist conference which for several months caused him serious anxiety. The December Election followed. O'Brien had hoped to win twenty seats. But he could put no more than twelve candidates in the field, among them an English Tariff Reformer, and kept only eight seats, all in the district of Cork. Throughout the United Kingdom the position of the parties remained unchanged. Redmond was still in a position to dictate his terms to the Cabinet. And the December Election had brought him the further gain of a formal undertaking by the Liberal and Labour members to introduce a Home Rule Bill in the new Parliament. The opposition of the House of Lords was no longer serious, since it was paralysed from the outset by the Parliament Bill passed in 1911. In 1913 the Government brought in a Land Bill which, if it had passed, would have given new vigour to the movement to expropriate the landlord. But it was a mere formality introduced at the close of the Session.[1] And though it was reintroduced in 1914, it was once more a formality. It was soon dropped.[2] Dillon continued his campaign against the policy of conciliation pursued by the followers of Lord Dunraven, Sir Horace Plunkett, and O'Brien,[3] and under his influence, favoured as it was by the situation, the official party succeeded in concentrating the entire attention of the masses in Ireland on the single question of Home Rule. The methods advocated by O'Brien and his friends were presented as out of date. There must be no longer any suggestion of going to Westminster cap in hand to beg the alms of a few immediate material benefits. The day was at hand when an independent Parliament in Dublin would deal with the land question as it pleased.

[1] H. of C., July 21, 1913 (*Parliamentary Debates*, Commons 1913, 5th Series, vol. lv, pp. 1722 sqq.).

[2] H. of C., July 20, 21, 22, 1914 (ibid., Commons 1914, vol. lxv, pp. 208, 261, 428).

[3] 'Some Phases of the Irish Question' (*Round Table*, March 1912, pp. 332 sqq. *Round Table*, June 1913, p. 509). Sidney Brooks 'Aspects of the Irish Question' (*Fortnightly Review*, November 1911; New Series, vol. xc, pp. 826 sqq.). See also the obituary notice of John Dillon in *The Times*, August 10, 1927.

To sum up: When in 1911 the battle between the two Houses ended, Redmond had nothing more to fear from O'Brien. But in another quarter the horizon was perhaps not so clear and dangers threatened which might one day prove serious. By his unyielding attitude on the question of Home Rule and his opposition to a policy of compromise Redmond, who, if he had ever been a revolutionary, was a revolutionary no longer, put himself at the mercy of the revolutionaries. It was all very well for him to promise that the Protestants would have nothing to suffer from Home Rule. He was the ally, indeed the leader, of all the Catholic zealots in Ireland.[1] And though he had been moulded by the civilizing influence of twenty years of Parliamentary life, the fact remained that he was identified with the United Irish League which Devlin had wrested from O'Brien and which as soon as the Land Act of 1909 had been passed had revived the campaign of agrarian outrages. If his policy were in the end defeated in the British Parliament, could he without losing his popularity at a stroke accept the defeat, even temporarily, now that the constitutional barrier to the passing of a Home Rule Bill had been removed? And if he did not accept it, on what grounds could he counsel prudence when the Irish called upon him to lead a revolutionary movement?

In fact, the policy of extreme courses never dead in Ireland was acquiring at this time fresh vigour. For the reasons mentioned above the year 1909 had been to a certain extent propitious to O'Brien and his following. In 1910 the situation was reversed and in the reaction against O'Brien's policy of moderation Redmond ran the risk of being himself outstripped and charged with being too moderate. The submission of the question of the House of Lords to a conference composed of Liberals and Unionists in equal numbers from which the Nationalists were excluded was calculated to alarm the latter. Then strange rumours got abroad of what was happening, if not at the conference itself, at least in its purlieus. Certain of its members, it was reported—Balfour was

[1] See Redmond's remarks in a conversation with Wilfred Scawen Blunt on February 13, 1910: 'In Ireland the defeat of the Government would be hailed with delight. There will be bonfires lit on every hill in Ireland. The alliance with the Liberals was very unpopular and the people wanted a fighting policy again for Home Rule.' (Wilfred Scawen Blunt, *My Diaries*, vol. ii, p. 301.)

mentioned on the Unionist side, Lloyd George on the Liberal—
had been attracted by the idea of applying this method of a committee of conciliation which had just settled the problem of the
unification of South Africa and might perhaps settle the conflict
between the two Houses, to the problem of the relations between
Great Britain and Ireland. Why should it not be examined by
another conference of similar composition? Might it not be possible to devise by amicable negotiations a solution which would
satisfy the desires of the Irish and the interests of the British people?
The sessions of Parliament were congested by the constantly increasing number of questions whose settlement was urgent. Why
not remedy the congestion by setting up subordinate Parliaments
not only in Ireland but in Scotland, Wales, and England itself?
When this Home Rule All Round was in operation the work of
the Parliament of Westminster would be confined to matters
which concerned the United Kingdom and the Empire as a whole,
fiscal questions, foreign politics, the army and navy. A number
of speeches delivered by Liberal politicians at public meetings
suggested that they found this programme attractive. In July
Birrell hinted at the possibility of incorporating Irish Home Rule
in a wider scheme of imperial federation.[1] At this juncture a
Scottish National Manifesto informed the public that a National
Scottish party was in existence at least in embryo.[2] In his youth
Lloyd George had been a Welsh Nationalist of a sort, and a
speech he delivered in September showed that he had not changed
his views.[3] Moreover in October the Conservative Press, as
though in obedience to an order from headquarters, adopted a
conciliatory attitude towards the Irish Nationalists.[4] And when
Redmond who was travelling in the United States, in an interview which he gave on October 4 to the New York correspondent of the *Daily Express*, expressed himself in terms which could

---

[1] Speech at the Eighty Club, July 25, 1910: 'To drag Ireland in the wake of England was
downright stupid policy. He believed that federation beginning here at home, as it was
called, was ripening for rapid and speedy decision. Such a federation once established
would be able to find room for our Dominions overseas as and when they wished to come
in. We should then have a truly Imperial Parliament.'

[2] Speech at the Eighty Club, July 25, 1910. Cf. the Master of Ellibank's speech at Belfast, October 18, 1910. In 1913 a *Government of Scotland Bill* setting up in Scotland a system
of Home Rule or of devolution at least passed the formality of a second reading in the
House of Commons (H. of C., May 30, 1913; *Parliamentary Debates*, Commons 1913, 5th
Series, vol. liii, pp. 471 sqq.).

[3] Speech at Cefnddwysarn Chapel, September 20, 1910.

[4] See in particular the *Observer*, October 16 and six articles in *The Times* signed Pacificus
on 'The Constitutional Conference'. October 20, 22, 24, 28, 31 and November 2, 1910.

be interpreted only as an acceptance of the programme of Home Rule All Round[1] it looked for a moment as though the politicians of all parties were prepared to overrule popular passions and effect an amicable settlement of the question of Home Rule. But it was not long before these passions once more gained the upper hand.

The Ulster Unionists called upon their English confrères not to yield an inch[2] and the attitude of the Conservative Press towards the Irish question once more became adamant. On the opposite side Redmond was compelled by his party to disavow the words put into his mouth by the *Daily Express*.[3] His attitude, he declared, was the same as Parnell's had been. The programme of devolution was dead. He had no objection to raise if the imperial Parliament having granted Home Rule to Ireland, proceeded to extend it to Scotland, Wales and England but he refused to wait for Irish Home Rule until the distant day when it might adopt such a far-reaching solution. Possibly Redmond in 1910 as in 1907 adopted this uncompromising attitude against his personal inclination. The extremists took exception to a speech he delivered at Waterford on November 27 in which he asked for a Parliament 'elected by the Irish people, with an Executive responsible to it, and with full control over all purely Irish affairs'. Parnell, it is true, had accepted the formula, but it was no longer sufficient for men determined to take nothing less than an immediate grant of complete autonomy.

4

We might be tempted at first sight to regard Sinn Fein as the centre of this new extremist agitation.[4] This however would be to misconceive the character of the party. Sinn Fein which lacked, as it has always lacked, a great leader was a group of eccentric intel-

[1] *Daily Express*, October 5, 1910.
[2] Meeting of the Joint Committee of the Unionist Association of Ireland, Dublin, October 18, 1910.
[3] *Daily Express*, October 18, 19, 1910. We should observe however that in an article published at this very time in *MacClure's Magazine* of New York and *Nash's Magazine* of London (See below p. 541 *n*.) Redmond while claiming for Ireland the status of a dominion expressed his willingness to leave the customs in the control of the imperial Parliament.
[4] For this revival of extremism in Ireland see Captain H. B. C. Pollard late of the Staff of the Chief of Police, Ireland, *The Secret Societies of Ireland. Their Rise and Progress*, 1922. R. M. Henry, *The Evolution of Sinn Fein*, 1920, pp. 87 and 90. Captain D. H. Sheeham, *Ireland since Parnell*, 1921, pp. 253 sqq.

lectuals, who refused to commit themselves to any definite strategy. They did not object in principle to an armed rising but, since an insurrection had no chance of success, unless England were absorbed in the conduct of a war abroad, the question was for the moment of purely academic interest. The novel tactics which in 1906 and 1907 they had loudly and most unsuccessfully advertised were a kind of peaceful strike by which Ireland would organize her own public life and without violence withdraw from the operation of English law. They had however consistently maintained that if at any time the Nationalists should be once more, as in the days of Parnell, masters of the parliamentary situation and in a position therefore to compel the British Parliament to concede Home Rule they would have no objection to the employment of this constitutional method. But in 1910 these conditions seemed to have been fulfilled and Sinn Fein officially declared that until further notice they would put no obstacles in the way of Redmond and his followers. For three or four years therefore Sinn Fein was for all practical purposes non-existent.[1] When later on it re-emerged it was a Sinn Fein rejuvenated and transformed by the influence of an extremist movement which came into being about 1910 and had originally nothing in common with Sinn Fein. For though the latter had been founded at the centenary of the 1798 rebellion it was not a republican group. It merely refused to regard the Act of Union of 1800 as legal and demanded a return of the constitution of 1782. But that constitution had been neither republican nor democratic, and Griffith's 'Hungarian' policy was prepared to accept an English monarch and an Irish aristocracy. At the outset the Sinn Feiners regarded with disfavour the birth of a movement both republican and revolutionary.

The new movement was led by two groups. The first of these, purely republican, dated from the foundation in the autumn of 1910 of a paper appearing every two months called *Irish Freedom*, *Saoirseacht na' h-Eireann* which set out to make Sinn Fein republican by reviving the old Fenian party the Irish Republican Brotherhood. The latter, discredited by the acts of violence of which its members had been guilty, its alliance with Parnell, and condem-

[1] 'From 1910 to 1913 the Sinn Fein party was looked on as a negligible association of cranks' (Captain H. B. C. Pollard, *The Secret Societies of Ireland*, p. 118). 'From 1910 to 1913 the Sinn Fein movement was practically moribund' (W. A. Philipps, *The Revolution in Ireland, 1906–1923*, p. 88).

nation by the hierarchy, had finally joined Sinn Fein in 1906. It was as a revolt against what was already termed the old Sinn Fein that it sprang once more into life. Its heroes were Wolfe Tone[1] and Robert Emmet the leaders of the 1798 rebellion, its directing group was called the Wolfe Tone Club, and John Mitchel and John O'Leary the conspirators of 1860. The movement was undenominational. Its leaders proposed 'to substitute the common name of Irishmen for that of Catholic or Protestant'. The objective of the Brotherhood was an Irish Republic, its method, violent revolution. It therefore soon made common cause with the Irish Socialist party which had already been in existence for fourteen years.

We have already had occasion to speak of the foundation in 1896 of this party, at once republican and Socialist, by an exceptionally hard-headed Irishman, Connolly. We have also related how in this critical year 1910, Connolly returned from a lengthy sojourn in America, and brought back with him the principles novel to himself and other agitators of the United Kingdom which he had borrowed from the Industrial Workers of the World and the French Syndicalists. And we have seen how in the person of Larkin the Irish Socialist party obtained what the other political groups lacked, a leader who in his ascendancy over the masses resembled O'Connell and Parnell. But we perhaps laid undue emphasis on the opposition between its programme of social revolution and the programme of national emancipation pursued by Redmond and Devlin. It is true that it had the entire Nationalist Press against it, that Devlin attempted without very much success to organize 'sane' trade unions in opposition to the frenzy of Connolly's great union, that the bishops distrusted it and shortly declared open war against it.[2] But all this must not blind us to the fact that the leading opponent of Larkin and Connolly during the Dublin strikes was Murphy, an opportunist and friend of O'Brien, whom Redmond and Devlin regarded with little favour. Nor

[1] The nationalist R. Barry O'Brien published in 1903 a new edition of Wolfe Tone's autobiography which he prefaced by a glowing panegyric. 'The overthrow of established government is a serious affair. The man who attempts it must be judged not only by the intrinsic justice of his cause but by the practical character of his plans. . . . Was there hope of success? This is the first question.' The introduction concluded with the ambiguous words: 'We live in better times and brighter prospects still are dawning on us' (pp. xxix, xxx, xxxi). Did O'Brien mean that the times were better because violent methods were no longer necessary or because rebellion had now a likelihood of success?

[2] J. M. Hone, 'James Larkin and the Nationalist Party' (*Contemporary Review*, December 1913; vol. civ, pp. 784 sqq.).

must we forget that if Larkin and Connolly were hostile to Sinn Fein it was because in their opinion it was anti-Socialist, undemocratic, and even, since it was prepared to accept an English monarch, unpatriotic.[1] They wanted a violent revolution to free the Irish worker at a single blow from the yoke of capitalism and England.[2] Should circumstances ever arise in which an armed rising had any prospect of success, they alone would have the desperate courage to hazard it. They might indeed prove its victims and others reap the fruits. But they would at least be its agents and heroes.

5

We must now return from Dublin to London and attempt to discover from the public utterances of the political leaders on what points the British ministers were in agreement with the Nationalist leaders. When Redmond speaking in the House of Commons demanded a measure 'giving to the Irish people the legislative and executive control of all purely Irish affairs',[3] he was simply repeating almost verbally the terms of the pledge Campbell-Bannerman had given in November 1905 a few days before Edward VII invited him to form a government. Campbell-Bannerman had announced his intention of placing 'the effective management of Irish affairs in the hands of a representative Irish authority',[4] and Asquith on the eve of the Election of January 1910, while explicitly safeguarding the indestructible supremacy of the imperial Parliament, had pledged himself to set up in Ireland 'a system of full self-government in regard to purely Irish affairs'.[5] But in the speeches delivered by these three statesmen—even by Asquith in spite of the misgivings, which, as everyone

[1] See in the first number of Larkin's paper, *The Irish Worker and People's Advocate*, his judgment of Sinn Fein: 'A party or group which, while pretending to be Irish of the Irish insults the nation by trying to foist on it not only imported economics based on false principles, but which had the temerity to advocate the introduction of foreign capitalists into this sorely exploited country. Their chief appeal to the foreign capitalists was that they should have freedom to employ cheap Irish labour.' 'For eleven years these self-appointed prophets and seers have led their army up the hill and led them down again and would continue to so lead them, if allowed, until the leader was appointed King of Ireland under the Constitution of 1782.' (Quoted by R. M. Henry, *The Evolution of Sinn Fein*, p. 92.)
[2] James Connolly, *Labour in Irish History*, 1910. *The Reconquest of Ireland*, 1911 (collected in a single posthumous volume entitled, *Labour in Ireland*, 1917).
[3] H. of C., March 30, 1908 (*Parliamentary Debates*, 4th Series, vol. clxxxvii, p. 116).
[4] Speech at Stirling, November 23, 1905.
[5] Speech at the Albert Hall, December 10, 1909.

knew, he entertained in regard to Home Rule—another formula made its appearance calculated to encourage the Irish to entertain more ambitious hopes. In 1907 Campbell-Bannerman had promised the Irish, if he were in a position to carry out his intentions, the powers that 'every self-governing colony has'.[1] Redmond had seized hold of the formula. 'What you have done for Frenchmen in Quebec,' he had declared in the House of Commons in 1908, 'what you have done for Dutchmen in the Transvaal, you should now do for Irishmen in Ireland.'[2] And when in 1910 Asquith, repeating the language employed by Campbell-Bannerman in 1907, claimed for his Irish policy 'the sympathy of the overwhelming majority of the great Dominions overseas who have learned how easy it is to combine local autonomy with imperial loyalty',[3] he was no doubt encouraged by the fact that at this very time Redmond was employing the same language in an article he published in an American review.[4] 'We are not seeking', he declared, 'an alteration of the Constitution or of the Imperial Parliament. We are simply asking to be allowed to take our place in the ranks of those other parties to the British Empire —some twenty-eight of them—which are governed, so far as their purely local affairs are concerned, by free and representative institutions, which are their own.' It was an ambiguous formula, and the ambiguity was perhaps deliberate. It was not the same thing to ask for a Home Rule confined to 'purely local affairs' and an autonomy of the kind enjoyed by the dominions.

When the principal Colonies had successively obtained parliamentary self-government the Statutes by which this autonomy had been conferred maintained side by side with the Colonial

[1] H. of C., February 12, 1907 (*Parliamentary Debates*, 4th Series, vol. clxix, p. 85). The serious implications of the formula did not escape the opposition which protested against it next day by the mouth of W. Long a former Irish Secretary under the Unionist Cabinet (ibid., vol. clxix, pp. 186–7).

[2] H. of C., March 30, 1908 (ibid., vol. clxxxvii, p. 133). Cf. his conversation with Barry O'Brien: 'I should like to know what Englishmen mean exactly when they ask: "What do the Irish want?" We have told them again and again—an Irish Parliament and an Irish Executive for the management of Irish affairs. Englishmen ought to know what a Parliament means; though from the questions which they ask us, one might suppose that the idea was quite new to them. They have their own Parliament; and there are the Parliaments of their Colonies and Dependencies—the Australian Commonwealth, New Zealand, The Cape, Canada, the Transvaal, and so forth. An English statesman has plenty of examples to study in framing a constitution for Ireland.' (Barry O'Brien, *Dublin Castle and the Irish People*, 1909, p. 415. Cf. pp. 416, 418, 420.)

[3] Speech at Hull, November 25, 1910.

[4] 'What Ireland Wants' (*MacClure's Magazine*, October 1910), vol. xxxv, p. 691. The entire article was reprinted in England in the Christmas number of *Nash's Magazine*.

ministers responsible to the local parliament a Governor appointed by the British Government and responsible to it. The Governor possessed the right to veto on the instructions of the British Cabinet, itself obedient to the wishes of the British Parliament, measures passed by the parliament of the Colony. But no Governor-General has attempted to make use of this right. A free-trade England had not even prevented the Colonies from placing duties on the importation of foreign and even of British products. Indeed, so far as the Australian Colonies were concerned it had formally sanctioned the system by an express enactment.[1] Nor had London ever attempted to compel the Colonies to contribute to the military and naval expenditure of the Empire. It was almost as a beggar that the Government of the mother country had asked them without very great success for voluntary assistance. No one in England dreamt of granting Ireland such a measure of freedom. If, however, there was no question of effecting between Great Britain and Ireland such a separation as had been made between the United Kingdom and a Self-Governing Dominion, was England prepared to establish a federal relation between the two countries, defined as strictly as the relations between Quebec and Ontario in the Canadian federation, or New South Wales and Victoria in the Commonwealth of Australia?[2] The logic of such a step involved that universal Home Rule which, as we have already seen at the close of 1910, suggested itself to several statesmen as a compromise. Short of this there were only such makeshifts as had been embodied in the Bills of 1885 and 1893. The former had proposed to set up in Dublin a legislature sovereign within a restricted sphere while reserving all questions which concerned the Empire as a whole to a Westminster Parliament in which the Irish by a glaring anomaly would not be represented. The latter envisaged two distinct classes of members in the Westminster Parliament. One of these, elected by the constituencies of Great Britain, would have the right to deal with all questions which did not exclusively concern Ireland, the other fewer in numbers than the Irish representatives under the Act of Union would have the right to deal with all questions which did not

---

[1] 36 Vict., Cap. 22: An Act to amend the Law with respect to Customs Duties in the Australian Colonies (*Australian Colonies Duties Act*, 1873).

[2] 'Local powers should be given similar to those enjoyed by the Provinces of Canada' (Sir Edward Grey, election address, December 1910). Frederick S. Oliver, *What Federation is Not*, 1912, p. 81.

exclusively concern England, Wales, and Scotland. The Irish Nationalists would have nothing to do with a universalized Home Rule which would reduce them to the position of a small-subject nation, forming part of the United Kingdom on the same footing as Wales. But they were prepared to accept without too meticulous a scrutiny of detail any solution which, explicitly or implicitly repealing the Union, left open the future concession, sooner or later, of an independence for which the imprudent formula of Campbell-Bannerman and Asquith permitted them to hope, similar to that possessed by Canada, Australia, New Zealand, and South Africa.[1]

6

The Government of Ireland Bill introduced on April 11, 1912, gave Ireland a Parliament. It would consist of two Chambers. There would be a Senate of forty members nominated for eight years, in the first instance by the Imperial Government, afterwards by the Irish. And there would be a Lower House of 164 members to be elected *on the existing franchise* in the proportion of one member for every 27,000 inhabitants, a franchise which the Irish Parliament might, if it chose, modify later. The financial powers of the Upper House would be limited like those of the House of Lords since 1911. In contra-distinction to the English procedure the members of either house would have the right to speak in the other. Disagreements between the two Houses would be settled by a joint session. The Lord-Lieutenant would give the royal assent to Bills passed by the Irish legislature, and would have the

[1] For the extension of the Dominion status to Ireland see Erskine Childers, *The Framework of Home Rule*, 1911 especially chap. x, pp. 188 sqq. *The Form and Purpose of Home Rule*, 1912, p. 25. The Home Rulers' present tactics were to exploit Imperialist sentiment. Erskine Childers, *The Framework of Home Rule*, 1911, pp. 144–5: 'Unionism for Ireland is anti-Imperialist. Its upholders strenuously opposed colonial autonomy and but yesterday were passionately opposing South African autonomy. To-day colonial autonomy is an axiom. But Ireland is a measure of the depth of these convictions. There could be no Empire to idealize if their Irish principles had been applied just a little longer to any of their oversea States which constitute the Self-Governing Colonies of to-day.' T. M. Kettle, *The Open Secret of Ireland with an Introduction by J. E. Redmond*, 1912, p. 120. 'The inevitableness of Home Rule resides in the fact that it is, as one might say, a biped among ideas. It marches to triumph on two feet, an Irish and an Imperial foot. If there were in Ireland no demand whatever for self-government it would nevertheless be necessary in the interest of the Empire to force it on her.' On the other hand, there is an excellent account of the difficulties which the Unionists discovered in the practical application of these formulas in A. V. Dicey's book, *A Fool's Paradise. Being a Constitutionalist's Criticism of the Home Rule Bill of 1912*, 1913.

right to withhold his assent for whatever period he thought fit. On the whole it was a constitution of the colonial type. But the powers of the Irish Parliament were made subject to special restrictions.

They concerned religion in the first place. The Irish Parliament was forbidden to establish any denomination or make financial grants to it, or favour or penalize anyone for his religious beliefs. The recent promulgation by the Vatican of the *Ne Temere* decree which rendered mixed marriages more difficult by pronouncing invalid marriages contracted by a Catholic without the presence of a priest had caused widespread irritation among Protestants and the Bill therefore provided that the Irish Parliament should have no power to render the validity of a marriage dependent on the faith of the parties or the performance of a religious ceremony. Of greater importance were the provisions which defined the relationship between the Irish and Imperial Parliament in such a way as to secure the permanent and sovereign interests of the Empire. The Irish Parliament would possess no competence in questions regarding the succession to the throne, foreign politics, imperial defence, the grant of peerages and other honours, coinage or weights and measures. Moreover, the Imperial Parliament reserved to itself the control of certain branches of the Irish administration itself; provisionally and for six years only control of the constabulary; as a temporary measure also, though the Irish Parliament could not demand its transfer until ten years had elapsed, the administration of the measures of social reform recently passed by the British Parliament, the collection of taxes, and legislation dealing with savings banks and friendly societies. And land purchase was permanently reserved. The mention of these latter reservations has brought us to the problem of the financial relations between Ireland and the rest of the United Kingdom.

The problem was always a delicate one but its aspect had changed of recent years. In the past Ireland could justly complain that she was exploited by England. This was the case no longer. The heavy burden of the new taxes just imposed by the Imperial Parliament fell on the wealthy and Ireland being a poor country escaped it. Moreover these taxes had been imposed to defray not only military expenditure but also the cost of social services by which Ireland benefited very considerably though she had not even expressed a desire for them. Old Age Pensions, Labour

Exchanges, National Insurance; Ireland, a rural and backward country, would never have thought of asking for such services if she had not been drawn into the orbit of her great industrial neighbour.[1] Official statistics proved that during the financial year 1910-11 Ireland paid taxes to the value of £10,350,000, and received in administrative services of every description £12,400,000.[2] The Bill therefore set up a complicated financial system to be in force only so long as the Irish deficit continued. The total amount of taxes levied in Ireland, together with a further sum which beginning at £500,000 would decrease annually until at the expiration of six years it would be fixed at £200,000, would be paid into 'the Irish Exchequer'. Whatever deficit there might be would be borne by the Imperial Treasury. It was hoped that it would become progressively less. The expenditure on the police, at present exorbitant, would diminish when the country had been pacified by Home Rule. Old age pensions would become fewer as the population continued to decline. And the cost of land purchase, if for some time to come it must continue to increase, would finally be extinguished altogether when the transfer had been completed. On the other hand, the yield from taxation would become higher if the economic position of the country improved and if the Dublin Parliament imposed additional taxation, as the Bill permitted; provided no new tariffs were imposed. When at last the Irish Budget was balanced another system would be adopted.[3]

7

Since the powers of the new Dublin Parliament were thus restricted Ireland, unlike the Colonies, must be given representation at Westminster. The Bill provided for forty-two Irish mem-

[1] Stephen Gwynn, *John Redmond's Last Years*, 1919.
[2] *Irish Finance. Report by the Committee on Irish Finance*, 1912, p. 24.
[3] Among the champions of Home Rule were a number of heretics who denied that in 1911 Ireland profited financially from her union with Great Britain (John J. Hogan, *Home Rule. A Critical Consideration*, 1911, pp. 54 sqq.), and others who, while admitting the financial advantages of the union, maintained that Ireland should be prepared to sacrifice them to secure financial independence. T. M. Kettle (*Home Rule Finance. An Experiment in Justice*) 1911: he even proposed that Ireland should make a contribution to the Empire, p. 71. Erskine Childers, *The Framework of Home Rule. A Lecture delivered at a Public Meeting Convened by the Young Ireland Branch of the United Irish League at the Mansion House, Dublin, on March 2nd, 1912*, pp. 23-4. But the system proposed was too generous to be welcome to the official Nationalist party. See Stephen Gwynn, *The Case for Home Rule Stated by*, with a preface by John Redmond, 3rd Edition, 1917. Preface.

bers of the Imperial Parliament. But the difficulties which we have just mentioned arose at once and the Bill made no provision for dealing with them. Asquith, it is true, in the speech in which he introduced the Bill promised a system of Home Rule All Round but it would be postponed to a later date and it was unpopular with the Irish. Moreover, the financial provisions of the Bill precisely because they were so generous—for an indefinite period Ireland would live on alms from England—placed severer restrictions on Ireland than were placed on any Self-Governing Colony: she was expressly forbidden to impose a tariff. The Unionists had therefore some reason to hope that Irish opinion would prove refractory and compel Redmond and his followers to break their alliance with the English Liberals. If they cherished any such expectations they were speedily undeceived. The Bill, like its predecessors of 1886 and 1893, gave Ireland a separate legislature. Moreover, names count for a good deal and Asquith conceded to the new Irish legislature what Gladstone had obstinately refused— the title of Parliament. When the Convention of the Nationalist party met in Dublin on April 24 it gave the Government Bill its unqualified and enthusiastic support. The meeting had been cleverly staged by Redmond and Devlin. The resolution was seconded by the Lord Mayor of Cork, who had just been elected to succeed an O'Brienite. A second resolution expressing the confidence of the assembly that the official party would introduce the necessary amendments into the Bill was seconded by a Protestant clergyman. And a Gladstone, a grandson of the great statesman, came from England to greet amid enthusiastic applause the dawn of the new era.

The debates in Parliament were prolonged until the end of the year. Once, in November, a Unionist amendment to the financial clauses of the Bill was adopted, and the Unionists exploited their victory for all it was worth. But they were well aware that it was a mere accident due to a poor attendance of the Liberal and Labour members. It was followed by an adjournment which gave time for angry passions to calm down and the damage was repaired a week later after violent debates.[1]

A few alterations were made in the Bill by the Government itself, of which one at least was important. After the expiration of

[1] H. of C., November 11, 12, 13, 1912 (*Parliamentary Debates*, Commons 1912; 5th Series, vol. xliii, pp. 1765 sqq., 1841–1842, 1993 sqq.).

five years the Senate would not be nominated by the executive but would consist of members elected in a fixed proportion for each of the four Irish provinces, a system of proportional representation being adopted to secure the representation throughout the country of racial and religious minorities—the Catholic minority in the north, the Protestant in the south. The Bill finally passed its third reading on January 16, 1913, by a majority of 110 votes. Eleven days later the House of Lords threw it out without debating its clauses by 326 to 96 votes.

If the debates had been lengthy they had not been passionate. On the contrary, interest had flagged, and the attendance of the public had often been scanty. Other and more pressing matters engaged the attention of Parliament and the nation. The iron machinery of the 'closure', peculiar to the British Parliament, discouraged all attempts at obstruction. Devised thirty years earlier to overcome the obstruction of the Irish members it now enabled the Irish Nationalists to crush the opposition of the English Unionists. And the Parliament Bill, employed this year for the first time, deprived the debates of much of their interest. For only urgent questions arouse strong passions. And the question at issue was not whether Dublin would or would not have its Parliament within a year. Nor would a decision be reached when the House of Lords rejected the Government of Ireland Bill. There would not even be an appeal to the electorate to decide the conflict between the two Houses. The House of Commons which passed the Bill of 1912 was sovereign but its sovereignty could not be made effective for a long while to come. It was the first act of a drama whose catastrophe lay two years ahead.

The session of 1913 did not begin until March, since the extraordinary session of 1912 had extended far into the following year. During the session of 1912 two Bills had been passed by the Lower, and thrown out by the Upper House—the Irish Bill and the Welsh Church Bill. A third, the Franchise Bill, had been provisionally dropped, hung up by the feminist difficulty before the Commons had even debated its clauses. In its place a more modest measure was introduced abolishing the plural vote. But this Bill was a year behind the others and if the House of Lords rejected it twice could not pass until 1915, provided no General Election were held in the interval. The Cabinet quickly passed the other Bills thrown out by the Lords through their second reading in the Commons and asked Parliament to sanction a special procedure for the third reading. Normally, the third reading of a Bill involved the individual discussion of its clauses. Such a discussion however would serve no purpose, since to fulfil the provisions of the Parliament Act the Bill must be returned to the Lords identical in every detail with the measure sent up the year before. The Cabinet therefore proposed that at the third as at the second reading both Bills should be passed *en bloc* after a cursory debate which must not exceed, particularly in the case of the Irish Bill, the limits of a single sitting. Asquith further pointed out that the Parliament Bill did not prevent the House of Lords from amending the Bill, or the Government from accepting its amendments. Clause two of the Parliament Act allowed the Opposition, even in the Commons, to suggest amendments which the Government might pronounce acceptable and which, if accepted in turn by the House of Lords might serve as the basis of a compromise.[1] But the Unionist Opposition, hostile to any compromise, refused to put any 'suggestions' forward and the Bill was passed *en bloc* by the Commons, rejected *en bloc* by the Lords. The debates were dreary, drearier even than in the previous year. This was the effect of the system set up by the Parliament Act of 1911. The second session of a Parliament had become a mere formality, an indispensable interlude between the first in which a genuine discussion took place, though the effects were too remote to make it interesting to the public, and the third, when a decision of the legislature already two years old, would be carried into effect and the will of the Lords overridden.

This final stage had been reached when Parliament reassembled for the new session in January 1914. The Cabinet after the Bill had

[1] 1 & 2 Geo. 5, Cap. 13, Sec. 2(4): '. . . Provided that the House of Commons may, if they think fit on the passage of such a Bill through the House in the second or third Session, suggest any further amendment without inserting the amendment in the Bill, and any such suggested amendments shall be considered by the House of Lords, and, if agreed to by that House, shall be treated as amendments made by the House of Lords and agreed to by the House of Commons. . . . ' To complete our account of the applications of the *Parliament Act* we may observe that it could also be employed *in terrorem*, to induce the House of Lords to accept a compromise without the need of recourse to the 'suggestions' for which the Bill made provision. This happened this very year 1913 in the case of a *Temperance (Scotland) Bill* which during the previous session had been mutilated by the amendments of the Upper House. The Government had announced its intention to drop the Bill, reintroduce it in the original form and pass it in this form in 1914 under the provisions of the *Parliament Act* if the House of Lords persisted in its attitude. The Bill was then passed a second time by the Commons but when it reached the Lords the latter restricted their amendments to those accepted by the Government and the dispute was settled by the compromise.

been passed for the third time by the Commons would possess the legal authority to disestablish the Welsh Church and give Ireland a Parliament. But was its legal matched by a corresponding moral and material authority? Brought suddenly face to face with facts after two years of unreal debate, it was obvious that the Cabinet, so far at least as Ireland was concerned, had no confidence in its own strength.

8

It was not that the Ministry need fear a revolt of British public opinion on the question. No doubt the Liberal party lost a certain number of seats. But in these cases the Unionist candidate owed his return to a split vote between the Liberal and Labour candidates.[1] The discontent which the National Insurance Act aroused in the working classes when it came into operation for the first time explains these Labour candidatures put forward to exclude the Liberal candidate. And the feminists financed them to further their cause. Labour headquarters gave a passive consent though not without anxiety at the prospect of a breach with the Cabinet which formed no part of its policy. The predominant feeling of the general public was boredom. The Liberals, besides the important measures actually introduced, promised universal suffrage and a reform of the law of real estate. They spoke also of an education Act and nationalization of the railways. But they aroused no enthusiasm. The Unionists promised conscription, protection, and the restoration of the rights of the House of Lords—not a popular programme. As regards the Irish question, opposition to Home Rule was still the fundamental plank of a party which for that very reason called itself 'Unionist'. But the Irish peril was no longer, as in 1886 and in 1895, an alarm which aroused the masses. Everyone was weary of a tedious problem, sickened by the dreary prospect that it might prove insoluble, and ready to welcome any solution a statesman might have the good fortune to discover. If ill-humour bulked largely in the attitude of the public towards political questions, there was also a large measure of indifference. There was a nonchalance encouraged by the

[1] Midlothian, September 10, 1912; Newmarket, May 16, 1913; Reading, November 8, 1913; South-West Bethnal Green, February 19, 1914; Leith, February 26, 1914 (the seat had been held uninterruptedly by a Liberal since 1832); North-East Derbyshire, May 20, 1914; Ipswich, May 23, 1914. Cf. Lloyd George speech at Criccieth, June 2, 1914.

continuous economic prosperity and the rapid increase of wealth in every branch of industry and commerce. And in consequence there was much moral anarchy, a spate of luxury and pleasure seeking. There was much social and political anarchy also. Labour seethed with unrest; the suffragettes raised their shrill war cries, and Ulster rebelled in advance against the Government of Ireland Act.

For it was in Ireland that the great, indeed well-nigh insurmountable, obstacle arose to the execution of this Statute accepted by the electorate of Great Britain. A quarter of its population—one million in four—was Protestant, and these million Protestants, determined not to endure the yoke of the majority, were not scattered uniformly over the island. In Munster and Connaught they were an insignificant minority, and in Leinster one in four. But in Ulster the situation was very different. In the west, in Donegal and in the south, in the counties of Cavan and Monaghan, the Catholics constituted five-sixths of the population; nearer the centre in Fermanagh and Tyrone they were only a little more than half and in the north in Londonderry,[1] and in the south-east in Armagh the Protestants were in a majority and their majority became overwhelming in the east, in Antrim, Down, and the city of Belfast. The Ulster Protestants worked hard and amassed wealth in their shipyards and linen factories. The firm of Harland and Wolff was the greatest firm of shipbuilders in the world. It had built the giant liners, the *Olympic* and the *Titanic*. It was the boast of the population of Ulster, or rather of its industrial districts, that they paid three-quarters of the Irish taxation. Proud of the example their hard-working community afforded to the rest of Ireland they were determined never to amalgamate with the race of babblers and merry-Andrews whose follies and vices the new school of Irish literature delighted, it would seem, to depict as though in defiance, a spectacle for the respectable Protestants of the north.

In September 1911, little more than a month after the House of Lords finally passed the Parliament Bill, Ulster was the scene of a vast popular demonstration which united Irish enthusiasm and Protestant gravity. 300,000 Irish Unionists assembled to express their thanks to Sir Edward Carson, an eminent barrister

[1] Where however the city of Londonderry itself returned a Home Ruler in 1912, giving the Home Rulers a majority of one vote in the representation of Ulster.

who had become the accredited leader of their party and at the same time to give him and his friends a commission to draw up a constitution for a 'provisional government' of Ulster, to come into operation the very day 'a Home Rule Bill of any description' became law. From that moment demonstrations of revolt against the Irish Government which the English Liberals proposed to set up in Dublin followed thick and fast. In January 1912 30,000 men marched past Sir Edward. In April 1912 at Balmoral near Belfast 100,000 men marched past Bonar Law, the official leader of the Unionists in the Commons, the son of a Presbyterian minister, and an Ulsterman by birth who on his return to England encouraged the Ulstermen by using, first at a public meeting, then in Parliament, the language of civil war.[1] Finally, a summer marked in Northern Ireland by perpetual brawls between Protestants and Catholics was concluded on the 28th of September by a solemn ceremony at Belfast. After a religious service the demonstrators formed a procession. It was headed by Sir Edward Carson, the Cromwell of the new movement. After him was borne an old banner of yellow silk embroidered with a red star in the centre and Saint George's cross in one corner, reverently preserved in an Ulster family and believed to have been carried two centuries earlier in the battle of the Boyne. Behind Sir Edward and his banner there followed an army of prospective rebels against the application of the Parliament Bill to Ireland. Then came Lord Londonderry, Lord Charles Beresford, and F. E. Smith, followed by a second army. The procession debouched on a public square. At a table set up for the purpose the demonstrators, 2,000 in number, were the first to sign what was called in Biblical language, the Covenant, a pledge taken in the presence of God to stand by each other 'in defending for ourselves and our children, our cherished position of equal citizenship in the United Kingdom, and in using all means which may be found necessary to defeat the setting up of a Home Rule

[1] Speech at Blenheim, July 27, 1912: 'Ireland was two nations. . . . The Ulster people would submit to no ascendancy, and he could imagine no length of resistance to which they might go in which they would not be supported by the overwhelming majority of the British people.' Also H. of C., July 31, 1912: 'In regard to what I said at Blenheim, I am very glad to have an opportunity of repeating it here. . . . I said the same thing in August a year ago. . . . I recognize . . . the difference and the great difference, between saying it when I was practically a private member and saying it as a leader of the Unionist party in this House. I have felt for months that sooner or later it would be necessary for me to say the same thing in the clearest and most explicit way.' (*Parliamentary Debates*, Commons 1912; 5th Series, vol. xli, pp. 2132–2133.)

Parliament in Ireland', and if they could not prevent its establishment never to recognize its authority.

The agitation redoubled in 1913 when it became clear that the Government intended to carry out its programme and would not, as some Unionists had maintained, evade the issue by dissolving Parliament before the Commons had passed the Government of Ireland Bill for the third time. In July, when the dismal session of 1913 was drawing to its close a monster demonstration of Carson's followers at Craigavon in Ulster, in which 150,000 men took part, inaugurated enlistments for the army of 'Ulster volunteers'. Before the end of the year 100,000 had enlisted.[1] On September 17 the Ulster volunteers were placed under the command of Lieutenant-General Sir George Lloyd Reilly Richardson and on the 27th all the organs of a prospective provisional government were constituted. There was an executive committee of seventy-six members; a military council; an Ulster Volunteer Committee; a Legal Committee; a Customs, Excise, and Post Office Committee. At the same time a public subscription was opened to raise a sum of £10,000,000 to provide pensions for the volunteers or their their families if they were wounded or killed in the course of the armed struggle so likely to occur in the near future.[2] But the leaders seem, at any rate at this period, to have regarded the collection of the fund as a diplomatic move rather than a genuine insurance against casualties actually expected. They defied the British Government to repress a movement which though in form a rebellion was in fact a Loyalist movement since it was directed against those Irish Catholics who had always adopted

[1] It was only at this juncture that the British public learnt of the constitution of this army of Ulstermen. But in a country where rebellion seemed everybody's natural vocation Ulster had long been preparing to arm. In his *Annals of an Active Life* (vol. i, pp. 172–3) General Macready mentions a manifesto of the Grand Orange Lodge of Ireland dated December 7, 1910, which, while urging the voters to go to the polls at the next election, calls upon the Irish loyalists to prepare to fight in the event of a Home Rule Bill being passed and adds 'Already steps are being taken to enrol men to meet any emergency.'

[2] Sir Edward Carson's speech at Belfast, September 20, 1912: 'I only want to say "Good Bye". I shall be longing for the time when I can come back, whether the occasion be for peace—I prefer it—or to fight, and if it be to fight I shall not shrink. One thing I feel perfectly confident of is that to-day we have taken a step which has put our enemies into such a state of difficulty that they are wondering what on earth they are going to do.' And his language at Belfast on November 4, 1913, was even more explicit: 'He had never had riots in his mind at all. All day he had cautioned their people not to risk their lives or liberties in fruitless action. What they meant was steady, unflinching, determined and continuous obstruction of the law so as to make government under Home Rule absolutely impossible.'

the attitude of rebels and whom the English had always regarded in that light.

9

And in fact the Cabinet began to find its parliamentary triumphs a source of embarrassment. What use should it make of the third victory in 1914, which nothing could prevent? Already, a year before, when the Home Rule Bill was first passed, Lord Dunraven and the small Irish party in favour of a policy of devolution had intervened and a member of the Cabinet, Winston Churchill, when sketching a scheme of federalism for Great Britain which divided the country into as many as twelve separate regions had let it be understood that he might be contemplating a similar division of Ireland which would safeguard the autonomy of Protestant Ulster.[1] In 1913 during the long parliamentary recess which extended until January attempts at conciliation became more insistent.

Lord Loreburn, a former Lord Chancellor, addressed a letter to *The Times* on September 11 in which to prevent a civil war in Ireland he urged 'that there should be a Conference or direct communication between the leaders'. On October 8 Churchill expressed his desire for what he called a settlement by consent or by agreement and pointed out that if only the parties concerned could be brought to agree, the text of the Parliament Act enabled 'far reaching' amendments to be made in the Government of Ireland Bill.[2] And Asquith himself on October 25 while rejecting the suggestion of a formal 'conference' proposed an 'interchange of views . . . for the adjustment of the position of the minority in Ireland'.[3] What was the 'adjustment' he had in mind? Was it Home Rule for Ulster within Irish Home Rule? Sir Edward Grey speaking at Berwick on October 27 seemed to favour that solution. That Ulster should be permitted to claim exclusion from a Home Rule Ireland either immediately or when sufficient time had elapsed to prove co-operation impossible? Sir Horace Plunkett suggested a plan of this kind. Or should Ulster, or more strictly speaking its Protestant portion, be excluded for a fixed term of

[1] Speech at Dundee, September 12, 1912.
[2] Speech at Dundee, October 8, 1913.
[3] Address at Ladybank to the East Fife Liberal Association.

years, to be incorporated only at a later date when it would have had time to become accustomed to the new conditions? *The Times* in November declared that this was in fact the plan favoured by the Government. At this juncture conversations were held between the leaders of the two great parties, Asquith and Bonar Law. No result was reached. Two proclamations issued on December 4 forbidding, the first the importation, the second the transport along the coast, of arms and munitions, seemed intended to recall men's minds to a sense of realities. It was in vain that the speech from the throne on February 10, 1914, after admitting the failure of the conversations held the previous November, insisted on the dangers which threatened the country if the problem were not handled 'in a spirit of mutual concession'. Very few traces of such a spirit were visible in Ireland. It was proposed to liberate a nation and there were two nations, one of which refused liberation. In Ireland the passions of the herd, the more embittered because they were religious as well as political, clashed and the very suggestion of a compromise was absurd. Policy was confronted with fanaticism, and parliamentary methods, official and unofficial alike, were faced by the stark reality of an incipient civil war.

Asquith, however, decided to put forward a compromise on his own initiative, since Bonar Law rejected the suggestion. On March 9 he explained his views to the House. He did not propose to employ, as he had thought of doing in 1913, the method of 'suggestions' for which Clause 2 of the Parliament Bill made provision. But simultaneously with the introduction for the third time of the Government of Ireland Bill, which must be passed without amendment to satisfy the conditions of the Parliament Act, he would introduce an Amending Bill which passed by both Houses would modify the Home Rule Bill as though its provisions had been incorporated as amendments in the latter. The Bill would enable each of the Ulster Counties to decide by a plebiscite in favour of exclusion for six years from the operation of the Government of Ireland Bill. At the end of the six years these counties would automatically be incorporated into a self-governing Ireland. This procedure would satisfy the Irish Nationalists who would concede to their adversaries nothing more than six years' respite. But it would also satisfy the Unionists. If, as was generally expected, Parliament were dissolved in the autumn, two General Elections would be held before the six years had elapsed. The Unionists therefore would have two opportunities of appealing to the country, and if the country gave them a mandate to do so, of settling the Irish question on a different basis. Possibly there were ministers who faced with a secret satisfaction the prospect of defeat at the next Election. The Government of Ireland Bill once passed they would be glad to see the Irish Nationalists confronted with a Unionist Government. But for this very reason perhaps the proposal did not attract the Unionist leaders. Moreover, it was confronted by the uncompromising attitude of the Ulster Protestants who were not prepared to abandon the rest of Ireland to the Catholics, unless the latter accepted the final, and not merely the temporary, exclusion of Protestant Ulster. While using conciliary language they demanded further concessions.

10

For a moment it seemed as though the Cabinet did not object in principle to this solution. From the time when at the close of 1910 he had appeared to entertain the hope of an amicable settlement of the Irish question, Lloyd George had maintained a deliberate silence. It was only at this juncture that he intervened once more. It was he who secured the assent of Redmond and his followers to the temporary exclusion of Protestant Ulster. He now again approached Redmond, Devlin, Dillon, and T. P. O'Connor and tried to obtain a further concession. They, however, refused. They had gone as far as they could without destroying their reputation as Irish patriots. Then the Cabinet decided to brave the opposition of Ulster. On March 14 Churchill spoke at Bradford words which seemed irrevocable. 'There are worse things than bloodshed. . . . We are not going to have the realm of Britain sunk to the condition of the Republic of Mexico.' On Monday, March 16, the Prime Minister in more Asquithian terminology made it plain that no further concessions would be made. And the Secretary for War, Seely, who had succeeded Lord Haldane when the latter was made Lord Chancellor in 1912, worked out in collaboration with Churchill, the First Lord of the Admiralty, what was nothing less than a plan of campaign in

Northern Ireland. The army would occupy all munition dumps and arsenals, and all strategic positions in Protestant Ulster. A small flotilla would be in readiness to transport by sea regiments which the railways would refuse to carry. A formidable concentration of troops would presumably nip any attempt at rebellion in the bud. If, however, Ulster replied to the military occupation by an actual revolt, the leaders would be arrested and the insurrection forcibly put down. It was indeed expected that certain officers of Ulster origin would find it difficult to obey the orders they would receive. Those officers therefore, whose principles would be outraged by the repression of the revolt and who could not be relied upon to employ the necessary severity, were invited to resign their commissions.[1] General Gough, who was in command of the Third Cavalry Brigade at the camp in the Curragh in Ireland, resigned and was immediately replaced. This happened on Friday, the 20th. The following day, Lloyd George speaking at Huddersfield used even stronger language than Churchill had employed. 'We are confronted', he declared, 'with the gravest issue raised in this country since the days of the Stuarts. Representative government in this land is at stake. . . . I am here this afternoon on behalf of the British Government to say this to you—that they mean to confront this defiance of popular liberties with a most resolute, unwavering determination, whatever the hazard may be.'

But General Gough was not the only officer at the Curragh who resigned on March 20. With a few exceptions all the officers of both cavalry regiments resigned with him. Against the rebellion of Ulster the army could be used, but what could be done if the army went on strike? Carson informed the King that the Cabinet proposed to arrest himself and the other Ulster leaders, and that if this step were taken, all the customs houses in Ulster would be seized in retaliation.[2] The King urged caution on Asquith, who gladly accepted his advice. The Prime Minister in the Commons, the Lord Chancellor in the Lords, denied the intention attributed to the Government of undertaking a military

---

[1] For the text of the instructions given on December 16, 1913, to the generals in command of the forces in England, Scotland, and Ireland by the Secretary for War, Seely, see Major-General The Rt. Hon. J. E. B. Seely, *Adventure*, pp. 160–1.

[2] Lieutenant-Colonel A'Court Repington, *The First World War, 1914–1918*, vol. i, p. 69: he repeats Carson's account of the matter in a conversation with himself on November 19, 1915.

campaign against Ulster. General Gough was summoned to London, withdrew his resignation and returned to Ireland bearing a written pledge signed by the Secretary for War that the army would under no circumstances be called upon to repress by force a movement of resistance to Home Rule. When the report of this surrender was triumphantly proclaimed by the Unionist Press, the Premier denied that the promise had been made or at least had received the assent of the Cabinet. Then the Secretary for War resigned. In reply, the Chief of Staff, Sir John French, resigned. The Secretary for War withdrew his resignation, then resigned a second time. What an example for the British proletariat! Speaking in the House of Commons J. H. Thomas declared that if the negotiations then in progress between the railwaymen and the companies failed and a strike broke out in November he would bear in mind the lesson taught by the events in Ulster and advise the men to arm.[1] Under these circumstances Asquith with a courage universally applauded, yielded to his colleagues' entreaties and took over the functions of Secretary for War. As expert Parliamentarian, taking Seely's place, he made a desperate attempt to preserve the semblance of discipline in the army, while as Prime Minister he did his utmost to preserve the semblance of legal government in the State.[2]

Ulster had won the first round. A month later it gained a further and even more striking victory. When in December a royal proclamation forbade the importation of arms into Ireland, the Ulstermen had replied that it came too late since they already possessed all the arms they needed. They had proceeded to argue in the courts, not always unsuccessfully, that the proclamation was illegal, since the Liberal Cabinet had repealed the Crimes Act. At the end of April they proved that it was in any case ineffective. In the course of a single night to the mystification of the police and customs officials 40,000 rifles and 1,000,000 cartridges were landed at three separate points on the west coast and immediately distributed throughout Ulster. Where did this mysterious vessel, which under a false name brought the arms and munitions, come

[1] H. of C., March 23, 1914 (*Parliamentary Debates*, Commons, 1914, 5th Series, vol. lx, pp. 80–1) also H. of L., same date. (ibid., Lords 1914, 5th Series, vol. xv, p. 639.)

[2] For the Curragh episode see Major-General The Rt. Hon. J. E. B. Seely, *Adventure*, pp. 166 sqq. General Macready, *Annals of an Active Life*, vol. i, pp. 176 sqq. Major-General Sir C. E. Callwell, *Field-Marshal Sir Henry Wilson*, vol. i, pp. 139 sqq. Field-Marshal Sir William Robertson, *From Private to Field-Marshal*, 1921, pp. 193–5. J. A. Spender and C. Asquith, *Life of Lord Oxford and Asquith*, vol. ii, pp. 44–6.

from? It came from Hamburg and the rifles were Mausers.[1] Far from being ashamed of this German aid these rebels, self-styled loyalists, blazoned the fact with a lack of restraint which shows how intensely Irish their temper was. They were delighted when a prominent German diplomat, Secretary to the German Embassy in London, Baron von Kühlmann, made a lengthy visit to Ulster[2] and a host of German journalists flocked to the scene to keep their public in touch with the incipient revolution. If England betrayed them, why should not William II prove another William of Orange, come like the former from the Continent to deliver them from the Catholic yoke?[3]

II

To this further manifestation of anarchy the Government replied at first by adopting a still more conciliatory attitude. Lloyd George had disappeared from the scene. He was absorbed in piloting through the House of Commons an ambitious and complicated Budget which imposed extremely heavy taxation and

[1] 'There was reason to think that the German Government had stopped the traffic in the Kiel Canal in order to let the *Fanny*, the steamer which carried them, get round Denmark into the North Sea and so escape the vigilance of the British Navy' (Richard Burdon Haldane, *An Autobiography*, p. 269).

[2] Captain Sheeham, *Ireland since Parnell*, pp. 273–4.

[3] James Chambers, M.P., speech at South Belfast, May 23, 1913: 'As regards the future, what if the day should come when Ireland would be clamouring for independence complete and thorough from Great Britain? . . . What side would they take then? (A voice "Germany".) He bound no man to his opinions. They owed to England allegiance, loyalty, gratitude; but if England cast them off, then he reserved the right, as a betrayed man, to say "I shall act as I have a right to act. I shall sing no longer God save the King"' . . . He said there solemnly that the day England cast him off and despised his loyalty and allegiance, that day he would say: 'England, I will laugh at your calamity, I will mock when your fear cometh' (*The Complete Grammar of Anarchy. By Members of the War Cabinet and their Friends* compiled by J. J. Hogan, 1919, p. 37). An utterance by Captain Craig, M.P.: 'Germany and the German Emperor would be preferred to the rule of John Redmond, Patrick Ford, and the Molly Maguires' (L. G. Redmond Howard, *Sir Roger Casement. A Character Sketch without Prejudice*, 1916, p. 30). Major F. Crawford speech at Bangor, April 29, 1912: 'If they were put out of the Union . . . he would infinitely prefer to change his allegiance right over to the Emperor of Germany or anyone else who had got a proper and stable government.' (D. Gwynn, *Life and Death of Sir Roger Casement*, p. 181.) It was more serious to find Bonar Law in open Parliament bestowing on this wild talk the semi-official sanction of the Unionist party: 'It is a fact which I do not think anyone who knows anything about Ireland will deny, that these people in the North and East of Ireland, from old prejudices perhaps more than from anything else, from the whole of their past history, would prefer, I believe, to accept the government of a foreign country rather than submit to be governed by hon. gentlemen below the gangway' (H. of C., January 1, 1913; *Parliamentary Debates*, Commons 1912; 5th Series, vol. lxvi, p. 464).

was the object of violent attacks.[1] But Churchill spoke in Parliament the language of peace with which Asquith associated himself. And on the other side of the House, Bonar Law and Sir Edward Carson himself made proof of considerable moderation. Unfortunately, the leaders on both sides always found themselves faced with the uncompromising obstinacy of the two factions, or rather, the two nations in Ireland. When on June 23 Lord Crewe introduced in the Lords the Amending Bill promised by Asquith at the beginning of March it was found to contain nothing more than the Prime Minister had indicated in his original sketch and which the Ulstermen and their allies had from the beginning refused to accept. Lord Crewe was content to mention incidentally that the Government were ready to consider certain amendments. The House of Lords replied by introducing into the Bill a series of amendments which changed its nature completely. Not only did they exclude Ulster without a plebiscite, *en bloc*, not county by county, finally, and not merely for six years but they modified the arrangements made by the Cabinet for the government of Catholic Ireland. The supporters of the Government in the Lords accepted this declaration of war passively and in silence. It was always the same impasse. If a Bill satisfied the Irish Catholics, the Irish Protestants would rebel against it. If a Bill was acceptable to Protestant Ulster and her English supporters, the Cabinet could not accept it without betraying its Irish clients. In despair, Asquith turned to the King.

The firebrands of the Unionist party had persistently pressed the King to intervene. They urged him to refuse his assent to the Bill when Asquith submitted it for his signature, or to dismiss immediately the Liberal ministers, form a Unionist Cabinet, and appeal to the country.[2] What did the King himself think? On the question of Ireland his personal opinions were those of the Unionist

[1] This is not the place to discuss the details of a Budget which Lloyd George carried only in part. We need only say that it exceeded the sum of £200,000,000, and presented a deficit and moreover that to provide for the increasing deficit of local government finance Lloyd George proposed to increase the contributions from the national exchequer to the local authorities in the spirit of that system of taxation of land values of which he never lost sight and that to make up the national deficit he proposed besides a considerable decrease in the sinking fund and an all-round increase of the taxes levied on large fortunes. Finally, the Speaker intervened to protest against the inclusion in a Money Bill of clauses not of a strictly financial character. For the difficulties in which Lloyd George was in consequence involved see Book 1, p. 349.
[2] For these demands see Sir John Mariott's reflections, *The Mechanism of the Modern State—a Treatise on the Science and Art of Government*, 1927, vol. i, p. 33.

party. Nor did he consider himself obliged to give his assent to the Government of Ireland Bill if it were not accompanied by the Amending Bill which the Liberal Prime Minister had himself admitted to be necessary.[1] But we can well believe that he shrank from taking so dangerous an initiative and forcing an appeal to the electorate after which it would be no longer as had been the case four years earlier the veto of the House of Lords, but the veto of the Crown itself which would be called in question.[2] It was because he was afraid to commit himself that during the last few months he had, though reluctantly,[3] come forward as a mediator. It was he who had approached Asquith and Bonar Law in November. It was he who in March acted as an intermediary between Carson and Asquith. Why should he not intervene again at the eleventh hour and attempt to secure, in accordance with the procedure which had suggested itself to Balfour and Lloyd George in 1910, and which Lord Loreburn had recommended in 1913, the appointment of an 'impartial' conference? When the Amending Bill reached the report stage—that is to say, when the measure as a whole must be put to the vote, an adroit use of the rules of procedure enabled Lord Dunraven to introduce and carry an amendment empowering the King to suspend by order in council the operation of the Home Rule Bill until a Royal Commission had reported on the constitutional relations between Ireland and the other parts of the United Kingdom.[4] Lord Morley opposed the amendment which he denounced as unconstitutional and it was carried in opposition to the Government. Nevertheless, Lord Dunraven was simply expressing, possibly in an unacceptable form, a desire to gain time, which the Government shared and which a few days later it would satisfy by another method. On Monday, July 20, after a week of feverish negotiations the

[1] Sir Almeric Fitzroy, *Memoirs*, June 16, 1914. Lord Morley's account of an audience with King George (vol. ii, p. 552).

[2] Christopher Addison, *Politics from Within, 1911–1918*, vol. i, pp. 34–6.

[3] Mensdorff Dispatch from London, October 10, 1913: 'King George is so preoccupied with the present difficulties of the domestic situation—that is to say, with Ireland and the responsibility laid upon the crown by both parties that he seems at the moment to give less attention to questions of foreign policy. His Majesty repeatedly complained to me of the extremely delicate position in which he was placed and the decisions he was called upon to take. No English sovereign, he said, had been confronted with such difficult problems. Fortunately he seems determined to maintain a strictly constitutional attitude and to resist the constant invitations made to him by members of the Opposition to intervene personally in the conflict' (*Österreich-Ungarns Aussenpolitik* . . . vol. vii, p. 430).

[4] H. of L., July 11, 1914 (*Parliamentary Debates*, Lords 1914, 5th Series, vol. xvi, pp. 1135 sqq.).

King summoned a conference of which the Speaker was chairman. It consisted of eight members: two Liberals, Asquith and Lloyd George; two Unionists, Lord Lansdowne and Bonar Law; two Irish Nationalists, Redmond and Dillon; and two Ulstermen, Carson and Captain Craig. The Labour party and the Liberal Press loudly denounced the Prime Minister's weakness and protested against a procedure which might be interpreted as an encroachment by the Crown upon the prerogatives of Parliament. Arthur Ponsonby raised the question in the House of Commons.[1] 'Republicanism', declared Ramsay MacDonald,[2] 'is at a discount in this country, but, if by the advice of responsible ministers or irresponsible court hangers-on the King is going to do something against the House of Commons' liberty, then the flames of Republican agitation will be lit at once.' But this doctrinaire opposition was indubitably artificial. It was obvious that the King in concert with his ministers was making a supreme effort not to assert his authority but to escape the necessity of using it, not to destroy the British system of parliamentary government but to save its imperilled tradition. The effort proved fruitless. The Conference held four meetings and the fourth, on Friday the 24th, ended in an impasse. The question of the treatment to be given to the two southern counties of Ireland, Fermanagh, and Tyrone where the Catholics were in a majority and the slight Protestant minority and the slight Catholic majority were so intermingled that it was impossible to separate them, was the point which the rival fanaticisms, each determined not to compromise with its opponent, chose on which to declare agreement impossible.[3] What then was the goal for which Ireland and England were heading?[4] Two days later another incident of civil warfare took place in Ireland more serious than any which had occurred in the previous spring.

[1] H. of C., July 22, 1914 (*Parliamentary Debates*, Commons 1914, 5th Series, vol. lxv, p. 454).

[2] Durham Miners' Annual Gala, July 25, 1914.

[3] For interesting details of the discussion on this question see Lord Ullswater, *A Speaker's Commentaries*, vol. i, pp. 163–4.

[4] General Macready, *Annals of an Active Life*, vol. i, pp. 193–4: 'On the 21st of July, 1914, the abortive conference took place at Buckingham Palace, and on the 24th of July I received a note from Mr. Asquith directing me to proceed to Belfast at once. There was to be no change from the former policy, troops were to 'sit tight' and make no moves of any kind. If a Provisional Government was proclaimed the consequential proclamation by Carson would be awaited to enable the Cabinet to determine their next move. A more thoroughly unsatisfactory position for any soldier it is hard to imagine, but the open support of the Conservatives by certain senior officers on the active list of the Army made it

The scene of the incident to which we allude was not Protestant but Catholic Ireland, the neighbourhood not of Belfast but of Dublin and to understand the events which led up to it we must go back a little. In telling the story of these last months of crisis we have said very little of the part played by Redmond, for the reason that it had been very subordinate. He had accepted the Government's Bill without reservation and obtained for it the support of his entire party. That support had ensured the passage of the Bill in three successive sessions. Redmond thus found himself as against the Ulster malcontents the representative of British constitutionalism and since thirty years of Parliamentary life had perhaps destroyed in him the revolutionary temper, he was delighted that under his leadership Catholic Ireland seemed to represent the forces of order against the forces of disorder. His position became more difficult when the Cabinet on the point of reintroducing the Government of Ireland Bill for the third time began to hesitate in face of the resistance of Ulster and to speak of compromise. In the teeth of many uncompromising utterances he capitulated for the first time in March when he accepted the Amending Bill as sketched by Asquith. He capitulated a second time in July when together with Dillon he consented to take part in a conference whose purpose could only be to explore the possibility of further concessions. But how difficult his position in Ireland had become! It is indeed surprising that he succeeded so long in maintaining his authority almost unimpaired. For at his back and without his recognition Catholic Ireland was following a year later the example set by Ulster and was arming.

The movement seems to have originated among Larkin's followers during the great strike in Dublin in the autumn of 1913. This host of workers mobilized for the strike provided the material of a genuine revolutionary army on the Ulster model, at once national and socialist, which would attempt to set up by

imperative in my view to see the business through no matter where it might lead.' To what extent the difficulties with which the Government was confronted were increased by the fear of alienating American opinion it is hard to decide in the entire absence of any reference to the subject either in the Press or in Parliament. It is however certain that the question must have caused the Cabinet considerable anxiety when it became clear that war with Germany was imminent. See *Royal Commission on the Rebellion in Ireland 1916, Minutes of Evidence*, p. 21: Evidence by the Rt. Hon. Augustine Birrell.

force an Irish proletarian republic.[1] A Citizen Army was actually organized under the patronage of an English crank, Captain White, son of one of the leading British generals who after following for some years his father's profession had conceived an antipathy to war and the army and had dabbled one after another in all the Utopias, Tolstoyan, Vegetarian, and Communist before his conversion to the cause of the Irish revolution. On October 25 we find him on the platform of a large public meeting held in Dublin where a more ambitious project was discussed—nothing less than the formation of a huge army of volunteers which, irrespective of social, political, and religious creed, would prepare to defend the independence of Ireland. Representatives of Irish republicanism and Sinn Fein took part in the meeting, and the Hibernians and the United Irish League were also represented though their representation was smaller.[2] Sir Roger Casement was also present.[3] A Protestant born in Ulster but of English parentage, he had for some time been in the consular service and had taken part in Africa in Morel's campaign against the companies exploiting the Belgian Congo. From Africa he had proceeded to South America, where his denunciation of the inhuman treatment of native labour by the planters in certain districts of Brazil had attracted the attention of the British public and earned him a Knighthood. He had finally quitted the consular service under circumstances about which his enemies circulated damaging reports and had become a champion of Irish independence. In a series of articles which he wrote or inspired for publication in the *Irish Review* he advocated an alliance between Ireland and Germany in the event of the imminent and inevitable war between England and the latter country. A German victory, he maintained,

[1] 'We see to-day two main kinds of collective revolt, that of subject races and subject classes. They may be (indeed generally are) quite distinct. A class may revolt against the pressure of a social system, although the race of which it forms part has evolved that system as part of its character and culture. Or a race may revolt without formulating any distinct class protest. The race revolt is an affair of the surface consciousness, concerned with the modification or reconstruction of external conditions. Where the two revolts unite in one the whole National Being is engaged.' (Captain White, *The Significance of Sinn Fein*, 1918.) Quoted by the writer himself on page 246 of a work entitled *Misfit* in which he tells the story of his inconsistent and incongruous career. See further for the history of the Citizen Army P. O. Catharaigh, *The Story of the Irish Citizen Army*, 1919.

[2] W. A. Phillips, *The Revolution in Ireland*, 1923, pp. 68–9. D. D. Sheeham, *Ireland since Parnell*, 1921, p. 279.

[3] L. G. Redmond Howard, *Sir Roger Casement. A Character Sketch without Prejudice*, 1916. Denis R. Gwynn, *The Life and Death of Roger Casement*, 1930. Casement's writings were collected and published at Munich in 1917 under the title *Gesammelte Schriften*.

would mean for Ireland complete independence or at the least independence under a German protectorate.[1]

The organization of the Irish Volunteers inspired by Casement made rapid progress. By December their numbers were 1,850. At the beginning of the following June there were more than 100,000 volunteers with 630 training centres. The movement was governed from Dublin and was under the despotic control of a Committee of twenty-five in which the representatives of the parliamentary party were an insignificant minority. It was an organization likely to have proved dangerous to the Nationalists if it remained in the hands of extremists anxious to destroy the authority of Redmond and his followers. In fact, it achieved such rapid progress during the summer of 1914 because in May Redmond ordered his party to join *en masse*, and on June 12 in an open letter Redmond called upon the twenty-five members of the Committee to co-opt twenty-five others, nominees of the party. In case of refusal he demanded the immediate formation in every county of committees to reorganize the volunteers on a new basis independently of the Dublin Committee. Of the twenty-five members of the Committee eight refused to yield. But the remaining seventeen accepted Redmond's conditions. It was in vain that the Republicans and Sinn Feiners who were beginning to join the movement and the Socialists of the little Citizen Army which had not amalgamated with the main body of volunteers, denounced the servility of the Dublin Committee. Redmond was taking control of a movement which had been organized without him and undoubtedly, in the intention of many of its founders, against him.[2]

---

[1] Batha Macrainn 'Ireland and the German Menace' (*Irish Review*, September 1912, vol. ii, pp. 343 sqq.). '*Shan Van Vocht*'—'Ireland, Germany and the next War' (*Irish Review*, July 1913, vol. iii, pp. 217 sqq.). Denis R. Gwynn (*The Life and Death of Roger Casement*, p. 194) ascribes the latter article to Casement. In the first number of *The Irish Volunteer*, April 7, 1914, Casement published an article entitled 'From Clontarf to Berlin' in which he advocated: 1. A review of the National Volunteers to be held on April 23 the ninth centenary of the great national victory of Clontarf; 2. The participation of Ireland as a separate nation in the Olympic Games to be held at Berlin in 1916. 'Ireland should there be ranked among the free countries of the world. She will be at least as free as Finland or Alsace.' When the ships of the Cunard Line ceased to call at Queenstown, the German Hamburg-Amerika Line decided to take its place. But the Irish prepared to welcome the arrival of the first liner with celebrations on so ambitious a scale that the Foreign Office took alarm and at its request the German Government asked the Hamburg-Amerika Line to abandon its intention.

[2] S. Gwynn, *John Redmond's Last Years*, 1919, p. 116. Cf. on the Irish Volunteers, *Royal Commission on the Rebellion in Ireland*, 1916, *Minutes of Evidence*, p. 45, Colonel Sir Neville Chamberlain's Evidence.

But the malcontents were to have their revenge. At first the Irish volunteers confined themselves to manœuvres and unarmed parades, or if they carried any arms they were wooden rifles. In July they decided to imitate Ulster and obtain arms from the quarters where the Ulstermen had obtained theirs, in Germany. A council of war was held in London at the house of Mrs. J. R. Green, the widow of an eminent English historian and an ardent Home Ruler. The meeting was attended by a young Englishman, Erskine Childers, a member of the spiritual family to which White and Casement belonged. A zealous patriot, he had fought in the Boer War and published the diary recording his life in the army. He had achieved success with a story about spying which called the attention of the British public to the danger of a German invasion, and had published studies of military tactics in which he discussed the lessons taught by the South African War as to the employment of cavalry. During the summer of 1910, spent with an Irish uncle, he was suddenly converted to Home Rule—in virtue of his British patriotism, he declared, and because he was an imperialist. Ireland must be treated as Canada had been treated in 1840 and South Africa a few years before and reconciled by complete liberation. His new creed led him to extreme courses. He collected and provided from his private means a portion of the funds necessary to purchase 25,000 German rifles. He commanded the yacht which took delivery of them in the neighbourhood of Hamburg and on July 26, 1914, two days after the failure of the conference, cast anchor with his cargo in the little port of Howth at the entrance to the harbour which led up to the capital.[1]

The Dublin volunteers were on the spot, prepared for a bold demonstration. They would unload the arms in broad daylight at the very gates of the city beneath the eyes of the powerless authorities. They occupied the pier, drove away the police and customs officers, kept whatever guns they required, piled the rest into motor lorries which disappeared from the scene, and set out on their return to Dublin, where they intended to make a martial and triumphant entry. They were met en route by a Scottish regiment which had been called out and which if it could not seize their arms, at least put them to flight. But when the Scotch

---

[1] For Erskine Childers see *Erskine Childers, 1870–1922. A Sketch* (by Basil Williams). For the Howth incident see Denis Gwynn. *The Life and Death of Roger Casement*, 1930, pp. 233 sqq. Conor O'Brien, *From Three Yachts. A Cruiser's Outlook*, pp. 1 sqq.

troops returned to Dublin they were greeted by the booing and missiles of an immense crowd. Alarmed and overwrought they fired. There were fifty casualties, among them three deaths.[1]

A loud cry of wrath arose throughout Catholic Ireland. This was the way in which the British Government, so long-suffering towards the Ulster rebels, met with shooting the first attempt of the genuine Irish to reply to the Ulster threat. But we cannot help asking whether the revolutionaries when they united their protests with the popular outcry were wholly sincere. For this bloody affray was a strategical success for themselves. Redmond was in a tight corner. He must either be the accomplice of a government of murderers or become in spite of himself the leader of an insurrection. The problem would in fact assume this form ere long, but meanwhile at the very moment when civil war seemed to have broken out in Ireland, Irish affairs became no more than an almost negligible episode in the tremendous struggle which was beginning and would array in mortal combat the nations and races of the globe.

[1] *Report of the Royal Commission into the Circumstances connected with the Landing of Arms at Howth on 26th July, 1914 and Minutes of Evidence with Appendices and Index, 1914.*

CHAPTER II

International Anarchy

I THE WEST AND THE PROBLEM OF ARMED PEACE

I

WE have already seen the effect produced in the West by the conclusion on November 4, 1911, of the agreement between France and Germany on the question of Morocco. It was not the reconciliation it might have been expected to produce. France did not forgive Germany the methods of intimidation she had employed in July and August. Germany could not forgive France for having snatched from her, six years after Tangier, the right to set up a protectorate in Morocco. Nor could she forgive England whose intervention in the dispute had rendered France less pliable than she had hoped. And in England we have observed loud expressions of dissatisfaction from a public eager for peace, a dissatisfaction which turned against Grey when it became known how close to the abyss the nation had stood. His position indeed was not seriously shaken. He had certainly not lost the confidence of the King, who in February bestowed upon him the signal honour of a Knighthood of the Garter, which had been conferred upon only four members of the House of Commons before him. But the triumvirs of Liberal Imperialism, Asquith, Haldane, and himself, perceived that the only way to satisfy public opinion was to do everything in their power to appease the anger of Germany without endangering either the *entente* with France or British naval supremacy.

Their task was made easier by the fact that certain members of the German Government entertained similar sentiments. For a long time the Chancellor, Bethmann-Hollweg, impressed by the persistence with which Metternich, the German Ambassador in London, urged a policy of caution on his Government, had been working for a *rapprochement* between the two countries. As we already know, negotiations had been opened, and had continued until they had been broken off unexpectedly by the despatch of the *Panther* to the harbour of Agadir. At the close of 1911 Bethmann-Hollweg had the support of the Minister of Finance, who shrank from the ruinous expenditure which the new naval law

demanded by the Emperor and Tirpitz involved. And his opposition was increased by the fact that the general staff was beginning
to demand a reinforcement of the army and to protest against the
excessive expenditure upon the navy which interfered with their
plans. The Emperor finally yielded to his Chancellor's arguments
and gave him leave to commence negotiations for a pact with
England. He did not believe they would be successful. To attempt
to reconcile the Anglo-French *entente* with an understanding between England and Germany was, he said, to attempt to square
the circle.[1] But the attempt would cost nothing. And its failure
would expose British bad faith.

Bethmann-Hollweg lost no time in sending Metternich instructions to begin the negotiations. But the Ambassador disagreed
with the procedure the Chancellor proposed. To attempt a formal
pact, a species of alliance or semi-alliance, was to invite failure. It
would be better to negotiate a colonial agreement on the lines of
those already concluded, with France first, then with Russia, and
which Grey's speech on November 27 seemed to envisage.[2] The
Chancellor left him free to negotiate in his own way and Metternich broached the subject on December 20. Grey, however,
showed no anxiety to follow up the suggestion. He was taken by
surprise. He could not decide upon his course of action until the
Reichstag election in January had determined the lines which
German policy would pursue in the immediate future. Moreover,
all the ministers were absent on their Christmas holiday and
would not return until the beginning of February. Nevertheless,
the negotiations continued. Like the negotiations between France
and Germany in 1905 and in 1911, they were conducted by business men who constituted themselves unofficial diplomats.[3]

[1] Note appended to a despatch from Metternich to Bethmann-Hollweg, December 20,
1911. (*Die Grosse Politik* . . . vol. xxxi, p. 86 n.)

[2] *Parliamentary Debates*, Commons 1911, 5th Series, vol. xxxii, pp. 61–2. Grey obviously was making a veiled allusion to the Portuguese colonies and it was in this sense
that Metternich interpreted his words in a letter written on November 28 to Bethmann-
Hollweg (*Die Grosse Politik* . . . vol. xxix, p. 274).

[3] See Sir Goschen to Sir A. Nicolson, February 9, 1912: '. . . the Chancellor . . . said
that he had just received a despatch from Metternich and that there was evidently some
misunderstanding. The idea seemed to prevail in London that Ballin had acted under
instructions from the Emperor. This was far from being the case, as neither the Emperor
nor he himself had anything to do with Ballin's first step ! In fact, he had been most surprised that Cassel had been chosen by His Majesty's Government as our intermediary in an
important matter which concerned the two Governments, and when there was a German
Ambassador in London. I said that I had certainly understood that Ballin had acted with
some authority, but the Chancellor denied it absolutely.' (*British Documents* . . . vol. vi,
p. 672.) The Same to the Same, February 10, 1912: 'The Chancellor's remarks to me about

They were Albert Ballin, the great shipbuilder, and Sir Ernest Cassel, the great banker, each a *persona grata* with the courts of Potsdam and Windsor respectively. Ballin sent Cassel to Churchill, who no doubt consulted Asquith, when the latter on January 8 spent a few hours in London. Ballin and Cassel favoured a personal meeting between the two naval ministers, Churchill and Tirpitz. Churchill refused. Such a meeting would commit the British Government too far, as the impression would be given that he had been sent to Berlin to apologize for Lloyd George's outburst. The utmost to which he would agree was to accompany King George to Berlin if the King should ever pay a visit to his cousin.[1] Nevertheless, he welcomed the suggestion of a conversation to discuss the possibility of a mutual limitation of armaments. Lloyd George, who was preparing his Budget for the financial year 1912-13, was asking for economies, and McKenna in one of the last speeches he delivered as First Lord of the Admiralty had promised that the navy estimates for 1912 would not exceed those for 1911, if Germany did not increase her navy.[2] Why not ask the German Government what its intentions were and undertake to call a halt in the armament race, if Germany did not speed it up? He obtained Lloyd George's consent when he returned on January 21 from the Riviera and the decision was taken by a small committee at the end of January before any meeting of the Cabinet

Ballin and Cassel were queer and there must be some—well call it misunderstanding—somewhere. Haldane says that the Chancellor was only trying to save Metternich's face, and that it was hardly necessary for him to allude to it. But then, how about my face if the Germans are allowed to give the impression that His Majesty's Government opened the conversations through Cassel and not through His Majesty's Ambassador at Berlin?' (ibid., p. 674) Szögyény. Despatch from Berlin, February 15, 1912: 'The papers comment at length on the fact that Sir Ernest Cassel visited Berlin at the same time as Lord Haldane. Herr von Kiderlen told me that on that occasion he had not met Cassel whom he regards as a busybody.' (*Österreich-Ungarns Aussenpolitik* . . . vol. iii, p. 83.) Kiderlen-Wächter was taking a holiday at Stuttgart when Haldane visited Berlin and was extremely annoyed because he was not consulted (F. Jaeckh, Kiderlen-Wächter, *Staatsmann und Mensch. Briefwechsel und Nachlass herausg.* Von F. Jaeckh 1924, vol. ii, p. 155). Hulderman's *Life of Albert Ballin* does not decide the question. The writer is content to say: 'It was Cassel and Ballin who suggested that another attempt should be made to reach an understanding and the suggestion found a ready welcome from Herr von Bethmann' (p. 248). It would appear that the idea of these conversations suggested itself spontaneously to these two magnates but that the offer of their services was immediately accepted, in what spirit we have attempted to conjecture, by both Governments and also, but with considerable reluctance, by the respective Foreign Offices. Cf. W. Churchill, *The World Crisis, 1911–1914*, p. 95. *Die Grosse Politik* . . . vol. xxxi, p. 97 n.

[1] Winston Churchill to Sir E. Cassel, January 7, 1912 (*British Documents* . . . vol. vi, p. 666).

[2] H. of C., March 13, 1911 (*Parliamentary Debates*, Commons 1911, 5th Series, vol. xxii, p. 1921).

was held. Churchill probably agreed to the negotiations in the same spirit as the Emperor William. He thought it advisable that they should be opened. He was sure they would fail.

The conversations began on January 29 by the presentation at Berlin of two diplomatic notes. Sir Edward Goschen handed one to Kiderlen-Wächter, Sir Ernest Cassel the other to Bethmann-Hollweg. The former was a long-delayed reply to the German note of June 27 respecting an interchange of naval information. The British Government gave an extremely guarded assent to the principle. Although it was the German Government which at the beginning of November had suggested further negotiations on the subject, the note met with an unfavourable reception in Berlin. It was regarded as an attempt to discover the secret of the German naval law to be introduced shortly.[1] The second was an extremely brief memorandum consisting of three clauses and approved by Grey, Churchill, and Lloyd George. It proposed as the subject of the negotiations a diplomatic agreement, a colonial agreement, and a reduction in the German programme of naval construction.[2] Those were the three points on which during the last two months the Emperor, Metternich, and Churchill had successively desired to negotiate. They were also the three questions unsuccessfully discussed by both Governments for two years, from the summer of 1909 to the summer of 1911. Agadir had not altered the policy of the British Government. The only difference was that the country seemed more anxious than before to reach an understanding. Would this greater anxiety make negotiations any easier than they had been before Agadir?

The German Emperor gave the note a favourable reply, but attached to his acceptance certain reservations of principle and invited Grey to discuss matters with him at Berlin. Before it had been Churchill, now it was Grey. German tactics were always the same. Germany wished to commit the British Government further than it was prepared to be committed. When, on February 2, the first meeting of the Cabinet was held the ministers decided in favour of a more cautious policy. The Minister for War, Lord Haldane—he had been made a peer a few months before—would visit Berlin, accompanied by his brother, a distinguished scientist

[1] *Die Grosse Politik, Parliamentary Debates,* Commons, 1911, 5th Series, vol. xxxi, p. 50 *British Documents . . .* vol. vi, p. 662.
[2] Ibid., vol. xxxi, p. 98.

and fellow of an Oxford college, ostensibly to study questions connected with the organization of higher education. Haldane knew German to his finger-tips, was a frequent visitor to the country, and had the *entrée* of the German Embassy in London. He could not fail to have the confidence of every English friend of Germany and every German friend of England. Moreover, he was an intimate friend of Asquith's and a still more intimate friend of Grey's. Both knew all he had done to secure a close co-operation between the British and French armies, if a German army should invade France. In short, the imperialist group in the Cabinet found in him their surest support. He arrived at Berlin on the 8th and left on the 11th after interviews with the Emperor, Tirpitz, Bethmann-Hollweg, and Jules Cambon. This visit, about which no secrecy was maintained, which the officials of the Foreign Office and the British Embassy at Berlin regarded with intense dislike, Conservative opinion greeted with a polite scepticism and Radical opinion welcomed with enthusiasm, produced a profound impression on the Continent. Haldane, it was believed, was going to Berlin to pave the way for a personal visit by Grey or Churchill in the immediate future, if the prospects of an agreement proved favourable. So many documents of every description bearing upon the visit have been published that nothing remains obscure.[1] We must discuss the three points on which the conversations turned and relate the immediate results achieved in respect to each and what forms the negotiation subsequently assumed.

2

It was the German Government which in 1909 had been the first to propose a pact between the two countries and the British Government which had refused, undoubtedly for very cogent reasons. Now the British Government was the first to revive the proposal, though the formula it put forward was more cautious and vaguer than the German formula of 1909. The Cassel note

[1] Th. von Bethmann-Hollweg. *Betrachtungen zum Weltkriege* 1 Teil. *Vor dem Kriege*, 1919, pp. 50 sqq. Viscount Haldane, *Before the War*, 1920, pp. 57 sqq., also *Autobiography*, 1929, pp. 238 sqq. A. von Tirpitz, *Erinnerungen*, 1920, pp. 185 sqq.; and *Politische Dokumente*, vol. i, pp. 280 sqq. *Die Grosse Politik* . . . vol. xxxi, pp. 95 sqq. *British Documents* . . . vol. vi, pp. 666 sqq. *Documents diplomatiques français*, 3e Série, vol. ii, *passim*. For Haldane's secret meetings at night with Cassel during his visit to Berlin see his disclosures to Sir Almeric Fitzroy (Sir Almeric Fitzroy, November 10, 1921, *Memoirs*, vol. ii, p. 765).

suggested 'mutual assurances denying each other the power of engaging in designs or combinations whose character might be aggressive to the other'. Metternich, to whom the note was communicated, wanted the word 'aggressive' expunged. England would always maintain that her *entente* with France was defensive. He also wanted the word 'wars' added to 'designs' and 'combinations'. The change would render the formula a pact of unconditional neutrality in the event of war. Germany wanted nothing more from England should she ever decide to crush France by her military strength. The interview between Bethmann-Hollweg and Lord Haldane took precisely the same turn. Haldane proposed a formula similar to that contained in the Cassel note. Bethmann-Hollweg put forward an alternative formula consisting of four articles in which the word 'aggression' was not used and it was expressly stipulated that, if either of the High Contracting Powers should find itself involved in a war with one or more powers, the other should observe towards it at least an attitude of benevolent neutrality and do everything in its power to localize the conflict. The original draft had been worded 'should be attacked by one or more powers'. This wording however raised the question how aggression should be defined and we have just seen why the German Government did not wish to raise the issue. Bethmann-Hollweg had therefore thought it prudent to give the formula a universal application. But the change made it dangerous. In the impossible supposition, Lord Haldane asked, of a British attack upon Denmark or Austria, did Germany really pledge herself to a benevolent neutrality? And on the other hand, how was it possible for England to promise Germany that if she ever made an unprovoked attack upon France, England would stand aside and even adopt an attitude of benevolence? Bethmann admitted the force of the objection. He returned to his original formula and even defined it more stringently. According to the new text, the promise of benevolent neutrality was made conditional. It was restricted to the eventuality that one or other of the contracting powers 'found itself involved in a war in which it was impossible to say that it was the aggressor'. This was the point the negotiations had reached when Haldane returned to England.

Conversations continued between Berlin and London. Haldane did not want a visit which had focused the attention of the entire world upon himself to end in a fiasco. Asquith and Grey would have been delighted to find a formula which, without alarming France or Russia, would give sufficient satisfaction to Germany to induce her to slacken the pace of her naval construction. But the Emperor William was perhaps right when he spoke of squaring the circle and Grey, preoccupied by efforts to settle the general strike of the collieries, had little time to spare for the question. The permanent officials, who had been extremely annoyed by Haldane's action, if only because their professional pride had been hurt by a procedure which seemed to imply that the conflict between England and Germany could be best settled without the assistance of the professional diplomats, now took their revenge. Nicolson, who for the last eighteen months had replaced Hardinge at the Foreign Office, was at pains to draw up a formula as meaningless as possible.[1] 'England will make no unprovoked attack upon Germany and pursue no aggressive policy towards her. Aggression upon Germany is not the object and forms no part of any Treaty understanding or combination to which England is now a party, nor will she become a party to anything that has such an object.' It was a formula so empty that Paul Cambon, to whom it was communicated, seems to have raised no objection. But for that very reason it was not likely to satisfy the German Government. It demanded the addition of the word 'neutrality'. Grey refused. The utmost to which he would agree was a slight modification of the opening words. Instead of saying 'will make no unprovoked attack', he was prepared to say 'will neither make nor join in any unprovoked attack'. This was not sufficient to satisfy Berlin. The Emperor lost his temper, talked of arming against England, of ordering a mobilization and finally wrote a personal letter to the King of England in which he proposed point blank the conclusion of a treaty of alliance to which France should be invited to adhere.[2] It was a western version of Bjorköe even

[1] 'A formula . . . which will be of as non-committal a character as possible, and also one which will not bind our hands in regard to any eventualities which may possibly arise in the future.' (Sir A. Nicolson to Sir E. Goschen, March 13, 1912; *British Documents* . . . vol. vi, p. 712.)

[2] March 18, 1912 (Von Tirpitz, *Politische Dokumente*, vol. i, p. 331). Cf. a note of the same date by the Emperor attached to a letter from Bethmann-Hollweg written the previous day 'I am proposing to England—since out of consideration for France she *refuses* to pledge us her neutrality—in place of a promise of neutrality an offensive and defensive alliance in which France will be included. If England rejects the offer *she will put herself in the wrong in the eyes of the entire world*, if she accepts, my position at home will be stronger. At the same time Schön in Paris must be informed that although France has behaved outrageously towards the German army and nation, the present Government entertains no

less likely than the latter to be taken seriously by professional diplomatists and which the Emperor himself did not take seriously. Though it was not until April 10 that Metternich officially informed the Foreign Office that since agreement had proved impossible the German Government considered the negotiations closed, by the middle of March, more exactly on March 20, the two Governments must be considered to have abandoned all hope of a satisfactory conclusion.

Nevertheless the affair had an unexpected sequel. On March 27 the British Ambassador in Paris, Sir Frances Bertie, alarmed by the continuation of negotiations of which he disapproved in principle, called on Raymond Poincaré, who for the past six weeks had been President of the Council and Minister for Foreign Affairs, asked leave to speak as 'though he were not an Ambassador', and denounced Grey's weakness. 'It is essential', he declared, 'that Cambon should express his dissatisfaction. If you will only employ firmer language in London, the false step I dread will not be taken.'[1] In London there was no difficulty in reassuring Cambon. Grey, speaking on behalf of the entire Cabinet informed him of his determination not to depart from his final declaration to Metternich. 'Sir Edward Grey', Nicolson explained, 'is fully aware of the situation and if he continues his conversations with Metternich it is simply a matter of tactics. He does not want the rupture to be his doing.'[2] Poincaré took the opportunity to make a new proposition through the intermediary of Cambon.

In 1905 Lord Lansdowne had proposed to reinforce and extend the *entente* with France. But when Delcassé wanted to accept the offer he was defeated by the opposition of Rouvier and his colleagues and compelled to resign. The following winter Rouvier had himself proposed to the British Government what he had refused when England offered it. It was then his turn to be defeated by the caution of the new Liberal Cabinet which had just taken office. In Cambon's opinion the time was ripe after the

---

unfriendly designs and in the course of negotiations with England has made known its willingness to include France in the alliance. If our proposal is refused the situation is clear. We have done our duty. If it is accepted the peace of Europe is assured. *The agreement which Haldane attempted to negotiate is dead.* I will have nothing more to do with it' (*Die Grosse Politik . . .* vol. xxxi, p. 187).

[1] Raymond Poincaré to Paul Cambon, March 28, 1912. (*Documents diplomatiques français*, 3e Série, vol. ii, pp. 264–5.)

[2] De Fleuriau to Raymond Poincaré, April 4, 1912 (ibid., vol. ii, pp. 309–10).

Agadir episode to revive Lord Lansdowne's project and attempt to define more precisely the obligations the *entente* imposed on the two Western Powers.[1] At the moment Cambon's proposal was not received favourably but it became evident in the course of the summer that if there was a majority in the country which desired better relations with Germany there was an active minority which favoured on the contrary a closer bond with France. The *Morning Post,* the *Daily Express,* the *Spectator,* the *Observer* and the *Pall Mall Gazette* conducted a campaign to transform the *entente* into a formal alliance. In the autumn Cambon renewed the attempt. The negotiations lasted a month, attended by difficulties akin in certain respects to those which had rendered the negotiations with Germany so difficult in the spring. But this time they were overcome. On October 22, Grey and Cambon exchanged letters in which it was agreed that, although the arrangements between the armies and navies of the two countries did not constitute 'an engagement obliging the two Governments to take action under circumstances not yet realized and which possibly might never arise', if either Government had serious reason to expect an unprovoked attack 'by a third power it would immediately consult with the other, whether both Governments should take concerted action to prevent aggression and maintain peace and in the event of an affirmative answer should discuss the concerted measures they were prepared to undertake'. What had been pronounced impossible between England and Germany seemed possible between England and France. The negotiations by which Bethmann-Hollweg had hoped to strengthen Germany's diplomatic position by weakening the *entente* had by a strange repercussion reinforced the latter. Hitherto purely verbal, a moral obligation and no more, it had assumed the character, in however guarded a form, of a written agreement. Hitherto when a British general had dealings with a French general, he represented only the War Office. When Major-General Wilson visited Paris in November he was in a position for the first time to speak on behalf of the Cabinet as a whole.

[1] Minute by Sir A. Nicolson, April 15, 1912. (*British Documents* . . . vol. vi, p. 747.)

But if it soon became clear that a pact of neutrality between England and Germany which should not violate the spirit of the Anglo-French *entente* was an impossibility, why should not England offer Germany a colonial agreement such as that which France had accepted in 1904 and Russia in 1908 without any alliance or pledge of neutrality? An agreement of this kind could not be difficult to achieve. For there was no question in dispute between the two powers. In 1898 a secret agreement had been concluded for the partition of the Portuguese colonies. It had never been put into operation. Had it lapsed? If so, why not revive it? On July 21, at the height of the Agadir crisis, Grey, while protesting against the German claim to settle the question of Morocco without consulting England, hinted to Metternich that England was prepared to make concessions to Germany in Africa if she were willing to negotiate with her instead of ignoring her. In his speech of November 27, as we have already had occasion to mention, he had used language susceptible of the same interpretation. The speech had scarcely been delivered when Metternich was bombarded with colonial offers of every description from Englishmen belonging to the most diverse sections of society and representing every shade of political allegiance.[1] When they were transmitted to the Emperor he repulsed them with indignation.[2] What had England to offer him? The property of other nations to embroil him with their possessors and thus promote the exclusive interest of British policy? But the Ambassador took these advances more seriously, and discussed them with Grey on December 20. In fact a possible colonial agreement was one of the three points of the Cassel note, and extensive concessions outside Europe were one of the inducements put forward by Haldane on his arrival at Berlin ten days later to persuade the German statesmen to abandon their new naval law.

What was the character of the negotiations conducted in this sphere by Haldane during his three days' visit? His account is extraordinarily reserved, and for obvious reasons. It would seem in fact that prepared as he was to purchase at a heavy price a halt

---

[1] Count von Metternich to Bethmann-Hollweg, December 9, 1911 (*Die Grosse Politik* . . . vol. xxxi, pp. 72–3).

[2] Memorandum of Kaiser Wilhelm II, January 11, 1912. (ibid., vol. xxxi, pp. 92 sqq.)

in the German naval programme, he expatiated imprudently on the numerous colonial concessions which, according to him, his country was prepared to make. In the event of a partition of the Portuguese colonies, Germany, if she gave up her claim to the Pacific island of Timor since Australia stood in the way, would receive Loango, which by the terms of the agreement of 1898 was to have formed an English enclave in Angola, and England might even promise the southern half of the Congo should it ever cease to be Belgian. Finally, he was willing to acquiesce in a German annexation of the islands of Zanzibar and Pemba if, in the negotiations pending on the question of Bagdad, Germany were willing to make more concessions to England in the region of the Persian Gulf than she had hitherto been prepared to make.

But when Haldane returned his colleagues made him understand that he had perhaps lost his way in the maze of his diplomatic metaphysics. The Foreign Office protested against the danger of employing an amateur in such serious negotiations; the Colonial Office complained that he had allowed himself to be duped by men better acquainted with the geography of Africa than himself. Nothing more was heard of the proposal for a colonial agreement similar to those already concluded with France and Russia. Nevertheless, the desire to improve the relations between the two countries was still active in England, and it was strengthened by circumstances to which we must return later. On the question of Bagdad conversations continued. And on the subject of the Portuguese colonies they were revived after an interval of fourteen years. The difficulties were not identical nor equally serious in both cases.

The entire aspect of the Bagdad question had been changed when, in November 1910, by an understanding ratified ten months later by a formal instrument, the Russian Government reached an agreement on the subject with the German. It was no longer possible in this region to confront Germany with the concerted policy of the Triple Entente. And the attitude of France on the question had always been ambiguous. French financial interests had been consistently in favour of an understanding in Turkey with German industrialism. But when the French Foreign Office, yielding to their pressure, had attempted to settle the basis of such an arrangement it had been confronted in 1900 with the veto of Russia, in 1903 with the veto of Great Britain. Now, though

French diplomacy was more hostile to Germany than it had been at that time, it was difficult for France to adopt a more uncompromising attitude than her Russian ally and her British friend. For months past England in view of Russia's change of front had realized the necessity of reaching a solution as speedily as possible. On July 31, 1911, when the *Panther* had been a month at anchor in the harbour of Agadir, she proposed to Turkey to internationalize the line between Bagdad and Bassorah, Germany, Russia, France, Turkey, and herself to hold equal shares; from Bassorah, whose port would be built by a British company to the sea if the railway should ever be taken beyond that point, the undertaking would be reserved exclusively to Turkey and herself. But neither Germany nor Turkey would agree to the proposal and for six months Turkey left it unanswered. At the beginning of 1912 she definitely rejected it.

The difficulties were great. The India Office adopted on political grounds an uncompromising attitude on any question which might affect British supremacy on the coast of the Persian Gulf. There were private interests to be considered, a British railway company in the district of Smyrna, an irrigation company in Mesopotamia, and an oil company. There were also French financial interests at stake. If France was ready to stand aside in Mesopotamia and on the Persian Gulf she demanded in compensation concessions to her railway enterprises in Asia Minor. A settlement of the entire question seemed to have been reached at last during the first half of 1914. A Franco-German agreement dealing with the railways in Asia Minor was signed on February 15, 1914. An agreement between England and Germany on the subject of the Bagdad railway, also the railway between Smyrna and Aidin, was initialled on June 15. Important concessions were made to Germany, whose right to extend the line to Bassorah was recognized. All that England asked was that two Englishmen should sit on the board of directors. Detailed provisions were laid down regulating the respective share of British and German capital in financing the construction of the ports of Bagdad and Bassorah, in the navigation of the rivers, irrigation, and the extraction of petroleum. An agreement was reached for the joint construction and control, without underhand competition, of the railway system of Anatolia; and England reserved the right eventually to construct a direct line between Egypt and the Persian

Gulf. After this the delays, deliberate or otherwise, of the Turkish officials, whose consent was essential, protracted the settlement so long that the Convention had not been signed by the end of July. Nevertheless, London and Berlin were anxious to reach a conclusion, Petersburg and Paris were consenting parties. On the eve of the Great War, the four great Powers were in agreement upon the division of spheres of influence throughout the territory which represented what was still left of the Ottoman Empire.[1]

The negotiations relative to the Portuguese colonies were more difficult. Not that agreement on the fundamental issue was impossible; a convention was in fact initialled in August 1913.[2] It was

[1] For the negotiation of the Anglo-German agreement respecting Bagdad see *Die Grosse Politik* . . . vol. xxvii, pp. 139 sqq. See further the interesting and mutually corroborating statements of Marquis Pallavicini (Constantinople, April 5, 1913) and Count Mensdorff (London, May 23, 1913) of the reasons for which in their opinion as a result of the Balkan War England regarded German expansion in Asia Minor with less anxiety than hitherto. (*Österreich-Ungarns Aussenpolitik*, vol. vi, pp. 40, 504.)

[2] The question of the Portuguese Colonies was in fact reopened by Grey on July 21, 1911—that is to say, at the beginning of the Agadir crisis and the very day on which Lloyd George delivered his bellicose speech. (Count von Metternich to Bethmann-Hollweg, July 21, 1911; *Die Grosse Politik* . . . vol. xxix, p. 199). He would seem to have believed at first that a friendly arrangement might be possible with Portugal, a bankrupt State, for the purchase of her African colonies. An allusion in his speech of November 27 is susceptible of this interpretation. Cf. in the *Naval Annual 1912*, pp. 17–18, the concluding paragraph of Lord Brassey's article entitled 'Suggestions on Naval Administration': 'If no clouds had arisen in Morocco, we might shortly have found ourselves under serener skies. It should have been possible to fulfil our obligations to France without giving offence to Germany. To indicate how reconciliation might be effected would carry us too far into politics. The cession of Walfisch Bay might fittingly be considered as a suitable opportunity. . . . Nor should it be impossible by friendly negotiations to obtain for South Africa full powers of administration in Delagoa Bay, under the flag of Portugal.' *Saturday Review*, January 20, 1912, p. 68: an article entitled 'An Anglo-German Deal': 'The time is now rapidly approaching when Portugal, urgently in need of cash, will offer Angola to German enterprise for a valuable consideration. . . . We have good grounds for saying that our Foreign Office privately intimated that to this acquisition of rich territory by Germany we should raise no objection. . . . We may assume that with Angola will pass the islands of S. Thomé and Principe, though they now form a separate province. . . . When the break-up of the Portuguese Empire begins, it will go on. We ought at once to make sure of Delagoa Bay. . . . Strategists will be less interested in the fate of Portuguese Africa than in that of the Islands. . . . Germany hankers after the Cape Verde group, but she clearly understands we could not permit her to settle there. But is there any valid objection to her acquiring the Azores, if we can buy the Cape Verde islands at the same time?'—also *Spectator*, January 27, 1912, p. 140, article entitled 'Germany and the African Colonies of Portugal': 'We have no doubt whatever that it would be greatly to the benefit of the world if Germany could acquire the African colonies of Portugal, or to put it more correctly, that portion of those colonies over which we do not possess a right of pre-emption—a right which belongs to us in the matter of Delagoa Bay. Not only would it be a great benefit to humanity that German rule, which if sometimes harsh, is, at any rate efficient and gives no sanction or encouragement to slavery, should be substituted for Portuguese rule; in addition Germany would be given the opportunity for expansion which she desires, and on the greatest scale. Her African Empire would thus only require a portion of the Congo Free State to make it stretch across the African continent from sea to sea.' But it soon became clear that Portugal had no intention of selling her colonies and it then became necessary to negotiate, as in 1898, over the head of the Portuguese Government.

more favourable to Germany than its predecessor of 1898. For if Germany renounced Timor and yielded to England in Mozambique a strip of territory to the north of the Zambesi and in Angola a district adjoining Belgian Katanga which constituted an enclave in Rhodesia, she obtained in recompense by the cession of Loango the entire African coast between the German colonies in South Africa and the Belgian Congo and in addition the islands of San Thomé and Principe off the Congo coast. But England insisted that the Convention should be laid before Parliament and thus made public. And the German Government was opposed to its publication.

For the new agreement, unlike that of 1898, had been drawn up in extremely cautious terms so as to deal only with the economic development of the Portuguese colonies, carefully avoiding all reference to the possibility of their political annexation by England or Germany. But in 1913 as in 1898 Germany cherished the design of establishing, sooner or later, her sovereignty over the regions which the convention allotted to her sphere of influence. And the indignation of the German public would be even greater, if, as England also demanded, the publication of the present agreement was accompanied by the publication of the agreement of 1898, whose secret clauses were far more explicit, and, moreover, by the publication of the treaty of Windsor concluded the following year, which expressly confirmed the clause of an old treaty of 1661 by which England pledged herself 'to defend and protect all the conquests and colonies pertaining to the crown of Portugal against all her enemies present or future'. German statesmen blamed this treaty of 1899, the work of Lord Salisbury,[1] for the fact that the convention of 1898 had remained inoperative.[2] In 1902 they had witnessed a British company

[1] For the Anglo-Portuguese agreements of 1898–9 see my *History of the English People* vol. v, pp. 55–6. My conjectures are confirmed and completed by the revelations, made in 1912 by the Marquis de Soveral to Paul Cambon (De Fleuriau to Raymond Poincaré, April 2, 1912; *Documents diplomatiques français*, 3e Série, vol. ii, p. 296 sqq.).

[2] Friedrich von Bernhardi, *Deutschland und der nächste Krieg*, chap. v. 'Weltmacht oder Niedergang,' p. 115: '... The financial or political collapse of Portugal might also provide us with an opportunity to take possession of a portion of her colonial possessions. There is even good reason to suppose that agreements are in existence between England and Germany which contemplate a partition of the Portuguese colonies, though they have never been published. Whether, should the circumstances arise, England would be prepared to carry out honourably the provisions of such an agreement, supposing it actually to exist, must indeed remain an open question. She could find ways and means to render it ineffective. It is indeed widely asserted, though the report is denied by others, that immediately after her convention with Germany for a partition of the Portuguese colonies Great Britain concluded a special treaty with Portugal guaranteeing the *integrity* of her colonial empire.'

undertake the construction of a railway linking Katanga with the port of Benguela and traversing the entire zone which the convention of 1898 had appeared to surrender to German industry. In 1913, the very year in which the British Government was prepared to confirm in a modified form the convention of 1898, the Benguela railway company was still refusing offers of collaboration from German capital.

And at this juncture, to increase the difficulties of the British Government, the French Government, to whom the negotiations had been communicated, united its protests on this point to the German protests. France, it is true, objected on grounds altogether different from those which inspired the protests of Berlin. The French Government disliked the agreement for its own sake, and if it were to be published like the Franco-British agreement of 1904, it would assume an equal status in the eyes of the world. It would be liable to be interpreted as the preface to an hypocritical alliance, a return to the policy of 1898, whose abandonment had been sealed by the *entente* with France. The French opposition was finally overcome, but Berlin held out. When at last the German Government agreed to publication it made a declaration of its reluctance and insisted on certain conditions. Publication was to be delayed until six months after the agreement had been signed and the British Government was to exert pressure at Lisbon in the interval to secure a particular concession Germany desired in Angola. We must also bear in mind the date at which the German Government finally agreed to the convention being published. It was July 27, 1914.[1] For three days the whole of Europe had been confronted with a problem of the most extreme gravity and German diplomacy was anxious to do everything in its power to conciliate England.

4

We have followed to 1914 the story of the two negotiations begun, or more accurately reopened, in February 1912 after Haldane's visit to Berlin, on the subject of the Bagdad railway, and the Portuguese colonies. But we must not forget that neither of these two questions, nor even the question of neutrality con-

[1] For the negotiations of the Anglo-German convention respecting the Portuguese colonies see *Die Grosse Politik* . . . vol. xxxvii, pp. 1 sqq.

stituted the essence of Haldane's mission. His real objective was to secure a slackening in the pace of German naval construction, and everything turned on the price, colonial concessions, a pact of neutrality, which England was prepared to pay. Germany's terms were onerous, but if England protested she could always reply that great sacrifices were being asked of her. She was being asked to regulate the size of her fleet, not in accordance with the standard she regarded as necessary to protect her commerce and uphold her prestige, but by the standard prescribed by the security and prestige of a foreign power. At every turn we are brought back to the struggle between the two navies. England needed her supremacy at sea to ensure supplies in time of war and to banish the danger of invasion which haunted the Continental nations and compelled them to bear the burden of conscription. But the habit of counting upon the protection of her navy was so deeply ingrained in the British mind that it had become an instinct. England was in love with her navy. Any threat to its supremacy was nothing short of an insult to the national honour. Von Bülow, who employed the leisure of his banishment from political life to meditate upon his country's policy and the international situation, was wide of the mark when he wrote: 'The mainspring of British policy is national selfishness, the mainspring of French policy, national idealism' and went on to draw the conclusion that 'one who seeks his interest with cold-blooded calculation will always prove at the decisive moment master of one who pursues an ideal'.[1] The English would have liked perhaps to settle their difference with the Germans as men of business. But it was impossible. Their navy had a sentimental value for them and Churchill expressed perfectly the true state of affairs when, in an interview with the German Ambassador, he attempted to make him understand that the German fleet was an Alsace-Lorraine between the two countries.[2]

It was the question of the rival navies which had reached a critical phase, this winter of 1911–12, partly as a result of the Agadir incident but also for two other reasons, of which one was directly connected with Agadir, the other had nothing whatever to do with it.

The former was the transference of Churchill to the Admiralty.

[1] Furst von Bülow, *Deutsche Politik* . . . 1916, p. 114.
[2] Prince Lichnowsky to Bethmann-Hollweg. April 30, 1913, *Die Grosse Politik* . . . vol. xxxix, p. 38. Cf. The letter written the same day to Tirpitz by the German naval attaché (Von Tirpitz, *Politische Dokumente*, vol. i, p. 391).

The real significance of this appointment was not immediately apparent. For five or six years he had been, together with Lloyd George, the foremost champion in the Cabinet of a policy of peace and disarmament, and at the time of the Agadir crisis it was not he but Lloyd George who had surprised Europe by an unexpectedly warlike speech. Had he then remained faithful to the principles he had professed before Agadir? Would he, like his father in a Conservative Cabinet, advocate a policy of naval retrenchment? He had begun his career in the army, and several later incidents had proved that this liberal, even ultra-liberal politician, had remained a soldier at heart. Possibly he felt that he had recovered his vocation, when, as Home Secretary, he despatched the police, his police, to put down a band of Russian anarchists in an East End tenement and like a genuine soldier had directed their operations on the scene of action. Nor can we be in any doubt as to the spirit in which he entered upon his duties at the Admiralty when we remember that he had left the Home Office because the too martial methods he had employed to put down the labour disturbances during the previous summer had rendered his position impossible. The Germans were greatly alarmed by the arrival at the Admiralty of a man whom they labelled 'an unscrupulous demagogue', 'a second edition of Chamberlain', 'a man of unbridled ambition', who could be trusted to make use of his new position to increase his popularity at the first international crisis by 'adding fuel to the flames'.[1] The fact that in a few months he had effected a complete change in the high command of the navy confirmed the estimate of those who had expected him to prove a fighter. He did not dare to recall Fisher and plunge the entire service into internecine feud, but he made him his confidant and corresponded regularly with him. Out of the four Sea Lords he got rid of three. Only the third, Rear-Admiral Briggs, retained his position. The term of office of Sir Arthur Wilson, the First Sea Lord, was due to expire. It was not renewed. He was replaced by Sir Francis Bridgeman, who a few months later was in turn brusquely dismissed,[2] Prince Louis of Battenberg

---

[1] The naval attaché in London Captain Widenmann to Tirpitz (*Die Grosse Politik . . .* vol. xxxi, p. 13). Note by the German Minister of Marine, November 1911. (Von Tirpitz, *Politische Dokumente*, vol. i, pp. 255–6.)

[2] For the dismissal of Sir Francis Bridgeman see the heated debate in the House of Commons between Churchill and Lord Charles Beresford (H. of C., December 11, 18, 20, 1912, *Parliamentary Debates*, Commons 1912, 5th Series, vol. xlv, pp. 433–4, 1469 sqq., 1875 sqq.); also A. MacCallum Scott, *Winston Churchill in Peace and War*, 1916, p. 43.

became Second Sea Lord in place of Sir George Egerton, and Captain Pakenham Fourth Sea Lord in place of Rear-Admiral Madden.[1] Immediately after his appointment Churchill satisfied what had been the general desire of the public ever since the scare in August by effecting at the Admiralty the reform Haldane had accomplished at the War Office. He instituted a Naval War Staff, the 'brain' of the British navy, to work out plans of campaign for future wars and through which all candidates for naval command must pass.[2] Its functions were purely advisory. The responsibility for the decisions taken rested with the First Lord of the Admiralty. Equipped with this novel bureau of information and surrounded by new councillors of his own choice, Churchill felt himself a naval commander. He divided his time between the Admiralty and its official yacht the *Enchantress*, in which he made voyages of inspection and study. His enemies complained that when he was present at manœuvres he interposed with advice which was almost a command and was too ready to play the admiral. In short, for the first time for many years, the First Lord of the Admiralty was not the mere mouthpiece of the Sea Lords. A statesman of the first rank had arisen at the Admiralty to confront Tirpitz.[3]

5

For at the moment when the Agadir crisis placed Churchill at the Admiralty the execution of the German naval law had reached a critical point, though the question of Morocco played no part in the matter. Ever since 1900 Berlin had been straining every nerve to build up a huge navy, but the question of personnel had not received corresponding attention. There were not sufficient sailors to man the German fleet and in autumn when one class of sailors having completed its two years service left the navy the vessels

[1] For these changes see H. of C., November 28, 1911 (*Parliamentary Debates*, vol. xxxii, pp. 359 sqq.).

[2] *Naval War Staff, Memorandum by the First Lord on a Naval War Staff*, January 1, 1912 (published as an appendix to the *Statement by the First Lord of the Admiralty explanatory of the Navy Estimates, 1912–1913*). See further the circular addressed on May 11, 1912 to all 'commanders-in-chief, captains, commanders and commanding officers' (*The Times*, March 14, 1912).

[3] For Winston Churchill at the Admiralty see an interesting chapter in A. MacCallum Scott, *Winston Churchill in Peace and War*, 1916, pp. 41 sqq.

were left for the moment practically empty. The navy was obliged
to ask for reinforcements. In place of an annual increase of 3,500
men which would produce in 1917 a total of 86,500 sailors, Tirpitz
obtained from the Reichstag 15,000 additional seamen of all
ranks which would raise the entire personnel of the navy in 1920
to the figure of 101,500. This would make it possible to maintain
three squadrons, instead of two, on active service—that is to say,
twenty-five capital ships instead of seventeen. On the other hand,
whereas the programme as originally laid down provided for the
construction of four capital ships every year up to the current year
1912, for the next five years—that is to say, until 1917—it made
provision for the annual construction of no more than two. As
we should expect, the Ministry of Marine and the Navy League
protested against this sudden decrease in naval construction. And
the entire shipbuilding industry echoed their protests. For it is the
tragic feature of modern industry—and of the armament industry
with the rest—that it leads of its very nature to over-production.
To increase the output the apparatus of production is extended,
and it therefore becomes impossible to slow down the rate of
production without throwing workmen and engineers out of
employment and tying up capital, and industry is condemned
to go on producing at a tempo it cannot slacken. Tirpitz asked
for an extra vessel to be laid down annually for the next six
years—that is, a total construction of three battle cruisers to
replace those condemned as obsolete and three Dreadnoughts
over and above those for which the programme of 1900 made
provision.

We have however already had occasion to speak of the opposition in official circles to a new naval law. It was so powerful that
the Emperor was obliged to make concessions. They were not
concerned with the increase of personnel or the formation of a
third squadron but solely with the construction of new ships. In
the first place the three cruisers were given up. Instead of laying
down six ships between 1912 and 1917 in addition to those provided by the original programme, only three would be built, the
first in 1912, the second in 1914, and the third in 1916. This was
the position when Haldane visited Berlin. The condition on which
the Emperor would agree to slacken the pace of German naval
construction was that England should abandon her programme
of laying down two capital ships for one German and accept the

proportion of three to two which Grey had himself proposed a few months before Agadir. Haldane made no direct reply. He expressed himself indifferent to the increase in the number of ships on the active list and its corollary an increased personnel. He gave the Germans with whom he talked to understand that only one subject caused his English colleagues anxiety—the programme of naval construction. He suggested that an understanding might be reached if Germany consented not to lay down an additional ship in 1912, but build the first in 1913, a second in 1915, and postpone indefinitely the construction of the third.

Perhaps he thought this clever tactics. When he returned to London he found that his colleagues were of a very different opinion. He might have taken warning from a speech made by Churchill at Glasgow on February 9, the day before the Berlin conversations opened. In this speech Churchill formulated the British attitude on the naval question in terms which became canonical: 'The British Navy is to us a necessity and, from some points of view, the German Navy is to them more in the nature of a luxury. Our naval power involves British existence. It is existence to us; it is expansion to them. . . . It is the British Navy which makes Britain a great Power. But Germany was a great Power, respected and honoured all over the world, before she had a single ship'. The effort which at the same moment the German Government was demanding from the Reichstag and the nation to increase the personnel of army and navy alike was the challenge of an overpeopled Germany, not only to France but to England herself; for the Germans were convinced that an England short of men and obliged to purchase crews for her navy could not maintain for long a struggle against Germany, where conscription was in force and the population increasing at the rate of a million a year.[1] Experts pointed out to Haldane that the formation of a third squadron on active service which he regarded so lightly constituted a new danger. It meant a German fleet permanently mobilized in the North Sea against England, ready when the signal was given to make a sudden attack. And the construction of ships in excess of the number laid down in the programme of 1900, however few, necessitated the construction

[1] Count von Metternich to Bethmann-Hollweg, November 1, 1911: '. . . England is convinced of her ability to sustain, if need be, a competition in armaments, longer than we, because she believes that she possesses the longer purse.' The Emperor wrote in the margin 'She has fewer men' (*Die Grosse Politik* . . . vol. xxxi, p. 21).

of additional English vessels. If the object of Haldane's visit had been to prevent this further competition he had failed.

And in fact when Churchill produced navy estimates lower by £307,000 than those for the current year he explained that they were provisional. He asked for an immediate increase of two thousand men. He proposed to lay down new cruisers. But he intended eventually to make further demands both for men and ships when the German estimates became known. As between the capital ships of the two nations he would accept a proportion of sixteen to ten, a proportion not far from the ratio of three to two which had been suggested. But only on condition that Germany did not exceed the programme of 1900. If in the course of the next six years she were to build additional vessels, England would accept her challenge and return to the old proportion of 'two keels to one'. If during these six years Germany laid down three extra ships, England would lay down six. If she built only two, England would build four. There was no note of aggression in this rejoinder; and Churchill put forward the novel suggestion that, if Germany were willing to proclaim a 'naval holiday' for one year during which she would not lay down a single new man-of-war, England would undertake to do the same. In May the German programme was made public. Bethmann-Hollweg and Haldane had defeated the Emperor and Tirpitz, though not without a hard struggle, in the course of which the Chancellor had been driven to the threat of resignation. Only two Dreadnoughts were to be built during the next six years instead of the three decided upon in February, and the six capital ships, ironclads and cruisers, for which Tirpitz had asked in November. When therefore Churchill presented in July his supplementary navy estimates, he was content with four additional Dreadnoughts to be built between 1913 and 1917. But at the same time he was obliged to take into account the German formation of a third active squadron and the increase in her personnel. Amid the chilly silence of the Radicals and the applause of the Opposition he asked for a supplementary grant of £990,000.[1]

[1] H. of C., July 22, 1912 (*Parliamentary Debates*, Commons 1912; 5th Series, vol. xli, pp. 838 sqq.).

No English Lord of the Admiralty since the century opened had spoken so frankly of the German peril, yet no English navy estimates were received with greater calm by German opinion. The official attitude in Berlin was satisfaction. And the following year Tirpitz astonished the world by his moderation. He rejected the imputation of harbouring hostility towards England. He would be satisfied with the proportion of sixteen to ten, with which England, or so at least he hoped, was now content. 'That proportion', he said, 'makes us sufficiently strong to be secure against attack. The naval law guarantees its maintenance. We desire nothing more.'[1] How are we to explain this sudden calm after such feverish activity? The Foreign Office thought it knew the answer and on March 5 Grey wrote as follows to the British Ambassador in Berlin: 'I do not wish you to say anything about Tirpitz's statement, unless something is said to you, because I agree that what Tirpitz said does not amount to much, and the reason of his saying it is not the love of our beautiful eyes, but the extra fifty millions required for increasing the German Army.'[2]

In October 1911, at the moment the Agadir crisis reached a solu-

[1] From a statement made by Tirpitz on February 6, 1913, to the financial committee of the Reichstag. Macnamara, Parliamentary Secretary to the Admiralty, speaking on behalf of Churchill in the House of Commons on February 11, expressed the satisfaction universally felt in England at the new tone adopted by Germany in regard to the naval question. (*Parliamentary Debates*, Commons 1913, 5th Series, vol. xlviii, p. 685.)

[2] Sir E. Grey to Sir E. Goschen, March 5, 1913 (Lord Grey of Fallodon, *Twenty-five Years*, vol. i, p. 257). Cf. Lloyd George, interview given to the *Daily Chronicle*, January 1, 1914. Of two reasons suggested for the relaxation of the naval competition between England and Germany Lloyd George chose the following 'that Continental nations are directing their energies more and more to the strengthening of their land forces. For years Germany seemed to have set her heart upon, and put her best thought into, the development of her naval power. But the experiences of the last two years have reminded her of a lesson which all European nations have had from time to time to learn. And that is, that if a country concentrates its energies upon one branch of its defensive forces, it is generally at the expense of the other. The German army is vital . . . to the very life and independence of the nation itself, surrounded as Germany is by other nations, each of which possesses armies almost as powerful as herself. . . . Certainly Germany has nothing' (so far as her army is concerned) 'which approximates to a Two-Power Standard. She has, therefore, become alarmed by recent events, and is spending huge sums of money on the expansion of her military resources. That is why I feel convinced that even if Germany ever had any idea of challenging our supremacy at sea, the exigencies of the military situation must necessarily put it completely out of her head' Cf. J. Ellis Barker, 'The Failure of Post-Bismarckian Germany' (*Nineteenth Century*, June 1912, vol. lxxi, pp. 1058 sqq., especially pp. 1075 sqq.) and a remarkable article by Crozier Long 'The End of Weltpolitik: a Letter from "Berlin" ' (*Fortnightly Review*, June 1914, vol. cxv, pp. 983 sqq.). For the article, possibly the best written before August 1914 on the origins of the war, see Lichnowsky's appreciative comments (Letter to Bethmann-Hollweg, June 10, 1914: *Die Grosse Politik* . . . vol. xxxix, p. 621).

tion, the first edition appeared of Bernhardi's famous work, *Germany and the Next War*.[1] The writer was far from suggesting that his country should give up her navy. But he was opposed in principle to any strategy which involved a conflict with the British navy on the high seas. Germany should be content to defend her shores against the attempts at invasion which were to be expected, and by reinforcing her fleet of torpedo-boats and submarines and evading the British blockade must place herself in a position to reply to it by destroying the greatest possible number of British merchant vessels. She must take the offensive on land and to free her hands in the east must begin under any circumstances by crushing France, whose army, too weak to invade German territory, would otherwise by its mere existence render an offensive on any other front impossible.[2] These views had been held for many years by the German staff. The novel feature of the situation was the fact that the civil authorities were coming round to them. We have already observed as an immediate repercussion of the Agadir incident, the pressure exerted in the counsels of the Government by the champions of a stronger army to secure, in the teeth of Tirpitz and the Emperor, a reduction in the new naval programme, while the Reichstag was to be asked to pass a new army law. It was also a novelty that these ideas were now publicly expressed, not only by Bernhardi, but by others whose opinions carried weight.[3] In January 1912, 'A League to secure a stronger

[1] *Deutschland und der nächste Krieg*. The sixth edition revised 'in view of the alterations in the military and political situation' was published in 1913.

[2] 'In the first place our political position would be enormously improved if we could free ourselves once and for all from the constant danger that France will attack us on the first favourable opportunity as soon as our hands are full elsewhere. One way or another *France must be put out of action* if we would be free to pursue the general aims of our policy. This is *the first and most essential condition* of a sound German policy, and since it is impossible to rid ourselves finally of French hostility by peaceful methods, we must do so by force. France must be so completely crushed, that she can never cross our path again' (*Deutschland und der nächste Krieg*, pp. 113–4).

[3] In a lecture entitled 'Deutschland und England. Heeres oder Flottenverstärkung? Ein historisch-politischer Vertrag, gehalten an 25 Jan. 1912 in der Heidelberger Ortsgruppe des Deutschen Flottenverein'. (Germany and England. Should we strengthen our Army or Navy? An Historical and Political Lecture delivered on January 25, 1912, to the Heidelberg group of the German Navy League), the German historian Hermann Oncken develops the argument that if Germany wished to help the English Radicals to overthrow Grey it was the worst possible tactics to build men-of-war. It was the army that must be reinforced. 'To strengthen our army is a real, indeed our best safeguard against England herself, and does not arouse her to violent action by a direct threat.' It is a protection on the Continent against the 'English dagger'. 'The demand for a stronger army is not therefore the expression of an uncalculating military enthusiasm. It is due simply and solely to a practical consideration of our opponent's strength with which we have to reckon and of the aims we intend to achieve. A powerful army is the weapon which will wound

Army' was formed which, copying the methods of propaganda employed by the Navy League, in a far shorter space of time effected for the army what the latter had done for the navy at the close of the nineteenth century. For several years Germany reassured by the complete disorganization of the Russian army and the increasing deterioration of the French had lost much of her interest in the army and turned her eyes to the sea. Given the enormous increase of the German population it was sufficient if half the young men of twenty were called to the colours. The position would soon be changed.

By the army law of 1912 two new army corps were formed, one on the Russian frontier, the other on the French, and measures were adopted to secure that on these two frontiers ten army corps out of twenty-five should be permanently maintained on what was approximately a war footing. The law of 1913 of a far more redoubtable character added a third battalion of eighteen infantry regiments, formed new regiments of cavalry and heavy artillery, and increased the effectives by 4,000 officers, 15,000 non-commissioned officers, 117,000 corporals and privates and 27,000 horses. As a result of these two successive measures Germany was maintaining under the colours in time of peace 870,000 instead of 625,000 troops, and in the event of war could put into the field an army of 5,400,000. The law of 1913 was passed amid an outburst of patriotic enthusiasm, stimulated by the celebrations which commemorated the centenary of the war of independence. And these celebrations inevitably lent German patriotism an aspect of hostility to France which replaced the anti-English feeling by which it had so often been coloured in the immediate past.

This powerful current of public opinion carried the Emperor with it. How could he long remain deaf to the appeal of a patriotic

him in his most vulnerable spot, his system of a Continental balance of power.' (*Historische politische Aufsätze und Reden*, vol. i, pp. 167 sqq.). Almost two years later Oncken contributed to the *Quarterly Review* (October 1913, Art. 13, *Germany under William II, 1888–1913*, vol. ccxix, pp. 566 sqq.) an article in which he argues that since Germany's policy had become continental instead of naval the moment is favourable for a *rapprochement* between the two nations. 'As this impression' (that the German nation desires peace) 'gains strength in England, it may be legitimate to hope that the *détente*, thus carefully prepared and utilized, will eventually lead to an Anglo-German agreement. An agreement of this kind embracing, as it naturally would, both the Near East and Central Africa, would inspire the German people with the conviction that England is prepared loyally to throw open to them the roads which have hitherto been kept systematically barred against them. In any case, the ties which bind the two nations together are, after all, stronger than the rivalries which divide them' and in support of his contention he refers to his lecture of 1912.

sentiment which, as he was well aware, charged him with weakness and held him responsible for the shameful retreats which had led Germany from Tangier to the agreement of November 4, 1911.[1] But he had done nothing to arouse it. On the contrary he was witnessing, and he knew it, the ruin of that dream of an anti-British naval expansion which had been his consistent ideal throughout his reign. It was a policy which necessitated friendship not only with Russia but with France. But it was becoming only too clear that, so far as France was concerned, it had failed. Caillaux's fall had brought into office the conscientious and industrious bourgeois and keen lawyer who for many years to come would embody French policy in the eyes of the world. Raymond Poincaré put an end to the attempts recently made by French diplomacy to explore avenues to an understanding with Italy, Austria, and Germany. These attempts had been marred by two defects. They were inconsistent and they tended to loosen the *entente* with England and the alliance with Russia and might perhaps leave France finally isolated when another crisis arose like those of Tangier and Agadir. Poincaré desired to strengthen the alliance with Russia, and make the *entente* with England for all practical purposes an alliance, so that the Triple Alliance might be permanently counterbalanced by a reorganized Triple Entente. The competition in armies began once more between the Continental Powers. After hesitating for several months and leaving unanswered the German law of 1912, which was itself the response to Caillaux's fall, France replied to the law of 1913 by the supreme effort of imposing three years' military service instead of two upon the entire youth of France. Russia also armed in answer to the German armaments. The ruling class indulged the belief that

[1] We may refer in this connection to Gerhart Hauptmann's topical drama, *Festspiel im deutschen Reimen*, a 'Memorial to the Spirit of the War of Independence'. The Crown Prince attended its production at Breslau and applauded the author's allusions to his father's incapacity. We may quote in particular the words Hauptmann places in Schnadhorst's mouth:

> A forest of heroes fills our land,
> Not spinsters we pass with a beck of the hand,
> Warriors march thick as the grains of sand.

> . . . . .

> If only a new old Fritz might grace
> To delight our hearts, the leader's place !
> But a man we lack to match the mood
> Of the hour, the monarch of Germanhood,
> Of prince and people to bow the knee,
> And show them the path to liberty.

the revolution had been finally defeated and began once more to alarm the world by the number, if not the organization, of Russia's armed forces. In his speech of November 27, Grey had conjured up the spectre of a Europe united against England. The danger had been dispelled. All the Great Powers of Europe were arming against each other. It was a guarantee for the security of Great Britain.

7

Unfortunately if the Foreign Office by the new system of *ententes* inaugurated in 1904 had dispelled certain risks, the system itself may well have involved England in a new danger—the danger of being dragged by the armed powers into a European war. There was a group of alarmists who were never weary of insisting upon the German peril and demanding the transformation of the *entente cordiale* into an alliance. They denounced the presumed designs of the German Government on the Dutch port of Flushing on the Belgian frontier. They sought opportunities to create a panic and as a further ground for alarm pointed out that England possessed few or no aeroplanes, few or none of those Zeppelins which were the pride of Germany. And from time to time the absurd rumour was circulated that a squadron of these airships had been seen flying above some English county or other.[1] But the scaremongers did not make the same impression on the public as they had done four years earlier. Throughout the country there was a widespread desire to loosen without actually breaking the network of *ententes* and it was to satisfy public feeling that the Cabinet despatched Haldane to Berlin and negotiated on the subject of the Bagdad railways and the Portuguese colonies. Anti-German literature no longer found readers.[2] The important

---

[1] F. W. Hirst, *The Six Panics and Other Essays*, 1913, pp. 103 sqq.

[2] Charles Sarolea, *The Anglo-German Problem*, Ed. i, December 1912. See especially pp. 36–7. '. . . *One of the crucial points* of the Anglo-German controversy—the naval policy of the German Empire. I advisedly said *one* of the critical points, for it is by no means the only one nor even, in my opinion, the most important one. As I shall presently endeavour to prove, *if Germany suddenly decided to reduce her naval armaments and to increase her army in proportion, England would have even more serious reasons for anxiety than she has at present.*' Why? Because (pp. 43–4) 'the greatest danger to England is not the invasion of England, it is the invasion of France and Belgium. . . . It is . . . in France and Belgium that the vulnerable point lies, the Achilles' heel of the British Empire'. But the book attracted no attention whatever. It was only after the declaration of war that it reached a second, third and fourth edition. (August, October 1914; February 1915.) See also: Archibald

reviews closed their columns to writers of articles against Germany. Among young intellectuals it had become more fashionable than ever to regard Germany as a second mother country.[1] After the Agadir crisis, as after the naval panic of 1909, conferences were held and committees formed to seek a basis of reconciliation between the two nations.[2] After the brief interregnum of Baron

Hurd and Henry Castle, *German Sea-Power, Its Rise, Progress, and Economic Laws* 1913. But its tone differs from that of Hurd's earlier works and the introduction ends with an appeal for a *rapprochement* (pp. xiv–xv): 'The only hope for the disappearance of the antagonism between the two peoples lies in a comprehension of each other's economic and strategical necessities; and, if this volume succeeds in giving to Englishmen a truer conception of German policy and German economic and maritime development, and to Germans a better appreciation of the position of the British people as the guardians of an Empire to which unchallengeable sea-power is a necessity, it will have done something to dispel those dark clouds which still hang menacingly on the political horizon.' J. A. Cramb, *Germany and England*, 1914 (A. C. Bradley's preface is dated April) is the posthumous publication of a course of lectures delivered in February and March 1913. The work is deliberately bellicose, but its bizarre conclusion deserves to be quoted (pp. 136–7). 'If the dire event of a war with Germany—if it *is* a dire event—should ever occur, there shall be seen upon this earth of ours a conflict which, beyond all others, will recall that description of the great Greek wars:
> "Heroes in battle with heroes,
> And above them the wrathful gods."
And one can imagine the ancient, mighty deity of all Teutonic kindred, throned above the clouds, looking serenely down upon the conflict, upon his favourite children the English and the Germans, locked in a death struggle, smiling upon the heroism of that struggle, the heroism of the children of Odin the War-God.'
[1] 'Germany which I feel to be my own country after England.' (F. H. Keeling to Mrs. Townshend, August 2, 1914. *Keeling Letters and Recollections*, 1918, p. 178.) Keeling continues: 'The best thing that can happen now is for Germany to be victorious everywhere on land and for us to come out top everywhere on sea.'
[2] See the two special numbers, devoted to a *rapprochement* between England and Germany, of Ludwig Stein's review, *Nord und Süd* (36 Jahrgang. Bd. 14. June and July 1912) also: *Deutschland und England in ihren wissenschaftlichen, politischen und kulturellen Beziehungen. Verhandlungen der Deutchs-Englischen Verständigungskonferenz (vom 30 Oktober bis zum 1 November 1912). Im Auftrage der Vereinigten Komittees. Herausgegeben von Ernst Sieper* 1913. (Germany and England in their scientific, political, and cultural relations. Proceedings of the German-English Conciliation Conference held from October 30 to November 1, 1912. Published for the Joint Committee by Ernst Sieper, 1913. Translated into English under the title *England and Germany*.) The questions discussed by the conference were: 1. Economic competition. 2. The Press. 3. The immunity of private property in wartime. 4. The demarcation of the colonial spheres of interest of both countries. The question of the navy was, therefore, prudently omitted. See further: *Germany in the Nineteenth Century*, five lectures by J. H. Rose, C. M. Herford, E. C. K. Gonner and M. E. Sadler. With an introductory note by Viscount Haldane. Manchester University Press, 1912. Holland Rose's article on 'political history' concludes with a defence of German policy (pp. 20–22): 'It is unquestionable that the formation of the German Empire has conduced to the peace of the world. . . . If we look at the past, we find that our forefathers dreaded France far more than the wildest alarmist now dreads Germany. And their dread was with reason. The position of France gives her great advantages for an attack on England and English commerce. . . . When France and Spain were leagued together against us, as was often the case, the blockade of their combined fleets was well-nigh impossible. That of the German naval ports is a far simpler task. Further the geographical position of Germany is far weaker than that of France. She has no natural frontiers on the East and poor barriers on the South and West. Her policy is therefore almost necessarily defensive. . . . By land she is easily assailable on three sides; by sea she is less vulnerable; but there she labours

Marschall, Prince Lichnowsky succeeded as German Ambassador in London Count Metternich, who had been recalled in disgrace. By his wealth, the lavish scale on which he entertained, and his affability he made the Embassy with his wife's help an important social centre. He was a friend of Asquith, Grey, and Haldane. Oxford gave him a public reception. When the summer of 1914 opened, he could boast that he had conquered British society.

Why did the public with a determination which seemed to increase in strength refuse to heed war cries which had evoked so wide a response in 1908. In the first place there was a keen desire to remain neutral in the event of a European war. And in the second place public attention was absorbed by serious domestic problems. A general strike in the collieries accompanied Haldane's mission and the speeches in which Churchill developed his naval programme. The threat of civil war in Ireland became ever more urgent. It was enough to face revolution without facing war as well. The *Daily News* and the *Manchester Guardian* every morning, the *Nation* every Saturday, denounced the policy of armaments. A general election was approaching. How could a Government which had avowedly been put into power at the opening of 1906 on a programme of opposition to a ruinous imperialism justify to its Radical voters the increase in the navy estimates since 1908? In the Cabinet itself Churchill had to face a determined opposition. Until 1911 it was he who, first at the Board of Trade then at the Home Office, had attacked McKenna, the First Lord of the Admiralty, for yielding to the exorbitant demands of his Board. Now he was at the Admiralty and McKenna at the Home Office retorted his former criticisms. Until 1911 the imperialism of Asquith, Grey, and Haldane had been attacked by the formidable combination of Lloyd George and Churchill. Now, after those few weeks when all five had agreed in opposing the German

under a great disadvantage, viz. that her oceanic commerce has to pass through the Straits of Dover and down the English Channel, within easy striking distance of the French and British fleets at Brest, Plymouth, Cherbourg, Portsmouth and Dover. This is what makes her nervous about her mercantile marine. This is what makes her build a great fleet; and again I say, were we in her situation we should do the same. . . . The events of the years 1866–1871 . . . helped her to build up on a sure basis a new European system which has maintained the peace for forty years. . . . German unification effected at one stroke what Great Britain with all her expenditure of blood and treasure had never been able to effect; namely, to assure the Balance of Power in so decisive a way as to make a great war the most risky of ventures.' For the entire movement in favour of a *rapprochement* between England and Germany see Bernadotte Everly Schmitt, *England and Germany, 1740–1914*, 1916, pp. 353 sqq.

threat, the three imperialists had become a moderate group pushed forward by Churchill, held back by Lloyd George. The recurrent disputes between these two statesmen when the annual Budget was drawn up were an additional source of embarrassment to a Cabinet battling with so many difficulties. No doubt the two demagogues were fully convinced of their sincerity when they championed their conflicting views in the Cabinet. Each had returned to his youthful creed—Churchill the aristocrat and soldier, Lloyd George the plebeian and humanitarian pietist. But we must not forget that the parliamentary struggle had its reverse. The two tribunes remained the intimate personal friends they had become between 1906 and 1911, and continued to hold long conversations almost daily at Westminster.[1] However sharply they might appear to disagree on one of the most serious issues of the day, on one point at least they found it easy to agree. In the Liberal Cabinet they alone counted for anything. All the others were ciphers.

At the close of 1913 the conflict assumed a dramatic character. In 1912 and in 1913 the Budget, on the new foundation laid by Lloyd George in 1909, met without additional taxation the increased demands of the Admiralty. But this time the Admiralty asked too much. The navy estimates had approached the figure of £43,000,000 in 1911-12, had exceeded £44,000,000 in 1913-14. Now the Admiralty was asking for £51,550,000. In December the National Liberal Federation organized an agitation on a large scale against the increased expenditure on the navy. On January 1, Lloyd George in a lengthy interview given to the *Daily Chronicle* spoke of the improvement in the relations between England and Germany, insisted that it justified a decrease in naval expenditure, and recalled how almost thirty years before Churchill's father had resigned his position as Chancellor of the Exchequer in a Conservative administration, because the Government had refused to reduce the army estimates. Churchill found it necessary to visit Paris to remove the anxiety of the French Minister of Marine. He

[1] Asquith to his wife, January 23, 1914: 'I think we shall get through our little troubles over the Navy without much more ado. Lloyd George squeezing in one direction, and Winston in the other. Neither of them wants to go and in an odd sort of way they are really fond of one another' (J. A. Spender and C. Asquith, *Life of Lord Oxford and Asquith*, vol. ii, p. 76). Sir Almeric Fitzroy, *Memoirs*, March 7, 1914: '. . . In the course of the dinner we had one Birrellism which is worth noting. Winston had said that no day of the session passed without his having half an hour's talk in the House of Commons with Lloyd George, upon which Birrell "In that case neither of you can be bored" ' (vol. ii, p. 540).

had indeed publicly pledged himself six weeks earlier to resign rather than accept the reductions in the expenditure of his department which the Cabinet was demanding,[1] and a fortnight before had brought up the question at a Cabinet meeting and announced his determination, if he failed to receive satisfaction, to resign for a reason the exact reverse of that for which his father Lord Randolph had resigned in 1886. In the end he carried the day. He introduced his huge estimates, merely promising reductions in the following years. The same promises had been made in 1911, and in a year's time, when the general election had been held, who could tell which party would be in office? We are indeed surprised by the ease with which he won his victory when we contrast the outcry raised by the Radical Press for the last two years with the extreme paucity of his opponents in the House. Only thirty-five and four members respectively voted against him at the solitary sitting during which a division was twice taken,[2] whereas a hundred and ninety Unionists supported a motion demanding a further reinforcement of the British navy.[3]

8

In a conversation with the German naval attaché Prince Louis of Battenberg spoke of the debt of gratitude which the British navy owed to Churchill. He had succeeded in extracting a larger sum from the Chancellor of the Exchequer than any previous Lord of the Admiralty.[4] How did he do it? Was it that his personal friendship with Lloyd George enabled him to employ persuasion successfully when another man must have used threats? In 1912 and in 1913 perhaps; but in 1914 he had been compelled to have recourse to threats. He spoke of resigning followed possibly by the four Sea Lords. He also hinted at a compromise with the Unionists on the Irish question, let it be rumoured that he was contemplating a return to his original allegiance. The Radicals took fright. The Irish crisis was enough without the further com-

---

[1] Speech at the Mansion House, November 10, 1913.
[2] H. of C., March 23, 1914 (*Parliamentary Debates*, Commons 1914, 5th Series, vol. lx, pp. 140 sqq., 143 sqq.).
[3] H. of C., March 17, 1914 (ibid., vol. lix, pp. 196 sqq.).
[4] Report of the naval attaché in London, February 6, 1913 (*Die Grosse Politik . . .* vol. xxxix, p. 13).

plication of a revolution at the Admiralty. They gave way and Churchill remained at his post. He purchased this complaisance on the question of armaments by again becoming an uncompromising champion of Home Rule.[1] In short his attitude was once more what it had been in 1912 and 1913. He had passed over to the imperialist camp. But on all questions except those of foreign policy he remained an advanced Liberal of Socialist sympathies. And even in his administration of the Admiralty he gave pledges to democratic opinion.

In speaking of Admiral Fisher's reforms we made only a brief mention of the discontent prevalent among the crews of the navy. For that great reformer did very little to allay it.[2] It was not it would seem until about 1906—that is to say, when Fisher had already effected the substance of his reforms—that the discontent assumed a definite shape, in consequence of the great explosion of Liberal ideas which produced the Radical victory at the election of 1906 and which that victory in turn intensified. In May 1905 the publication commenced of a weekly paper called *The Fleet* edited by Lionel Yexley, a former blue-jacket, which enjoyed a wide circulation among the sailors, whose claims it championed with considerable skill.[3] And shortly afterwards their grievances began to be presented annually in a more concise form in a publication composed by sailors and entitled *Naval Magna Charta; An Appeal from the Lower Deck.*

For a long time the Press kept silence about this agitation which had no direct interest for its regular readers, to whom this extension of syndicalist methods to the navy was repugnant from the outset. It was however inevitable. Living in these armour-plated barracks, the new ironclads, under conditions more akin to those of a factory than a battleship of the old style and mingling at the large naval bases with the civilian proletariat during the long periods when their vessels were in port the sailors could not escape the contagion. The concentration of the squadrons in home waters

[1] Winston S. Churchill, *The World Crisis, 1911–1914*, pp. 177–8.
[2] For what was accomplished particularly in improving the conditions of life on board see Charles Watney and James A. Little, *The Workers' Daily Round*, 1913, pp. 60 sqq. A. S. Hurd, 'Progress or Reaction in the Navy' (*Fortnightly Review*, April 1906; n.s. vol. lxxix, p. 710).
[3] See further a work by the same author describing the conditions under which the sailors lived. *The Inner Life of the Navy. Being an Account of the Inner Social Life led by our Naval Seamen on board Ships of War, together with a detailed Account of the Systems of Victualling and Uniform in vogue during the latter Part of the Nineteenth and the opening Years of the Twentieth Century*, 1908; also *Our Fighting Sea Men*, 1911.

in accordance with the new policy of the Admiralty increased the opportunities of infection,[1] and the Admiralty was alarmed by the growing tendency of officers and men to interest politicians in their demands. A writer of syndicalist sympathies, Stephen Reynolds, was probably the first civilian to concern himself with the conditions of the seamen on the Lower Deck and bring their grievances to the notice of the public. He began his agitation at the time Churchill went to the Admiralty.[2] The political motives which induced Churchill to seek popularity by taking up the question are obvious. But at this particular juncture he had further inducements to do so. The Government was increasing the naval effectives. In a country where conscription was in force nothing could be easier or cheaper. This was not the case in England. So long as it was a question of building three ironclads for every two German or even two for one, England could sustain the struggle. She possessed the necessary wealth. But it was not so easy to secure by voluntary enlistment the sailors required to man a fleet constantly increasing in size, if the population of the sea-board and ports looked askance at the service, joined in insufficient numbers or after joining found that they had made a mistake and sought to leave the navy as soon as possible.

The sailors complained of the unhealthy conditions in which they lived, confined as they too often were to narrow, damp, and ill-ventilated quarters, while the public cherished the poetic picture of Jack Tars buffeted all day by the sea breezes. Though Fisher had begun to improve their conditions and food, complaints were still raised. And they also complained of the inadequate pay. During the sixty years from 1852 to 1912 their pay had risen from

---

[1] 'The concentration of the Fleet in home waters whatever its political advantages may be has had a most detrimental effect. So long as a ship is on foreign station the very nature of circumstances causes a bond of union between officers and men which draws them closer together. The fact of their all being foreigners in a foreign land creates in itself a solidarity as nothing else can. With identical interests, sharing one another's work and play, the officers obtain a moral hold over their men such as is impossible in British ports. Here the men's minds naturally incline more to their homes and less to their ships; they are filled with a desire for longer leave and a constant wish to get away to visit their friends and families is the natural result, which the monotony of service in home waters but serves to intensify. Here too they are exposed to the wiles of the Socialist agitator, never backward in working up the molehill of some trumpery grievance into a mountain of discontent and doing his best to imbue them with that class hatred quite foreign to their natures, now so prevalent in England.' (Trafalgar the Soul of the Navy, *National Review*, November 1912, vol. lx, pp. 448 sqq.).

[2] Stephen Reynolds, *The Lower Deck. The Navy and the Nation*, 1912. For the spirit, at once revolutionary and patriotic, which inspired his book see the remarkable conclusion of his preface (p. vii) to which we have already had occasion to refer, p. 412 *n*.

1s. 7d. to 1s. 8d. a day, an increase of 6 per cent. How different during the same period had been the increase of wages for labourers of every description.[1] And when the rise in the cost of living during the last sixty years is taken into account it is evident that the sailors' real pay had seriously fallen. The men demanded nothing less than an increase of 20 per cent. And finally they complained that the discipline was too strict.

It was impossible to turn a deaf ear to these demands at a time when trade was prosperous, unemployment at a minimum, and wages constantly rising and when though the factory had become a dangerous competitor with the man-of-war the demand for seamen was steadily increasing. The men did not indeed secure the increase of a fifth for which they asked. But they obtained an increase of 3d. a day for able seamen and stokers after six years' service,[2] and certain other advantages for seamen of every category which were equivalent to an increase of pay. And Churchill let it be understood that he was trying to obtain further increases from the Exchequer. It was however the question of discipline which most occupied the attention of the Admiralty. Already McKenna had carried a Naval Discipline Bill,[3] which made a distinction between the disgraceful punishment of imprisonment to be inflicted on seamen guilty of crimes against the laws of the land and a new penalty called detention to be inflicted on those guilty only of infringing regulations. In September 1912 Churchill carried out a general reform whose character he explained to the sailors in an official circular.[4] Humiliating forms of punishment which seemed to treat the sailors more like schoolboys than adults were abolished, the guard room officers were empowered to inflict a number of slight punishments without the formality of a report to the Commander, which gave the matter an exaggerated importance, and sailors who considered themselves unjustly sentenced were given the right of appeal. Shortly afterwards it was made impossible to deprive petty officers of their rank with-

[1] *Royal Navy (Pay) Statement showing the Present and New Rates of Pay for the Royal Navy and Royal Marines*, December 4, 1912.
[2] H. of C., March 26, 1913 (*Parliamentary Debates*, Commons 1913, 5th Series, vol. l, p. 1778).
[3] 9 Edw. 7, Cap. 41: An Act to enable the punishment of Detention to be substituted for the punishment of Imprisonment for offences against Naval Discipline under the Naval Discipline Act (*Naval Discipline Act*, 1909). It extended to the navy a measure already adopted for the army in 1906.
[4] *Circular Letter dealing with Naval Discipline*, September 7, 1912 (*The Naval Annual*, 1914, pp. 447 sqq.).

out the sentence of a court martial.[1] These concessions did not satisfy the sailors who continued to complain. Neither did they satisfy the Admiralty, which elaborated and even introduced experimentally on certain ships a far-reaching system of reforms designed to render discipline on board ship less harsh, and the Sunday rest more real, and to increase the hours off duty.[2]

The sailors or rather the petty officers complained that they were debarred from the possibility of promotion. And if exceptionally one of their number became an officer, he felt uncomfortable in an alien social sphere in which moreover he could not keep up his position on his pay. On this point Lord Selborne's reforms had amounted to very little;[3] a declaration of principle which had apparently remained a dead letter. As we have seen, Fisher had approached the problem from another angle and he was widely criticized for making the navy a more plutocratic profession than before by increasing the cost of an officer's training. The need of a sufficient number of officers became more pressing every year. Since it took seven years according to the existing rules to turn out an officer, only two to build a Dreadnought, it became urgently necessary to draw officers from a wider class. Churchill reached the Admiralty at the very moment when it was awakening to the urgency of the problem and had just adopted a measure—the first of its kind—to enable common sailors, among the marines for a start, to be promoted as officers.[4] He vigorously prosecuted the new policy. Not only did he shorten the interval required before a midshipman could be made a sub-lieutenant,[5] make it possible for cadets from the public schools to enter the navy directly,[6]

---

[1] Letter of September 27, 1912 announcing the decision to this effect of *the Lords Commissioners of the Admiralty* (*The Times*, September 28, 1912).

[2] For the experiments conducted on board the cruiser *Queen Mary* and the question as a whole see *The Times*, April 2, 1914.

[3] *Navy (Personnel) Memorandum dealing with the Entry, Training and Employment of Officers of the Royal Navy and the Royal Marines*, December 16, 1902, p. 11.

[4] August 14, 1911. See the article in *The Times* for February 3, 1914, entitled 'Officers for the Navy'.

[5] H. of C., March 18, 1912. Winston Churchill's speech. *Parliamentary Debates*, Commons 1915, 5th Series, vol. xxxv, p. 1571.)

[6] Disregarding the report of a Committee (H. of C., March 26, 1913, Winston Churchill's speech; *Parl. Deb.*, Commons 1913, 5th Ser., vol. l, p. 1782). See *Navy (Education) Reports of the Committee appointed to inquire into the Education and Training of Cadets, Midshipmen and Junior Officers of His Majesty's Fleet*, May 18, June 14, September 13, 1912. Also the article in *The Times Educational Supplement* dealing with these reports April 1, 1913, p. 61. Thirty might be accepted in this way every year on passing an examination. See the Admiralty Circular entitled 'Special Entry of the Naval Cadets' in *The Times* for March 6, 1913.

raise the age limit for admission to Osborne,[1] and establish partial scholarships in that college,[2] but he issued two regulations on August 5, 1912, the first of which ordered the selection from the lower ranks of the fleet of a number of men anxious and suitable for promotion, to serve after two or three years' training as commissioned officers, while the second ordered all warrant officers whose conduct had been satisfactory to be promoted after fifteen years' service to the rank of commissioned warrant officer.[3] It remained to solve the more difficult problem of making the social position of an officer who had risen from the ranks tolerable. Everything that could be done to solve it by administrative measures Churchill did. During the period of training future lieutenants who had risen from the ranks would receive additional pay and on promotion as lieutenants a gratuity of £50 to pay for their uniform. The pay of captains, commanders, and lieutenants would be raised.[4] And for the first time in the history of the British navy he made an officer from the ranks a Commander on active service.[5]

Another liberal and humanitarian reform was the abolition of the system of prize money announced by Churchill when he introduced the estimates of March 1914. The Government did not go so far as to abolish the right to capture the private property of enemy subjects on the high seas, as it should have done to conform to the Declaration of London and give full satisfaction to the readers of the *Manchester Guardian* and the *Nation*. But it promised that a future naval war would no longer, so far as the English were concerned, be authorized piracy, and then when British sailors captured a merchant vessel of the enemy they would do so, not in their personal interest, but solely on behalf of the State.[6]

The suggestion of a naval holiday put forward by Churchill for the first time in 1912 and twice repeated in 1913[7] was also inspired by pacific intentions. Both fleets, he proposed, the English

[1] *The Times*, August 6, 1912.
[2] *The Times*, November 24, 1913.
[3] *The Times*, August 6, 1912.
[4] *Royal Navy (Pay) Statement showing the Present and New Rates of Pay for the Royal Navy and Royal Marines*, December 4, 1912, pp. 9–10.
[5] Lieutenant Lyne (Stephen Reynolds, *The Lower Deck*, p. 99).
[6] H. of C., March 17, 1914. Winston Churchill's speech. (*Parliamentary Debates*, Commons 1914, 5th Series, vol. lix, p. 1926.) Churchill declared that he was considering the idea of giving the sailors by way of compensation a special bounty in wartime.
[7] H. of C., March 18, 1912 (Introducing the Navy Estimates; ibid., vol. xxxv, p. 1557). H. of C., March 26, 1913 (Introducing the Navy Estimates; ibid., vol. l, p. 1757). Speech at Manchester, October 18, 1913.

and German should agree to call a year's truce to their battle during which neither would lay down any new capital ships. Since the British naval programme was more extensive than the German, how could the German Government object to a plan which was equally in its own advantage? It objected all the same. It pointed out—and Churchill was obliged to agree[1]—that the example must be followed by other navies, in the first place by the French and Russian. But they would certainly refuse. France was extremely hostile to the suggestion of a naval agreement between England and Germany which would leave the latter free to increase her army. Germany might therefore have been well advised to saddle the French and other *entente* powers with the responsibility of defeating the suggestion. But in fact she entertained towards the suggested naval holiday that instinctive repugnance every powerful nation feels towards any suggestion of disarmament, even reciprocal. The German attitude therefore justified the scepticism expressed by the entire British Press without distinction of party, and entertained by the Admiralty, the Foreign Office and Grey, who thought fit to disavow Churchill's proposal publicly after it had failed. [2]As for Churchill himself it is not easy to guess what he really thought. He was a man of imaginative temperament, a journalist as well as a statesman. And a project of such a journalistic character as the naval holiday may perhaps have made a passing appeal to him.[3] But we must bear in mind that in his *Memoirs* he makes only the briefest allusion to his suggestion of 1912 and 1913. Are we to conclude that while prepared to face the risk of succeeding he was indifferent to the prospect of failure? Possibly his intention in making this dramatic move was to cajole Lloyd George and the champions of disarmament.[4]

[1] H. of C., March 26, 1913 (*Parliamentary Debates*, Commons 1913, 5th Series, vol. 1, p. 1754).

[2] *Speech at Manchester*, February 3, 1914: 'If you wish to please foreign nations and to get on well with them, do unto them as they would be done by. . . . It is no good making to them appeals which they will not welcome and are not prepared to receive. We have to bear in mind that in a large part of the continent of Europe, at any rate in many great countries of Europe, they still regard their expenditure on armaments as an internal affair and resent as an intrusion demands from any foreign country that their expenditure on armaments should be open to disarmament or arrangement.' Cf. Lord Grey of Fallodon, *Twenty-Five Years, 1892-1916*, vol. i, p. 300. But in this work, written after the war, Grey expresses much more surprise at the German opposition than he appears to have shown in 1913.

[3] Prince von Lichnowsky to Bethmann-Hollweg, April 30, 1913: 'He is thoroughly in earnest about the naval holiday and regards it as undoubtedly practicable.' (*Die Grosse Politik* . . . vol. xxxix, p. 38.)

[4] For the entire episode see, from the German standpoint, *Die Grosse Politik* . . . vol. xxxix, pp. 3 sqq.

Among the objections to Churchill's proposal which the German Government raised was one we have not yet mentioned. The Germans feared that under the cover of the proposed naval holiday the Admiralty intended to strengthen the British fleet by various underhand methods while pledging themselves not to strengthen it. Of these devices, these indirect methods, something must be said if the reader is to understand how the naval struggle between the two powers continued unabated at the very time when on both sides of the North Sea there was talk of diplomatic conciliation and intellectual *rapprochement*.

The conciliatory formula accepted by Churchill in the spring of 1912 prescribed a 60 per cent superiority for the British fleet (in Dreadnoughts and Post-Dreadnoughts, of course), a superiority very little higher than the 50 per cent formula, three ironclads to two, put forward by Grey at the opening of 1911. It may therefore surprise us to find him in March 1912 demanding as the indispensable condition of maintaining this superiority the construction of two to every one German Dreadnought and thus apparently accepting the formula of two keels to one. But when we reckon up the number of capital ships laid down from the construction of the first English Dreadnought begun in 1905, we find that the English had built thirty Dreadnoughts and Post-Dreadnoughts as against twenty-one German vessels of the same type, that is to say the British superiority was slightly below not the 60 per cent but even the 50 per cent standard. To attain the level of 60 per cent the pace must be speeded up. England must therefore build twenty-five large ironclads as against fourteen German, a ratio of over 17 to 10, almost 18 to 10. But the programme would involve by 1917 the construction of fifty-five capital ships since the introduction of the Dreadnought as against thirty-five German, a ratio of 15.7 to 10, that is something under 60 per cent. The devices to which Churchill and the Admiralty had recourse must be sought elsewhere.

One of these was the deliberate omission by the experts of the British Admiralty when they compared the British and German naval programmes to take into account the respective speed of building in both countries. Boast as Germany might of her industrial progress, in the field of shipbuilding England retained her old

superiority. And if Germany had watched with delight the syndicalist unrest interfere seriously in 1911 with the work of the Clyde
shipyards, the crisis once passed, England had made up the time
lost. The calculations of the British Admiralty showed, and the
results were much the same for other vessels, that the *Orion* had
taken two years and one month to construct, the German *Thurin-
gen* three years and three months.[1] That is to say, the ratio between
the respective speed of British and German naval construction was
two to three. Suppose therefore that in accordance with the rule
formulated in 1912 England laid down that year four capital
ships whereas Germany laid down two the four English ships
would be ready in 1914 but not a single German. Nor was this all.
In 1913 and again in 1914 the Admiralty decided to anticipate by
eight months the date at which the annual quota of ships, three
in 1913, two in 1914, should be laid down.[2] This was more time
gained in the armament race with Germany. By doing his utmost
to speed up by appropriate subsidies the construction of battleships and by advancing within the year the date when their
construction began, Churchill sought to hoodwink, if not
experts, at least the general public as to the meaning of the
official figures.

Another device was to count as equivalent units all the ironclads
posterior to the first Dreadnought. In reality improvement had
followed improvement until with the construction of the *Orion*
begun in 1911 a standard was reached which was known as the
Super-Dreadnought. The speed was the same but the displacement was 23,500 instead of 17,900 tons. The thickness of the main
belt armour was now from twelve to eighteen instead of eleven
inches. The armament consisted of ten guns of a calibre of 13.5
inches (instead of ten of twelve inches). And if in 1913 England
possessed only fourteen Dreadnoughts to eleven German, she had
twenty Super-Dreadnoughts built or in process of construction
as against only twelve German. The advantage was therefore
clearly passing to England. Even before Churchill's arrival at the
Admiralty plans had been made by which in March 1914 England
would possess twelve capital ships furnished with 13.5 inch guns,

[1] H. of C., February 27, 1912, Winston Churchill's reply to a question by Robert
Harcourt (*Parliamentary Debates*, Commons 1912, 5th Series, vol. xxxiv, pp. 1331-2) also
H. of C., March 4, 1912, Churchill's reply to Chiozza Money (ibid., vol. xxxv, p. 173-4).
[2] H. of C., June 1913, Churchill's speech (ibid., Commons 1913, vol. liii, pp. 1043-4);
March 2, 1914, Churchill's speech (ibid., 1914, vol. lix, pp. 90-1).

while not a single German ironclad would possess a gun with a calibre of more than twelve inches. Would the Admiralty at least be content with the Super-Dreadnought equipped with 13.5 inch guns and the other ironclads built since 1911 which had already attained a displacement of twenty-five thousand tons? Many people believed that the tremendous expense would soon prove intolerable—the latest Super-Dreadnoughts built before 1914 cost £2,250,000—and that the moment was at hand when the torpedo boat and submarine would so revolutionize naval warfare as to render these monster vessels useless. Churchill however trod faithfully in Fisher's steps and laid down in 1913 in the utmost secrecy the formidable vessels of the type represented by the *Queen Elizabeth*. The cost of construction was £3,000,000. The displacement was 27,500 tons; the speed twenty-five instead of twenty-one knots. There were only eight large guns, but they had a calibre of fifteen inches and were able to fire at a single target and over a distance of eleven miles a charge of seven tons, an increase of about a ton over the charge which the *Orion's* ten guns of 13.5 inches could fire.

Evidently in the construction of these monsters the Admiralty was not sacrificing speed to the size of the vessel or its armament. The reason was that all the new English Dreadnoughts were driven by petrol. Given equality of size the use of petrol enormously enhanced the vessel's speed, made it far easier to reach full speed, and refuelling on the open sea a far speedier process, and one requiring fewer hands. The amount of energy derived from petrol was 40 per cent greater than that derived from the same weight of coal. How were the necessary supplies of petrol to be insured? And how was the Government to overcome the opposition of those powerful private interests at home whose profit demanded that the British navy should use coal fuel? And what could be done to prevent the State as a consumer of petrol being held to ransom by the Societies which had a monopoly of the wells? Churchill hit upon the daring plan of making the British Government joint owner of the wells in Southern Persia. He had many difficulties to surmount, deep-rooted prejudices against State ownership, and the suspicion at a juncture when the Marconi scandal was before the public, of a personal interest in the undertaking.[1] Backed however by the report of a parliamentary com-

---

[1] His real motive however was to free the Admiralty from the pressure of the great oil companies in Mexico and even in the British colony of Trinidad. Moreover, the political

mittee of which he had dared to make Lord Fisher chairman he won the victory. By thus obtaining possession of considerable supplies of petroleum the British State assured her supremacy at sea when that supremacy had become more than ever necessary to protect her free communications with the Persian coast.[1]

10

Moreover, all these calculations were concerned exclusively with Dreadnoughts and Post-Dreadnoughts. For the Admiralty had for the reasons given above adopted that principle in its calculation. But were these reasons so decisive as they were said to be? It is true that ironclads of the pre-Dreadnought types were being superseded and that in consequence of the dramatic innovation constituted by the advent of the Dreadnought it was wise to look forward to the day when they would disappear altogether. But it had not yet arrived. In 1914 England would possess fifty-eight battleships less than twenty years old as against only thirty-five German, and when we compare the battleships of pre-Dreadnought type, England's superiority was overwhelming. There were two ships of the *Lord Nelson* type of 16,500 tons built immediately before the Dreadnoughts and so closely akin to the latter that satisticians could reckon or refuse to reckon them as such, as they wished to prove the strength or the weakness of the British navy. There were eight ships of the *King Edward* type of 16,350 tons, eight of the *Formidable* type of 15,000, six of the *Canopus* type of 12,950 and nine of the *Majestic* type of 14,900 tons. To all these Germany could oppose from the pre-

---

activities of the Mexican company created diplomatic difficulties with the United States (see Burton J. Hendrick, *The Life and Letters of Walter H. Page*, vol. i, pp. 175 sqq.). And one of its chief shareholders was Lord Murray, one of the politicians involved in the Marconi affair. See the debates H. of C., July 17, 1913 (*Parliamentary Debates*, Commons 1913, 5th Series, vol. lvi, pp. 1477, 1561 sqq.).

[1] 4 & 5 Geo. 5, Cap. 37: An Act to provide Money for the purpose of the Acquisition of Share or Loan Capital of the Anglo–Persian Oil Company Limited (*Anglo-Persian Oil Company [Acquisition of Capital] Act*, 1914). By its provisions a sum of £2,200,000 was placed at the disposal of the Treasury and added to the Consolidated Fund. For the Bill see the important debate in the House of Commons on June 17, 1914 (*Parl. Deb.*, Commons 1914, 5th Ser., vol. lxiii, pp. 1131 sqq.). One of the difficulties involved in the substitution of oil for coal in the navy was to placate the coal industry. The Government therefore explained that they intended to conduct experiments in the extraction of petrol from coal. See on the question, *Navy (Oil Fuel) Agreement with the Anglo-Persian Oil Company Limited*, 1914, p. 5.

Dreadnought era only twenty-two ironclads not one of which exceeded 13,000 tons, and which included two old-fashioned little ironclads of the *Hagen* type which displaced no more than 4,000.[1]

If we take further points of comparison and consider the old cruisers, whose type was obsolete but which were still capable of active service, and the light cruisers British superiority was more than double.[2] And the British advantage in submarines both already built and in course of construction was more than double.[3] In 1912 the Admiralty asked Parliament to vote the sums required to maintain a personnel of 137,500 as against the 66,700 sailors of the German fleet. Here again the proportion was more than double and the Admiralty and Churchill were determined to maintain by a progressive increase which would produce in 1920 a total of 230,000 seamen, a ratio far removed from that ratio of 60 per cent with which they professed to be content.

We must add that in her dockyards England was building not only for her own needs but for those of foreign countries. In the event of war it would be easy to commandeer vessels originally destined to fight under a foreign flag which could be transformed in the twinkling of an eye into British men-of-war. In July 1914 four large vessels of respectively 23,000, 27,500, 26,200, and 28,000 tons were being built in British dockyards—two for Turkey, and two for Chile.[4] That is to say, there were four Super-Dreadnoughts which the Admiralty knew were at its disposal which had never formed part of any programme of naval con-

---

[1] *Fleets (Great Britain and Foreign Countries) Return Showing the Fleets of Great Britain, France, Russia, Germany, Italy, Austria-Hungary, United States of America and Japan, on the 1st day of January, 1914, omitting Battleships, Battle Cruisers and Cruisers, over twenty years old from date of launch and distinguishing, both built and building, Battleships, Battle Cruisers and Cruisers, Light Cruisers, Torpedo Vessels, Torpedo Boat Destroyers, Torpedo Boats and Submarines:—Return to show Date of Launch, Date of Completion, Displacement, Horse-Power, and Armaments reduced to a Common Scale. Admiralty, February 1914.* The publication which began in 1896 and had been annual since 1911 was generally known as the Dickinson Return. Churchill himself warned Germany that England would be satisfied with a superiority of 60 per cent in Dreadnoughts, only so long as the pre-Dreadnoughts remained in commission. (H. of C., March 18, 1912; *Parliamentary Debates*, Commons 1912, 5th Series, vol. xxxv, p. 1556.)

[2] Cruisers of an old type: 40 British to 9 German. Light Cruisers already finished: 60 British to 43 German, under construction 19 British to 6 German.

[3] Submarines already built: 69 British to 24 German: under construction 27 British to 14 German.

[4] The Russian Government wanted to purchase the two Chilean ironclads, but the Government of Chile refused, pointing out that the British Admiralty possessed a right of pre-emption. (The Russian naval attaché in London, to the Chief of Staff of the Russian navy; Graf. Benckendorff's *Diplomatischer Briefwechsel*, vol. iii, p. 281.)

struction or been counted in any comparison between the German and British navies. Add to this the powerful reserve which the Admiralty possessed in England's immense mercantile marine, large vessels easily transformed into auxiliary cruisers or transports, small vessels which could be employed in a great variety of ways for the defence of the coast. When Germany devoted the new fleet of which she was so proud to a single purpose, to harass England on the seas where admittedly she could not hope to wrest the supremacy from her, she could not have committed herself to a more ungrateful and futile task.

II

Nevertheless, she succeeded in harassing England and the latter to make her position still more secure sought additional strength beyond her borders. She called upon her Colonies for assistance. And she transformed or was preparing to transform her diplomatic *ententes* with France and Russia into naval agreements.

We have already seen how from the date when the first of the Imperial Conferences met, one of the principal aims of the British Government which summoned them was to obtain from the Self-Governing Dominions a contribution, direct or indirect, to imperial defence. As time went on and the German fleet grew the appeal from the Home Government became more pressing. In 1909 a special conference had been summoned devoted exclusively to studying military and naval problems.[1] The aim the Admiralty had in view was clearly explained in the official note which wound up the proceedings of the Conference. The common interest of all parts of the Empire demanded a single fleet under a single command with identical training and discipline for all its crews. All that required to be settled was the proportion in which each colony should contribute to the support and expansion of the British navy.

But it was necessary to take account of the sentiments of local patriotism which had grown up in the Colonies and the desire of every colony to possess a fleet of its own. For a long time Australia

---

[1] The discussions were private and no reports were published. For the conclusions reached see Asquith's statement H. of C., August 26, 1909 (*Parliamentary Debates*, Commons 1909, 5th Series, vol. ix, pp. 2310 sqq.).

had cherished an explicit programme on this point, to which the Imperial Conference of 1903 had made concessions. A compromise suggested by *The Times*, by which Australia and New Zealand would undertake to defray the cost of building and maintaining a special squadron which would be the imperial squadron in the Indian Ocean and the Pacific, met with scant success. New Zealand alone formally promised to pay for the construction of a Dreadnought to be placed at the disposal of England for the purposes of imperial defence on condition that England promised in return to send New Zealand a certain number of light vessels for the defence of her shores. Australia would pay the cost of another Dreadnought but it was to form part of the Australian fleet. Canada was even more refractory and the sole result of the conference was to draw up a programme of naval construction as unambitious as possible. A small navy, strictly local, would be built to be divided between the Atlantic and Pacific coasts and amounting only to five light cruisers and six torpedo boat destroyers, and even this extremely modest programme remained on paper.

The Conference of 1911 brought the question no further. The utmost the mother country could obtain from her Self-Governing Colonies after lengthy discussions, and when the principle had been admitted that 'the naval forces of the dominions of Canada and Australia would be subject only to the direction of their respective Governments' was that the regulations governing the training and discipline of the crews should be identical with those in force in the mother country, that the officers and men should be 'interchangeable' and that 'in time of war, when the fleets of the dominions, in whole or in part, should have been placed under the authority of the Imperial Government, the vessels would make an integral part of the British fleet and would remain under the direction of the British Admiralty for the whole duration of hostilities'.[1] But in 1912, when Churchill was at the Admiralty, it seemed as though the mother country would succeed at last. The Admiralty had secured from the native chiefs of Malaya the gift of an ironclad. And at the General Election in Canada the Conservative party, under Borden, defeated Laurier and his Liberal followers. Its programme, frankly imperialist, involved the con-

---

[1] *Imperial Conference 1911. Dominions No. 9. Papers laid before the Imperial Conference: Naval and Military Defence*, p. 2. Resolutions, 1, 2, and 19.

struction of a genuine navy including three battle cruisers of the most modern type.

What use would the Admiralty make of these ironclads or battle cruisers? In the two important speeches he delivered in the House of Commons in March 1913 and in March 1914 to present the navy estimates, Churchill pointed out that the real danger to which the Self-Governing Colonies of America and Australasia were exposed lay in European waters. If England perished, their safety perished with her. He therefore urged the formation of an 'Imperial Squadron' with its base at Gibraltar which should 'cruise freely about the British Empire, visiting the various Dominions, and showing itself ready to operate at any threatened point at home or abroad'.[1] It would consist of the *Malaya*, the *New Zealand* and the three battle cruisers which Canada proposed to build. But Churchill did not despair of witnessing the day when Australia would make her contribution to it. What good purpose could be served by the Dreadnought for which she had decided to pay and which was launched in the summer of 1913, if it remained in Australian waters? It would serve only to flatter Australian vanity. The defence of the coast could be performed equally well by cruisers, torpedo boats, and submarines. And might we not hope that the latest addition to the Dominions, South Africa herself, would one day take her part, when the reconciliation between the two races who had colonized her had been completed, in the perils and glory of the Empire?

This ambitious project disturbed naval experts in Germany. Was this the meaning of the proposals made by Churchill in the House of Commons, and Lord Haldane at Berlin? They had spoken of eight English squadrons to five German, and of a superiority of 60 per cent in Dreadnoughts. Now it was explained that the formula as interpreted by England referred only to the seas of Northern Europe, and excluded the battleships contributed by the Empire.[2] In 1913 and the three following years the British Empire would lay down four ships of the line, the *Malaya* and the three Canadian battle cruisers, over and above the twenty-one whose construction had been officially announced. Six capital

---

[1] H. of C., March 26, 1913 (*Parliamentary Debates*, Commons 1913, 5th Series, vol. l, pp. 1760–3); March 17, 1914 (ibid., 1914, 5th Ser., vol. lix, pp. 1933–5).

[2] Despatch from the Capitain de fregate de Saint-Seine, French naval attaché in London, quoted by Lieutenant-Colonel de La Panouse, military attaché in a letter to Millerand, Minister for War, June 24, 1912 (*Documents diplomatiques français*, 3e Série, vol. iii, p. 164).

ships would thus be built in 1913 to three German, five to two in 1914 and 1915, five to three in 1916 and four to two in 1917. That is to say, during the six years from 1912 to 1917 England would build twenty-nine ships instead of twenty-five as against fourteen German—more than double. Germany had good reason to declare herself duped.

Her anxiety was dispelled by a new revolt of local patriotism. In 1913 Borden was unable to obtain the consent of the Ottawa Parliament to the first instalment of his naval programme and though he expressed his intention to persist with his plan and fight the Liberal opposition, he was not very likely to find future conditions more favourable than on the morrow of his triumph at the polls in 1912. In Australia the Ministry of Defence protested that Churchill's plan amounted to a repudiation of the agreement of 1909. The Dreadnought had been built as part of an exclusively Australian fleet. If the First Lord of the Admiralty was right in suggesting that vessels of this type were useless in the Pacific, Australia ought not to build them. Even loyal New Zealand complained. England, while incorporating the *New Zealand* in her imperial navy, had not given her colony the two light cruisers and the submarines she had promised in 1909. If she did not keep her promise within a year New Zealand would build a cruiser at her own cost, but it would be stationed in home waters. In short, England must content herself, for the present at least, with only two vessels to reinforce her imperial navy, the *New Zealand* and the *Malaya*. Churchill, disappointed in this direction, was driven back upon the expedient of which we have already spoken to advance the date every year when the construction of the new vessels was put in hand.

12

There were indeed imperialists to whom it was repugnant to depend upon the colonies for the security of the United Kingdom. How much more repugnant it must have been to them to see England seeking help, not from these young nations who were after all British, but from foreign nations so lately her mili⸱ and naval rivals.

The Admiralty no doubt acted prudently when the⸱ selves with the French navy against the Germ⸱

dominated the Triple Alliance. In obedience to her instructions, Austria was beginning to build Dreadnoughts and these could hardly be left out of account in a calculation of the forces Germany could employ against England in the event of war. Italy was also building them and though the Italian fleet was probably intended to combat Austria rather than her enemies, and though it was most unlikely that Italy would ever take part against England in a naval war between Austria and the latter, the fact remained that Italy like Austria was Germany's ally. England must therefore put forward a still greater effort or trust to France to guard the Mediterranean. The surprising thing is indeed that the Admiralty waited till 1911 before deciding upon a naval understanding with France, though the two armies had been collaborating for the past five years. The explanation is that the British army, taught humility by the disillusionments of the Boer War, was forced to admit that although the German army was far stronger than the French, the British had much to learn from the latter, whereas the contempt for the French navy entertained for many years by the British prevented the latter from entertaining the idea of concerted action. The Agadir crisis in August 1911 brought home to the British Government the danger involved by this attitude of haughty isolation adopted by the Admiralty. When Churchill succeeded McKenna he determined to inaugurate a new policy. A month had not passed before the English authorities made overtures to the French naval attaché,[1] and since the French Government soon passed into the control of a statesman who, reversing his predecessor's policy, was anxious to tighten the *entente* with England, the understanding between the two armies was soon completed by an understanding between the two navies.

When he introduced the navy estimates on March 18, 1912, Churchill announced his intention to redistribute the squadrons charged with the defence of the United Kingdom.[2] In future there would be three fleets comprising in all eight squadrons of eight battleships each. The first of these, four battle squadrons of Dreadnoughts, would be kept permanently on active service,

[1] Capitain de fregate Le Gouz de Saint-Seine, naval attaché in London, to Delcassé, Minister of Marine, December 11, 1911 (*Documents diplomatiques français*, 3e Série, vol. i, p. 328).

[2] H. of C., March 18, 1912 (*Parliamentary Debates*, Commons 1912, 5th Series, vol. xxxv, pp. 1564 sqq.).

ready for action without any previous mobilization. The second consisting of two squadrons, also on active service, would nevertheless be obliged in the event of war to visit the bases of its units to obtain supplementary crews. The third, also consisting of two squadrons, would be a reserve fleet, but a special reserve would be formed to man it, the 'immediate reserve', which could be called up in advance of a general mobilization.

These measures were a direct reply to the new German naval law. Germany was increasing the number of her permanently mobilized ships. England would follow suit. But to form the 'first fleet' the 'Atlantic fleet' must be withdrawn from its base at Gibraltar for which English ports would be substituted. The 'Mediterranean fleet', now the fourth fleet, would take its place at Gibraltar, leaving the Mediterranean without English capital ships. The step intensified the concentration of the British navy, which in response to the pressure of the German navy was withdrawing it from the extremities to the centre of the Empire. Did this mean that British interests in the Mediterranean would be left unprotected? Or would England count upon the French fleet to protect the common interests of the *entente*? Was not the purpose of Asquith's visit to Malta in May to discuss this question with Fisher, who came from his Italian villa, and Kitchener, who came from Egypt to meet him? Were not the journalists who at this moment were advocating the transformation of the *entente* into an alliance in the councils of the Foreign Office and the Admiralty? What truth was there in the rumour, current in August, of negotiations between England and France for a naval *entente*? The answer to these questions seemed to have been given in September when it was announced that six ironclads of the third French squadron had been transferred from Brest to Toulon to form, together with the vessels already stationed in the latter port, a single fleet of eighteen ironclads and six armoured cruisers. It was not a powerful fleet; there were no Dreadnoughts. But it was sufficiently strong to counterbalance the combined fleets of Austria and Italy, supposing the latter were allied, for like France neither of these powers had as yet completed a Dreadnought. Thus France assumed before the whole world the task of protecting against possible attacks by the allies of Germany the route to India between Gibraltar and Port Said, now stripped of English capital ships. On the other hand England made herself responsible for the defence of the French coast on the North Sea, the Channel, and even the Atlantic, henceforward devoid of French ironclads.

Rumour had spoken the truth; a naval convention was being negotiated between the two Powers. Negotiations had in fact been begun at the beginning of September 1911 to prepare for the danger which many regarded as imminent, of war between the three Western Powers and a verbal agreement had been reached as to the respective spheres of action to be allotted to the British and French fleets in the event of hostilities.[1] They were revived on the basis of the new distribution of the British squadrons in July 1912. At first Churchill, not to commit the Foreign Office, asked for an explicit declaration in the preamble that the agreement should be operative only if Great Britain and France were actually engaged in conducting a joint war and should not restrict the political freedom of each Government to participate or not to participate in such a war.[2] When the technical agreements were concluded in January and February 1913 they bound the contracting parties only to take the necessary steps for co-operation in the Mediterranean or elsewhere 'in the event of a war in which Great Britain and France are allied against the Triple Alliance' and to defend the Straits of Dover and the Channel 'in the event of being allied with the French Government in a war with Germany'. It was onto these naval negotiations that Paul Cambon grafted the diplomatic negotiations which ended in the exchange of notes in October. Thus little more than a year after Agadir the diplomatic *entente* was committed for the first time to writing, the military understanding ratified for the first time by the Cabinet and, most significant of all, the diplomatic and military agreements completed by a naval agreement.

The naval agreement was and remained secret, but the new distribution of the British and French fleets could not be concealed and it caused considerable dissatisfaction in England. Churchill was attacked by a formidable combination of critics.

---

[1] Capitain de fregate Le Gouz de Saint-Seine to Delcassé, Minister of Marine, July 10, 1912 (*Documents diplomatiques français*, 3e Série, vol. iii, pp. 235–6. Cf. vol. i, p. 328 *n*.).

[2] Capitain de fregate Le Gouz de Saint-Seine to Delcassé, July 10 and 18 (*Documents diplomatiques français*, 3e Série, vol. iii, pp. 235, 270). Delcassé to Poincaré, September 17, 1912, letter enclosing a preliminary draft of a naval convention with notes (ibid., pp. 506 sqq.); Paul Cambon to Poincaré, September 19, 1912 (ibid., pp. 523 sqq.). Poincaré to Paul Cambon, September 20, 1912 (ibid., p. 530). Capitain de fregate Le Gouz de Saint-Seine to Vice-Admiral Aubert, September 21, 1912 (ibid., p. 546). (*Documents diplomatiques français*, vol. v, pp. 486, 490.)

The imperialists disliked entrusting the Mediterranean communications of the Empire to the protection of a foreign Power.[1] The pacifists objected to the British fleet taking charge of the French coast of the Channel as involving the subordination of British policy to the French Foreign Office. To disarm his critics Churchill promised in July 1912 to send to Malta four cruisers of the *Invincible* type to compensate for the departure of the fourth fleet, transferred a month before to Gibraltar. And it was no doubt to dispel the same misgivings that a little later he contemplated the formation of an imperial squadron, with its base at Gibraltar, which would release five Dreadnoughts for the Mediterranean. When the project failed, he despatched to the Mediterranean in November 1913[2] a division of the first squadron, four Dreadnoughts, and a division of the third squadron of cruisers, four large armoured cruisers, to take part in joint manœuvres with the Mediterranean fleet. Finally, on March 17, 1914, when he introduced the annual navy estimates he explained that the acceleration effected in building the three Super-Dreadnoughts laid down in 1913-14 would enable the Admiralty by the end of 1915 to send to Malta a squadron of eight battleships, of which at least six would be Dreadnoughts to replace the four battle cruisers stationed there in 1912.[3] The imperialists were satisfied; British prestige in the Mediterranean was secure. But nothing had been done to reassure the pacifists, the opponents of any intervention in a European war. The defence of the north coast of France was in fact entrusted to the British fleet, and so great was the naval weakness of France, that just because it obliged her to entrust her safety to British aid, it was her surest guarantee that that aid would not be withheld.

13

When the negotiations for a naval convention between England and France opened in July 1912, a naval convention between France and Russia had just been concluded. France adopted a

---

[1] See Lord Esher's essay entitled 'Naval and Military Situation' in his book, *The Influence of King Edward and Other Essays*, 1915. At the Malta Conference in May 1912, Kitchener had expressed himself strongly against abandoning the Mediterranean to the French fleet. (Sir George Arthur, *Life of Lord Kitchener*, 1920, vol. ii, p. 336.)

[2] H. of C., July 22, 1914 (*Parliamentary Debates*, Commons 1914; 5th Series, vol. xli, p. 855).

[3] H. of C., March 17, 1914 (ibid., 1912, 5th Ser., vol. lix, p. 1929).

programme of naval construction which would at last give her Dreadnoughts and produce by 1920 a fleet of twenty-eight large ironclads. The Russian Government, confident that it had overcome the danger of revolution, was actively engaged in creating a new navy, since her old navy had been practically annihilated by Japan. Four Super-Dreadnoughts had already been launched and the Duma had just sanctioned the construction of three more large ironclads and four battle cruisers. The German Government hoped, it would seem, to alarm England by calling her attention to the danger she might one day incur from these French and Russian armaments. In 1914 Tirpitz was careful not even to allude to the naval power of Britain and to justify the naval expenditure of his country as her inevitable reply to the expenditure of France and Russia. England however did not regard with disfavour the understanding between the Russian and French navies and the reinforcement of both. If Germany were challenged in the Baltic, France stronger in the Mediterranean, England would be freer to meet the German menace in the North Sea. When, therefore, in April 1914, King George visited Paris, accompanied by Grey, whose presence invested the visit with an exceptional importance,[1] the French Prime Minister, at the suggestion of the Czar, asked the English Government to empower the Admiralty to negotiate with the Russian naval authorities an agreement similar to that concluded between France and Russia in 1912, and between France and England in 1913. Grey, whom the Czar had already approached directly,[2] made no objection.

Conversations took place in London at the beginning of May between Grey, Benckendorff, Paul Cambon, and Isvolsky, who had come from Paris for the purpose. Subsequently Grey would seem to have followed the procedure he had inaugurated in 1906 and left the Admiralty a free hand to conduct negotiations in

[1] Valuable information about this visit will be found in the Austrian diplomatic documents. Despatch from their councillor to the legation Count Karl Trauttmansdorff, London, April 24, 1914. Report from the Ambassador Mensdorff, May 8, 1914; *Österreich-Ungarns Aussenpolitik* . . . vol. vii, p. 1085; vol. viii, pp. 21–2. With the approval of the Foreign Office *The Times* invited the French historian Ernest Lavisse to write an article on the occasion of the King's visit celebrating the *entente cordiale* which this very month of April had reached its tenth anniversary. But when *The Times* asked Arthur Balfour, the Prime Minister of 1909 and Lord Lansdowne his Foreign Secretary to supplement the French by an English article, they refused, disapproving it would seem of the excessive importance which *The Times* and, indirectly, the Foreign Office attributed to the royal visit. (H. Wickham Steed, *Through Thirty Years*, vol. i, pp. 388 sqq.)

[2] For the conversation on April 3 between the Czar and Sir George Buchanan see Sir George Buchanan, *My Mission to Russia*, vol. i, p. 183.

which from that moment he took no further part.[1] When indiscretions were committed at Petersburg, the German Press denounced these suspicious conversations, the Radical Press took alarm and a question was asked in Parliament. Grey gave the stereotyped answer: 'If war arose between European powers, there were no unpublished agreements which would restrict or hamper the freedom of the Government or of Parliament to decide whether or not Great Britain should participate in a war. That answer . . . remains as true to-day as it was a year ago. No negotiations have since been concluded with any Power that would make the statement less true. No such negotiations are in progress, and none are likely to be entered upon, so far as I can judge.'[2] There was not a word in the reply which was not literally true. The accuracy of the semi-official statement published in the *Westminster Gazette* that 'there is no naval agreement, nor any negotiations with a view to a naval agreement, between Great Britain and Russia',[3] was more dubious. The statement was certainly true, if it meant that in consequence of the awkward revelations the negotiations had been suspended. At the moment when the article in the *Westminster Gazette* appeared they were not in progress. But it had been decided it would seem that they should be renewed in August under conditions of greater secrecy when Prince Louis of Battenberg, at once a Prince of the blood royal and a Sea Lord, was expected to visit Petersburg.[4]

British policy during the two years preceding the war was marked by curious inconsistencies. On the one hand the Government wished to remain free, and perhaps genuinely believed itself free, to intervene or not to intervene in an eventual war. To preserve this liberty it had attempted a policy of *rapprochement* with Germany, which it regarded as consistent with the *ententes* with

---

[1] Lord Grey of Fallodon, *Twenty-Five Years*, vol. i, pp. 284–5.

[2] H. of C., June 11, 1914 (*Parliamentary Debates*, Commons 1914, 5th Series, vol. lxiii, p. 458).

[3] *Westminster Gazette*, June 13, 1914.

[4] Count Benckendorff to Sazonov, May 20, June 2, 1914 (*Un Livre Noir*, vol. ii, pp. 324 sqq.). Secret report by Captain Wolkoff, Russian naval attaché in London, May 24, June 6, 1914. (Graf Benckendorff's *Diplomatischer Briefwechsel*, Ed. 1928, vol. iii, pp. 281–2) Count Benckendorff to Sazonov, May 29, June 11, 1914 (*Un Livre Noir*, vol. ii, p. 326, *Der diplomatische Briefwechsel Iswolskys*, vol. iv, p. 133). Count Benckendorff to Sazonov, June 19, July 2, 1914 (Graf Benckendorff's *Diplomatischer Briefwechsel*, Ed. 1928, vol. iii, pp. 281–2). Sir Edward Grey's despatch to Sir George Buchanan of June 25, 1914 is not the denial which it appears at first sight. Grey simply protests against the report that a convention had been actually concluded and that it comprised an agreement on the question of the Dardanelles. (*British Documents . . .* vol. xi, p. 6.)

France and Russia. On the other hand it strengthened the defences of the Empire, and with this object sought to achieve a closer co-operation with the Colonies, France, and Russia, measures which had no meaning apart from the eventuality of an armed struggle between England and Germany. But the paradox of this double-edged policy did but accentuate, say if you like caricature, the paradox of that European system it had become customary to term armed peace.

To confine ourselves to the two rival nations with which we are particularly concerned here, we observe that the military and naval expenditure of Great Britain had more than doubled between 1895, the year in which the imperialists came into power and 1913 when the Liberals had held office for eight years. In Germany during the same period they had been quadrupled and on the eve of the Great War exceeded the British figure by £21,000,000, more than a fifth. In an extremely pessimistic speech in which, while calling attention to the evil he avowed himself at a loss for a remedy, Lloyd George estimated at £40,000,000 the annual increase in the world's expenditure on armaments. It is not surprising that this ruinous competition terrified those who retained sufficient independence of judgment not to be swept away by the tide. In the United States the head of the Government, President Wilson, who in consequence of the geographical position of his country could adopt towards the affairs of Europe the attitude of an impartial umpire, took alarm. When at the close of 1913 Sir William Tyrell, Grey's private secretary, visited Washington to discuss grave questions outstanding between England and the United States, which he settled to the satisfaction of both countries, the suggestion took shape of an unofficial mission to be undertaken by Colonel House to the rulers of the great European Powers with the object of devising some safeguard against the danger of war. An alliance between England and the United States, an alliance between England, the United States, and Germany, an organized *entente* of all the great Powers, were the various projects which entertained the dreams of Anglo-Saxon politicians and formed the subject of their confidential discussions until late in July, at the very time when the British Admiralty was negotiating or preparing to negotiate with Russia.[1]

---

[1] *The Intimate Papers of Colonel House* arranged as a Narrative by Colonel Seymour, vol. i, pp. 266 sqq. See especially for the rigorous secrecy with which the conversations

But by the end of May, Colonel House had lost heart. 'The situation is extraordinary,' he wrote from Berlin. 'It is militarism run stark mad. Unless someone acting for you can bring about a different understanding, there is some day to be an awful cataclysm. No one in Europe can do it. There is too much hatred, too many jealousies.'[1] Nevertheless, if we consider only the Western nations of Europe it is by no means so clear that the imminent war was the natural consequence of the system of armed peace, as it had been in operation for many years past.

The cost was ruinous. But can one purchase too dearly the blessings of peace? And many competent thinkers regarded a democratic system which enfranchised the masses and imposed military service on the wealthy as favourable to peace and stable international relations. In support of their contention they could appeal to the fact that the host of diplomatic conflicts, between England and France, England and Germany, and France and Germany, which during the last forty years had seemed to place the nations on the brink of armed conflict, had never led to war. One of the two parties had given way or a compromise had been arranged. Bloodshed had been avoided. Why should it be different in 1913 or 1914? There was no issue likely to provoke a direct conflict between England and Germany. War between the two countries could arise only from a war between Germany and a third Power. From a war with France? What matter of dispute between the two nations could be foreseen, sufficiently serious to lead to war? Morocco? A considerable section of German opinion had not renounced the hope that Germany would regain a footing in that country. But the German Government would certainly not be so foolish as to strengthen the *entente* between France and England by another Tangier or Agadir at a time when its chief anxiety was to consolidate its position in Europe by allaying British mistrust. Alsace? The issue had been revived in some quarters both in Paris and in Alsace itself. But what French Cabinet would undertake the responsibility of a war of revenge? The politicians knew that nothing was more remote from the

were conducted House's conversation with Tyrell: 'Tyrell brought word to me to-day that Sir Edward said he did not wish to send anything official or in writing, for fear of offending French and Russian sensibilities in the event it should become known. He thought that it was one of those things that had best be done informally and unofficially.' (Colonel House to President Wilson, July 3, 1914; vol. i, p. 277.)

[1] *The Intimate Papers of Colonel House*, vol. i, p. 255. Cf. Burton J. Hendrick, *The Life and Letters of Walter H. Page*, vol. i, pp. 270 sqq.

thoughts of the country as a whole, and it was fear of a German attack not the desire to undertake a war of aggression which had won the nation's consent to a reinforcement of the army. They also knew that France unaided was too weak to sustain a war with Germany and that they could not count on British aid in a war of this kind. Indeed, they were aware that to raise the question of Alsace would be the surest way to alienate British sympathies. In pontifical tones The Times, an organ by no means unfriendly to France, had solemnly warned the French against the consequences of such imprudence. 'If the French people cannot help thinking of it, they should bear Gambetta's counsel in mind, and keep their thoughts to themselves.'[1]

If, nevertheless, the danger of war became serious about the beginning of 1914, it was for reasons, though many Frenchmen and Englishmen were not aware of the fact, which had nothing to do with problems of western politics. It was the result of a sudden change in the relations between Germany and Russia. In spite of the Franco-Russian alliance, the rapprochement between Russia and England, and the formation of the Triple Entente they were as we have seen still good, when the storm kindled by the episode of Bosnia had blown over, and continued to be good until after Agadir. They suddenly became very bad at the close of 1912 and the German Staff could never have wrested from the Government and the Reichstag the army law of 1913, which made the European war inevitable, if the diplomatic situation in Eastern Europe had not aroused with good reason a host of new anxieties in Berlin. Was the Russian or the German Government responsible for these new risks of war? The Governments themselves still desired peace. Not individuals or governments but the collective passions of the masses must bear the responsibility. In their own despite the Governments were pushed forward by their subjects' irresistible pressure. To understand the chain of events which led England on August 4, 1914, to declare war on Germany we must acquaint ourselves with the nature and origins of these currents of popular feeling which from Asia to the Balkans, from the Balkans to the southern frontier of Germany, swept onward from struggle to struggle, from one national revolution to another until they had submerged the West in the deluge of war.

[1] March 3, 1913.

II THE EAST AND THE PRINCIPLE OF NATIONALITY

I

We have already had occasion at the beginning of this volume to comment upon the important part in human history played by the victory of Japan over Russia in 1905. It was an example to the whole of Asia, indeed to all those races which Europe had branded as permanently inferior. There was however a fundamental distinction between Japan and the other Asiatic civilizations. Under its theocratic and feudal monarchy Japan had successfully resisted all the attempts of the Western Powers to establish themselves in her territory. Elsewhere the situation was completely different. Everywhere else the native monarchies and aristocracies had been conquered or corrupted and had allowed their dominions to be more or less completely annexed. If, therefore, the Asiatic peoples were to throw off the yoke of the West, their liberation must begin by a revolt against their own Governments —and the watchword of revolt had been taught by the West. In the nineteenth century the principle of nationality had changed the face of Europe. That principle demanded that national independence should be achieved by political autonomy, democratic parliamentary government, and universal suffrage. It no longer enjoyed its former credit in the West, where since parliamentary democracy had been established universally, other problems aroused popular enthusiasm and Socialism was gaining ground at the expense of Nationalism. But it had now taken hold of Asia, which it would completely revolutionize.

Of China in the first place. A revolt against foreign penetration and the Manchu dynasty had already followed the Japanese victories of 1895, when everyone expected China to be partitioned between the Western Powers and Japan. The movement redoubled its strength as a result of the Japanese victory of 1905. In 1906 an edict was published promising political reforms, and shortly afterwards a constitution was drawn up by which the Emperor would share the government with a representative, if not a democratic, assembly. In 1908, after the mysterious deaths within two days' interval of the Emperor and the dowager Empress and the accession to the throne of an infant of three,

changes followed rapidly and assumed a revolutionary complexion. In 1911 the Emperor granted the assembly a responsible
Cabinet. But when a rebellion broke out on the Yang-Tsé-Kiang
it was only partially suppressed by the Prime Minister, Yuan-Shi-
Kai, an armistice was concluded with the rebels, and the Emperor
abdicated having first set up a provincial Government to administer the country until the meeting of the Convention, which in
1912 proclaimed a Republic. Had Republicanism conquered or
been defeated? A year later Yuan-Shi-Kai made himself dictator
and his Government displayed the same vices which had discredited the former Imperial Government. But this did not alter
the enormous significance of a revolution which had overthrown
the oldest of the great military monarchies.

The Chinese revolution proved detrimental to British influence.
The control of the Chinese customs which England had exercised
for the last fifty years was disputed and diminished, and if she
succeeded in obtaining for one of her subjects the control of the
duty on salt she renounced by a formal declaration her right,
accepted without question hitherto, to audit the balance sheet of
the railways built with British capital. Nor was it only the Chinese
who extorted concessions from England in China. It was all very
well for the new Chinese Governments to charge the former Imperial Government with weakness—they were weaker still. And
although a consortium of the four Great Powers had been established to harmonize their respective economic ambitions, the
struggle for concessions, the scramble for Chinese spoils recom-
menced. An agreement between Russia and Japan compelled the
English and Americans to retreat from Manchuria. France secured
concessions in the south-west. And since Germany was intriguing
against England on the Yang-Tsé-Kiang and England needed, not
only in China but elsewhere, the diplomatic support of Russia,
Japan, and France, her diplomacy was obviously faced with a
checkmate. Under these circumstances it might have expected
the support of the United States. For in many respects American
policy in China was identical with British and it was in concert
with America that in 1902 England had persuaded the Powers to
proclaim the principle of the open door in China. But how much
was left of that principle by 1914? And what weapons were at
the disposal of the two great English-speaking nations to enforce
it? The American Government was opposed to any kind of

military intervention. And the British was compelled by the pressure of the German navy to withdraw gradually all its ships from Chinese waters.[1]

Meanwhile the revolt of China was spreading and provoking outside the country a far more direct opposition to British imperialism. We have seen how in India the Indian Councils Bill of 1909 had inaugurated an era of concessions to Hindu nationalism. But would the Nationalists be content with what was obviously a mere instalment? They made use of the elective element thus introduced into the provincial legislative councils to render British administration difficult throughout the entire country. And they made their way into the branches of the Civil Service. Moreover violent agitation continued. There were assassinations and bomb throwing. England hoped to strike an effective blow by despatching King George and the Queen to preside in person at the solemn Durbar, which inaugurated at Delhi the new capital of British India. The royal visit would, it was believed, endear the monarch to his Indian subjects and give a sentimental consecration to Hindu loyalty. The Hindu reply to this theatrical demonstration was the outrage committed a year later, on December 23, 1912, in this very city of Delhi. The Viceroy, Lord Hardinge was seriously wounded by a revolutionary, who successfully made his escape. England was clearly faced with a problem of extraordinary difficulty. 'The English', wrote a contemporary sadly, 'are interested in this problem. But they are also tolerably anxious and they make the mistake of letting this anxiety be seen.'[2]

We have seen how in Egypt the 'Young-Egyptian' movement cast a cloud over the final period of Lord Cromer's administration. The administration of his successor, Sir Eldon Gorst, coincided with years of economic depression, financial difficulties, and a nationalist agitation amounting to rebellion. Sir Eldon continued his predecessor's methods, though in consequence of the assassination of the Prime Minister and the discovery of a plot against his own life and the Khedive's he found himself obliged to enforce the Press laws more stringently than hitherto. He extended local self-government, giving greater powers, particularly in the matter of education, to the provincial councils. But he firmly

[1] For the situation in China on the eve of the War see an excellent article by J. O. P. Bland entitled 'The Future of China' (*Edinburgh Review*, October 1914, No. 450, pp. 427 sqq.).
[2] India and the English (*Round Table*, November 15, 1910; vol. i, No. 1, p. 45).

refused to introduce anything in the nature of a representative parliament. The first concessions to the Young-Egypt party were made by Kitchener, who succeeded Eldon in 1911. While taking energetic measures to improve the economic situation of the *fellahin* and attempting without success to solve the problem of the mixed tribunals, he drew up a constitution which was published in 1913. The Legislative Council and General Assembly were superseded by a single body, the 'Legislative Assembly,' composed of eighty-nine members of whom sixty-six were elected. It would have the right to initiate legislation, which the council of ministers could veto for reasons stated. Moreover the council would be obliged to submit any measure of legislation it thought desirable to the assembly, on which the new constitution conferred a suspensive veto. Only the civil list and foreign policy would be entirely excluded from its control. It would be elected indirectly by universal suffrage. In a document explaining the principles of the reform the hope was expressed that it would educate politically the native population and 'little by little' enable it to secure from its legislature 'a faithful representation of its interests'.[1]

2

In Persia the revolt of Asia assumed the same form as everywhere else. To strip of his power a sovereign whom they accused of being in the pay of Russia, the Nationalists of Teheran demanded a democratic constitution, an assembly elected by universal suffrage, and a responsible Government. They could count upon the sympathy of England, so that in Persia the same phenomenon could be witnessed which had occurred so often in other countries during the past century, a pre-established harmony between British interests and the cause of liberty. Twice during the year 1906 several thousand of the population of Teheran encamped on the huge piece of ground which was the property of the British legation, and obtained by this gesture of passive protest first the

[1] Report for year 1913. Sidney Low, *Egypt in Transition* with an Introduction by the Earl of Cromer, 1914, pp. 230 sqq. Sir George Arthur, *Life of Lord Kitchener*, 1920, vol. ii, especially for the constitutional question, pp. 330 sqq. The account is far from clear but makes it plain that when he granted Egypt a 'Legislative Assembly' Kitchener had no intention of fostering the growth of a genuine system of parliamentary government in Egypt.

grant of a constitution by the Shah, then an actual election. But at this juncture the Anglo-Russian Convention of August 31, 1907, was concluded. The Convention brought into line the policy of the two empires in Asia and particularly in Persia. While affirming the 'integrity and independence of Persia', it recognized Russia's 'special interest' in the northern portion of the country, which included Teheran, and the meaning of the phrase, as employed by European diplomacy, is obvious. England was therefore obliged by the pact of 1907 to betray at Teheran the Nationalist party, which had become accustomed to regard itself as the English party. The problem became even more difficult when, in 1910, Isvolsky, who had negotiated on behalf of Russia the agreement of 1907, was succeeded as Foreign Minister by Sazonov, who was far less friendly to England.

The Shah, driven from Teheran by a revolt, fled to Russian territory where he continued his intrigues. He was replaced on the throne by a child of twelve, a tool of the Assembly. But a Russian army occupied Tabriz and kept the capital under the constant threat of armed intervention. The Nationalist Government placed an American named Shuster in control of the Persian finances. He constituted himself the whole-hearted champion of the pro-British as against the pro-Russian party. At the very moment of the Agadir crisis when Russia was openly betraying her Western friends and allies but when it was more than ever necessary to avoid quarrelling with her, Shuster appointed Englishmen to the most important posts in the government departments—that is to say, in the very zone in which the Convention of 1907 admitted Russia's special interest, since it included Teheran. The Russian Government protested and the British was obliged to recognize that the protest was justified. The Government of Teheran dismissed Shuster and shortly afterwards was overthrown by a Russian army. The Shah was restored to his throne with despotic authority. Then Russia increased her demands. She proposed a partition of the zone hitherto left neutral between the British and Russian zones, and spoke of a trans-Persian railway to run through Teheran from the Caspian to the Persian Gulf. The British Government, its hands tied as they were by the necessities of its general policy, found itself in a humiliating position, powerless to oppose openly these projects of Russian expansion. The English opponents of Grey's policy were furnished with an excellent ground of attack. The advanced Liberals, foes of the Anglo-Russian *entente* and champions of a *rapprochement* with Germany, found powerful allies among the imperialists, particularly those who took a special interest in India and the Middle East. They had always regarded the Convention of 1907 as too favourable to Russia. Now they saw the Mohammedans of India, England's most certain allies against an eventual rising of the Hindus, denouncing the crime committed by the Foreign Office in abandoning Teheran, one of the last remaining Moslem capitals, to Russian rule. It was therefore a formidable attack, for it kept up an incessant fire and was conducted on two fronts by Arthur Ponsonby on one side, by Lord Curzon on the other, which Grey had to face when he defended his Persian policy as best he could, whether in the Press or in Parliament.[1]

These anxieties however, serious though they were, were nothing in comparison with those caused by events nearer home. For the revolt of Asia had reached Turkey and not only Turkey in Asia but Turkey in Europe and had kindled in the Balkans a conflagration destined shortly to spread until it had set the whole of Europe on fire.

It was in July 1908 that the 'Young-Turk' movement broke out at Salonika. On July 23 two army corps revolted and the following day Abdul Hamid capitulated. The conspirators had no need, as in Persia or China, to construct a completely new constitution. It was sufficient to restore the constitution of 1876 based on indirect election by universal suffrage, which the Sultan had abolished thirty years before. Once reorganized, the Ottoman Empire, as we have already had occasion to point out, would confront Europe not as a State formed by the subjection of several conquered people to a conquering race, but as a State of the Western type, in which the entire population, without distinction of race, language, or creed would consist of Turkish citizens on an equal footing. And for this very reason there could no longer be any ground for the constant interference of the great Christian powers in 'the domestic affairs of Turkey'. Turkey would no longer be humiliated in the person of her Sultan. The national honour had been saved by the accession to power of the 'Jacobins', the Young Turks.

The hope was disappointed. Three months after the Young-

[1] For the events in Persia see Edward G. Browne, *The Persian Revolution of 1905–1909*, 1920 and W. Morgan Shuster, *The Strangling of Persia, a Record of European Diplomacy*, 1912.

Turk revolution Austria-Hungary annexed Bosnia and Herzegovina. Three years later Italy occupied the coast of Tripoli. The
disintegration of Turkey followed. It is susceptible of two alternative explanations.

The first of these attributes the overthrow of Turkish authority
in the Balkans to the intrigues of the great powers. The war between Turkey and Italy dragged on. Fear of losing face prevented
the young Turks from making peace. The Italian Ambassador in
Paris, Tittoni, entered into conversations with Isvolsky, now
Russian Ambassador to France, who wanted to avenge the humiliation inflicted upon him by Austria and Germany in 1909 by a
further attempt to establish Russian hegemony over the Dardanelles. Why not provoke a rising of the Eastern Christians against
Turkey, a joint attack upon her by the Balkan powers? Under
Isvolsky's auspices an alliance was concluded between Serbia and
Bulgaria, the germ of the triple alliance of the Serbs, Bulgars, and
Greeks. When this war or revolution broke out, Turkey would be
compelled to abandon the last remnants of her African dominions
to Italy, and Russia would make use of the opportunity to secure
a free passage of the Dardanelles for her warships, possibly to
effect a military occupation of Constantinople.

We do not believe that diplomacy exercises such power over
human affairs. It is by internal causes that we explain the dissolution of the Ottoman Empire. No diplomatic intrigue provoked
the rebellion of the Assyrians, the Arabs in Asia, and the Albanians
in Europe against the Young Turks.[1] When the Young Turks surrendered to the Albanians and granted them a measure of autonomy the Macedonian Christians inevitably demanded the same
concessions. The very fact of the Young-Turk revolution gave
such impetus to the movement for emancipation that for a time
the enmity between Serbs, Bulgars, and Greeks was forgotten. The
Russian diplomats witnessed rather than inspired the alliance between Bulgaria and Serbia,[2] and if they deemed it advisable to
take the movement under their patronage, they were soon dis-

[1] If in the case of Albania intrigue played a part it was Austrian. See De Saint-Aulaire
to Raymond Poincaré, January 18, 1912; Krajewski to Raymond Poincaré, January 22,
1912 (*Documents diplomatiques français* . . . 3e Série, vol. i, pp. 496–7, 518–20). Duchesne to
Raymond Poincaré, August 4, 1912 (*Documents diplomatiques français* . . . 3e Série, vol. iii,
pp. 321-2).
[2] Bompard to Raymond Poincaré, August 4, 1912 (ibid., p. 320). Laroche to Briand,
August 20, 1912 (ibid., p. 377). Bompard to Raymond Poincaré, September 21, 1912
(ibid., p. 547).

mayed by the violent passions unloosed at Sofia and Belgrade. In any case no Russian or Italian action had anything to do with the *rapprochement* between Greece and Bulgaria, and Greece and Serbia. If any foreign influences were at work here they were British, official or private.[1] To overthrow Abdul Hamid, the Young Turks had appealed to the principle of nationality. That revolutionary principle was now being turned against themselves. What would be the issue of the conflict? Turkey was certainly weak, but the prestige of her army stood high. Europe which hardly knew what to expect or desire was soon relieved of uncertainty. On October 17 and 18 Bulgaria, Serbia, and Greece recalled their Ambassadors from Constantinople. Four days later in Thrace at the historic Battle of Kirk-Kilissé the Bulgarian army routed the Turkish.

3

For a moment the allies were expected to make a triumphant entry into Constantinople. And when at the beginning of December they halted before the lines of Chataldja after investing Adrianople, Turkey in Europe, apart from the environs of Constantinople and a fragment of Thrace, could be regarded as a thing of the past. An historic event of such grave import threatened the equilibrium of Europe. How could Austria witness without anxiety this sudden aggrandisement of Serbia which brought the Serbs to the coast of the Adriatic? And if she intervened by force to debar the Serbs from access to the Adriatic, or perhaps to take possession of the Salonika route, would the Russian Government tolerate her intervention? In the name of Slavonic racial solidarity and pushed forward by the pan-Slavs Russia might perhaps intervene, if need be in the teeth of certain Balkan Slavs, to obtain possession of Constantinople and a free access to the Mediterranean. But Austria was the ally of Germany. She could not go to war without her ally's approval, and if a war against Serbia became a war against Russia, the German army would come to the aid of the Austrian. France in turn was Russia's ally. An alliance which at the end of the nineteenth century might have been regarded as protecting France against the danger of a German invasion now exposed her to it.

---

[1] *Documents diplomatiques français* . . . 3e Série, vol. iii, p. 303 *n.*; Deville to Raymond Poincaré, August 1, 1912 (ibid., p. 314).

But it was quite impossible for France to break free from the alliance. The German Government left her no choice in the matter. The mere existence of a large French army in its rear while it was fighting the Russian forces constituted too great a military danger for the German Staff to accept. A march on Paris and the annihilation of the French army would be the first act of the European war, as its scenario had been drawn up in Berlin. But if France were involved in war, England, her cordial friend, could not remain a disinterested spectator. What would her attitude be?

We must bear in mind that it was at the very time when the Balkan War was brewing and finally broke out that the Foreign Office and Admiralty concluded the double negotiations which led on the one hand to a written definition of the *entente* in November 1912, on the other to the conclusion in February 1913 of a naval convention, which completed the alliance between the two armies, effected six years before, by an agreement between the two navies for concerted action against the common enemy. But it was at the same moment that Grey made the most marked advances to Germany he ever made while he was at the Foreign Office. On October 7 he sent for the chargé d'affaires, Von Kühlmann, communicated to him the conversations which had taken place between himself and Sazonov, who had just visited London, and expressed his wish, indeed his anxiety, to remain in touch with him.[1] At a second interview with Von Kühlmann on the 14th he seemed disappointed to hear that the German Government had not thought fit to reply to his advances,[2] and that very evening his chief secretary, Sir William Tyrell, dining with Von Kühlmann tendered him 'the olive branch' in the name of the Foreign Secretary and expressed the wish for 'an intimate collaboration between the two powers' not only in Europe, but in China, Persia, Turkey, and Africa.[3] The following morning Tyrell returned to the German Embassy to explain—presumably on Grey's behalf—that the evening before he had simply expressed his chief's personal views and that for the moment no communication would be made either to Sir Arthur Nicolson the permanent under-secretary, or to Sir

[1] Von Kühlmann to the German Foreign Office, October 7, 1912 (*Die Grosse Politik* . . . vol. xxxiii, pp. 175–6).
[2] Von Kühlmann to Bethmann-Hollweg, October 14, 1912 (ibid., vol. xxxiii, p. 221).
[3] Von Kühlmann to Bethmann-Hollweg, October 15, 1912 (ibid., vol. xxxiii, p. 228 sqq.).

Edward Goschen, the British Ambassador at Berlin.[1] The prospect of an Anglo-German *entente* delighted the German chargé d'affaires. The Wilhelmstrasse was more sceptical though quite ready to take advantage of the British minister's friendly attitude.[2] What interpretation are we to put upon this secret advance by Grey? What light does it throw on the methods of British diplomacy at this juncture?

It suggests a disagreement between Grey's views and those current at the Foreign Office. For Sir Arthur Nicolson, as for his 'assistant', Sir Eyre Crowe, the distinction between an '*entente*' and an alliance was purely verbal: the Triple Entente was simply another Triple Alliance, a counterblast to the Triple Alliance between Germany, Austria, and Italy.[3] When Grey, before he took office had championed a *rapprochement* with France and Russia, his views probably did not differ from those of Sir Arthur Nicolson, his predecessor Lord Hardinge, and any diplomats he might choose to help him at the Foreign Office. But we have already seen how as a responsible minister he became the link between these permanent officials and a parliamentary majority and a Cabinet whose attitude was different. He was obliged to take their views into account and was perhaps himself affected in the long run by the arguments of those who were opposed to a policy of continental alliances. The result of these cross-currents was the elaboration of what we may term the doctrine of an *entente* as distinct from an alliance. The *entente* meant preparations complete to the last detail for concerted military action, to be taken automatically and immediately, by the parties to it, if ever they found themselves jointly engaged in war. And in the autumn of 1912 a further step was taken and France and England agreed that if a serious situation arose they would take joint diplomatic action without waiting for the outbreak of war. But this was all. There was no agreement to make war, in circumstances defined beforehand. Whatever the *casus belli* England reserved to the last moment her

---

[1] Von Kühlmann to the German Foreign Office, October 16, 1912 (*Die Grosse Politik* . . . vol. xxxiii,p. 232).

[2] Von Kiderlen to Von Kühlmann, October 20, 1912 (ibid., vol. xxxiii, p. 233).

[3] Count von Benckendorff to Sazonov, November 1–14, 1912: '. . . Nicolson told Cambon with the utmost emphasis that in the event of war between the Triple and the Dual Alliance England would not in his opinion remain neutral. I must however add that Nicolson's views are not always the same as Grey's.' (Graf Benckendorff's, *Diplomatischer Briefwechsel* Band, ii, p. 491. Cf. Mensdorff's despatch from London of June 6, 1913 (*Österreich-Ungarns Aussenpolitik* . . . vol. vi, p. 608).

freedom to intervene or remain neutral. She even claimed the right, if the Power against which the *entente* was directed were willing to abstain from any step which would embroil England with her friends on the Continent and refrained from challenging her in a competition of armaments, to complete the *ententes* with France and Russia by some kind of *entente* with Germany. It was an *entente* of this kind which Grey offered Germany at the very moment when the first Balkan war broke out and Sir William Tyrell was his agent in the private negotiations he conducted with the two Great Powers of Central Europe,[1] while Sir Arthur Nicolson, kept in ignorance of Sir William's action, remained his agent in all dealings with France and Russia with whom he was determined to maintain cordial relations.[2] As for Grey himself, the language he used to the Ambassadors of France and Russia was not altogether the same as that employed by his

[1] For the part played at this junction by Sir William Tyrell see Prince Lichnowsky *Meine Londoner Mission*, Eine Denkschrift, verfasst in August 1916, p. 26, 'After the Foreign Secretary, Sir A. Nicolson and Sir W. Tyrell were the most influential persons at the Foreign Office. The former was no friend of ours. . . . He was in the confidence of my French colleague with whom he was in permanent contact. He even wanted to replace Lord Bertie in Paris. . . . Sir Edward Grey's private secretary, Sir W. Tyrell possessed far greater influence than the permanent under-secretary. A man of very high intellectual gifts he had studied at a Gymnasium in Germany. He adopted a diplomatic career but had served abroad only a short time. Though he shared at first the anti-German attitude popular among young British diplomats he became later the convinced advocate of an understanding with our country. He has influenced Sir Edward Grey with whom he was on intimate terms in this direction.' For the confidential relations between Tyrell and Count Mensdorff throughout the Balkan wars see the latter's despatches. April 11, 15, May 9, June 4, 1913, *Österreich-Ungarns Aussenpolitik* . . . vol. vi, pp. 105, 159, 397, 596-7. This would seem to have been his attitude since the beginning of 1911 (see Count Mensdorff's despatches March 17, May 26, 1911. ibid., pp. 214-252. In the spring of 1914 we find von Jagow the German Foreign Minister attempting to arrange a meeting with Tyrell. But the latter refused (G. von Jagow, *England und der Kriegsausbruch. Eine Auseinandersetzung mit Lord Grey, mit einem Nachwort von Alfred von Wegener*, 1925, p. 32 *n*.).) But at this very time Tyrell was the diplomatic agent whom Grey employed to explore the possibility of effecting a *rapprochement* with Germany through the mediation of the United States (see above p. 618).

[2] Notice how Grey himself on the eve of the World War described the relations between England and France and Russia. Sir Edward Grey to Sir Edward Goschen, June 24, 1914: '. . . I said to Prince Lichnowsky that I felt some difficulty in talking to him about our relations with France and Russia. It was quite easy for me to say, and quite true, that there was no alliance; no agreement committing us to action; and that all the agreements of that character that we had with France and Russia had been published. On the other hand, I did not wish to mislead the ambassador by making him think that the relations that we had with France and Russia were less cordial and intimate than they really were. Though we were not bound by engagement as allies, we did from time to time talk as intimately as allies. . . .' (*British Documents* . . . vol. xi, pp. 4-5.) Colonel House to President Wilson, August 1, 1914: '. . . Sir Edward Grey told me that England had no written agreement with either Russia or France, or any formal alliance; that the situation was brought about by a mutual desire for protection; and that they discussed international matters with as much freedom with one another as if they had an actual written alliance.' (*The Intimate Papers of Colonel House*, vol. i, p. 485.)

Under-Secretary, nor was the language he used to the German Ambassador exactly the same as that employed by his private secretary. In particular he was careful to explain to Lichnowsky that if he was so anxious for German assistance in his efforts to maintain peace, it was because in the event of a war between the Continental Powers England could not avoid intervention and if she intervened it would not be on the side of Germany.[1] On the other hand when King George, speaking to Prince Henry of Prussia, used the firm language which Sir Arthur Nicolson might have employed had he been King instead of a mere official at the Foreign Office, Grey expressed his entire approval.[2] The system was a maze in whose windings Lord Haldane had all but lost himself a few months earlier. But its architect, Grey, threaded his way with an imperturbable *sangfroid*.

4

The policy of the British Government, as we have just described it, proved successful since the Balkan crisis was settled without a European war. The success however was due in reality to the fact

[1] Prince Lichnowsky to the Minister for Foreign Affairs, December 4, 1912: 'If a European war broke out as a result of Austrian action against Serbia, and Russia, yielding to the pressure of public opinion and to avoid another humiliation such as she suffered in 1909, invaded Galicia, a step which would involve our intervention, France could not avoid taking part in the war and the further consequences could not be foreseen. This is the second occasion on which he has made use of this latter circumlocution whose significance cannot be misunderstood. In this connection several persons in his intimacy have told me during the last few days that the present government is determined to do everything possible to prevent European complications arising because it fears they might hinder the *rapprochement* with ourselves which it desires to bring about, and it is a matter of life and death for her, though England has no secret agreements with France to prevent our inflicting a crushing defeat upon France. England would therefore find herself compelled in the event of our victory over France to intervene on her behalf.' (*Die Grosse Politik* . . . vol. xxxiii, pp. 417, 453.) Notice on the other hand the caution with which Grey refused to inform Benckendorff, the Russian Ambassador, what attitude England would adopt should the war become general. (Count von Benckendorff to Sazonov, November 1–14, 1912; Graf von Benckendorff, *Diplomatischer Briefwechsel*, vol. ii, p. 490.)

[2] Mensdorff telegram despatched from London, December 22, 1912. 'When Prince Henry of Prussia visited England not long ago and the King told him he was sorry that Herr von Bethmann in his speech in the Reichstag had directly alluded to the possibility of war and had not maintained the same reserve as Count Berchfeld, M. Sazonov and Sir Edward Grey Prince Henry asked him the direct question whether in the event of a war between Austria-Hungary and Germany and Russia and France England would intervene on behalf of the latter. King George replied, "Certainly under certain circumstances". When Prince Henry displayed annoyance and surprise the King proceeded: "Do you imagine we have less sense of honour than you? You have formal alliances, we have unwritten understandings. But we cannot allow either France or Russia to be defeated."' (*Österreich-Ungarns Aussenpolitik* . . . vol. v, pp. 212–4.)

that throughout the crisis the policy of the other Governments resembled in many respects that of the British. In every European capital the desire to preserve peace proved stronger than the spirit of warlike adventure and the sentiment of what was once more termed by the revival of an old phrase the 'European concert' prevailed over the spirit of national and racial animosity which inspired the two rival groups. In the first place we must remember that the web of international relations was so complicated that the system of alliances could not always be consistently worked. In Constantinople France was obliged to support Russia for political reasons, but her financial interests inclined her rather to the side of Germany, and it often happened that the French Ambassador, speaking as the mouthpiece of the French colony, expressed himself in a sense hostile to Russia and sometimes even to England. Germany was the ally not only of Austria, but of Italy, and to prevent Italy leaving the Triple Alliance the German Government was compelled to discourage any Austrian attempt at expansion in the Mediterranean area. In the second place the revival in the three Courts of Berlin, Vienna, and Petersburg of that spirit of monarchical solidarity on which the Holy Alliance had been based a century earlier was a powerful factor making for peace. The Emperor Francis Joseph sent an Austrian noble of high rank to Petersburg on a mission of conciliation. At Petersburg the Conservative party, the determined champion of an understanding with the Prussian monarchy, held office in the person of Kokovtsov. King George and the Emperor Nicolas visited Berlin for the marriage of a royal Princess and their friendly conversations with the German Emperor, if apparently devoid of any political character, helped nevertheless to relax the diplomatic tension.[1] Finally the great civilized nations had for close upon fifty years grown unaccustomed to war, though making unremitting preparations for it, and statesmen on the brink of the gulf which divides peace and war, were sensible of the abyss at their feet and shrank from taking the plunge.

The British attitude however differed in one respect from that of

---

[1] See the private letter written by Szögyény from Berlin on May 20, 1913: '. . . I have been able to have a few words only with Herr von Jagow since his return from Vienna. He and the other officials of the Foreign Office are at present so busy making preparations to receive the royal guests who are coming to Berlin for the wedding of Princess Victoria Louise that as the Secretary of State assured me, they have at present no time for politics and are thinking of nothing but the marriage.' (*Österreich-Ungarns Aussenpolitik* . . . vol. vi, p. 467.)

the other Governments. The British Government wanted the European states to settle the Balkan crisis by joint action, to forget as far as possible their membership of opposite political groups and think only of the supreme interest of peace. The other Powers, however, refused to lose sight of their alliances even for the moment. They regarded the European concert as an understanding between two combinations which even while acting together must act as such. One Government perhaps pursued a slightly different policy. The German Government sought to drive a wedge into the Triple Entente by separating France from Russia, as it had successfully done in 1909 and in 1911, or England from France and Russia, and though on this occasion it failed to achieve the former object, it could cherish or at least spread the belief that it had achieved the latter. Foreign policy during the last few years has been too rigid, Haldane told Lichnowsky on December 3, it must be made more gelatinous.[1] And since this was precisely the aim which the Prussian Government was pursuing, at least so far as the Triple Entente was concerned—it wanted to reduce it to a jelly—we often receive the impression during the long months for which the Balkan wars dragged on that a reconciliation had begun between England and Germany. It was loudly advertised in Germany. And the English were delighted.

For the real difference between British policy and that of the other nations must be sought not in the attitude of their respective Governments but in the attitude of the people. On the Continent the Governments of the great nations were more cautious than the public, at least that opinionated and violent section of the public which finds utterance in the Press. As regards Austria this is a truism. In Russia reaction against the schemes of annexation entertained by the military party in Austria had provoked a pan-Slavonic campaign in the Press which caused the ministers considerable embarrassment. It was only natural that the Germans of Germany should make common cause with the Germans of Austria in the event of a conflict with the Slavs. In France the news of the first Turkish defeats was the signal for an enthusiastic celebration by almost the entire Press of the victories won by the allies which were regarded as victories won by Le Creusot's cannon over Krupp's, victories therefore of the French over the

[1] Prince Lichnowsky to Bethmann-Hollweg, December 3, 1912 (*Die Grosse Politik* . . . vol. xxxix, pp. 121-2).

German army. Moreover, we must remember that the German and French Governments were faced by special difficulties in pursuing a policy of peace. For at the opening of 1913 the German Government thought it necessary to make provision against the dangers of the moment by asking for an enormous increase in the army, to which the French Government replied by asking for a return to the system of three years' service. But in two countries possessing universal suffrage an elective assembly could be induced to shoulder such burdens only by inflaming the patriotic sentiments of the masses. It was no easy task to pursue at the same time a foreign policy of peace and a European concert. England was confronted by no such difficulties.

When we read English newspapers of the period we gather at first the impression of a profound cleavage in public opinion. Generally speaking the Conservative Press, attached though it might be to the principle of an *entente* with Russia when the threat from the German navy had to be met in the West, detected Russian pan-Slavism at work behind the Balkan alliance, pictured the Russian army already on the Bosphorus and upheld the traditional English policy of protecting Turkey against Russia. And how could Great Britain, a great Moslem Power, favour a war which had the aspect of a crusade without giving offence to millions of her subjects? When, lastly, the owner of an important Unionist paper was a Jew his indignation against the barbarities of Russian anti-semitism strengthened his mistrust of the policy pursued at Petersburg. Among the Liberals on the contrary the spectacle of Bulgarians, Serbs, and Greeks reconciled against the Turk revived the old Liberal-Christian tradition of Gladstone. A year earlier the prospect of a war in which the English would shed their blood to serve the interests of French against German imperialism was anathema to the staff of the *Nation* and the *Manchester Guardian* and to combat it the utilitarian philosophy of peace at any price made fashionable by Norman Angell was accepted without reserve. It was altogether different now. War, it was allowed, might be noble, if waged for justice and liberty. But where was the Gladstone to lead this movement of public opinion? Churchill who blew the war trumpet[1] did not possess, as everyone admitted,

---

[1] Speech at Sheffield, October 30, 1912: '. . . We have sometimes been assured by persons who profess to know that the danger of war has become an illusion and that in these modern days that danger would not exist at all but for the machinations of statesmen and diplomatists, but for the intrigues of financiers, aided by the groundless suspicions of

the temperament of a Gladstone. Conceivably Lloyd George might have been attracted by such a role. But he had other concerns. Moreover if a new Gladstone could have been discovered, not only would he have failed to arouse popular enthusiasm, he would not even have found a Lord Beaconsfield to combat. The time had gone by when parties were divided by questions of foreign policy. The nation, completely absorbed by social and Irish questions, made the Press, whatever its political complexion, understand that it must be more moderate in the expression of its preferences. When he adopted an attitude of strict neutrality and impartial opposition to the war and tried to induce the other powers to do the same, Grey was pursuing to the letter the policy the British people wished him to pursue.

Count Berchtold was the first statesman to appeal to the powers to intervene: in August 1912 he invited them to put joint pressure on the allies to prevent them from declaring war, and on Turkey to secure the adoption of reforms which by satisfying its Christian subjects would deprive the former of every pretext for hostilities. The initiative was coldly received by the Foreign Office, which saw nothing but danger in the suggestion of putting pressure on the Turkish Government. When, at the end of September, the allies had mobilized and war was imminent it was the turn of Raymond Poincaré, Prime Minister and Foreign Minister and shortly to become President of the Republic, to intervene. He suggested joint action by the Powers to inform the allies that no alteration in the map of the Balkans would be tolerated, the Turks that they must carry out long-promised reforms in favour of the Christian population of their empire. The British Government was the last to accept the French proposal, which in its opinion bore too hardly upon the Turks. But hostilities had

generals and admirals and fomented by the sensationalism of the Press—all directed upon the ignorance and credulity of the people. Well, here is a war which has arisen from none of these causes, which has broken out in spite of all that rulers and diplomatists could do to prevent it, a war in which the Press has had no part, a war which the whole force of the money power has been subtly and steadfastly directed to prevent, which has come upon us, not through the ignorance and credulity of the people, but on the contrary, through their knowledge of their history and their destiny, and through their intense realization of their wrongs and of their duties, as they conceived them, a war which from all these causes has burst upon us with all the force of a spontaneous explosion, and which in strife and destruction has carried all before it. Face to face with this manifestation, who is the man who is foolish enough to say that force is never a remedy? Who is the man who is vain enough to suppose that the long antagonism of history, and of time can in all circumstances be adjusted by the smooth and superficial conventions of politicians and ambassadors?'

already opened and it was obvious that no diplomatic action could prevent thoroughgoing changes in the boundaries of the Balkan States. Poincaré was the first to suggest mediation by the Great Powers and an international conference to decide the conditions of peace, and his proposals were finally accepted though not without very considerable modifications.

In the first place there was no new Congress of Berlin at which the Powers carved up the Balkans as they thought fit. There was simply a conference at a European capital of delegates from the belligerent nations and at the same time a 'meeting'—nothing more—of the ambassadors of the Great Powers to deliberate on the questions, strictly limited in number, which the Balkan war had raised and which might endanger the peace of the world. In the second place Poincaré had wanted the Conference to be held in Paris. Sazonov made the proposal on his behalf and it was warmly welcomed by Grey, who wished to escape the responsibility and vexations a conference in London would involve. But the Central Powers wanted London—not Paris. In Paris Russia would be represented by Isvolsky. Obsessed by the desire to avenge the humiliation he had endured in 1909 as Foreign Minister, Isvolsky was making unwearied efforts to conquer the Press and the political world. It would be preferable to deal with Benckendorff, the Russian Ambassador in London, a man of mature wisdom, a diplomat of the old school, and a supporter of the policy of a European concert. In Paris a partisan Press treated the Balkan war as if it were a French war. The atmosphere of London was more favourable to a conference of arbitration. Finally Poincaré was too energetic a statesman, too obviously eager to play a leading part as chairman of the Conference. Grey would make a better chairman, for the very reason that he had no desire to preside.

We must not therefore imagine that the British public or even the Londoners were flattered that London had been chosen as the scene of so important an event. The general feeling was one of indifference, if not boredom. The presence of this host of Levantines from Constantinople, Athens, Sofia, and Belgrade who merely added their quota to the social chatter in the lounges of the great cosmopolitan hotels passed almost unnoticed. As for the conversations between the ambassadors Grey was at pains to give them as unceremonious and private a character as possible. He was often absent even at the most critical moments and his place as the representative of the Cabinet was taken by Asquith or Lord Morley. These disappearances surprised the foreigners who attributed to the British minister when he absented himself motives of which he was completely innocent.[1] He simply wanted a rest. 'There is some prospect of rain and if so the sport will be very good. It seems almost too much to expect that everything including both Balkan crises and salmon should go well simultaneously, but things seem to prosper so well in my absence that it would not be in the public interest for me to curtail it. I am in rude health with an appetite for everything except office work.'[2] This British indifference has always nonplussed and exasperated Continental diplomats. Listen to Lichnowsky, after his first meeting with Grey on the latter's return from holiday. 'I have just had an interview with Sir Edward Grey in which we discussed the situation fully. He regards it with his usual imperturbability and icy calm. He even found time to tell me all about the fish he caught on his holiday.'[3]

5

The Chataldja armistice was not the inauguration of peace. Outstanding questions remained to be settled—the Greek claim to the islands and the Bulgarian claim to Adrianople. For the Greeks had not taken the islands, nor the Bulgars Adrianople. A renewal of hostilities was expected daily. If they broke out, pan-Slavic opinion in Russia demanded a demonstration against Turkey whose obstinacy was delaying peace. Sazonov proposed a joint naval demonstration. Grey, his colleagues in the Cabinet and the Foreign Office hung back. If the Young Turks refused to yield, it would mean war and England would not have war under any circumstances. Fortunately for England the German Government flatly rejected the suggestion of a naval demonstration. To pacify Russia Grey was content to propose, if the Bulgarians captured Chataldja and anarchy prevailed at Constantinople, the despatch of an international squadron, not to carry out a naval

[1] See the report of Commander Horvath, military attaché to the Austro-Hungarian Embassy in London, April 24, 1913 (Feldmarshall Conrad von Hötzendorf, *Aus meiner Dienstzeit*, vol. iii, pp. 264 sqq.).

[2] Sir Edward Grey to Sir Arthur Nicolson, April 19, 1913 (Harold Nicolson, *Lord Carnock*, p. 389).

[3] Prince Lichnowsky to the Minister for Foreign Affairs, April 28, 1913 (*Die Grosse Politik* . . . vol. xxxiv[ii], p. 756).

demonstration, but merely to protect Europeans whose lives might be in danger. Again Germany refused, maintaining that the vessels already stationed in the Dardanelles would be sufficient for the purpose. And the British Government, a faithful mirror of public feeling, was only too pleased to yield to the German objection. Meanwhile the war party gained the upper hand in Constantinople, imprudently broke the armistice and when hostilities were renewed, lost Adrianople. Slowly and under great difficulties negotiations began in London between the delegates of the allies and the Turkish delegates. But new questions now occupied the meetings of the ambassadors, in the first place that of Albania.

When, in 1912, the Balkan Powers formed a league against Turkey, Serbia, and Greece had divided Albania, and Montenegro demanded her share of the spoils. But neither Italy nor Austria would accept such an extension of Greece and still less of Serbia to the Adriatic coast. They agreed to invoke against Greece and Serbia the principle of nationality which the latter had invoked against the Ottoman Empire. They claimed Albania not for themselves, deadly foes in spite of their alliance, but for the Albanians. To define the status of this new country, trace its frontiers, and find a way without giving Serbia the territorial outlet on the sea which she demanded and upon which the Russian Government, defying the Pan-Slavists' anger, refused to insist, of granting her at least certain facilities of commercial transit were the problems which from December onwards were the ordinary topics of discussion at the ambassadors' meetings.

But the Montenegrin army, assisted by Serbian reinforcements and commanded at one moment by a Serbian general, defied the prohibition of the Powers and continued to invest the town of Scutari. Would this involve war with Austria? And if a war broke out between Austria and Serbia would it in turn involve a European war? There was only one way by which the danger could be removed; the European concert must prove its solidarity by a joint demonstration which would compel Montenegro to yield. On March 22 the ambassadors' meeting decided to make the proposal. On the 25th Grey and Asquith, speaking in the House of Commons, advised Montenegro not to persist in a war from which she would not be allowed to reap any advantage and warned her that she would 'be confronted . . . with the united pressure of all the Powers'.[1] But what form should this pressure take? Berlin proposed a naval demonstration by Austria and Italy as mandatories of all the Powers. Grey thought it inadvisable that the mandatories should be two members of the same group. He suggested a naval demonstration in which the fleets of the six Great Powers should participate. But fear of the Pan-Slavists compelled the Russian Government to refuse. It advised the French Government to take part in the demonstration but dared not give it an official commission to do so. And without that commission the French Government shrank from associating itself with the demonstration, for it dared not brave the anger of the French Press, more Slavophil than the Russian Government itself. For a moment England was faced with the danger of being involved in a step in which her only associates would be the three members of the Triple Alliance. In the end the danger was averted. A French man-of-war joined the rest acting in the name of France and at the invitation of Russia. As a result of the joint action of the Powers the Serbian Government withdrew its forces from the walls of Scutari. But the Montenegrins persisted with the siege and took Scutari unaided. What was the use of the naval demonstration, if this affront was not met by the landing of troops? This however England would not hear of. Scutari was not worth the life of a single bluejacket.[2] Grey was content with informing King Nicolas 'that if he submitted to the wishes of the

[1] Sir Edward Grey's speech: '. . . Once an announcement has been made to Servia and Montenegro that the Powers have come to an agreement and of their decision, there ought to be a cessation of hostilities in what is in future to be Albania. . . . If the decision of the Powers is not respected, then I trust that those who dispute it will be confronted, not with any separate action on the part of one Power, which may divide the Powers, but with the united Pressure of all the Powers.' He adds the following characteristic qualification: 'This is only a mediation of the Powers. I do not mean to say that the Powers have made up their minds to enforce a compulsory arbitration or to impose terms.' (*Parliamentary Debates*, Commons 1913; 5th Series, vol. l, pp. 1499–1500.)

[2] Prince Lichnowsky to the Minister for Foreign Affairs, April 24, 1913: '. . . I am convinced that the present Government will never take the responsibility of exposing British troops to the danger of being fired upon by the Montenegrins, if only because such a war would be unpopular.' Von Tschirschky to the Minister for Foreign Affairs, April 24, 1913: '. . . Mr. Asquith and Sir A. Nicolson have given me to understand that they will not take the risk of British soldiers being fired upon.' Prince Lichnowsky to the Minister for Foreign Affairs, April 25, 1913: 'Mr. Asquith . . . asked me not to persist with a proposal involving the participation of British troops. Public opinion as it is at present would not support the Government in such action and the Cabinet as was agreed at the last Cabinet council was therefore not in a position to hazard the lives of British subjects.' Von Tschirschky to the German Foreign Office, April 28, 1913: 'The King (King George in the course of conversation with the Austrian) expressed himself strongly against the despatch of troops. He would not take the risk that British soldiers might be fired upon.' (*Die Grosse Politik* . . . vol. xxxiv[1], pp. 724, 727, 734, 760.)

Powers, they were prepared to discuss reasonable concessions *after the evacuation of Scutari*. If on the contrary he refused their request the British Government would give him no support and leave him to his fate'.[1] Paris followed suit. Did this not give Austria a free hand to take independent action if Montenegro proved obstinate? But the inaction of the British ministers was justified by the event. Vienna found no support at Berlin and was afraid of provoking by its intervention a counter-intervention by Italy. The King of Montenegro on the other hand was not encouraged by Petersburg and yielded. Austrian militarists were disappointed in their hope of a war of conquest. But the Slavs lost Scutari.

6

On May 30 a general pacification seemed imminent. At Grey's invitation the delegates to the Conference signed the 'Preliminaries of London'. By its terms Turkey surrendered to the allies the district of Adrianople and Crete and left the fate of the islands and the Athos peninsula to the decision of the six Great Powers. But it did not mean peace, for the allies had still to divide the spoils of victory and it had long been known in London that there was dissension between them. Serbia and Greece deprived by the powers of Albania, which they had partitioned in anticipation in 1912, demanded compensation in the east in Macedonia. The agreement of 1912 had assigned part of Macedonia to Bulgaria and left the other part to the Czar's decision. But it was occupied at present by Serbian and Greek forces. It was for the Bulgarians to conquer it by force if they dared. They dared and war broke out afresh. The Bulgarians were attacked in the rear by Roumania, which for months had demanded a rectification of the frontier to the disadvantage of Bulgaria—a conference of ambassadors at Petersburg had attempted in vain to arrange an amicable settlement—and in front by Turkey, delighted to have this opportunity to take her revenge within a few months for such crushing defeats.

It was a sordid struggle but its ignobility actually favoured the maintenance of peace, for it cut across the two rival systems of

[1] Pichon to Doulcet, April 29, 1913 (*Ministère des Affaires étrangères. Documents diplomatiques. Les affaires balkaniques* [1912–1914], 1920. T. 11, p. 174).

the Triple Alliance and the Triple Entente. The German Government supported Roumania, as also did the French, though hampered by fear of jeopardizing the alliance with Russia. On the other hand Austria, the foe of Serbia, and Russia, the foe of Roumania, found themselves unexpectedly united in a common support of Bulgaria. Once more Austria wanted to go to war, once more Germany held her back. For some weeks relations between the two allies were extremely strained. Finally, when the Turkish army reconquered Adrianople the position of the Powers became still more awkward. For it was the preliminaries of London of which they were guarantors which the Turkish Government was tearing up. The Russian Government demanded an armed demonstration, naval to begin with. In England, the conflict between Turkey's friends and foes broke out anew. The latter were the more numerous in the Liberal party and Asquith thought it safe to threaten Turkey at a public meeting.[1] But her friends proved finally the more powerful, not only in the country as a whole but even in the Liberal ranks, because their policy was one of inaction. Grey was willing to agree to independent intervention by Russia, provided it had the approval of Berlin, or alternatively to a joint naval demonstration if all the Powers took part in it. In other words he opposed from the outset any naval demonstration, because he knew Germany objected. He suggested financial action, but the financiers, particularly the French, would not hear of a measure from which Turkey's French creditors would be the first to suffer. Nothing was done and on July 29, tired out and as usual impatient to begin his holiday, Grey proposed that the ambassadors' meeting should be adjourned *sine die*. It was in vain that Cambon and Benckendorff protested against a decision which seemed to denote a rupture between the Powers. In a fortnight's time the ambassadors were forgotten.

At last peace was signed on August 10 at the capital of a victorious Roumania between Bulgaria on the one hand, Roumania, Serbia and Greece on the other, and the treaty of Bucharest was completed on September 17 by a treaty signed at Constantinople between Bulgaria and Turkey. Bulgaria lost the entire basin of the Vardar; Salonika and a considerable portion of Thrace, including the fort of Cavala, went to Greece. Roumania annexed a large strip of Bulgarian territory between the Danube and the

[1] Speech at Birmingham, July 21, 1913.

sea. And the Bulgars lost Adrianople, only a few weeks after the Serbo-Montenegrins had lost Scutari. It was on this final point that the agreement concluded in London was directly violated. The defeated party was therefore entitled to call upon the Powers to intervene or at least to protest. The Russian and Austrian Governments demanded that the Treaty of Bucharest should be revised and for a moment Grey seemed disposed to agree. A considerable section of the British Press and of the Liberal Press in particular was clamouring for a revision of the treaty. But he was confronted by the opposition of the German and French Governments, and he retreated. He soon perceived that the public indignation was superficial and that the dominant sentiment throughout the country was delight that peace had been restored on any terms whatsoever. The public would not admit that the European concert had failed. For although it had not succeeded in preventing war from breaking out, and twice recommencing and had dictated only to a very slight extent the conditions of peace, it had at least kept the struggle localized in the Balkans and prevented it from developing into a European war.[1] Men of all parties were grateful to Grey for having done more than any other statesman to achieve this result, by his firm determination to do nothing. His popularity, eclipsed at the beginning of 1912 because he had committed England more deeply than she desired to Continental entanglements in the train of France, was greater than ever at the close of 1913 because he had adopted the contrary attitude on dealing with Balkan affairs.

---

[1] It is amusing to read in the *New Statesman*, within a fortnight's interval, two diametrically opposite estimates of the diplomacy of the Powers during the Balkan wars, both supported by equally good arguments. November 15, 1913: '. . . The Concert of Europe . . . during the past twelve months has come to grief over many fences there. It ordered the Balkan allies not to go to war with Turkey—and they went to war. It ordered the Montenegrins not to take Scutari—and they took Scutari. It forced Greece and Servia to sign the Treaty of London with the Turks—and then let the Turks break the Treaty. It commanded the Turks to leave Adrianople—and allowed them to stay there. It looked on and let Austria egg on Bulgaria to attack her allies and egg on the Albanians to raid Servia. It extracted a promise from Italy to leave the Ægean—and is permitting her to make open arrangements to remain there. It has alternately worried the weak and yielded to the strong and has been by turns meddlesome, callous and helpless.' November 29, 1913 (an article by Lord Esher): 'The art of diplomacy has been justified in 1913. A Balkan war, annually prophesied as impending and to be certain to precipitate Armageddon, has come and gone. Europe, in the sense of what are called the Great Powers, remained at peace. This was due, not to the special friendliness of nations, certainly not to the restraint of the Press but to the governments concerned and to their representatives: in short, to the art of diplomacy.'

But was the peace likely to prove lasting? This was very widely doubted, and when the King of Roumania in a telegram of thanks which he sent to the Emperor William swore that the 'peace would be definitive', a diplomat unkindly added 'definitive for the moment'. *The Times* comforted itself by reflecting: 'The moment may be a long one.'[1] The moment was not destined to last long—less than a year—and a succession of incidents immediately warned the diplomatists that at any time a third Balkan war might break out in the South-East of Europe. In that event would the miracle of the months which had just passed be repeated and the Great Powers continue to be neutral?

Throughout the winter and the following spring the question of Albania caused anxiety to the Governments of Europe. For this petty barbarian state was their work, created to keep the Serbians from the sea and prevent the Austrians and Italians from coming to blows. Its frontiers must now be drawn, the Serbian on the north, the Greek on the south. The task was entrusted to two international commissions. On both commissions the attitude of the British members was strictly impartial. The English member of the commission appointed to demarcate the northern frontier openly professed himself in favour of a *rapprochement*, if not an actual alliance, between England and Germany and refused all the suggestions for common action made by the French and Russian commissioners: 'England', he said, 'desired a friendly understanding with all nations.'[2] The English member of the southern frontier commission was, like his wife, a keen traveller, delighted with the prospect of hunting in the Albanian mountains. 'His Government', he explained, 'cared only for one thing, that peace should be preserved in the Balkans, he did not care in the least whether Albania was a little larger or a little smaller.'[3] Nevertheless incidents ensued of a nature to disturb the sangfroid of the British Government and its agents. On October 18th the Austrian Government called upon Serbia to evacuate within a week areas

[1] *The Times*, August 11, 1913.

[2] Commander von Laffert, German member of the commission delimiting the northern frontier of Albania to Bethmann-Hollweg, November 14, 1913 (*Die Grosse Politik . . .* vol. xxxvi, p. 223).

[3] Commander Thierry, German member of the commission delimiting the southern frontier of Albania to Bethmann-Hollweg, September 4, 1913 (ibid., vol. xxxvi, p. 140).

which Europe had assigned to Albania. Threatened with an Austrian invasion the Serbian Government submitted. Grey made energetic protests to the Austrian Government. What need of this bellicose and isolated action when the peaceful pressure of the Great Powers acting in concert would have been sufficient?[1]

The Austrian ultimatum was a serious matter. For in the present instance Austria's action was taken with the approval and encouragement of Germany, withheld on previous occasions. The very day the ultimatum was despatched, the Emperor William, celebrating at Leipzig amid a vast concourse of spectators the centenary of the Battle of the Nations, held a long conversation with Field-Marshal Conrad von Hötzendorf in which he maintained Austria's right to destroy Serbia.[2] At Vienna a week later he expressed himself still more strongly to the same effect.[3] A week later still in a conversation with the King of the Belgians at Berlin he made it plain that in his opinion a European war was imminent and inevitable.[4] In short, for the first time, instead of holding the Austrian Government back or following it reluctantly when it took a step likely to lead to war, Berlin encouraged Vienna to pursue a bellicose policy. London indeed knew nothing of this. The newspapers devoted very little space to the Austrian ultimatum.[5] The Irish question, which had reached an acute stage, occupied public attention and provided ample material to fill their columns. But at Petersburg this new success won by Austria at the expense of the Southern Slavs aroused the anger of the Pan-

[1] Von Kühlmann to the Minister for Foreign Affairs. London, October 20, 1913 (*Die Grosse Politik* . . . vol. xxxvi, p. 407).

[2] Conrad von Hötzendorf, *Aus Meiner Dienstzeit*, vol. iii, pp. 496 sqq.

[3] S. Berchtold. Account of a conversation with the German Emperor William II on October 28, 1913 (*Österreich-Ungarns Aussenpolitik* . . . vol. vii, pp. 512 sqq.).

[4] Baron Beyens, *Deux Années à Berlin 1912–1914*, 1921, vol. ii, pp. 38 sqq. Cf. Jules Cambon to the Minister for Foreign Affairs, November 22, 1913 (*Ministère des affaires étrangères. Documents diplomatiques 1914. La Guerre européenne*, vol. i, p. 20).

[5] In its number of October 21 the *Daily Telegraph* speaks of 'the high-handed action of the Austrian Government which I have good reason to add, was strongly backed, if not encouraged, by the Berlin Government' but, while deploring the methods adopted by Austria expressed its pleasure that Serbia had yielded thus ensuring a peaceful issue of the conflict. Both *The Times* and the *Manchester Guardian* informed their readers of the ultimatum without comment and devoted a leader to the anniversary of the Battle of Leipzig. The only difference between the two papers was that the *Manchester Guardian* gave an entire column to the commemoration of the Battle. The *Observer* of the 19th published a despatch from Vienna in five lines without comment and a leading article on the Leipzig celebrations. The *Sunday Times* (October 19 and 26) treated the matter with the utmost sangfroid. Russia and Austria were agreed and Serbia could no longer exploit their differences. 'Thus ends the latest, and probably the last, trouble arising out of the Balkan Wars, for an eventual understanding between Greece and Turkey is also confidently expected.'

Slavists, who thought themselves entitled to demand their revenge when, on November 6, it became known that the Turkish Government had invited to Constantinople to act as instructor of the Turkish army and take command of a division in the capital itself, the German General Liman von Sanders.

The Russian public called upon a Cabinet which the more fiery patriots had long blamed for excessive complaisance towards the Central Empire to take action in face of this new German encroachment. This time Kokovtsoff did not dare to ignore public opinion, and the Ministers under the pressure of the Pan-Slavists, who found a champion in Sazonov even considered—though they finally rejected it—the suggestion of armed intervention in Asia Minor.[1] The ambassadors of the three Entente Powers jointly asked the Porte to revoke a step which gave Russia legitimate cause for complaint. But if the German Government gave way it was not to avoid offending Great Britain. For it was obviously only for form's sake that she took part in the Russian protest. British public opinion was still completely indifferent to events in the Balkans and Grey's hands were further tied by the fact that the Turkish Government as a counterpoise to German influence had just given the command of the fleet to a British Admiral.[2] The German Government yielded because it did not want a pro-German Government at Petersburg turned out of office, as was likely to happen if its prestige were persistently weakened. Liman von Sanders kept the training of the Turkish army in his hands. But the Turkish Government raised him to the rank of a Field Marshal. This made it impossible for him to remain in command of a division in Constantinople and the Russians were satisfied.

This question had no sooner been settled when the Albanian

[1] *Die Grosse Politik* . . . vol. xxxviii, pp. 191 sqq. M. Pokrowski, *Drei Konferenzen* (*Zur Vorgeschichte des Kreiges*) 1920, pp. 32 sqq. The project of military action, this time in the Dardanelles, was again examined by the Russian Government on February 21, 1914. But it was not a step to be taken immediately. It was a plan of campaign against Turkey in the supposition of a European war already begun. (M. Pokrowski, *Drei Konfernzen* . . . pp. 46 sqq.) In fact the chief of staff refused to consider the suggestion, which he said would unduly divide the armed forces of Russia, which must be employed wholly against Germany. This was what actually happened. Russia had not sufficient strength to make an attack on the Dardanelles from the north, and left it to England to make the attack, with French help, from the south, how unsuccessfully we know.

[2] Mensdorff. Report from London, December 17, 1913: 'When I called on Sir Edward Grey yesterday to take leave our conversation touched upon the German Military Mission to Constantinople. The Secretary of State remarked that "it is one of the most uncomfortable questions we have to deal with".' (*Österreich-Ungarns Aussenpolitik* . . . vol. vii, p. 663.) On this affair of General von Sanders see Sir George Buchanan, *My Mission to Russia*, vol. i, pp. 148–150.

question began once more to preoccupy the diplomatists. This time it was a question not of the frontier between Serbia and Albania, but of the frontier between Albania and Greece. Grey, shaking off for once his inertia, suggested a settlement by which Greece would be enabled to make in Albania the territorial concessions demanded of her without loss of prestige, because in return Turkey would abandon to her the islands of the Archipelago. It was an imprudent proposal. It did not succeed in putting an end to the conflict between Albania and Greece, for in March Epirus revolted against the Albanian Government and it aggravated the conflict between Greece and Turkey at the very time when the persecution of the Greeks in Thrace and Asia Minor by the Turks was becoming more severe. At one moment towards the middle of June war seemed imminent. Finding it impossible to persuade the Powers to take concerted action to put pressure upon Turkey, Grey, weary of the Balkan imbroglio, contemplated standing aside altogether and leaving affairs in the Near East to take their course.[1] But it was impossible to stand aside from a dispute which might result in closing the Dardanelles to British commerce. And was it so certain that a third Balkan war would be confined to Greece and Turkey? Would not Bulgaria and Roumania intervene? And in their train the Great Powers? Once more Grey spoke the language of 1912 and 1913 and sought the best method of 'localizing' the conflict.[2]

Once more the danger was staved off, but only that the Adriatic might again become the focus of attention. The Powers had undertaken not only to draw the frontiers of the new state of Albania but to provide it with a government and constitution. They chose as King, a German, Prince von Wied. But he was unable to establish an effective sovereignty over the country. The whole of Albania was in revolt. Besieged in Durazzo the King

---

[1] See already Mensdorff Report for London, February 13, 1914: 'It may well be disappointment at the course of events in Constantinople together with a certain weariness of spirit which has prompted Sir Edward Grey during the last few days to consider the possibility of withdrawing and keep open the possibility of doing so. Ever since my return the Foreign Secretary has shown, I have noticed, an increasing "lassitude". He is constantly using such language as "I am sick to death of the whole thing". The domestic situation and many other questions make large drafts upon his time and strength, and he had, I believe, entertained the confident expectation that his last proposals would have settled the questions of Albania and the islands—so far as the Powers are concerned.' (Österreich-Ungarns Aussenpolitik . . . vol. vii, pp. 866–7.)

[2] Memorandum communicated by the British Ambassador, June 17, 1914 (Die Grosse Politik . . . vol. xxxvi, pp. 817–8).

was watching his opportunity to take refuge on board a British man-of-war, whose presence in these waters had no other purpose. What was to be done? Give him the necessary troops to enforce his sovereignty? Not one of the Great Powers was prepared to do this, England least of all. Substitute for his government an Austro-Italian condominium of Austria and Italy? But in Albania nothing short of a war was being waged between the agents of the two Powers, and the supporters of the Prince von Wied accused Italy of fomenting the insurrection of Albania against a ruler too friendly to Germany and Austria. Leave the Albanians to settle their own fate, the Powers being content to guarantee their territorial integrity? But how could this integrity be guaranteed against an eventual invasion by the Serbs or Greeks except by that use of force to which England would not consent? Meanwhile the situation in Albania became worse every day. On June 27 the Austrian Government communicated to its Ambassador in Rome the text of an ultimatum addressed to the Italian Government demanding the immediate recall of the Italian Consul at Durazzo. The same day a recruiting agency was opened in Vienna to enlist volunteers to support Prince von Wied. Would the third Balkan war break out in Albania and take the form of a war between Austria and Italy?

8

It was unlikely. Germany had too much interest in settling the dispute, and preventing a war which began with a split in the Triple Alliance. But before the situation could be cleared up or further embroiled in Albania, a conflagration was kindled a little farther to the north, where the diplomats did not expect it, because the occasion did not come within their competence. It was not a question of foreign policy in the technical sense but of domestic. It was an episode which occurred within Austria-Hungary itself.

In fact, the domestic problems of the Austro-Hungarian monarchy hardly differed, if the diplomatists had viewed them in the right light, from the problems with which they were professionally concerned. For the struggle here was not between different classes of a single nation, but between nations within a composite State. Two races shared power and oppressed a minority of subject races, Czechs, Slovaks, Slovenes, Croats, and Serbs. As time went on, their discontent grew. The more intense it became, the stronger became the temptation felt by the two Governments, particularly the Hungarian, to settle the problem by force. All Europe was ringing with the story of the Agram trial and the documents forged by the Austrian police to secure the condemnation of the accused by a Hungarian court.

How are we to explain the increasing strength of national feeling within the Dual Monarchy? In the first place by the progress of democratic institutions. Universal suffrage had been introduced in Austria, the franchise considerably extended in Hungary. In consequence the disorder which prevailed in the legislatures became worse every year. In the Bohemian Diet the obstruction practised by the Germans had reached such a pitch that it became necessary to dissolve the Diet at the close of 1913. In revenge the Czechs organized such powerful obstruction in the Parliament at Vienna that in March 1914 the sittings had to be adjourned indefinitely. For if in the states of Northern and Western Europe democracy meant international Socialism, in the South-East of Europe it meant national independence. In the former rebellion was rebellion against war. In the latter it was war—hence the second reason why the domestic situation in Austria became so grave at this juncture, the recent events in the Balkans. The principle of nationality re-awakened in Asia had just destroyed the Ottoman Empire. Pursuing its revolutionary and fanatical course it was now issuing from the Balkan peninsula and invading the Danube basin, where it threatened to destroy in turn the Austro-Hungarian monarchy. Three million emancipated Serbs exercised upon the six million Yugo-Slavs under the dominion of Austria the same attraction Piedmont had exercised upon the rest of Italy half a century before. At Belgrade there was a widespread desire for war, but many Serbians believed that the unification of the Southern Slavs would be achieved without fighting. Within the next three or four years the Austro-Hungarian empire would have broken up and the Serbs of Bosnia, the Croats and Slovenes would peacefully unite with Serbia.[1]

[1] See Sir George Buchanan's account of a conversation with the Emperor of Russia on April, 14, 1913: 'The Emperor spoke of Austria without any bitterness, but as a source of weakness to Germany and as a danger to peace, owing to the fact that Germany was bound to support her in her Balkan policy. He further expressed the opinion that the

Threatened by the revolt of their Slav subjects, the Germans in Austria were naturally led to draw closer to their brethren in Germany. A species of fusion was effected between the organizations and institutions of the two countries—churches, political parties, universities, and armies. Only court circles still displayed anxiety to safeguard national independence and saw with displeasure the Austrian Germans look up to the German Emperor as the head of their race. The courts apart, the two states composed a single nation, as Austria-Hungary on the other hand was a single state composed of several nations. Nor did the Germans of Austria simply ask the Germans of Germany to come to their help if the integrity of Austria-Hungary were endangered by an internal revolt. An entire party led by the Chief of Staff of the Austrian army, Marshal Conrad von Hötzendorff, advocated an offensive against Serbia and the conquest of that country. Once annexed, Serbia would be absorbed in a Yugo-Slav kingdom under the sovereignty of the Emperor Francis-Joseph. The dual system of Austria-Hungary would be replaced by a triple system, Austrian, Magyar, and Yugo-Slav, and the 'Greater Serbia' thus called into existence by the action of Austria would henceforward be a bulwark against the anti-Austrian Pan-Serbs of Belgrade. But the stroke would certainly have a repercussion in Russia, and it was at this point that the Austrians counted on the German army, perhaps to intimidate Russia and prevent her from declaring war on Austria, but more probably to make war on Russia. The plan of such a war had been in existence for many years past. It would open with a march on Paris through Belgium. Then when the French army had been wiped out and Germany's western frontier was secure, a march on Petersburg or Moscow would follow. But if the first part of the plan were carried out and Germany reduced France and Belgium to subjection, what would England do?

---

disintegration of the Austrian Empire was merely a question of time, and that the day was not far distant when we should see a kingdom of Hungary and a kingdom of Bohemia. The Southern Slavs would probably be absorbed by Serbia, the Roumanians of Transylvania by Roumania, and the German provinces of Austria incorporated in Germany. The fact that Germany would then have no Austria to inveigle her into a war about the Balkans would, His Majesty opined, make for peace. I ventured to observe that such a recasting of the map of Europe could hardly be effected without a general war.' (*My Mission to Russia*, vol. i, p. 182.)

While the two Balkan wars were in progress, a few isolated voices had been raised from time to time in the Press in an attempt to make the British public realize the serious danger to the peace of Europe presented by the domestic situation of Austria-Hungary.[1] An eminent journalist, Wickham Steed, *The Times*' correspondent at Vienna, in a work on the Austro-Hungarian monarchy which was widely read, pointed out how enormously it had been weakened by the Serbian victories of 1912 and 1913, and that all the Germans were being drawn closer together in face of the Slavonic peril. In conclusion he suggested the possibility that Austria and Germany might attempt to meet it by embarking on a war with Russia, which if the two Central Empires were victorious would result in their aggrandisement at the cost of Russia, if they were defeated, would mean the end of the Austrian Empire, and perhaps of the German also 'at least in its present form'.[2] It was an interesting prophecy from the pen of the man who at the end of 1913 would take charge of the foreign news department of *The Times* and make the policy of the paper more decisively anti-German than it had been for several months. But if he was determined to champion and make his country champion the cause of the Slavs against the Germans those among his fellow countrymen who had made a special study of the problems affecting the peace of the Continent were by no means unanimously of his opinion. Seton Watson, who of all the English had studied most thoroughly the Slavonic question in Austria-Hungary, was strongly opposed to Pan-Serb ambitions. He regarded the absorption of Croatia and Slovenia in a Greater Serbia of which Belgrade would be the capital as a defeat of the West by the East, that is to say, of civilization by barbarism. A severe critic of the administrative methods employed by Austria and Hungary in Yugo-Slavia he dedicated

[1] See especially in the *Round Table*, June 1913 (vol. iii, pp. 395 sqq.) the excellent article entitled 'The Balkan War and the Balance of Power'.

[2] Henry Wickham Steed, *The Habsburg Monarchy*, 1913, p. 294 (last page but one of the book). He continues, it is true: 'But catastrophic hypotheses are best left out of account in these days of intertwined interests and of armies so colossal that defeat could hardly fail to be attended by revolutions fatal to thrones and to the existing social order; and calm consideration of the complicated factors involved leads rather to the conclusion that the Habsburg Monarchy has but one sure way of escape from its difficulties into a more prosperous and tranquil future—the way of evolution, gradual or rapid as circumstances may permit, towards an internal organization better adapted than the Dual System to the permanent needs of its people.'

his book 'To that Austrian statesman who shall possess the genius and the courage necessary to solve the Southern Slav question.' What solution did the author envisage? Apart from the conquest of Serbia it resembled closely the 'triple system' advocated by the followers of Marshal von Hötzendorff.[1] Other writers went even further. In his book *The War of Steel and Gold* Brailsford attacked Grey's policy for encouraging Russia too much and paralysing the action of Austria in the Balkans. He regretted that she had not been allowed during the last five years to annex Serbia and the greater part of Macedonia.[2] Brailsford no doubt was an extreme anti-capitalist and pacifist. But an eminent publicist of much more moderate opinions, Sir Harry Johnson, a Liberal imperialist and retired colonial governor, professed on Austria's Balkan policy opinions identical with Brailsford's.[3] He even contemplated the possibility of the struggle between the Yugo-Slavs and Austria-Hungary provoking a European war and maintained that in that event British sympathies should be with the Germans against the Russians and French.

Such were the conclusions of those Englishmen who interested themselves in the problem of Austria-Hungary. They were divergent but there can be no doubt that the majority of those who made a special study of the question were sympathetic to German aims in Central and South-Eastern Europe. We must remember that during the years immediately preceding 1914 the Russian empire was regaining in the opinion of the West almost all the prestige it had possessed before the disastrous war with Japan. Once more it was fomenting trouble in Mongolia and in Persia, where the Russian penetration was directly opposing the British. In the Balkans the Czar's Government had displayed a moderation which the Pan-Slavs found intolerable, but it had begun to reassert itself in the affair of Liman von Sanders. Russia was strengthening her army, building Dreadnoughts, and doing everything which lay in the power of her Government to do to persuade Europe

[1] R. W. Seton Watson, *The Southern Slav Question and the Habsburg Monarchy*, 1911, pp. 335 sqq. See by the same author, *Corruption and Reform in Hungary. A Study of Electoral Practice*, 1911. *Absolutism in Croatia*, 1912.

[2] H. N. Brailsford, *The War of Steel and Gold. A Study of the Armed Peace*, 1914, pp. 33-4.

[3] Sir Harry Johnson, *Common Sense in Foreign Policy*, 1913, pp. 48 sqq. It must be added that in the opening pages of his book (pp. 15-16) Sir Harry mentioned among the possible events on the Continent which would justify England in declaring war upon Germany any violation of the independence of Belgium or an attack upon the territorial integrity of France. But for that very reason he disliked the solidarity it was sought to establish between the policy of France and England and the policy of Russia.

that she had banished the peril of revolution. But as she became or appeared to become stronger the question arose whether the maintenance of the European balance of power required a victory of the German or the Russian army in the plains of Hungary and Poland.[1] It was therefore only under considerable difficulties and almost in secret, careful to avoid giving offence to a considerable section of public opinion, whose arguments could not be lightly dismissed, that the Foreign Office remained faithful to the policy of the Triple Entente. We must however remember that only a handful of Englishmen took an interest in these questions of Eastern Europe, that the attitude of the general public towards the Austrian question, as towards the Turkish the year before, was one of indifference, and that its attention was now more completely absorbed by the increasing gravity of the domestic situation.

For in the United—or Disunited—Kingdom of Great Britain and Ireland the principle of nationality was operating as disastrously as in Austria-Hungary and in the spring of 1914 the Irish question reached, as we already know, a critical phase. The German military law of 1913 and the French and Russian replies which it provoked had not shaken British apathy. The law had even had the paradoxical result, of which we have already had occasion to speak, of improving Anglo-German relations. The more money Germany spent on her army, the less she could spend on her navy. In this state of somnolent perplexity the British public watched with indifference the Government declare that it was bound by no military pledge to France, couching its declaration in terms sufficiently ambiguous to permit it to maintain contact with the French staff, Lloyd George advocate a *rapproche-*

---

[1] 'Her (Russia's) efforts to improve her army may distract Germany's attention from naval development—there is no doubt that Russia is spending huge sums on a new fleet. It may well be—though it would be idle to prophesy one way or the other—that in a few years' time the balance of power will be threatened, no longer by Germany but by the advancing strength of Russia. The chief danger then would be no longer the German menace in the North Sea but the Russian advance in Asia Minor, Persia or Northern China.' ('The Balkan War and the Balance of Power,' *Round Table*, June 1913, vol. iii, p. 423.) See further the curious article published in the *Daily Chronicle* of July 29, 1914, on the eve of the Great War, the day after the Austrian declaration of war on Serbia (the writer is the Sir Harry Johnson of whose book we have just spoken): '. . . We should like to see all participants in the great renaissance of Eastern Europe happy and contented and satisfied as to their ambitions. But if they are not, and are about to resort to the arbitrament of arms to adjust their claims, well, it should be no concern of ours, provided it did not lead to two developments—the aggrandisement of Russia in Europe or the defeat of France by Germany, with a consequent German irruption into Belgium and Holland.'

ment with Germany, Churchill reinforce the British fleet, the Parisian crowd cheer King George, and a British squadron on its return from Cronstadt pay an official visit to the Emperor William in Kiel Harbour. Whether it were a question of the social problem at home, of Irish Home Rule, or of the balance of power in Europe the British put their trust more or less consciously in that method of keeping cool and doing nothing which for two centuries of national greatness had served it so well in all matters of domestic policy. Only keep cool and wait till crises settled themselves. A few months' or a few years' patience and everything would come right. Were not the Balkan wars a proof that British *sangfroid* was as successful in foreign as in internal politics? England had set the Powers an example of calm, they had followed it and the Balkan had not become a European war. There was no reason to foresee in the course of the next few months any disturbance equally serious. The British, who wanted to be optimistic, found in the events of 1912 and 1913 excellent reasons to justify their optimism.

10

It was at this moment on June 28 that a wholly unexpected event happened. The Archduke Francis-Ferdinand, heir to the throne of Austria, visited that day the city of Serajevo, the capital of Bosnia and Herzegovina. He was believed to favour the annexationist views of Marshal von Hötzendorff, and his visit to Bosnia wore the appearance of a challenge to Belgrade. For he had chosen for a military review the anniversary of the day on which the great Serbia of the Middle Ages had been overthrown by the Turkish army in 1389. While the Prince and his wife were driving through the streets of Serajevo two attempts were made upon their lives, the second of which was successful. The two assassins were Bosnians, but both had come from Serbia, their weapons from Serbian depots. Obviously they were emissaries of a secret society known as the 'Black Hand', which if openly at war with the Government of Belgrade, intimidated and blackmailed it, and the Court in particular. It had been members of this society who only a few years before by the double murder of the last of the Obrenoviches and his wife had seated the Karageorgevitches on the throne. Now once more they were attracting

the attention of the whole of Europe by another double assassination even more sensational than the former.

The Serbs were not popular in England. The crime of 1903 had
provoked an outburst of indignant horror. Alone among the
sovereigns of Europe King Edward had refused to enter into diplomatic relations with King Peter until he had agreed to banish
from his Court the leaders of the plot which had placed him on
the throne at the cost of regicide. Only two papers, politically at
the opposite poles, expressed after the murder of the Archduke
distrust of Austria. One was the Tory *Morning Post*, the other the
Labour *Daily Citizen*, a paper with no circulation and the organ
of a party which was as yet an opposition with no chance whatever of holding office. With practically no other exceptions the
entire Press declared it perfectly justifiable for Austria to require
the Serbian Government to take all the necessary steps to prevent
the recurrence of similar outrages. They expressed the hope that
the latter would take the initiative in opening an inquiry.[1] The
direction in which the wind was blowing in England can be
gauged from the articles written in July by the demagogue
Bottomley for his weekly *John Bull*. For years he had never been
weary of demanding the destruction of the German fleet. Now he
felt himself in no danger of disgusting his readers when he demanded every week with equal vehemence the annihilation of
Serbia.

Was the British public then blind to the possible repercussions
of the assassination of June 28; that the double murder might
prove the signal for the Slavs of Austria-Hungary to revolt
against Austrian and Magyar oppression, and battle be joined
between Teutons and Slavs throughout Central Europe? We
know that the German Ambassador, Lichnowsky, urged by his
superiors to take every step in his power to ensure the neutrality
of British statesmen and journalists, never ceased to warn his
Government against excessive optimism,[2] and at first sight the

---

[1] For the views voiced by the Press between the assassination at Serajevo and the declaration of war see the excellent work by Irene Cooper Willis, *How we went into the War, A
Study of Liberal Imperialism* [1919]. Jonathan Frank Scott, *Five Weeks. The Surge of Public
Opinion on the Eve of the Great War*, 1927, chap. ix; Caroline E. Playne, *The Pre-War Mind
in England; an Historical Review*, 1928; and in particular for the policy of *The Times*,
H. Wickham Steed, *Through Thirty Years, 1892–1922, A Personal Narrative*, vol. ii, pp.
1 sqq.
[2] Lichnowsky to the Minister for Foreign Affairs, July 14, 1914 (*Die Deutschen Dokumente . . .* vol. i, p. 68), July 15, 1914 (ibid., p. 77).

language used by Grey in his conversations with Lichnowsky during the first fortnight of July seems marked by a certain nervousness. Grey counted on Germany to press a circumspect policy on Vienna and wanted the two Governments of London and Berlin to unite in the same conciliatory action which they had taken with such success on several occasions during the Balkan crisis.

'The greater the risk of war,' Grey informed Lichnowsky on July 9, 'the more closely would I adhere to that policy.'[1] And indeed it was obvious to anyone who understood the situation that the risk was greater than it had ever been during the Balkan wars. It was then a question of conflicts between the Balkan States in which all the Great Powers without exception including Austria declined to be mixed up. Now the 'third Balkan war' so dreaded in London threatened to open with a struggle between a Balkan state and one of the Great Powers. How could the rest be prevented from following Austria's lead? But we have only to look a little closer to see how little at this date Grey realized the gravity of the situation.

His interviews with the German Ambassador after the assassination continued others which had taken place before it and throughout them all his principal concern was to appease the indignation aroused in Berlin by the publication of the negotiations for a naval agreement between England and Russia. No doubt the murder at Serajevo complicated the international situation, but the English were far from ascribing to it the importance we should imagine today. On the very morrow of the assassination the House of Commons held a debate on foreign policy. It was a hurried affair, and the audience scanty and unattentive. The one question which aroused a little more interest than the others was the dispute between England and Russia in Persia.[2]

[1] Sir Edward Grey to Sir H. Rumbold, July 9, 1914 (*British Documents* . . . vol. xi, p. 34 sqq.). The phrase we have quoted is not to be found in Lichnowsky's report of this conversation which he concludes with the following words: 'Generally speaking the minister's mood was one of confidence and in cheerful tones he assured me that he saw no reason to take too tragic a view of the situation' (Lichnowsky to Bethmann-Hollweg, July 9, 1914; *Die Deutschen Dokumente zum Kriegsausbruck*, vol. i, p. 52).

[2] *Parliamentary Debates*, Commons 1914, 5th Series, vol. lxiv, pp. 53 sqq. See especially the following Statement by the pacifist Noel Buxton: 'It is pleasant in a time of considerable international difficulties in many parts of the world to congratulate the Foreign Secretary to-day upon the fact that matters which are likely to be raised are not questions of *haute politique* at all, but they are comparatively minor questions not involving matters of great danger' (ibid., p. 59).

Colonel House was in London. The warlike spirit he had observed in government circles in Berlin even before the murder of the Archduke had caused him serious anxiety, but he was unable to communicate his fears to Grey.[1] And what was true of Grey was true of his subordinates. 'I have my doubts', wrote Sir Arthur Nicolson on July 9, 'as to whether Austria will take any action of a serious character, and I expect the storm will blow over.'[2] The British representative in Sofia to be sure feared another Balkan war in the near future, but by this near future he meant October and what Sir Henry Bax-Ironside expected about October was a declaration of war by Turkey on Greece; Austria would remain at peace so long as the Emperor lived.[3] When after a short holiday Sir Francis Bertie returned to Paris, his instructions mentioned only Albania.[4] President Poincaré paid a visit to the Czar. He was expected to persuade the Russian Government to restrain its agents' encroachments in Persia. And that was all.[5]

The days passed by and the Austrian Government took no action at Belgrade. Tisza addressing the Parliament at Budapest used reassuring language. People were beginning not so much to fear the possible stringency of the Austrian demands as to feel surprise at her longsuffering. They were asking themselves whether Baron von Aehrenthal by his violent stroke in 1908 had not given Europe a false impression of the real power of the Austro-Hungarian monarchy and whether now that he had disappeared from the scene it would not prove incapable of meeting the dangers by which it was threatened at home and abroad and begin to break up. Under these circumstances the English did what they most of all wanted to do—stood aside from the racial conflict in the Danube valley. They had sufficient trouble of their own to face when the Irish Catholics and Protestants were arming against each other and the Lords were mutilating so severely the measure of compromise to which the Cabinet had with the

[1] Colonel House to President Wilson, July 31, 1914: '. . . I tried to convey this feeling to Sir Edward Grey and other members of the British Government. They seemed astonished at my pessimistic view and thought that conditions were better than they had been for a long time.' (The Intimate Papers of Colonel House, vol. i, p. 283).

[2] In a note to a despatch sent by Sir Maurice de Bunsen from Vienna on July 5 (British Documents . . . vol. xi, p. 33).

[3] Private letter from Sir H. Bax-Ironside to Sir Arthur Nicolson, July 1914 (ibid., vol. xi, p. 35).

[4] Sir F. Bertie to Sir Edward Grey, July 30, 1914 (ibid., vol. xi, p. 230).

[5] Private letter from Sir G. Buchanan to Sir Arthur Nicolson, July 9, 1914 (ibid., vol. xi, p. 39).

greatest difficulty obtained the assent of the Irish Nationalists that they seemed anxious to precipitate the conflict. The country was heading for civil war. How could it think of anything else? In a speech which he delivered on July 17 at a banquet in the city and to which we have already had occasion to allude Lloyd George had taken for his theme peace, domestic and foreign, the 'one thing that is of paramount importance'. But he passed lightly over the questions which concerned peace abroad, reminding his hearers that the international situation had been more serious in 1913 and hinting that, if there were still clouds on the horizon, it was because 'you never get a perfectly blue sky in foreign affairs'. He therefore urged a policy of disarmament and turning to other matters enlarged upon the imminent peril which threatened peace at home—civil war in Ireland complicated by a general revolutionary strike in Great Britain.[1]

II

Two days after this speech an important German newspaper, in fact the unofficial organ of the Government, the *Norddeutsche Allgemeine Zeitung*, published a *communiqué* which prepared European opinion for a step to be taken immediately by the Austrian Government. It expressed the wish that the Serbian Government would give Austria the satisfaction due to her and Europe display the same solidarity she had shown during the Balkan crisis and permit the issue between Austria and Serbia to remain localized. Two things therefore were evident; on the one hand that Germany had given *carte blanche* to Austria, on the other that when the German Government invited the British to take joint action for the maintenance of peace as during the Balkan wars, the two Powers did not attach the same sense to the proposition. Let us work together to preserve peace, said Grey, you by urging moderation upon Austria, we by urging it upon Russia. Let us work together, replied Von Jagow: prevent Russia interfering while Austria inflicts a richly deserved chastisement on Serbia.[2]

[1] Speech at the Mansion House, July 17, 1914.
[2] Von Jagow to Prince Lichnowsky, Berlin, July 18, 1914: 'Sir Grey [*sic*] is always speaking of the balance of power to be maintained by the two groups of Powers. He must clearly understand that this balance would be totally destroyed if we abandoned Austria

Then the Foreign Offices began to move. Grey proposed to Petersburg direct negotiations between the Russian and Austrian Governments before the latter had committed itself irretrievably. But the suggestion was not welcomed in Russia and Poincaré, who had just arrived in Petersburg, proposed that the Ambassadors of the Triple Entente should make a joint representation to the Austrian Government. The proposal was immediately rejected in London. For it ran counter to the policy the Foreign Office had consistently pursued for the past two years, never to oppose to each other the two groups, the Triple Entente and the Triple Alliance. But all these suggestions and conversations remained secret. It was in vain that *The Times*, in a magnificent leader, began to warn its readers of the danger to which the Austrian policy might within a few days expose the peace of Europe. The public had other preoccupations. The more critical the European situation became, the more critical also became the situation in Ireland. It was on July 21 that the King, in a desperate effort at conciliation, summoned the representatives of the opposing parties, and on the 24th the readers of the British newspapers learned, one after the other, two disastrous pieces of news. In the morning they were informed of the despatch by Austria to Serbia of a list of demands, the last of which was tantamount to Serbia's renunciation of her independence, to be accepted unconditionally within forty-eight hours. A refusal would mean war. In the afternoon, they were informed of the failure of the Buckingham Palace Conference, which seemed to signify that Protestants and Catholics had no other solution of the Irish problem than the arbitrament of force. On the following day, a Saturday, the Serbian Government returned the Austrian a reply as conciliatory as was possible without surrendering the rights of a sovereign state. But it was not the unconditional acceptance which Austria demanded and the latter, as had been expected, immediately broke off diplomatic relations with Serbia. On Sunday the gun-running at Howth occurred with its loss of life. Europe was hastening towards a general war, Ireland towards civil war.

Taken thus unawares in the middle of so serious a domestic crisis by an even more serious international crisis, we might have

and left her to be destroyed by Russia and would be very considerably shaken by a world war. If therefore he is logical and his intentions honourable he must support us and localize the conflict.' (*Die Deutschen Dokumente* . . . vol. i, p. 100.)

expected confusion to prevail in the counsels of the British Government. There was nothing of the kind. The Cabinet, or rather an 'inner Cabinet' composed of Asquith, Grey, and Churchill—perhaps also *sub rosa* of Lord Haldane—took with all the necessary decision the military and diplomatic measures the situation required.

In place of the extensive manœuvres in the North Sea carried out in former years Churchill had adopted this year a programme, less costly but equally instructive, by which the third squadron was mobilized and at the same time the three squadrons which made up the home fleet were concentrated in home waters. 20,000 reservists obeyed the summons and their period of service which began on July 13 ended on the 25th. The German naval command, anxious not to do anything to alarm the British Admiralty and prevent at such a critical juncture the dispersal of their immense force had ordered the German fleet to make no movement[1] and on the 26th the German spies were able to inform the Government which employed them that its strategy had been so far successful that the 20,000 reservists had returned home.[2] But the first and second squadrons remained concentrated at Plymouth. Acting in concert with Grey, Churchill inserted a *communiqué* in the papers on Monday morning which informed England, Germany, and the entire world that the first squadron would not leave Portland and that the vessels composing the second squadron would remain at their bases within call of their crews.[3] England was thus the first of the Great Powers with the exception of Austria to make ostensible preparations for war.

Meanwhile Grey proposed to the various Governments that the Powers not directly concerned in the dispute, Germany and Italy in the Triple Alliance, England and France in the Triple Entente should make an attempt to mediate. On Saturday he suggested

[1] In contravention of the Emperor's instructions. Bethmann-Hollweg to the Emperor July 25, 1914 (*Die Deutschen Dokumente* . . . vol. i, p. 193.) The Same to the Same, July 26, 1914 (ibid., vol. i, p. 211).
[2] Memorandum by the Under-Secretary for Foreign Affairs, Berlin, July 25, 1914: The naval attaché in London—reports: the fleet dispersed according to plan. So far as he knows no extraordinary movements. (ibid., vol. i, p. 187.) The German naval attaché in London to the Minister of Marine, July 26, 1914 (ibid., vol. i, p. 211).
[3] For the text of the *communiqué* see Winston Churchill, *The World Crisis 1911-1914*, p. 198. Grey prudently explained to Benckendorff that in preventing the dispersal of the fleet he had in view only diplomatic action. (Sir Edward Grey to Sir G. Buchanan, July 27, 1914; *British Documents* . . . vol. xi, p. 211.)

joint intervention by the four Powers at Petersburg and Berlin.[1]
On Sunday accepting a slightly different proposal put forward by
Sazonov,[2] he proposed at Nicolson's advice[3] a conference, to be
held in London, of the German, French, and Italian Ambassadors
and himself to explore an amicable solution of the dispute. While
the conference was in session Austria must suspend all military
operations. Rome accepted the suggestion. Paris also, through the
acting Premier, for the minister who was at once Premier and
Minister for Foreign Affairs, Viviani, was at sea hurrying home
from Cronstadt with President Poincaré and out of touch with
events. But Berlin was hostile. This return to the methods employed a year before during the Balkan crisis would involve treat-
ing not only Serbia but Austria-Hungary itself as a 'Balkan' state
under the tutelage of the West.[4] Berlin was extricated from the
difficulty by Petersburg. On the morning of the 27th the French
Ambassador, Paléologue, proposed to the British Ambassador
Buchanan, on behalf of Sazonov a different method of procedure
—direct conversations between Russia and Austria-Hungary.[5]
The German Government welcomed the new suggestion and
made use of it to reject the British proposal.

Grey's diplomacy had suffered an initial defeat. It suffered a
second, still more serious, the declaration of war by Austria on
Serbia, of which the Foreign Office was officially informed during
the night between Tuesday the 28th and Wednesday the 29th and
which was followed immediately by the bombardment of Belgrade. Again the British Government gave the necessary orders.
In pursuance of a decision reached on the Tuesday morning and
to which Churchill had obtained Grey's assent the fleet sailed
through the Straits of Dover during the night with all fires banked
and took up its station in Scottish waters at Scapa Flow in face of
the German fleet. On Wednesday Churchill despatched to all the
commands the warning telegram they had been expecting since
Monday ordering them to make all the necessary preparations

---

[1] Sir Edward Grey to Sir George Buchanan, July 25, 1914 (*British Documents* . . . vol.
xi, pp. 86–7).

[2] Sir G. Buchanan to Sir Edward Grey, July 25, 1914 (ibid., vol. xi, p. 93).

[3] Sir A. Nicolson to Sir Edward Grey, July 26, 1914 (ibid., vol. xi, p. 100).

[4] Out of regard for Austrian susceptibilities Grey expressed to the Austrian Ambassador
his regret at having used the word 'conference' and explained that he had in mind only
meetings of ambassadors, similar to those held in 1913 (Telegraphic despatches from Mensdorff, July 28, 1914, and from Berchtold to Mensdorff same date (*Österreich-Ungarns
Aussenpolitik* . . . vol. viii, pp. 839, 941).

[5] Sir George Buchanan to Sir Edward Grey (*British Documents* . . . vol. xi, p. 125).

to begin war as soon as the order was received.[1] At the same time he persuaded the Cabinet to take all the measures which in virtue of decisions reached some years before by the Committee of Imperial Defence were involved in the proclamation of a precautionary period, that is to say to issue a series of instructions addressed to the authorities concerned throughout the Empire ordering immediate preparations for war.[2] Grey now sent for Lichnowsky and informed him, 'in a quite private and friendly way' and, without waiting for the Ambassador to question him on the subject, that 'the situation was very grave' and that if Germany, and in consequence France, should be involved he must not conclude from the friendly tone of their interview that England would stand aside. If England believed that her interests required her intervention she would intervene at once and her decision would be no less rapid than those of the other Governments.[3]

12

On the evening therefore of Wednesday, July 29, the British Government had, it would seem, done everything in its power, openly and in secret, from the naval and diplomatic standpoint alike to prepare for war and confront hostile powers with the prospect of her entry into the war. But days of hesitation followed. Only four—but to those who lived through them they seemed an eternity. We must be clear as to the nature and reasons of this halt on the brink of the abyss.

What did most to mislead public opinion, not only in England, but on the Continent was the imperturbable calm, the persistent *sangfroid* which the British public maintained, when the entire condition of Europe, political, financial, and military, proclaimed

[1] Winston S. Churchill. *The World Crisis*, pp. 206–7.

[2] Winston S. Churchill, ibid., p. 208; H. H. Asquith, *The Genesis of War*, p. 184 (cf. for the import of the steps taken pp. 118, 136). Field-Marshal Sir Henry Wilson's *Diary*, July 28 (29?), 1914: 'The Russians have ordered the mobilisation of 16 Corps. The Austrians are mobilising 12 Corps. The Germans and French remain quiet. At 3 p.m. a note came to Douglas from Asquith ordering the "Precautionary Period". This we did, I don't know why we are doing it, because there is nothing moving in Germany. We shall see. Anyhow it is more like business than I expected of this government.' (Major-General Sir C. E. Callwell. Field-Marshal Sir Henry Wilson. 1927, vol. i, p. 152.)

[3] Sir Edward Grey to Sir E. Goschen, July 29, 1914 (*British Documents* . . . vol. xi, p. 182). Prince von Lichnowsky to the Minister for Foreign Affairs, July 29, 1914 (*Die Deutschen Dokumente* . . . vol. ii, p. 86).

the catastrophe already begun. The annual holiday season had commenced; for the workers the week-end would be exceptionally prolonged by the fact that the following Monday was a bank holiday, and on Friday, and even on Saturday, while Russia, Austria, Germany, and France were arming English holidaymakers of every class were hastening to the stations and the Channel ports in search of rest and pleasure. It was not surprising that foreign observers concluded that the country had determined to stand aside from the Continental war, and that Grey, who at the beginning of the week had taken an extremely pessimistic view of the situation, should shrink from taking action too far in advance of an indifferent public opinion and consider how best to restrain the warlike zeal of the Government departments, and that pacifist doctrinaires misinterpreted this calm as a determination to maintain peace at any price and hugged the illusion that they had the entire country on their side.

Certain signs however enable us to interpret more correctly the temper of the nation. The minority of writers in the Press who regarded it as inevitable that England should enter the war in support of Russia and France expresssed themelves cautiously and took care not to adopt a censorious attitude towards the Cabinet. On the other hand the measures of preparation for naval warfare which had been already adopted by the Admiralty on Monday morning had aroused no protest from the leading Liberal organs, and the more direct measures taken by the Cabinet on Wednesday were not made public by the indiscretion of any journalist. Finally, when the Irish Amending Bill came up for discussion on Thursday, all parties—the Conservatives, Liberals, and Labour members of Great Britain, the Ulstermen and the Irish Nationalists—agreed to adjourn the debate indefinitely, because, Asquith explained, it was essential that the country, 'which has no interest of its own directly at stake, should present a united front, and be able to speak and act with the authority of an undivided nation'.[1] In the past no doubt there had been occasions when England had displayed a more belligerent temper. In 1898 and 1899 for example public opinion had pushed the Government into war. But the country had now returned to its normal state. Both instinctively and deliberately the average Englishman distrusts the imagination.

[1] H. of C., July 30, 1914 (*Parliamentary Debates*, Commons 1914; 5th Series, vol. lxv, p. 1601).

He does not want to redouble a danger by the dread of it. So long as the situation was in the hands of the diplomatists, it was a duty to believe that they were sincere in their efforts to preserve peace, a duty moreover to believe success possible and to contribute to that possibility by giving the British Government the assistance of calm and silence.

But this calm and silence were carried so far that they became a hindrance instead of a help to the Government. There were moments when Grey wondered whether it would be possible to arouse the British public from its slumber and rally it to the cause of the mother country by declaring war. This was one reason for hesitation and even if it had not existed there were a host of others, some common to all the Governments alike, others peculiar to the British.

There was in the first place a fear which all the Governments felt and which made them shrink back when the moment arrived to declare war, the fear of revolution. In the latter part of the nineteenth century Karl Marx's great disciple and friend Friedrich Engels had foretold 'a world war' provoked by 'Prussia-Germany' 'of unsuspected length and violence' during which 'eight to ten million soldiers would slaughter each other and strip Europe bare like a swarm of locusts'. He predicted that 'the artificial structure of commerce, industry, and finance would be destroyed and the irreparable chaos result in general bankruptcy; the old states and their traditional ideas would be overthrown, crowns would roll by dozens on the pavement and no one would pick them up, and the universal exhaustion would provide the conditions under which the working class would at last achieve victory'.[1] Now, when Europe was at last threatened by the immediate prospect of a general war, many people, judging from a considerable number of signs—the first Russian revolution, the propaganda of revolutionary syndicalism, the growth of Marxian Socialism in Germany—were inclined to predict a world revolution in its train. On the very eve of the Austrian ultimatum, while President Poincaré was visiting the Emperor of Russia, serious rioting broke out at Petersburg, with casualties extending to loss of life and the German Ambassador remarked with amusement that while the band of the Imperial Guard greeted Poincaré at Krasnoié-Sélo

---

[1] Preface to a pamphlet by Borkheim 1887 (quoted by Lenin). (Report on the Modifications in the Party Programme, March 8, 1918, *Works*, vol. xv, p. 149—French. tr.)

with the strains of the 'Marseillaise' the workers of the Petersburg suburbs were receiving a charge of the Cossack cavalry to the same accompaniment.[1] In Great Britain the syndicalist leaders had indulged in too many outbursts of anti-patriotism not to alarm the ruling class. Might not the reply to a war or the economic crisis it would immediately provoke be that general strike of railwaymen, transport workers and miners which had been threatened for months past? And must we not attribute to considerations of this kind a share in the explicit declaration of neutrality made on July 26 by King George to Prince Henry of Prussia? May not the court have shrunk at first from being drawn into a revolutionary war opened by a regicide? 'Be careful,' Grey told the Austrian Ambassador, Mensdorff, when on July 23 the Ambassador came to prepare him for the despatch of the ultimatum, 'a general war would be accompanied or followed by a complete collapse of European credit and industry in these days in great industrial States. This would mean a state of things worse than that of 1848.'[2] 'In the present temper of labour,' Lord Morley warned his colleagues a few days later almost in the same words, 'the atmosphere of war cannot be friendly to order, in a democratic system that is verging on the humour of '48.'[3]

[1] Count von Pourtales to Bethmann-Hollweg. July 24, 1914 (*Die Deutschen Dokumente* . . . vol. i, p. 207). Cf. Despatch by Count Berchtold, September 7-8, 1912: 'In Baltic-Port he had received the impression that Russia would pursue a peaceful policy for many years to come. Herr Kokovtsov had determined to carry out an extensive economic programme. Moreover the Russian Premier was convinced of the very serious dangers which in view of the social situation in Russia foreign complications would involve.' (*Österreich-Ungarns Aussenpolitik* . . . vol. iii, p. 415.) See further Prince von Bülow's *Memoirs* (French trans., vol. ii, p. 291): 'In May 1914—in Rome I asked Kokovtsov the former Russian Prime Minister who had just quitted office, if he believed there would be a war and he answered without hesitation: "War? No. Unless you compel us, we will not go to war. But I believe a revolution in Russia not only possible but likely." '

[2] Sir Edward Grey to Sir Maurice de Bunsen, July 23, 1914 (*British Documents* . . . vol. xi, p. 70). Cf. Mensdorff telegram from London, July 23, 1914: 'He (Sir Edward Grey) recognized the difficulty of our position and spoke very seriously of the gravity of the situation. If four great powers, Austria-Hungary, Germany, Russia and France became involved in war, the consequence for all intents and purposes would be the bankruptcy of Europe. No more credit would be obtainable, and the centres of industry would be plunged into a state of chaos, so that in many countries it would cease to matter which side was victorious when so many existing institutions had been swept away.' (*Österreich-Ungarns Aussenpolitik* . . . vol. viii, p. 603.) For another summary of the same conversation also by Mensdorff see his despatch of July 29. (*Österreich-Ungarns Aussenpolitik* . . . vol. viii, p. 878.) Mensdorff concluded his despatch with the remark: 'It made a great impression on my German colleague, a nervous man at the best of times.'

[3] Viscount Morley. *Memorandum on Resignation*, p. 5. Cf. H. of C., August 3, 1914, Wedgwood's speech: 'Starvation is coming in this country and the people are not the docile serfs that they were a hundred years ago. They are not going to put up with starvation in this country. When it comes you will see something far more important than a European War—you will see a revolution.' (*Parliamentary Debates*, Commons 1914; 5th Series, vol. lxv, p. 1838.)

But to this fear of revolution and revolutionaries which the British Government shared with the government of every other country there was added in England another anxiety which no Continental government felt to the same degree, dread of seeing the machinery of exchange paralysed and that vast republic of commerce and finance collapse which in peace time knew nothing of frontiers and was conterminous with the globe. On Tuesday the 28th the crisis which had already played havoc with all the exchanges of Europe reached the Stock Exchange and after it closed prices fell still further on the news that Austria had declared war on Serbia. After a slight recovery on Wednesday morning the crisis went from bad to worse until on Friday the Stock Exchange Committee decided to close the Exchange until further notice. The supreme scandal had actually occurred which Norman Angell had pronounced improbable, indeed practically impossible, in the West—warlike passion had triumphed over organized financial interests. It was, it is true, an infection caught from the East. Might not England prove the last bulwark of Western civilization against the plague? Had she not still time to take the necessary steps to arrest its ravages at the Straits of Dover? While the British public displayed to a tormented Europe the mask of their impassivity, the business world took action. The aged Lord Rothschild led the movement. For years, the consistent champion of an *entente* between England and Germany,[1] he tried to bring pressure to bear upon the editorial staff of *The Times*, and upon his relatives in Paris,[2] and he wrote to the Emperor William a letter of entreaty, whose naïveté is heartrending.[3] And in addition to all this in an attempt to influence the British Government he put himself at the head of a deputation from the City, which called on Lloyd George on Friday morning to urge him by preserving the neutrality of England at all costs to save the country from disaster and possibly enable her to stretch out a helping hand to the Continent.

[1] 'For a period extending over nearly forty years I have been personally acquainted with the different German ambassadors of the time, and this personal intimacy has allowed me on more than one occasion to be of service to the respective governments. What have we . . . not got in common with Germany? Nothing perhaps except their army and our navy. But a combination of the most powerful military nation with the most powerful naval nation ought to be such as to command the respect of the whole world, and ensure universal peace.' (Articles entitled 'England and Germany' in the collection which bears the same name and which was published in 1912, pp. 21–3.)

[2] Henry Wickham Steed, *Through Thirty Years*, vol. ii, p. 8.

[3] *Die Deutschen Dokumente* . . . vol. iii, pp. 77–8. The Emperor appended the note: 'An old and honoured acquaintance of mine! Between 75 and 80 years old!'

The choice of leader aroused protest. The *Morning Post* and *The Times* depicted the crisis on the Stock Exchange as a device, engineered by the German-Jewish banks, to create a panic in the business world and paralyse the diplomatic and military action of the Government, and at the Foreign Office itself Sir Eyre Crowe repeated the legend.[1] But Lloyd George and Grey[2] were impressed by Lord Rothschild's action; if the City was opposed to to war, would the country be in favour of it?

We may add that in shrinking from the final decision the British Government did but give evidence of the same alarm which all the Governments of the Great Powers, with the exception of Austria, felt at this juncture at the prospect of war as such with its horrors and dangers. The Emperor William, after urging Austria forward for months, particularly during the last few weeks and still scornful, while he cruised off the coast of Norway, of Count Berchtold's delays, suddenly took alarm and returned in haste to Berlin to embarrass the more warlike of his ministers by his nervousness. President Poincaré, who in Petersburg before the Austrian ultimatum had done everything in his power to draw closer the bond which united France with Russia and had spoken in haughty terms to the Austrian Ambassador, had no sooner returned to his native country after the ultimatum when face to face with the immediate prospect of war he too became anxious and timid. Grey, the impassive architect of the ambiguous system of *ententes*, lost his impassivity when brutal realities compelled him to speak in terms which could not be misunderstood.[3] In every capital the same dialogue was held between the chiefs of the army, the mouthpieces of fate, who demanded mobilization and the civil rulers who revolted against it and would fain believe themselves still free to decide their course of action. And everywhere they submitted to fate, in Russia first, then in Germany, then in France, and finally in England. Is it surprising that England was the last to submit? On the contrary, should we not be surprised that her decision followed the French so closely? For

[1] Memorandum by Sir Eyre Crowe, July 31, 1914 (*British Documents* . . . vol. xi, p. 228).
[2] See Grey's remarks to Paul Cambon on the 31st: 'The commercial and financial situation was exceedingly serious; there was danger of a complete collapse that would involve us and every one else in ruin; and it was possible that our standing aside might be the only means of preventing a complete collapse of European credit, in which we should be involved. This might be a paramount consideration in deciding our attitude (Sir Edward Grey to Sir F. Bertie, July 31, 1914: ibid., vol. xi, pp. 226–27).
[3] Harold Nicolson, *Sir Arthur Nicolson, First Lord Carnock*, pp. 419, 422.

her position was not the same as that of France. France had no choice but to prepare with more or less haste, and more or less efficiency for the inevitable day when Germany would declare war upon her. It was on the other hand certain that Germany would never declare war on England. She would not allow Russia to crush Austria-Hungary and had made up her mind to crush France before attacking Russia. But she needed the neutrality of England. It was for the latter to abandon it, if she dared, by taking the responsibility of declaring war. She would take it, it was inevitable that she should: but it is one thing to submit to fate, another to make oneself fate's active accomplice.

13

How are we to summarize the history of these breathless days? On the evening of Wednesday the 29th, the very day on which the news of the bombardment of Belgrade reached London, the Foreign Office was officially informed that the Russian Government had decided upon a partial mobilization, while still holding out against the wishes of the army which demanded a general mobilization. On the 30th vague reports were received from Germany that mobilization had begun or was at any rate imminent. On the 31st in the late afternoon the Foreign Office was informed, almost simultaneously, that Russia had ordered a general mobilization, that Austria had done the same, and that Germany had declared 'a state of danger of war' which constituted a preliminary mobilization. At the same time, the German Government despatched a double ultimatum, to Russia, calling upon her to revoke within eighteen hours the order to mobilize and to France, requiring her to pledge herself, within the same interval, to remain neutral. In case of refusal, war would be declared on both fronts. On Saturday August 1, almost at the same moment, Germany and France ordered mobilization. Shortly afterwards, Germany declared war on Russia.

Meanwhile, British diplomacy, though steadily retreating, persisted in seeking a peaceful solution of the dispute between Austria and Serbia. The Austrian army could no longer be prevented from occupying Belgrade. Even so, let the conquest go no further and Belgrade be occupied merely as a pledge until Serbia had accepted the Austrian terms and then be evacuated. It was no longer possible to hope that the Austrian army would be content with the occupation of Belgrade. Let it then advance farther but let Austria promise to respect in the last resort the sovereignty of Serbia. The German Government gave an official promise to England not to annex any European territory of France in the event of victory, to respect the neutrality of Holland, and to restore to Belgium her territory intact, if she allowed the German army to cross it. On these terms England had only to pledge herself to remain neutral and 'a general pact of neutrality' might be concluded between the two nations. Grey refused even to consider these promises. But three days later he aroused vain hopes in the mind of the German Emperor and his Chancellor by letting it be known that, if only Germany would abstain from attacking France, England would not intervene. On Thursday, Paul Cambon called at Downing Street to remind him of the letters exchanged in October 1912, and the undertaking then given by the British Government to act in concert with the French and deliberate in common upon the joint measures to be adopted by both Powers if the peace of Europe were seriously endangered. The following day, when the question had been discussed by the Cabinet, Grey replied that the Government could not at the moment bind itself by any pledge. The same evening a special messenger brought King George an autograph letter from President Poincaré calling upon England to come to the aid of France in her danger. A long and courteous, but guarded, reply ended with the words: 'Events change so quickly that it is impossible to foresee their future developments.'

They changed quickly indeed. The deputation from the City to Lloyd George on Friday was in truth the first sign that the champions of neutrality were beginning to perceive that they no longer had the entire country behind them. And their anxiety must have been increased when they saw the Secretary for War calling up the special reserve, armed sentries making their appearance wherever there were depots or railway bridges and level crossings to be guarded,[1] and the villages along the coast emptied of their

---

[1] Lord Ullswater, *A Speaker's Commentary*, vol. i, p. 166. Cf. Sir Arthur Griffith Boscawen, *Memories*, p. 167: 'Sir James Grierson had arranged to come and see us at work on the following Wednesday and lunch in Mess; but when Wednesday morning came I received a message from him that things looked so threatening that he was obliged to go to the War Office. On the following Saturday precautionary measures were being adopted and I received an order to send a detachment off at once to guard the seaplane station at

fishermen whom the Admiralty had called up by what amounted to a secret mobilization.[1] On Friday, in contravention of Grey's express desire, hitherto strictly observed, that there should be no collective demonstration on the question of war, a number of Members of Parliament organized in the lobbies of the House of Commons a demonstration in favour of neutrality. But it was a feeble affair.[2] On Saturday the advocates of peace at any price took more definite action. Two committees to organize propaganda on behalf of neutrality were formed. They drew up two manifestoes for which they secured a number of important signatures among the pacifist intelligentsia.[3] Would these signatories succeed in rousing the opinion of the country against the war party? Perhaps with the simplicity characteristic of the English propagandist they thought so. But it was very late in the day.

On Friday, the most impetuous member of the Cabinet, Churchill, exasperated by his colleagues' calm, made overtures to Bonar Law for the formation of a Coalition Cabinet in the event of a split among the Liberals. Bonar Law however still hung back and would negotiate only with the Prime Minister in person. But in the afternoon of the following day, Saturday August 1, the Opposition leaders, hastily summoned by a group of alarmed supporters, hurried back from the country and renouncing their week-end met at Lansdowne House to concert a joint approach to the Government. A letter was composed and despatched to the Prime Minister on Sunday morning in which the Opposition promised him its unreserved support in the crisis through which the country was passing.[4] Its timely receipt strengthened Asquith's

Westgate.' L. J. Maxse, 'Retrospect and Reminiscence' (National Review, vol. lxxi, p. 746): 'The organizers of the British Expeditionary Force were decidedly "doing their bit" all the more because a genius among them had invented the phrase "precautionary period" which permitted certain measures to be taken on the ipse dixit of the Secretary of State, without reference to the Cabinet and without a civilian realizing how important they were when time was the only thing that mattered.' For these measures of preliminary mobilization see further Robert Burden Haldane, An Autobiography, p. 276.

[1] Stephen Reynolds to Miss Jane Reynolds, August 1, 1914: 'I expect you are very startled and worried over these threatenings of war. It has hit us very hard here: for the British mobilization—newspapers to the contrary—is undoubtedly very complete; all our navy people are at sea and we don't know where.' (Letters of Stephen Reynolds, p. 191.)

[2] Christopher Addison, Politics from Within, 1911–1918, vol. i, p. 37.

[3] Irene Cooper Willis, How we went into the War. A Study of Liberal Imperialism, p. 61.

[4] Lord Beaverbrook, Politicians and the War, 1914–1916, pp. 22 sqq.—also for the circumstances which led up to this step see L. S. Maxse 'Retrospect and Reminiscence' (National Review, August 1918, vol. lxxi, pp. 745 sqq.). Cf. Charles Roux, Trois Ambassades françaises à la veille de la guerre, pp. 43–52, a lively account, unfortunately damaged by inaccuracies of detail, which on this point affords Maxse's account the interesting support of the author's personal recollections.

position at a decisive moment. For that same morning the ministers were informed at a meeting of the Cabinet that Churchill with the approval of the Premier and some of his colleagues had taken the responsibility of ordering the mobilization of the fleet. The majority of the Cabinet approved the step.[1] The partisans of neutrality who only a few days, perhaps even a few hours before, had cherished the illusion that the majority of the Government was of their opinion announced their intention to resign.

Who were they? John Burns, a self-opinionated man and perhaps even more anti-French than pacifist. Lord Morley, a man of less violent temper who was obliged to recognize that the arguments of the war party were not always easy to answer and who disclaimed any desire to persuade his younger colleagues to follow his example. Nevertheless, an heir of Gladstone's policy and a veteran of peace, the old man made it a point of honour not to take part in a war Cabinet in which he would hamper than rather help his colleagues.[2] Neither of the two had the necessary prestige to become the leader of a Radical opposition against a Liberal Cabinet which had become a War Cabinet. Nor had Sir John Simon who adopted their position, a skilful barrister, and an active politician but not a great statesman. But for a few hours the pacifists thought they had found a leader in the person of Lloyd George.

At the beginning of the week Lloyd George is said to have inclined to the side of Grey and Churchill and had seemed disposed to adopt once more the belligerent attitude he had assumed once before, three years earlier, at the time of the Agadir crisis. But how could he forget that in the interval and indeed down to the very eve of the crisis provoked by the Austrian ultimatum[3] he had

[1] Winston S. Churchill, *The World Crisis, 1911–1914*, p. 217.

[2] 'What should I be doing in a War Ministry?' Words used by Morley on September 13, 1914, and reported by J. H. Morgan. (John Viscount Morley, *An Appreciation and some Reminiscences*, p. 42.).

[3] See his speech in the House of Commons on July 23, during the debate on the third reading of the Finance Bill: 'It is very difficult for our nation to arrest this very terrible development' [of armaments]. 'You cannot do it . . . I realize that, but the encouraging symptom which I observe is that the movement against it is a cosmopolitan one and an international one. Whether it will bear fruit this year or next year, that I am not sure of, but I am certain that it will come. I can see signs, distinct signs, of reaction throughout the world. Take a neighbour of ours. Our relations are very much better than they were a few years ago. There is none of that snarling which we used to see, more especially in the Press of those two great, I will not say rival nations, but two great Empires. The feeling is better altogether between them. They begin to realize they can co-operate for common ends and that the points of co-operation are greater and more numerous and more important than the points of possible controversy.' (*Parliamentary Debates*, Commons 1914, 5th Series, vol. lxv, pp. 727–8.)

been the champion of a *rapprochement* with Germany and disarmament. It was therefore only natural that on Friday he should have been affected by the deputation from the City and made himself its advocate in the Cabinet. An eye witness describes him following with his thumb the course of the Meuse Valley on a map of Belgium and asking his colleagues if it were really worth while going to war to prevent the German army taking that route.[1] Then he appears once more to have hesitated. On Saturday he denied that in laying the arguments of the City financiers before the Cabinet he had intended to make them his own, and his frequent talks with Churchill alarmed Lord Morley.[2] His moral repute had been shaken by the Marconi scandal, his great Insurance Act had aroused inevitable dissatisfaction, his programme of land reform was hanging fire, his Budget for the current year had just ended in a fiasco, and the Irish crisis would involve for him, as for other English statesmen, nothing but mortification. The unexpected outbreak of a great European war opened new prospects in which he must take his bearings within a few hours. It was an anxious problem for a man of his imaginative and impressionable temperament, a decision in which his career as well as his conscience was at stake. On Sunday morning he joined Burns, Morley, and Simon in upholding the policy of neutrality.

The same evening, when the Cabinet reassembled, Burns definitely resigned. At Asquith's request Lord Morley consented to keep the matter open until Monday morning. Next day he resigned. But Simon, and what was a more serious blow for the supporters of neutrality, Lloyd George, remained in the Cabinet. There was no longer in any real sense a Liberal split. There were simply two resignations from the Cabinet, whose importance was moral, rather than political and a third, Charles Trevelyan's, in the subordinate ranks of the Ministry. The great Liberal organs continued for a day longer to kick against the pricks. But the entire party was being swept along by the current which was bearing the nation into war.

[1] Lord Beaverbrook, *Politicians and the War*, p. 29.

[2] His biographer, J. Hugh Edwards, depicts him writing on Saturday evening a letter to one of his fellow ministers in which he protested with the utmost vigour against the entry of England into the war and then keeping the letter in his pocket as the result of a conversation with the Belgian minister who had suddenly converted him to the cause of war. But is not the incident misdated and should it not be placed on the evening of Sunday, August 2? (J. Hugh Edwards, *The Life of David Lloyd George*, vol. iv, p. 211.)

The best way to explain this decision, made almost instantaneously by millions, will perhaps be to go back to the conversations between Grey and Cambon on Friday. 'Up to the present', Grey declared 'we did not feel, and public opinion did not feel, that any treaties or other obligations of this country were involved.' But he added that 'further developments might alter this situation,' and that the preservation of the neutrality of Belgium might prove an important factor, deciding England to enter the war.[1] And almost immediately after Cambon left him he officially asked the two Governments of Berlin and Paris for a pledge to respect Belgian neutrality. Paris gave it at once, Berlin refused. England was therefore morally, if not even juridically, bound to declare war on Germany. Nevertheless, on Saturday when Lichnowsky asked Grey whether, if Germany gave an undertaking not to violate Belgian neutrality, England would promise to remain neutral, he replied: 'I cannot say that; our hands are still free.'[2] For he had just seen Cambon who had pressed him even more insistently than the day before. Moreover, an exceedingly close tie united the French and British navies. France, relying on her agreement with England, had transferred her entire navy to the Mediterranean, leaving the defence of her northern coast to the British fleet. How then could England without dishonour, indeed without confessing that she was no longer a first-class power, allow her fleet to look on while the German navy made itself master of the Channel, sank the French mercantile marine, and bombarded the French ports? This was the question Grey laid before his colleagues on Sunday morning and it was his answer to it which secured the assent of the majority against the still formidable opposition of a group of dissidents of which Lloyd George seemed likely to take the lead. Was this then the immediate cause of England's entrance into the war? But next day Sir Edward Grey was informed that the German Government which had declared war on France would undertake not to allow its men-of-

[1] Sir Edward Grey to Sir F. Bertie July 30, 1914 (*British Diplomatic Documents* . . . vol. xi, p. 227).
[2] Sir Edward Grey to Sir Edward Goschen, August 1914 (*British Documents* . . . vol. xi, pp. 260–61). Cf. Prince Lichnowsky to the Minister for Foreign Affairs, August 1, 1914, who however adds in conclusion: 'He returned constantly to the question of Belgian neutrality which in his opinion would in any case play a very important part.' (*Die Deutschen Dokumente* . . . vol. iii, pp. 89–90.)

war to enter the Channel, and England declared war all the same.[1] We are therefore driven back to the conclusion that the factor which determined irrevocably the patriotic insurgence of the nation was in fact the despatch on Sunday evening of the German ultimatum to Belgium, followed on Monday morning by the appeal of the King of the Belgians to the King of England, asking for his diplomatic intervention. But we must understand why the German invasion of Belgium possessed this decisive importance.

In the first place, the violation of Belgian neutrality by the German army, if it enabled Germany to win in France a Napoleonic victory, would mean, whatever pledges the German Government might have given, the annihilation of Belgium as a nation. The war therefore in the West assumed from the very first the character it possessed in the Balkans and the Danube valley of a war in which the principle of nationality was at stake. There was, however, a difference between western and south-eastern Europe. In the latter case, the nation Austria was preparing to destroy was a focus of rebellion which sought by revolution and assassination to liberate the Yugo-Slavs at present subject to Hungarian or German rule—in other words, to change the existing territorial arrangement. In the west on the contrary the nation attacked was innocent of any annexationist ambitions or intrigues against Germany and its existence guaranteed by international treaties, constituted in the fullest sense an integral part of the European territorial arrangement. To go to the assistance of Belgium was therefore to embark upon a conservative not a revolutionary war, a war to protect at once the principle of nationality, the established order, and the sanctity of treaties. But if Belgium had not been so close to the British coast would England have been stirred so powerfully, or rather would she ever have guaranteed Belgian neutrality? If the English were disposed to regard the independence of Belgium as the keystone of the European balance of power, it was because her very existence was in a sense a masterpiece of British diplomacy. By creating Belgium England had

[1] H. of C., August 3, 1914, Sir Edward Grey's speech: '. . . Things move very hurriedly from hour to hour. Fresh news comes in, and I cannot give this in a very formal way; but I understand that the German Government would be prepared, if we would pledge ourselves to neutrality, to agree that the fleet would not attack the Northern Coast of France. I have only heard that shortly before I came to the House, but it is far too narrow an engagement for us. And, Sir, there is the more serious consideration—becoming more serious every hour—there is the question of the neutrality of Belgium.' (*Parliamentary Debates*, Commons 1914; 5th Series, vol. lxv, p. 1818.)

intended to make it finally impossible for the greatest European power—France formerly, Germany at present—to occupy Antwerp and thus permanently threaten the mouth of the Thames with its navy. The Belgian question had further complicated a situation already bristling with thorny problems, the south-eastern problem of nationality, the western problem of armed peace, and the naval rivalry between England and Germany. British foreign policy was less concerned than one might suppose to preserve the balance of power in Europe. What she would not permit—and the entire nation was instinctively of the same mind—was that the strongest military power in Europe, now also the strongest naval power on the Continent, should endanger England's naval supremacy by establishing what would amount to a European balance of power at sea.

On Monday morning the Government decided to follow up the mobilization of the navy by mobilizing the army. Lord Haldane offered to return to the War Office, at which for six years he had accomplished so much for military reorganization. The Premier, whom a political accident had placed at the War Office, was delighted to make way for him. Did Haldane wish, as has often been said and is possible in spite of his denials, to become once more the official Secretary of State for War? Could he have failed to understand that his famous visit to Berlin rendered him suspect to the public? Nevertheless, from the strictly professional point of view he was perhaps the only man who could save the War Office from the confusion which prevailed. For at the very moment of mobilization no one at the War Office, it would appear, knew what use to make of the men being called to the colours, whether they should be despatched immediately to France, or kept for imperial defence or whether the plan long cherished by the Admiralty should be adopted, the fleet despatched to win a new Trafalgar and an invasion organized at some point on the German coast.[1] One thing at least was certain, there would be war.

[1] According to Lord Beaverbrook (*Politicians and the War*, pp. 43 sqq.), even Haldane hesitated to order the despatch of the expeditionary force. But this is flatly contradicted by Lord Grey of Fallodon (Sir Edward Grey) in his speech at Fallodon on August 23, 1928: 'When the crisis came he alone among the civilians, according to my recollection, was at once unreservedly for sending the whole of the Expeditionary Force abroad immediately, showing himself to be as prompt and courageous in action as he had been energetic and wise in preparation.' It is also contradicted by J. H. Morgan, an intimate friend of Lord Haldane, who in an article entitled 'The Riddle of Lord Haldane' (*Quarterly*

This was what Grey explained in the afternoon to the House of Commons. His speech, cool, restrained, and devoid of rhetoric won the almost unanimous assent of the House. A handful of pacifists, not one of whom represented a party or even a group protested. 'What is the use', asked Ramsay MacDonald, 'of talking about coming to the aid of Belgium, when, as a matter of fact, you are engaging in a whole European war which is not going to leave the map of Europe in the position it is in now?'[1] They received a courteous hearing from an audience coldly hostile. In the streets the crowd were singing patriotic songs, and the young men gathering in queues outside the recruiting stations. Next morning, the Prime Minister, without troubling to consult the Cabinet and confident of the silent support of the entire country, authorized Grey to send Sir Edward Goschen a telegram calling upon the German Government to pledge itself before midnight to respect the neutrality of Belgium. What reply could be given? The invasion of Belgium had already begun. Night fell. England entered the war.

Review, January 1929, vol. ccxlii, p. 18) writes as follows: 'Not only were all the civilians for nursing the Expeditionary Force to defend our shores, but so were even some of the soldiers. I have high authority for saying that Lord Roberts, who, as I know, was called in by the Cabinet, wished to hold the Expeditionary Force back, believing then, as he did, in the possibility of immediate invasion. As for Lord Kitchener, invasion was to him, as a former member of the Army Council recently expressed it to me, an "obsession" to the very end.' And finally it is contradicted by Lord Haldane himself whose statement is explicit and detailed: 'I need hardly say that there was never the slightest foundation for the suggestion presently to be launched that I had wished to delay the sending of the Expeditionary Force. I had desired to send off all the six divisions from the outset. Careful consultation with the Admiralty had made it plain that they would guarantee that there would be no practical possibility of serious invasion, and after the War was over I ascertained that the Germans had never thought seriously of attempting it. In the afternoon of Monday (the 3rd) the Prime Minister had asked me to summon a War Council, and to select those who should attend. Among others I summoned Lord Roberts and Lord Kitchener, who happened to be in London. The Council proved a little timid about invasion, and did not like the idea of all the six divisions leaving the country, but it decided that four should go at once and that the fifth should follow . . . Sir John French and I wanted all the six to start, but we were in a minority. There was available, as we pointed out, a seventh, the sections of which would have to be brought in part from Egypt.' (R. B. Haldane, *An Autobiography*, pp. 277-8.)

[1] *Parliamentary Debates*, Commons 1914, 5th Series, vol. lxv, p. 1830.

Index

A

Abdul Aziz, 135, 379

Abdul Hamid, 372–3, 626–8

Acts of Parliament:

1834, Poor Law Amendment Act, 512n.

1835, Municipal Corporations Act, 512n.

1857, Matrimonial Causes Act, 490–3

1858, Matrimonial Causes Amendment Act, 491n.

1858, Combination of Workmen Act, 95

1864, 1866, 1868, 1869, Contagious Diseases Acts, 498–9

1869, Municipal Franchise Act, 513n.

1870, Married Women's Property Act, 495; Education Act, 512n.

1873, Supreme Court of Judicature Act, 324; Supreme Court of Judicature (Commencement) Act, 325n.; Australian Colonies Duties Act, 543n.

1874, Married Women's Property Amendment Act, 495n.

1875, Supreme Court of Judicature Act, 325n.

1876, Appellate Jurisdiction Act, 325n.; Trade Union Act Amendment Act, 483

1877, Married Women's Property (Scotland) Act, 496n.

1878, Matrimonial Causes Amendment Act, 493n.

1881, Married Women's Property (Scotland) Act, 496n.

1882, Married Women's Property Act, 496; Municipal Councils Act, 504n.

1884, Married Women's Property Act, 496; Matrimonial Causes Act, 497

1885, Criminal Law Amendment Act, 499

1886, Guardianship and Custody of Infants Act, 497; Married Women Maintenance in Case of Desertion Act, 497; To Repeal Contagious Diseases Acts, 498

1888, Appellate Jurisdiction Act, 325n.; Local Government Act, 512n.

1889, Local Government (Scotland) Act, 513n.

1891, Factory and Workshop Act, 247–8

1892, Indian Councils Act, 46, 51

1893, Elementary Education (Blind and Deaf Children) Act, 82; Married Women's Property Act, 496

1894, Merchant Shipping Act, 23; Local Government Act, 513n.

1895, Factory and Workshop Act, 247–8; Conciliation (Trade Disputes) Act, 477;

Summary Jurisdiction (Married Women) Act, 496

1896, Poor Law Guardians (Ireland) Act, 513n.

1897, Workmen's Compensation Act, 99

1898, Vagrancy Act, 499n.; Local Government (Ireland) Act, 513n.

1899, London Government Act, 513n.

1900, Commonwealth of Australia Constitution Act, 23; Workmen's Compensation Act, 99; Railway Employment (Prevention of Accidents) Act, 108

1901, Factory and Workshop Act, 248

1902, Patents Act, 16; Education Act, 65–9, 512n.; Immoral Traffic (Scotland) Act, 499n.

1903, Land Act (Ireland), 54–7

1906, Merchant Shipping Act, 15; Labourers (Ireland) Act, 56; Town Tenants (Ireland) Act, 56; Education of Defective Children (Scotland) Act, 80–1; Education (Provision of Meals) Act, 81; Trade Disputes Act, 93–8, 363, 453; Workmen's Compensation Act, 100–2, 497; Justices of the Peace Act, 315n.

1907, Patents and Designs (Amendment) Act, 16; Patents and Designs Act, 16–17; Evicted Tenants (Ireland) Act, 56, 102–3; United Methodist Church Act, 75; (Administrative Provisions) Act, 82; Small Holdings and Allotments Act, 102; Factory and Workshop Act, 103; Employment of Women Act, 103–4; Companies Act, 103; Territorial and Reserve Forces Act, 175–84, 315; Married Women's Property Act, 496; Deceased Wife's Sister Marriage Act, 497; Qualification of Women County and Borough Councils Act, 519; Qualification of Women County and Town Councils (Scotland) Act, 519

1908, Acts to Regulate the Indian Press and to deal with Explosive outrages in India, 50; Act subjecting Anarchist Plots in India to Special Jurisdiction, 50; Education (Scotland) Act, 82; Children Act, 82n., 285n.; Small Holdings and Allotments Act, 103; Coal Mines Regulation Act, 240–2; Old Age Pensions Act, 280–4; Married Women's Property Act, 496; Public Meetings Act, 520; Irish Universities Act, 529–30

1909, Commonwealth of South Africa Act, 36, 296; Indian Councils Act, 51,